Building Trust, Effective Communication, and Transparency Between Police and Community Members

Christopher Lee Bush
Allen County Community College, USA

Jennifer Matthews
Metra Police Department, USA

A volume in the Advances in Criminology, Criminal Justice, and Penology (ACCJP) Book Series

IGI Global
PUBLISHER of TIMELY KNOWLEDGE

Published in the United States of America by
IGI Global
Information Science Reference (an imprint of IGI Global)
701 E. Chocolate Avenue
Hershey PA, USA 17033
Tel: 717-533-8845
Fax: 717-533-8661
E-mail: cust@igi-global.com
Web site: http://www.igi-global.com

Library of Congress Cataloging-in-Publication Data

Names: Bush, Christopher L., 1974- editor. | Matthews, Jennifer, 1981- editor.
Title: Building trust, effective communication, and transparency between police and community members / edited by Christopher Bush, Jennifer Matthews.
Description: Hershey, PA : Information Science Reference, [2024] | Includes bibliographical references and index. | Summary: "The main objective of this publication is to provide a bridge for police and community social change"-- Provided by publisher.
Identifiers: LCCN 2023040613 (print) | LCCN 2023040614 (ebook) | ISBN 9781668485699 (hardcover) | ISBN 9781668485705 (paperback) | ISBN 9781668485712 (ebook)
Subjects: LCSH: Community policing. | Police-community relations.
Classification: LCC HV7936.C83 B855 2024 (print) | LCC HV7936.C83 (ebook) | DDC 363.2/3--dc23/eng/20231130
LC record available at https://lccn.loc.gov/2023040613
LC ebook record available at https://lccn.loc.gov/2023040614

This book is published in the IGI Global book series Advances in Criminology, Criminal Justice, and Penology (ACCJP) (ISSN: pending; eISSN: pending)

British Cataloguing in Publication Data
A Cataloguing in Publication record for this book is available from the British Library.

For electronic access to this publication, please contact: eresources@igi-global.com.

Advances in Criminology, Criminal Justice, and Penology (ACCJP) Book Series

ISSN:pending
EISSN:pending

Editor-in-Chief: Liam J. Leonard, Winchester University, UK

MISSION

Criminology has never been more relevant. Violence, serial murder, crime and victimization continue to remain an unfortunate staple of society. Crime is a key issue globally, nationally, and regionally. Law enforcement personnel within the criminal justice system must keep pace with ever changing modes of crime. As officials work to predict and prevent crimes, as well as apprehend offenders, they will need to devise new tools and strategies to preserve the safety of society and ensure proper justice is served.

The **Advances in Criminology, Criminal Justice, and Penology (ACCJP)** Book Series explores emerging research behind crime control strategies, crime motivation, new methods and the utilization of technology for committing illegal acts, criminal justice and reform strategies, and the effects of crime on society and its victims. The publications contained within this series are valuable resources for government officials, law enforcement officers, corrections officers, prison management, criminologists, sociologists, psychologists, forensic scientists, security specialists, academicians, researchers, and students seeking current research on international crime.

COVERAGE

- Gang Violence
- Criminology
- Drug Trafficking
- Human Trafficking
- Serial Murder
- Gaming
- Criminal Psychology
- Penal System
- Victimology
- Hacking

IGI Global is currently accepting manuscripts for publication within this series. To submit a proposal for a volume in this series, please contact our Acquisition Editors at Acquisitions@igi-global.com or visit: http://www.igi-global.com/publish/.

The Advances in Criminology, Criminal Justice, and Penology (ACCJP) Book Series (ISSN pending) is published by IGI Global, 701 E. Chocolate Avenue, Hershey, PA 17033-1240, USA, www.igi-global.com. This series is composed of titles available for purchase individually; each title is edited to be contextually exclusive from any other title within the series. For pricing and ordering information please visit http://www.igi-global.com/book-series/advances-criminology-criminal-justice-penology/212650. Postmaster: Send all address changes to above address.

Titles in this Series

For a list of additional titles in this series, please visit:
http://www.igi-global.com/book-series/advances-criminology-criminal-justice-penology/212650

Comparing Black Deaths in Custody, Police Brutality, and Social Justice Solutions
Janelle Christine Simmons (Independent Researcer, USA)
Information Science Reference • © 2023 • 296pp • H/C (ISBN: 9781799893042) • US $215.00

Restorative Justice and Practices in the 21st Century
Holli Vah Seliskar (Purdue University Gloal, USA)
Information Science Reference • © 2023 • 324pp • H/C (ISBN: 9781668461457) • US $215.00

Realizing the Purpose and Benefits of Juvenile Transfer to Criminal Court
Joseph B. Sanborn, Jr. (University of Central Florida (Retired), USA)
Information Science Reference • © 2023 • 516pp • H/C (ISBN: 9781799879237) • US $245.00

Cases on Crimes, Investigations, and Media Coverage
Liam James Leonard (University of Winchester, UK)
Information Science Reference • © 2023 • 254pp • H/C (ISBN: 9781799896685) • US $215.00

Paths to the Prevention and Detection of Human Trafficking
Sharon K. Andrews (University of Houston-Clear Lake, USA) and Caroline M. Crawford (University of Houston-Clear Lake, USA)
Information Science Reference • © 2022 • 422pp • H/C (ISBN: 9781668439265) • US $215.00

Comparative Criminology Across Western and African Perspectives
Simeon P. Sungi (United States International University-Africa, Kenya) and Nabil Ouassini (Prairie View A&M University, USA)
Information Science Reference • © 2022 • 322pp • H/C (ISBN: 9781799828563) • US $250.00

IGI Global
PUBLISHER of TIMELY KNOWLEDGE

701 East Chocolate Avenue, Hershey, PA 17033, USA
Tel: 717-533-8845 x100 • Fax: 717-533-8661
E-Mail: cust@igi-global.com • www.igi-global.com

To my family with a special feeling of gratitude for their love and support – I love you all. To my wife Dr. Alishia S. Bush (Doctor of Education in Educational Leadership), for always believing in me, and giving me words of encouragement and push for tenacity, in which I often replayed her voice saying, "You can do it." To my sons Christopher and JaqSon your curiosity about the book through my journey kept me going to reach the destination – a finished book

Table of Contents

Detailed Table of Contents

of America (USA). BWCs have become very common among law enforcement officers, including police officers, sheriff deputies, state patrol, and federal agents. No national law forces law enforcement to wear BWCs. Since no national policy outlines when footage can or cannot be released to the public, which leaves states and municipalities to deal with the legality and practicality of releasing BWC footage. This chapter will provide an overview of how BWC policies have developed and the impact of BWCs on police and community relations.

This chapter provides a discussion on the best practices for the reintegration of offenders into the community. More than one approach is necessary to address the emerging needs of this population. This chapter discusses some of the most prevalent barriers to reintegration and the stigmas ex-offenders face as they reintegrate into the community. This chapter also evaluates recidivism reduction strategies and community corrections strategies to facilitate the transition of offenders into the community. It then discusses the need for relationship building between law enforcement and the community to assist in reintegration strategies for justice-involved people. The chapter concludes with best practices for reintegrating offenders into the community and a review of reintegration strategies in California, Florida, and Texas state prisons.

In today's modern world, trust between the interactants is shrinking, since while communicating with each other, there is almost always the fear of being misled by means of disinformation or miscommunication. The chapter discusses the necessity of the application of five expression management techniques formerly proposed by Andersen and Guerrero, namely 1) intensification, 2) de-intensification, 3) simulation, 4) inhabitation, and 5) masking, which, according to the studies of the authors of this chapter, have the potential of raising the level of emotional connection between the speaking partners, who then gain the ultimate chance of influencing each other's viewpoint by means of heightening the trust level through the application of these emotion expression management techniques for the benefit of both parties both in the business field and in our everyday lives. To elucidate this, extracts from contemporary English fiction are discussed by the author that show the impact of emotion management to achieve emotive impact on the listener(s).

In the age of the internet, the criminal trial, while respecting constitution guarantees, cannot be insensitive to technological innovation which by now concerns every sector of human activity and every public service, which is also justice. The use of technology is able to redesign the new process of security and forensics, to improve government and law. The advanced technology in the application of the law provides efficiency. The Italian criminal justice system is currently under an important transformation by means Cartabia reform. The aim of the Italian reform is modernizing and simplifying the criminal process as well as increasing its efficiency and transparency. The chapter aims to explore the items relating to the Italian reform of criminal justice focusing to technology making changes. The work also intends to reflect on the role of technology in generating the self-reinforcing trust of criminal justice.

The landscape of law enforcement is changing. Mental health needs are on the rise, and the vast majority of law enforcement calls for service are already related to social issues. Public safety today requires greater attention to justice, innovation, and new technology. It also requires additional professionals, like social workers, for social service delivery. The future of public safety is clearly a serious situation for police and emergency services organizations and their professional employees. This chapter will (1) discuss the situation that communities and organizations face, (2) identify some of the alternative strategies that can be employed, and (3) provide a process planning model for creating new approaches on the ground in communities. This model emphasizes a data-informed and collaborative approach to the issue.

Punishing offenders and the type of punishment to be given has been one of the fundamental questions of criminal law. The concept of punishment has been associated with revenge in history; however, after the 1940s, it has been formed through a different understanding of the idea of rehabilitating offenders and reintegrating them into society. After the 1970s, with the concept of "reparation," models emerged in which offenders analyze the consequences of the act committed within the scope of restorative justice and display a constructive attitude towards eliminating the damage. Therefore, the understanding of making offenders pay for, atone for, or compensate for the consequences of the act committed, the question of what the

Foreword

"Trust between law enforcement agencies and the people they protect and serve is essential in a democracy. It is key to the stability of our communities, the integrity of our criminal justice system, and the safe and effective delivery of policing services." (President Barack Obama, 2015)

Often there are critical points in time whereby we are confronted with making decisions relative to events occurring around us. Such was the case when Former President Barack Obama charged for the formulation of a strategy to enhance policing in America. The resultant report from the 21st Century Task Force identified several areas that necessitated attention by those engaged in public service. Much like that report this book explores areas that are essential if there is to be a demonstrable change in public safety and communities in our democracy.

Fast forward to 2020, five short years later following the death of George Floyd, policing in America was once again challenged to address policies and procedures that were inimical to engendering trust and legitimacy in communities. Often the juxtaposition of concepts of guardianship against those of being a warrior contain values that are perceived differently and as polarities. Managing such polarities or values are essential to garnering trust between the police and the communities they serve. Such navigation necessitates the integration of values that shouldn't be seen as an either/or proposition but as AND principles. This book navigates topics that are essential if we are to see discernable progress towards changing the dynamics of such relationships across America.

Trust is a fundamental commodity that police departments must develop and maintain between themselves and the communities they serve. Effective communication is the salient ingredient necessary to build the level of trust that can be counted on when challenging situations present themselves. Some would suggest policing in America can't be reformed to embrace values that enhance community relationships. I strongly disagree. This book navigates these very concepts with material that provides a roadmap for such institutional reformation and successful engagement in communities. This is a must-read book by Dr. Bush and Dr. Matthews for those seeking change between those called upon to serve and those being served.

Joseph A. McMillan
Polarities of Democracy Institute, USA

Joseph A. McMillan *has served in law enforcement positions with the United States Air Force, the Air Force Office of Special Investigations, and the Defense Criminal Investigative Service. He has held a variety of field and Headquarters positions culminating in his selection as the Special Agent in Charge, Mid-Atlantic Field Office. Dr. McMillan received his appointment in the Senior Executive Service and was appointed the Assistant Inspector General for Investigations for the Nuclear Regulatory Commission Office of the Inspector General. Dr. McMillan retired from federal service with over 41 years of public service. Dr. McMillan is a Past National President for the National Organization of Black Law Enforcement Executives, a Senior Fellow with the Polarities of Democracy Institute, a Contributing Faculty member in the Walden University School of Criminal Justice, a member of the International Association of Chiefs of Police, the Police Executive Research Foundation, the American Society of Criminology, and Alpha Phi Alpha Fraternity, Incorporated. Dr. McMillan is married with two daughters and resides in Bowie, MD.*

Preface

In the ever-evolving landscape of criminal justice, the demand for transparency, effective communication, and trust between law enforcement and community members has never been more pressing. The quest for universally aligned practices, policies, and procedures that resonate through the lens of trust has become imperative as our society navigates the intersection of longstanding traditions and the rapid advancement of technology.

This edited reference book, spearheaded by Christopher Lee Bush of Allen County Community College and Jennifer Matthews of the Metra Police Department, USA, delves into the critical juncture where the criminal justice system meets the digital age. As our world undergoes unprecedented technological transformations, the criminal justice system stands at a crossroads, grappling with the need to adapt its policies, practices, and procedures to meet the demands of the 21st century.

The pages that follow are a testament to the urgent need for systemic change and the exploration of innovative avenues to bridge the gap between police and community for positive social change. With a focus on prevention, awareness, and intervention practices, this publication serves as a comprehensive guide for criminal justice professionals, policy writers, students, business leaders, and technologists alike.

The contributors to this volume address key themes, including the advancement of law enforcement technology, the digital evolution of the criminal justice system, and the impact of technology on community policing. The exploration extends to the effective use of body-worn cameras (BWCs) not only within law enforcement but also in other venues such as schools, hospitals, and security locations.

Chapter 1 addresses how Police officers are often first responders to crisis situations that involve natural disasters, large-scale accidents, and acts of terrorism. Yet, the importance of a proper communication plan is often overlooked and rarely addressed within police agencies. There is also a scarcity of literature that explores how these crisis communication plans can be effectively implemented via social media platforms. As such, the lack of research in this area warrants a conceptual framework to examine the police agencies' role when facilitating crisis communication through social media. The purpose of this article is to use the CAST-Informed crisis educational leadership (agile decision-making, influencer, and coordinator) framework (CICELF) to examine the crisis communication mechanisms for police officers using social media.

Chapter 2 addresses how Body-worn cameras (BWC) policies can have a significant impact on police-community relations in various ways, which this chapter will examine. BWCs have been implemented internationally, especially in the developed world. This chapter will primarily focus on law enforcement policies within the United States of America (USA). BWCs have become very common among law enforcement officers, including police officers, sheriff deputies, state patrol, and federal agents. No national law forces law enforcement to wear BWCs. Since no national policy outlines when footage can or cannot be released to the public, which leaves states and municipalities to deal with the legality and practicality of releasing BWC footage. This chapter will provide an overview of how BWC policies have developed and the impact of BWCs on police and community relations.

Chapter 3 provides discussion on the best practices for the reintegration of offenders into the community. More than one approach is necessary to address the emerging needs of this population. This chapter discusses some of the most prevalent barriers to reintegration and the stigmas ex-offenders face as they reintegrate into the community. This chapter also evaluates recidivism reduction strategies and community corrections strategies to facilitate the transition of offenders into the community. It then discusses the need for relationship building between law enforcement and the community to assist in reintegration strategies for justice-involved people. The chapter concludes with best practices for reintegrating offenders into the community and a review of reintegration strategies in California, Florida, and Texas state prisons.

Chapter 4 addresses what is happening In today's modern world, trust between the interactants is shrinking, since while communicating with each other, there is almost always the fear of being misled by means of disinformation or miscommunication. The present paper discusses the necessity of the application of 5 expression management techniques formerly proposed by Andersen and Guerrero, namely 1) intensification, 2) de-intensification, 3) simulation, 4) inhabitation, and 5) masking, which, according to the studies of the authors of this article, have the potential of raising the level of emotional connection between the speaking partners, who then gain the ultimate chance of influencing each others' viewpoint by means of heightening the trust level through the application of these emotion expression management techniques for the benefit of both parties both in the business field and in our everyday lives. To elucidate this, extracts from contemporary English fiction are being discussed by the author, which show the impact of emotion management to achieve emotive impact on the listener(s).

Chapter 5 aims to shed light on the practices of community policing in Egypt, show its most prominent forms, and highlight its social role in solving and settling social and criminal problems in Egyptian society. The chapter will rely on the descriptive analytical approach to identify the practices of community policing in Egypt. The chapter plans to introduce community policing and its theoretical framework, by addressing its definition, components, goals, and requirements and reviews the most prominent applications of community policing in Egypt, the most important of which are community participation committees in police departments, police reconciliation committees, and community participation committees in police stations. Reform and rehabilitation, and finally the societal role of the police in community initiatives aimed at reducing the living burdens on citizens. The chapter concluded with the importance of the community policing model in enhancing public participation in maintaining security and combating crime and its reflection on building confidence in the police.

Chapter 6 addresses how Dearborn, MI is the enclave of Arab Americans in the United States. Arabs migrated to Dearborn, MI, many as refugees of war, seeking prosperity. The Arab American experience is invisible because this population is classified as "White'" according to the U.S. Census. However, many Arab Americans do not identify as "White." Therefore, interpretations using "White" statistics may be flawed. It is imperative that the Office of Management and Budget include a Middle Eastern North African (MENA) category to separate the "White" data and disaggregate MENA data. The Obama and Biden Administrations have submitted proposals on collecting MENA population data. It is unknown if the 2030 U.S. Census will include MENA categories. Law enforcement and other organizations can incorporate both quantitative and qualitative data collection methods to capture MENA population statistics and their lived experiences. Until then, the MENA population and their needs will remain invisible to the general population and justice may be elusive.

Chapter 7 provides how the In the age of the internet, the criminal trial, while respecting constitution guarantees, cannot be insensitive to technological innovation which, by now, it concerns every sector of human activity and every public service, which is also justice. The use of technology is able of redesigning the new process of security and forensics, to improve government and law. The advanced technological in the application of the law provides efficiency. The Italian criminal justice system is currently under an important transformation by means Cartabia reform. The aim of the Italian reform is modernizing and simplifying the criminal process as well as increasing its efficiency and transparency. The chapter aims to explore the items relating to the Italian reform of criminal justice focusing to technology making changes. The work also intends to reflect on a role of technology in generating the self-reinforcing trust of criminal justice.

Chapter 8 addresses the landscape of law enforcement is changing. Mental health needs are on the rise and the vast majority of law enforcement calls for service are already related to social issues. Public safety today requires greater attention to justice, innovation and new technology. It also requires additional professionals, like social workers, for social service delivery. The future of public safety is clearly a serious situation for police and emergency services organizations and their professional employees. This chapter will (1) discuss the situation that communities and organizations face, (2) identify some of the alternative strategies that can be employed and (3) provide a process planning model for creating new approaches on the ground in communities. This model emphasizes a data-informed and collaborative approach to the issue.

Chapter 9 addresses punishing offenders and the type of punishment to be given has been one of the fundamental questions of criminal law. The concept of punishment has been associated with revenge in history however, after the 1940s, it has been formed through a different understanding of the idea of rehabilitating offender and reintegrating them into society. After the 1970s, with the concept of "reparation", models emerged in which offenders analyze the consequences of the act committed within the scope of restorative justice and display a constructive attitude towards eliminating the damage. Therefore, the understanding of making offenders pay for, atone for or compensate for the consequences of the act committed, the question of what the punishment given over time or the result of the criminal justice system reveals for offenders has also begun to be asked. At this point, the question asked within the scope of our study is how effective restorative justice models are in reconciling and reintegrating offenders with society.

Chapter 10 addresses how the Royal Canadian Mounted Police (RCMP) are in the process of implementing body-worn cameras (BWCs) across the country. This chapter reports on a pilot project designed to evaluate the implementation of these cameras that was conducted in Iqaluit, Nunavut, a northern community of Canada where most residents identify as Inuit. The community engagement and consulation process that was undertaken is described, and the findings from two surveys – one focusing on community members and the other focusing on RCMP officers – are presented. These findings suggest that BWCs are generally supported by the public and are thought to have a positive impact on both public safety and police-community relations. RCMP officers are also generally satisfied with their BWCs and the training they received about their use. We believe the steps for this pilot project helped develop community trust around the use of BWCs by RCMP officers in Iqaluit. We hope the report of these steps within this chapter provides a blueprint for other agencies to follow as they work through their own implementation of BWCs.

Chapters unfold to illuminate the intricate relationships between law enforcement and various facets of society, including community reintegration of offenders, collaboration with loss prevention efforts, and community preparedness for unforeseen circumstances involving law enforcement incidents. The book also examines the often-overlooked aspects of mental health and psychological diagnoses within law enforcement and explores the influential role of athletes and coaches in increasing accountability in community policing, from high schools to professional entities.

As editors, we are grateful to the contributors for their insightful perspectives and dedication to addressing the critical issues at the heart of police-community relations. It is our hope that this volume stimulates meaningful dialogue, inspires positive change, and serves as a valuable resource for those committed to building trust, effective communication, and transparency in the criminal justice system.

Editors,

Christopher Lee Bush
Allen County Community College, USA

Jennifer Matthews
Metra Police Department, USA

Acknowledgment

Over the past five years the country has been met with some challenging times. We must not turn away from what has garnered attention globally with police, communities, and technology with the emphasis being around trust and transparency. It is vital that criminal justice practitioners and others address bridging the gap, connecting police, community, and technology. All these must be intertwined with trust and transparency.

We often look to leaders to take command to bridge the gap between communication and efforts to work interactively. To help close the gap we will need to hear from the voices that are often left out, or do not have a platform where the voice can be heard. of youth and young adults. Criminal justice professionals, practitioners, and leaders should make their efforts intentional to engage youth and young adults to be at the table. When we engaged in a robust diverse setting, we can unleash different prospectives from multiple lens that can open new doors for better prevention and intervention measurements for *Building Trust, Effective Communication, and Transparency Between Police and Community Members.*

I have spent the last 20 years engaged in the criminal justice field. I have also been a member of the community my entire life and have lived experiences of positive and negative events indirectly and directly. My experiences have shaped my passion to provide scholarship to the field topics surrounding community policing, and why I wanted to be an editor of this reference book. This title of the reference book and some of the chapters will draw discussion with colleagues, friends, and family that will not be easy.

I would like to thank all the authors who contributed to this book. Your chapters will be resources to help make a change globally. Dr. Jennifer Matthews, thank you for your commitment from the beginning and helping to see this book get to its final preparation. Your expertise in and knowledge on body worn cameras and experience as a past law enforcement sheriff provided clarity for the reference book that help draw attention to our diverse authors chapter submissions.

Acknowledgment

I would like to thank all those at IGI-Global who provided guidance and management to help this reference book come to life. I would like to personally say special thanks, to our Assistant Development Editor, Elizabeth Barrantes for being available to answer emails, calls and assisting with some of the technical assistance in the editor's portal. I like to say thanks to my chair who encouraged me to continue to pursue publishing work around my dissertation "community policing and body worn cameras" and to Walden University who helped me understand what *social change* is and how to incorporate this practice into my research and work efforts globally.

Finally, I cannot end without acknowledging my wife Dr. Alishia S. Bush, and our two sons Christopher and JaqSon for all their unwavering encouragement and excitement about being an editor of a reference book.

I am thankful ad grateful to God for the guidance that have been poured into my life to remain being a branch attached to his vine to be a voice utilizing my gifts that I have been blessed with to provide education in the criminal justice field.

Building Trust, Effective Communication, and Transparency Between Police and Community Members provides scholarships about what must be intentional efforts from police and community individuals to demonstrate transparency from a global perspective. The front cover is a true testament of filling in the missing puzzle in which both the police and community hold the key pieces to complete the puzzle to build the bridge to close the gap. My inspiration behind my research was to gain understanding from families and community members perspectives on how body worn cameras delayed video release impact their trust in in police and what efforts can be done to strengthen community policing. To extend to my research this book provides research from the lens of scholars who has contributed to perspectives from literature review, data and analysis addressing what can further be implemented to building trust, effective communication and transparency between police and the community globally… *~Dr. Christopher L. Bush*

This book has been a labor of love for everyone involved. I would like to thank all of the contributing authors for their hard work, dedication, and perseverance in bringing this project through to fruition. Without their contributions, Dr. Bush and I would not have been able to convey our message to the world. In today's modern age, the lessons and knowledge gained from their research are invaluable. I am grateful to IGI Global for giving us such a powerful platform to be able to share our voices with the masses. I am honored daily to be able to share my talent and the talent of my fellow respected scholars with such a dynamic audience. I am thankful daily for all the gifts that God has bestowed upon me that have enabled me to be a beacon of light, knowledge, and voice of authority in the field of Criminal Justice… *~Dr. Jennifer Matthews*

The criminal justice system is currently under a microscope for transformation, whereas the demand for universally aligned practices, policies, and procedures can be framed through one lens. American citizens have been demanding an overhaul of the criminal justice system since its inception of advanced technology. Taking an in-depth look for systematic changes is far overdue. Many criminal justice procedures and interventions are no longer parallel to what was applied over a century ago and will take some effort to change, but little is applied to the recent inception of technological advancement.

Technology is evolving rapidly, whereas the criminal justice system's position on technology policies, practices, and procedures is stagnant. The progression to making change is viewed as untrusting by current and new coming professionals in the field which is also carrying over into the community. Addressing the need for research towards better practices around prevention, awareness, and intervention is a step into the 21st century to expand on positive social change. Providing research on this can change the perspective of the criminal justice system as new technology is adapted that can be applied to these efforts.

Chapter 1
Building an Effective Crisis Communication Plan for Police Agencies

Tomicka Williams
https://orcid.org/0000-0003-1528-2429
Purdue University Global, USA

Chloe Robinson
https://orcid.org/0000-0002-7860-4627
Indiana University, South Bend, USA

ABSTRACT

Police officers are often first responders to crisis situations that involve natural disasters, large-scale accidents, and acts of terrorism. Yet, the importance of a proper communication plan is often overlooked and rarely addressed within police agencies. There is also a scarcity of literature that explores how these crisis communication plans can be effectively implemented via social media platforms. As such, the lack of research in this area warrants a conceptual framework to examine the police agencies' role when facilitating crisis communication through social media. The purpose of this chapter is to use the CAST-informed crisis educational leadership (agile decision-making, influencer, and coordinator) framework (CICELF) to examine the crisis communication mechanisms for police officers using social media.

Police officers are often first responders to crisis situations that involve natural disasters, large-scale accidents, and acts of terrorism (Brinser & King, 2016; Hine & Bragias, 2020; Rojek & Smith, 2007; Bonkiewicz & Ruback, 2012). Compared

DOI: 10.4018/978-1-6684-8569-9.ch001

to other emergency services, police departments often comprise the largest presence (Hine & Bragias, 2020). These capricious and sometimes tragic events can greatly impact the communities that the police are called to protect and serve. During these events, police officers must simultaneously employ multiple skills to successfully mitigate the situation while also protecting the community from future harm. Large-scale crisis events are even more complicated not only because of the size of the event but also because they require multi-agency coordination across various jurisdictions (Rojek & Smith, 2007). Far-reaching disasters require proper communication plans. Without the implementation of an appropriate plan, citizens' trust in the police can falter which could then lead to a legitimacy crisis for the agency. The importance of a proper communication plan is often overlooked and rarely addressed within police agencies (McElroy, 2019). This lack of attention devoted to the proper dissemination of information during the time of a crisis also means that there is a dearth of literature devoted to creating and establishing best practices in the field. There is also a paucity of literature that explores how these crisis communication plans can be effectively implemented via social media platforms. A model that can guide police leadership during these tenuous situations is needed in the field. The purpose of this chapter is to showcase how the CAST-Informed crisis educational leadership (agile decision-making, influencer, and coordinator) framework (CICELF) can be used to better facilitate crisis communication plans for police officers via social media.

SOCIAL MEDIA USE BY POLICE AGENCIES

Most American police departments claim that they utilize social media consistently. Scholars have found that police departments employ several different social media platforms to promote public safety, recruit new officers, investigate crimes, showcase effective police work, and communicate possible threats (Hu, Rodgers & Lovrich, 2018; Liberman, Koetzle & Sakiyama, 2013; Walsh & O'Connor, 2019). Most of the research that examines social media and the police is predicated on understanding how departments use social media to shape their image and effectively interact with the communities that they serve (Steele & Blau, 2023). Police executives and policy analysts have also begun to examine the importance and prevalence of the use of social media by police officers. In late December 2014, President Obama created a task force to strengthen community policing and trust among police officers and citizens (President's Task Force, 2015). The task force was charged with creating recommendations to build and sustain better police departments. The task force's final report argued that the American police needs to establish legitimacy in the eyes of the public. This means that citizens have confidence and trust that the police will serve them fairly and equitably. To effectively establish legitimacy, the task force recommended an action plan which centered around six main pillars. The use of technology and social media was one of the main pillars. The inclusion of this pillar in the final task force report showcases the importance of social media use amongst police departments.

In 2016, the International Association of Chiefs of Police (IACP) published the results of a nationwide survey of police departments. Survey results revealed that 96% of the police departments who responded to the survey had used various social media platforms to communicate with their community members (International Association of Chiefs of Police, 2016). IACP's survey results revealed that Facebook, Twitter, and YouTube were among the three social media platforms most used by police departments. It was found that 94 percent of the police agencies used Facebook, 71.2 percent used Twitter and 40 percent used YouTube (International Association of Chiefs of Police, 2016). These statistics indicate that the use of social media by police agencies is quite prevalent. Therefore, social media can serve as a powerful tool during a time of crisis.

SOCIAL MEDIA AS A COMMUNICATION TOOL

Social media and the police officer's role are limited but warranted in building relationships with the community and understanding their role in using social media mechanisms to resolve and manage a crisis (Beshears et al., 2019; Schneider, 2020). During a crisis, people tend to comprehend, process, and act on information differently than they would normally (CDC.gov., 2019). The attempts to adequately handle the information being disseminated are further hindered by the emotional and psychological barriers that the individual must contend with during these emergencies (CDC.gov., 2019). Crisis communicators must also take into account how feelings of uncertainty, fear, anxiety, dread, hopelessness, helplessness, and denial can influence the way someone acts during these precarious events (Addo, Jiaming, Kulbo & Liangqiang, 2020; CDC.gov., 2019).

Therefore, when a crisis happens, rapid communication is essential. Social media can serve as an important crisis response tool because it encourages open access and exchange of information via public conversation and interaction (Yates & Paquette, 2011). Social media platforms cultivate discourse communities that can help spread important messaging during a time of crisis. The conversational aspect of social media eliminates many barriers in public communication that some governmental agencies may endure (Bertot, Jarger, Munson & Glaisyer, 2010). Hence, social media can promote effective collective action during a crisis (Tsui, Rao, Carey, Feng & Provencher, 2020).

THE UNDERPINNINGS OF A CRISIS COMMUNICATION SYSTEM

To achieve a comprehensive understanding of a police officer's role when using social media to respond to and manage a crisis, one must first define the underpinnings of a crisis communication system. A crisis communication system comprises interconnected components that work interdependently to enable swift and effective responses (Zhang and Li et al., 2023). According to Williams and Liou (2023), a transparent chain of command and defined roles and responsibilities ensure that communication channels are streamlined, avoiding misunderstanding during a crisis. Additionally, advanced communication technology such as social media monitoring tools used by police agencies to respond to and manage crises, plays a pivotal role in disseminating timely and accurate information for overall public safety (Jungblut & Kümpel et al., 2022; Mayes, 2021). Police agencies worldwide are increasingly recognizing the power of these digital tools as an intricate instrument in their crisis communication system to manage crises effectively, disseminate timely information, and engage with the community in unprecedented ways (Steele & Blau, 2023; Jungblut, Kümpel, et al., 2022).

In addition to using a crisis communication system as a mode to manage channels of communication and avoid chaos, the system encompasses the policies, protocols, and various technologies that organizations deploy to effectively communicate with internal and external components during times of crisis (Stuart, 2013; Zhang and Li et al., 2023; Williams, 2019). The internal and external components comprise various stakeholders working as agents to manage human and nonhuman details in both a timely and effective manner (Erickson, 2021; Thornton-Lugo & Rupp, 2021; Veil & Husted, 2012). These components are a culmination of first responders' personnel, technology, tools, and methods to manage the flow of information timely and accurately (Adubato et al., 2021; Veil & Husted, 2012). In the digital age, leveraging technology is instrumental in fortifying the flow of information. A police agency's ability to incorporate social media technology within a crisis communication system in responding to and managing a crisis is critical in protecting the community.

According to Eriksson and Olsson (2016), the social media platform serves as a conduit for both disseminating official information and sources of real-time feedback from stakeholders. Researchers suggested that a community crisis challenges communication systems, officers who apply communication mechanisms, and the person reporting the crime (Adubato et al., 2021; Thornton-Lugo & Rupp, 2021). Communication technologies within a crisis communication system, such as social media, can support police departments in effectively transmitting information to the communities they serve during a crisis. Therefore, using a conceptual framework to examine the police officer's role in using social media to respond to and manage a crisis is warranted (Beshears et al., 2019).

POLICE AGENCIES UTILIZATION OF SOCIAL MEDIA DURING A TIME OF CRISIS

There is a paucity of research that examines the use of social media by police agencies during or directly after a crisis (Crump, 2011; Procter et al., 2013; Dong & Wu, 2022). Most of these studies also focus on post-crisis communication following use-of-force incidents. Most recent research examined how police agencies across the country reacted on Twitter following a major legitimacy crisis (Dong & Wu, 2022). Researchers identified 115 large police departments in the United States that all had a regular presence on Twitter. The tweets from these departments were collected over a 4-month period between April 2020 and July 2020 (Dong & Wu, 2022). This time series design allowed the scholars to observe how social media was used by police departments before, during, and following the death of George Floyd. It was found that police agencies tweeted more frequently directly after the killing of George Floyd. It was also found that police agencies posted more civil-unrest related tweets. The public also showed signs of engaging more with the police through the rate at which they favorited or retweeted police tweets. This rate of engagement stayed higher throughout the rest of the study period (Dong & Wu, 2022).

A few earlier international studies also examined the use of Twitter by police departments following the death of Mark Duggan, a Black man who was killed by the police in 2011. This police-involved shooting caused 5 days of rioting in several cities in London. The authors analyzed the tweets of the London Metropolitan Police (MET) and the Greater Manchester Police (GMP) during the riots (Denef, Bayerl & Kaptein, 2013). The comparison of the Twitter communication from both departments demonstrated that they used varying communication techniques. The MET utilized a more distant approach to remain in control while the GMP cultivated a more personalized and expressive approach (Denef, Bayerl & Kaptein, 2013). Procter and colleagues (2013) analyzed social media communication following the same public crisis event in England. The authors found that although the number of people who followed the police on Twitter increased during this time, the police did not capitalize on this increased following. The police took a more distant approach and would disseminate information rather than interact with community members (Procter, Crump, Karstedt, Voss & Cantijoch, 2013).

These few research studies highlight the importance of utilizing effective crisis communication plans via social media. Research on crisis communication in social media for policing is necessary to (a) enable police officers to protect the community, (b) serve and maintain order in the community, and (c) develop and maintain relationships within the community and other agencies. As such, the lack of research in this area warrants a conceptual framework to examine the police agencies' role when facilitating crisis communication through social media.

As social media continues to evolve, its integration into law enforcement crisis communication systems is a testament to the adaptability of policing strategies in the digital age. The embracement of social media platforms strategically by police enables them to effectively respond to and manage crises, fosters transparency, builds community trust, and enhances overall public safety (O'Connor & Zaidi, 2021). This chapter seeks to explore the critical role of a police officer when using social media platforms to respond to and manage a crisis, drawing from the lens of CICELF. According to Beshears et. al. (2019), using a conceptual framework to examine the police officer's role in using social media to respond to and manage a crisis is warranted. Officers are pivotal in proactively shaping public understanding, dispelling misinformation, and fostering community cooperation through these digital platforms. Therefore, exploring the critical role of police officers through social media platforms is necessary in order to enhance community resilience, build community trust, and improve overall public safety. The following aims to contribute to the field of policing by demonstrating how an innovative conceptual framework can be employed so that police officers can better understand their role when using social media platforms during times of crisis.

PROPOSED CONCEPTUAL FRAMEWORK

CAST-Informed crisis educational leadership framework (CICELF) is relevant in examining the role of police officers as they use social media platforms to facilitate crisis communication. CICELF was derived from complex adaptive system theory (CAST). CAST was founded by John Holland, Murry Gell-Mann, Kevin J. Dooley, and other philosophers, at the Santa Fe Institute, in the 1980s (Holland & Miller, 1991; Pohl, 1999). The agents of CAST's analyzed how agents self-organize in a system that is influenced by chaos (Coetzee et al., 2016; Hammer et al., 2012; Palombo, 2013). Holland, one of the pioneers of CAST, described the theory as multiple diverse agents working proactively and reactively together to respond to events in the systems' environment (Pohl, 1999). According to Brownlee (2007), Holland found that cohesiveness by agents is necessary to achieve resilience amid chaos. As such, police officers working with social media platforms work cohesively with digital communication systems, the community, and policies to ensure the overall safety of citizens and officers in the field (Elphick et al., 2021).

During an American Educational Research Association Conference, Williams and Liou (2023) described the framework, CICELF, as a tool to examine the role of school leaders stepping into a crisis leader's role to respond to and manage a crisis (2023). The characterization and philosophy of the CICEL Framework are described as a crisis leader role, attributes in the educational environment influenced by a crisis, yet the school leader is working with various agents to manage communication and resources (Williams & Liou, 2023). As police work with social media to manage crisis communication, they work with citizens, department leaders, social media policies, and a digital platform to respond to and manage a crisis (Mayes, 2021; Heverin, & Zach, 2010). CICELF explains that the role of agile decision-maker, influencer, and coordinator is significant in understanding the core competencies of an officer stepping into the role of an effective crisis leader through a social media platform (Williams & Liou, 2023). As an officer uses social media platforms to manage a crisis before, during, and following, Elphick (2021) found that through digital technology, police officers are making decisions, influencing outcomes, and coordinating the flow of information for the overall well-being of the community and officers to solve a crime. Hence, the CICEL Framework can be used to examine and understand the role and attributes necessary for police officers to be effective in strengthening their social media crisis communication skills when responding to and managing a crisis.

Through decision-making, the police officer applies safety protocols and procedures to make rational decisions and ensure communication is clear, concise, and flexible (Williams & Liou, 2023). The communication that the agent-leader (police officer) conveys and receives is used to make decisions, yet the police officer is flexible in their communication. The flexibility and clear and concise information allow the officer to be agile in their decision-making based on pre-established safety protocols and procedures. Agile decision-making requires the officer to be knowledgeable of the safety protocols and procedures to ensure the community's and field officers' overall safety (Williams & Liou, 2023). Through the decision-making role, the officer screens information conveyed to the public and solicited from the public for clarity and conciseness to make informed decisions. As the officer labor in making informed decisions based on information received from the public and transmitted to the public by the police—the lead officer ensures communication flowing through the social media platform is constant and concise, yet flexible in nature. The flexibility component is pertinent in determining the type of information transmitted to and received from the public in resolving a crisis. According to Mayes (2021), flexibility builds trust in the community, encourages citizens to transmit information through social media platforms, and portrays officers as open and transparent. Trusted communication through social media outlets is necessary to receive cooperation from citizens (Elphick et al., 2021). Citizens yearn to be informed and engage in protecting their communities through open and transparent information received by police. Thus, as citizens labor to convey information regarding crime, the officer(s) are working to make agile decisions as they work through information for the overall safety of citizens.

Next, the police officer as the influencer denotes the officers' actions of demonstrating calmness, confidence, and guidance through social media communication. This role requires the officer to gain the trust of citizens by demonstrating calm and confident communication through social media (Williams & Liou, 2023). Calm and confident communication allows the officer to gain the trust of the public to guide them through the crisis (Williams & Liou, 2023). When police provide instructions that are direct, simple, and practical, citizens can find confidence in police (Steele & Blau, 2023). Scholars found that proper dissemination of information via social media provided citizens with a sense of confidence in the police during the protests following the killing of George Floyd (Steele & Blau, 2023). Likewise, Mayes (2021) found that communication from police through social media positions the police in a role of influence, and the public will follow and trust the information provided. The influence attributes are accomplished through a culmination of leadership and social media policies (Mayes, 2021). Likewise, Williams and Liou (2023) found that the CAST-Informed crisis educational leadership framework (CICELF) draws on a leader stepping into the role of a crisis leader having knowledge of safety protocols to resolve the crisis. According to Elphick al el., (2021), social media privacy policies are essential for police to gain the trust of the public. The policies provide citizens with a sense of protection, guidance, and assurance that their communication is protected (Elphick et al., 2021). As such, Fielding (2023) found that ongoing social media communication between police and citizens calms fears and grows the confidence of citizens. Ongoing communication through social media platforms allows citizens to engage with officers and obtain guidance (Fielding, 2023). Williams and Liou's (2023) conceptual framework, CICELF, postulates that effective crisis leaders require influence to guide individuals impacted by the crisis.

As the officer works to gain the influence of the community, the officer coordinates communication and resources. The influence attribute requires the officer to identify and distribute resources through established relationships (Williams & Liou, 2023). According to Adubato (2021), developing relationships before and during a crisis is vital for officers to manage crisis communication. At this stage, the officer must understand and survey the community as they communicate, access, and distribute information for the community's and other officers' overall safety. Likewise, Schneider (2022) found that organized information through social media is paramount in social media as officers disseminate, distribute, and manage information through various social media platforms. Scholars have emphasized the importance of building trust through transparent communication as officers work to gather and disseminate information (Mayes, 2021; Fielding, 2023; Elphick et al., 2021). Transparent communication through social media enables the community to trust and accept distributed communication (Elphick et al., 2021; Mayes, 2021). As officers coordinate communication through social media, the community is inclined to work with the police to resolve a crisis (Mayes, 2021). Likewise, Williams and Liou's (2023) conceptual framework, CICELF, found that coordination and influential communication with internal and external stakeholders is paramount in resolving a crisis. As such, relationship building between the officer and the community is monumental as the officer steps into the role of the coordinator, influencer, and agile decision-maker for the overall safety of citizens and field officers. According to Mayes (2021) and Fielding (2023), social media communication is a culmination of disseminating and distributing information.

The proposed framework (CAST-Informed crisis educational leadership framework - CICELF) supports an important contribution to the literature as it relates to the police officer's role of responding to and managing a crisis via social media. CICELF focuses on the leader laboring to make agile decisions, influencing others within the system, and coordinating resources. Each attribute is paramount in ensuring the community's overall safety, while the officers are responding to and managing the crisis via various social media platforms. Through this approach, police officers are equipping themselves with tools to effectively manage a crisis. As such, police agencies can effectively support officers in the field while simultaneously protecting the communities that they serve.

REFERENCES

Addo, P. C., Jiaming, F., Kulbo, N. B., & Liangqiang, L. (2020). COVID-19: Fear appeal favoring purchase behavior towards personal protective equipment. *Service Industries Journal*, *40*(7–8), 471–490. doi:10.1080/02642069.2020.1751823

Adubato, B., Sachs, N. M., & Fizzinoglia, D. F. (2021). Gatekeepers: Controlling communication in a time of crisis. *Atlantic Journal of Communication*, *29*(5), 275–291. doi:10.1080/15456870.2020.1779724

Bertot, J. C., Jaeger, P. T., Munson, S., & Glaisyer, T. (2010). Social Media Technology and Government Transparency. *Computer*, *43*(11), 53–59. doi:10.1109/MC.2010.325

Beshears, M. L., Beshears, M. L., & Bond, M. (2019). Improving police social media use practices. *International Journal of Social Science Studies*, *7*(5), 34–42. doi:10.11114/ijsss.v7i5.4449

Bonkiewicz, L., & Ruback, R. B. (2012). The Role of the Police in Evacuations. *Police Quarterly*, *15*(2), 137–156. doi:10.1177/1098611112442808

Brinser, K. L., & King, W. R. (2016). Organizational Permeability to Environmental Conditions. *Police Quarterly*, *19*(4), 387–409. doi:10.1177/1098611115626409

Centers for Disease Control and Prevention (CDC). (2019). *CERC: Psychology of a crisis*. https://emergency.cdc.gov/cerc/ppt/CERC_ Psychology_of_a_Crisis.pdf

Coombs, W. (2005). Crisis and crisis management. In R. L. Heath (Ed.), *Encyclopedia ofpublic relations* (Vol. 2, pp. 218-221). Sage. https://doi-10.4135/9781412952545.n103

Crump, J. (2011). What are the police doing on Twitter? Social media, the police and the public. *Policy and Internet*, *3*(4), 1–27. doi:10.2202/1944-2866.1130

Denef, S., Bayerl, P. S., & Kaptein, N. A. (2013). Social media and the police. *Proceedings of the SIGCHI Conference on Human Factors in Computing Systems*. 10.1145/2470654.2466477

Dong, B., & Wu, X. (2022). Reaching and engaging people: Analyzing tweeting practices of large U.S. police departments pre- and post- the killing of George Floyd. *PLoS One*, *17*(7), e0269288. doi:10.1371/journal.pone.0269288 PMID:35834505

Elphick, C., Philpot, R., Zhang, M., Stuart, A., Walkington, Z., Frumkin, L. A., Pike, G., Gardner, K., Lacey, M., Levine, M., Price, B., Bandara, A., & Nuseibeh, B. (2021). Building trust in digital policing: A scoping review of community policing apps. *Police Practice and Research*, *22*(5), 1469–1491. doi:10.1080/15614263.2020.1861449

Erickson, S. (2021). Communication in a Crisis and the Importance of Authenticity and Transparency. *Journal of Library Administration*, *61*(4), 476–483. doi:10.1080/01930826.2021.1906556

Eriksson, M., & Olsson, E. (2016). Facebook and Twitter in crisis communication: A comparative study of crisis communication professionals and citizens. *Journal of Contingencies and Crisis Management*, *24*(4), 198–208. doi:10.1111/1468-5973.12116

Fielding, N. G. (2023). Police communications and social media. *European Journal of Criminology*, *20*(1), 316–334. doi:10.1177/1477370821998969

Heverin, T., & Zach, L. (2010). Twitter for city police department information sharing. *Proceedings of the American Society for Information Science and Technology*, *47*(1), 1–7. doi:10.1002/meet.14504701277

Hine, K. A., & Bragias, A. (2020). Effective communication during major crises: A systematic literature review to identify best practices for police. *Police Practice and Research*, *22*(5), 1492–1507. doi:10.1080/15614263.2020.1821681

Holland, J. H., & Miller, J. H. (1991). Artificial adaptive agents in economic theory. *The American Economic Review*, *81*(2), 365.

Hu, X., Rodgers, K., & Lovrich, N. P. (2018). We are more than crime fighters": Social media images of police departments. *Police Quarterly*, *21*(4), 544–572. doi:10.1177/1098611118783991

IACP, International Association of Chiefs of Police. (2016). *Social media survey results*. Retrieved March 4, 2023, from https://www.theiacp.org/resources/technology-and-social-media

Jungblut, M., Kümpel, A. S., & Steer, R. (2022). Social media use of the police in crisis situations: A mixed-method study on communication practices of the German police. *New Media & Society*, *0*(0). Advance online publication. doi:10.1177/14614448221127899

Lieberman, J. D., Koetzle, D., & Sakiyama, M. (2013). Police departments' use of Facebook: Patterns and policy issues. *Police Quarterly*, *16*(4), 438–462. doi:10.1177/1098611113495049

Mayes, L. (2021). Social media and community-oriented policing: Examining the organizational image construction of municipal police on Twitter and Facebook. *Police Practice and Research*, *22*(1), 903–920. doi:10.1080/15614263.2020.1843459

McElroy, J. (2019). *Uncovering the police: Converging trends threaten public accountability of local and state law enforcement across the United States*. Middle Tennessee State University: College of Media and Entertainment. https://www.mtsu.edu/seigenthaler/UncoveringThePolice.pdf

O'Connor, C. D., & Zaidi, H. (2021). Communicating with purpose: Image work, social media, and policing. *The Police Journal*, *94*(3), 333–352. doi:10.1177/0032258X20932957

Pohl, J. G. (1999). Some notions of complex adaptive systems and their relationship to our world. In *Proceedings of InterSymp-1999: The 11th International Conference On Systems Research* (p. 9). Informatics and Cybernetics. https://digitalcommons.calpoly.edu/cadrc/34

President's Task Force on 21st Century Policing. (2015). Final report of the president's task force on 21st century policing. *Office of Community Oriented Policing Services*. https://cops.usdoj.gov/pdf/taskforce/taskforce_finalreport.pdf

Procter, R., Crump, J., Karstedt, S., Voss, A., & Cantijoch, M. (2013). Reading the riots: What were the police doing on Twitter? *Policing and Society*, *23*(4), 413–436. doi:10.1080/10439463.2013.780223

Rojek, J., & Smith, M. R. (2007). Law Enforcement Lessons Learned from Hurricane Katrina. *The Review of Policy Research*, *24*(6), 589–608. doi:10.1111/j.1541-1338.2007.00301.x

Schneider, C. J. (2021). Police use of social media as bureaucratic propaganda: Comments on state violence and law enforcement use of social media in 2020. *Criminology, Criminal Justice, Law & Society*, *22*(2), 1–8.

Steele, J. L., & Blau, N. (2023). An Analysis of Police Department Crisis Communication via social media. *Police Quarterly*, *0*(0), 520–544. Advance online publication. doi:10.1177/10986111221150505

Thornton-Lugo, M. A., & Rupp, D. E. (2021). The Communication of Justice, Injustice, and Necessary Evils: An Empirical Examination. *SAGE Open*, *11*(3). Advance online publication. doi:10.1177/21582440211040796

Tsui, E., Rao, R. C., Carey, A. R., Feng, M. T., & Provencher, L. M. (2020). Using social media to disseminate ophthalmic information during the #COVID19 pandemic. *Ophthalmology*, *127*(9), e75–e78. doi:10.1016/j.ophtha.2020.05.048 PMID:32502595

Veil, S. R., & Husted, R. A. (2012). Best practices as an assessment for crisis communication. *Journal of Communication Management (London)*, *16*(2), 131–145. doi:10.1108/13632541211217560

Walsh, J. P., & O'Connor, C. (2019). Social media and policing: A review of recent research. *Sociology Compass*, *13*(1), 1–14. doi:10.1111/soc4.12648

Williams, T., & Liou, Y.-H. (2023). Framing K-12 school leaders' roles and competencies in times of crisis. *Journal of School Leadership*, *0*(0). Advance online publication. doi:10.1177/10526846231187576

Williams, T. N. (2019). *Crisis Communication Systems Among K-12 School Principals* (Order No. 13807361). Available from ProQuest One Academic. (2198700438). https://www.proquest.com/dissertations-theses/crisis-communication-systems-among-k-12-school/docview/2198700438/se-2

Yates, D., & Paquette, S. (2011). Emergency knowledge management and social media technologies: A case study of the 2010 Haitian earthquake. *International Journal of Information Management*, *31*(1), 6–13. doi:10.1016/j.ijinfomgt.2010.10.001

Zhang, J., Xie, C., Chen, Y., Dai, Y. D., & Yi-Jun, W. (2023). The matching effect of destinations' crisis communication. *Journal of Travel Research*, *62*(3), 491–516. doi:10.1177/00472875211067548

Chapter 2
How the Police Released Body-Worn Camera Footage Matters

Angelo Kevin Brown
Arkansas State University, USA

ABSTRACT

Body-worn cameras (BWC) policies can have a significant impact on police-community relations in various ways, which this chapter will examine. BWCs have been implemented internationally, especially in the developed world. This chapter will primarily focus on law enforcement policies within the United States of America (USA). BWCs have become very common among law enforcement officers, including police officers, sheriff deputies, state patrol, and federal agents. No national law forces law enforcement to wear BWCs. Since no national policy outlines when footage can or cannot be released to the public, which leaves states and municipalities to deal with the legality and practicality of releasing BWC footage. This chapter will provide an overview of how BWC policies have developed and the impact of BWCs on police and community relations.

There was an impetus for BWCs under the Obama administration, including the implementation of the President's Task Force in 21st-century policing provided 75 million dollars for BWCs, and funding was continued under the Trump administration (Smith, 2019). President Obama was quoted as saying, "There's been a lot of talk about body cameras as a silver bullet or a solution. I think the task force concluded that there is a role for technology to play in building additional trust and accountability, but it's not a panacea, it has to be embedded in a broader change in culture and a legal framework that ensures that people's privacy is respected and that not only police

DOI: 10.4018/978-1-6684-8569-9.ch002

officers but the community themselves feel comfortable with how technologies are being used." (White House, 2015).

President Biden signed the Executive Order to Advance Effective, Accountable Policing and Strengthen Public Safety of May 2022, which ordered all federal law enforcement agents and officers to be equipped with BWC when possible (White House, 2022). The Executive Order was met with much support, especially from Democratic representatives like Don Beyer, who stated, "The steps President Biden announced today would improve accountability for police misconduct while boosting transparency and support for officer wellness, and approach that supports police by improving community trust." (White House, 2022).

Federal agencies, including the Department of Interior, announced soon after the Executive Order that they were implementing the policing outlined in the order. The order requires federal law enforcement officers to wear BWCs while patrolling and interacting with the public and the requirements for documenting, downloading, and storing the data. Over 130,000 federal law enforcement personnel are in the country (Brooks, 2022), and this order may help guide their work.

The employment of BWCs was projected to help progress the country's public perception of law enforcement (Bush, 2020). Cameras have shown that people become more self-aware when they are watched and change their conduct when being watched (Farrar and Ariel, 2013). This was thought to appeal to the law enforcement community to reduce civil liability and potentially alter citizen behavior. As more departments started to adopt BWCs, the public perception of police had decreased, the opposite of what was intended, especially for the Black community. Using BWC footage for research has helped verify and quantify racial disparities. For example, Voigt et al. (2017) showed that police treat African American with significantly less respect than they do White people.

IMPACT OF BWCS

BWCs can impact community relations, including increasing accountability and transparency for community-police relationships, which can impact the trust between the community and law enforcement (Maskaly et al., 2017). BWCs were also designed to give protection of citizens from excessive use of force and police brutality from being overlooked. The research has shown that the implementation of BWCs has been followed by a reduction in complaints against law enforcement and an improved perception of police officer behavior (White et al., 2017). This trust, accountability, and transparency depend on the agency's policies. When law enforcement selectively releases footage or does not release it promptly or transparently, it can greatly erode the legitimacy people in the community have for law enforcement and exacerbate tensions between law enforcement and the community (Bush, 2020).

Sometimes, the BWC footage is held for years before being released without any reasonable explanation. One example of such a delay is the shooting of Laquan McDonald in Chicago, Illinois, in 2014 (Licht, 2018). The BWC footage was held for over a year before being released (Bush, 2020). This delay can lead to protests and legal trouble. In 2021, for example, the city of Columbus, Ohio, had to pay around 10 million dollars to the family of Andre Hill, an unarmed African American man whose life was taken in December 2020 by a law enforcement official. The lawsuit involved the failure of the officer to properly activate his BWC and the delay in releasing the captured video. However, when law enforcement agencies can prioritize the transparent and effective means of releasing the footage, it can help improve the relations between law enforcement and the public and support police legitimacy.

BWCs are generally a new technology for police, but the use of cameras and video footage is not. The use of video technology and surveillance for police officers has been implemented since the 1950s. The use of CCTV technology has also been a way that law enforcement has used video footage to their advantage (Nieto et al., 2002).

Police citizen encounters have always been an important factor for police perceptions, and the ability to share these interactions with thousands or millions of others instantly online has made these interactions even more important. The sharing of videos can have a significantly negative impact on police perceptions (Parry, 2017). As the effects are not just on those directly involved in police encounters but also on the surrounding witnesses may also be impacted by what they see and lose trust and legitimacy in police (Mastrofskiet al., 2002; Skogan, 2005). Overaggressive and disrespectful police behavior especially have a negative impact on police legitimacy, trust, and over-perceptions of the police (Paternoster et al., 1997; Skogan, 2006, Tyler, 1990; Tyler, 2003).

Police legitimacy and trust are essential for effective police work. As people perceive the police as legitimate, they are significantly more likely to provide information to the police, report crimes, cooperate with investigations, and comply with law enforcement orders (Tyler, 1990). While in communities that do not have trust and legitimacy in the police, officers often have a more difficult time being effective investigators, keeping their communities safe, and holding criminals accountable.

Personal police experience is known to help shape a person's attitude toward police officers, but the typical American has little direct contact with police officers (Gaines & Kappeler, 2011). So, the main experience that some people have with the police is through watching BWC footage. The videos that are released and watched by most people are disproportionally the videos of violent and abusive actions of police officers. For example, the murder of George Floyd by a police officer was watched by millions of people within a short period of time (Ellison, 2021).

BWC are cameras that police officers wear and capture audio and video from the perspective of the police officer wearing it. BWCs are generally worn on the upper body of the officer. The first implementation of BWCs was in 2005 with officers in the United Kingdom (Smykla et al., 2016). Through the years BWCs have improved with high-definition quality, night vision, and infrared and have spread to departments worldwide, especially in the United States, which will be the focus of this chapter. Research on BWC has helped support their adaptation in response to criticism of poor policing (Ariel, 2016). For the first decade of BWCs, there was very little research and knowledge about their impact on police-community relations (Berdjis, 2016). Police officers often need to provide the proper training and resources on what should and should not be shared with the public so that community members may have a clear understanding of policing operations and procedures (Escutia, 2016).

It is important for police agencies to increase the level of rapport with community members to help provide effective dialogue to improve community problems. Police agencies can reduce barriers and skepticism in the community through such conversations (Hemmer, 2017). Community input can help allow police agencies to know what current policies are acceptable and which are not (Bush, 2020). This community involvement can help give community members a stake in the changes, which can help empower the community and ensure their voice is heard.

Police unions have been a problem that has decreased the transparency of BWC footage. The Police Benevolent Association (PBA) had even sued the city to stop the release of any footage from police BWC footage to be released to the public, the PBA lost the case but appealed the findings. The PBA argued that each time the NYPD releases BWC footage, they arbitrarily harm the officer's safety (Toor, 2018).

BWCs were first implemented to help create trust between the police and the community, increase the transparency of policing, increase the sense of safety and accountability, and give officers a sense of being supervised to improve their behavior and decrease the likelihood of corruption and wrongdoing going unchecked (Ariel et al., 2015). Community members and groups had demanded that all police agencies be required to adopt BWCs to help ensure transparency and accountability. These factors were thought that the relationship between the police and the community would be improved through this innovative technology (Cao, 2015).

Many states have mandated their use by law enforcement officers, including Colorado, Connecticut, Illinois, Maryland, New Jersey, New Mexico, and South Carolina. Before May 2020, only one state (South Carolina) required BWCs (Mullinax, 2016; NCSL, 2021). The officers generally required to wear BWCs are those interacting with the public, but there are exceptions, for example, officers in undercover work, in courtrooms, in confidential settings, and administrators. The

BWC expansion in the US increased around 2014, as the shooting of Michael Brown was seen throughout the nation and abroad, leading to major protests around the country (Fallik et al., 2020).

One feature to highlight for many BWCs is the automatic triggers for the recording of the camera, such as when an officer grabs their taser or firearm, when the patrol car door opens, when the siren is activated, etc. (Taylor & Lee, 2020). Another important capability of BWCs is the ability to pre-record the activation of the camera. The BWCs are meant to be recorded so that when the officer manually records, the prior thirty seconds will also be saved. This is an important feature because situations can happen without warning, and the context of the situation can be necessary for trials and investigations. This, for example, can give the public a better understanding of why the person was approached, any type of actions that the citizen may have done to make an officer react in a certain way, or also provide evidence to show that the officer had not acted in the proper way.

During a serious event like an officer-involved shooting, the memory of victims, officers, and the public is often unreliable, to be precise (Artwohl, 2002). As officers and civilians will often underestimate or overestimate certain factors like the timeline and the number of bullets fired. The BWC footage is often crucial to get a full picture of the reality of the situation.

BWC footage is used for many distinct aspects of policing, from community accountability to criminal and civil trials, internal investigations, training, and more. The policies surrounding BWC can vary from different agencies and are continuously changing, making it hard for the community to understand the legality of camera usage. Some footage is shared only with the specific department, while others are shared or held in outside agencies, including district attorneys. The inconsistent and problematic release of BWC footage became a national issue, prompting community leaders and politicians to attempt to support policy changes (Parry, 2017). As most police departments are engaged in community policing, it is important for our law enforcement agencies to work with community members in an active partnership to establish proper BWC protocols. A community-approved public policy has started to be implemented in different states.

DELAY IN FOOTAGE

The delay of footage can create issues for the legitimacy of police agencies (Grabiner, 2016). This is especially problematic when the media has publicized an incident, and the public is eager to see the video for themselves. Delays can be important for various reasons, including the need to edit the footage to protect victims and witnesses and the potential impact on ongoing investigations can make a delay necessary. These delays can impact the transparency of departments in an era where police have been mistrusted by many, especially minority communities (Bush, 2020).

The police may have legitimate or perceived reasons to keep BWC footage secured, and police often work with confidential information (Farmer, 2016). Police may have illegitimate reasons to keep the footage secure such as to protect officers from legal consequences, hide corruption, or lack of effort and incompetency.

BWC policies and practices can directly impact the legitimacy of the police and procedural justice (Escutia, 2016). When BWC footage is significantly delayed, it can often worry community members, especially the victim and their families (Mateescu & Rosenblat, 2016). Many communities have viewed BWC implementation as positive and have been supportive of police having BWCs (Grabiner, 2016). Bush (2020) found that poor communication of police regarding the BWC video release can have a negative impact, especially on family members and their perception of the police and if the police are being honest and legitimate with their duties. Many of the participants did not believe that there was justification for the videos to be delayed and that the editing of the videos was not warranted.

Public criticism has helped ensure that police departments implement policies related to the release of video footage (Parry, 2017). One significant case occurred in Topeka, Kansas, after an officer-involved shooting that led to the death of Dominque White. The family members attempted to access the video footage. They learned there was no policy related to BWC footage which made it difficult to obtain the footage for the family, which upset the community. Eventually, the department allowed White's father to view the BWC footage (Bush, 2020), and since the incident, the department has implemented policies related to releasing the BWC video.

There have been many issues communities have with the unknown practices of police and BWCs. Common concerns have been the lack of understanding of when the cameras are recording and when they are not, and why police have to turn the cameras on. This has led to many departmental policies for the officers to inform citizens that the camera is actively recording (Roy, 2014). The lack of policies that law enforcement agencies have had with BWCs has led to numerous lawsuits, including the death of Marcus Deon Smith, who died after being hogtied by officers and the department not releasing the video.

Different departments have different policies and practices for releasing video footage, which has negatively impacted public opinion of law enforcement and can impact public distrust (Paulsen, 2016). This can be incredibly impactful when the videos have been believed to be edited.

STATES

There are various state laws that govern the release of BWC footage. The statutes that govern the release of video footage are often aligned with their public record legislation and differ from each other (Thomas, 2016). The lack of consistency of states shows a lack of uniformity which can impact trust in law enforcement because of the lack of understanding for many citizens.

In states like Connecticut, Nevada, North Dakota, Ohio, Oklahoma, and Texas, they treat BWC footage as a public record (NCSL, 2021). For Maryland, BWC footage is released under the public information act. The State laws often provide mechanisms for police to withhold data, including video, for various reasons, including if an investigation is in progress, if the video needs to have footage redacted to protect witnesses, or if consent is needed from victims who appear in the video. For Ohio, a video that includes children, nudity, crime prevention tactics, personal information unrelated to law enforcement activity, a video that could identify domestic violence or sexual abuse victims, protected health information, and death not caused by a law enforcement officer can be restricted from release.

New Mexico regulates the release of footage when it can reveal certain information that is meant to be confidential such as the use of confidential informants, or when it may reveal people who are accused but not yet charged. In New Jersey and South Carolina, the BWC footage is provided to those people involved in the footage and their legal counsel. The state of New Jersey does provide exemptions for the release of the footage when the public interest outweighs the requirement for confidentiality (Delaney, 2019).

Some have criticized some police for being too restrictive and not providing sufficient protection for citizens. In California, for example, law enforcement officers can review the BWC footage before writing their reports, which can lead to biased reporting but has also been shown to help improve accuracy (Boivin & Gendron, 2022). Some policies give the officer a wide range of discretion regarding when to activate their camera or not, which can lead to disproportionate practices and bias.

State laws also regulate how long agencies can keep the BWC footage before releasing it, and how long it should be kept (Parry, 2017). In Illinois, for example, the BWC data is to be held for at least 90 days, and if the footage is flagged, it must be held for two years. While in South Carolina, the requirement is 14 days. While in Colorado, the footage must be released to the public within three weeks of a complaint being received, with stipulations that if an ongoing investigation could be compromised, it can be released after 45 days.

There are exceptions to the rule that departments have with their days of releasing the video. The officer-involved death of 17-year-old Laquan McDonald was an example of the Chicago Policeman and the City of Chicago not releasing the video even within the 90-day policy that was in place. This shooting was eventually charged with murder. Officer Van Dyke was found guilty about three years after the shooting for second-degree murder and sixteen counts of aggravated battery with a firearm. The incident was first reported as McDonald refusing the officer's orders to put down a knife and accusations of McDonald lunging at the officers with a knife which officials first deemed the shooting justified, and the officer not initially being charged. The video was not released for thirteen months after the incident. The video was only released because of the work of a freelance journalist and an attorney working with the Better Government Association to release the tape under the Illinois Freedom of Information Act. The video showed a completely different story for McDonald and the officers, where he was not threatening the officers (Bush, 2020). The Freedom of Information Act provides a compliance time of five to ten business days to meet requests for governmental material, including audio or video.

Some cities have most of their videos released the next day or at least the same week unless there is a need to protect an ongoing investigation that could jeopardize if there was release of the footage. This difference in the video's release time can be another factor that exacerbates the mistrust between the police and community members.

CONCERNS OF THE COMMUNITY

People have often been critical of officers' discretion and use of their cameras (Roy, 2014). For example, the public has questioned why officers turned off the audio, why only part of the event was recorded, and why the event was not recorded at all. These questions can show a lack of transparency with the police and a lack of knowledge of the public regarding police policy and the job of a police officer. This has helped lead to policies and practices of officers informing citizens when they activate their BWC.

With the use of social media and most people having access to phones with video recording abilities, the public can often get quick access to videos of police and community interactions, including deadly interactions. Since 2013 most Americans have had cell phones with video capability (Sterling, 2013). The uploading of such ideas can seriously impact reducing the trust and legitimacy of the police. This instant access to negative interactions can impact police legitimacy and trust. When police take a long time to release the video, many people in public may have already seen other versions of the incident. They may have already decided on their perceptions of the incident. To improve trust in police in the community, transparency and proper communication must be established (Bush, 2020).

NEGATIVE REACTIONS FROM THE RELEASED VIDEO

The release of a video showing police brutality and corruption can cause serious societal reactions. The murder and death of Tyre Nichols in Memphis, Tennessee, by Memphis police officers, was caught on BWC footage as well as footage from a SkyCop. Nichols had not committed a crime, and there was no evidence to suspect him of committing a crime. As he was pulled out of his care, the officers did not give him a chance to have any dialogue or understanding before the start of their violence toward Nichols (Yearwood, 2023). The video was released only after multiple statements from the department and other government officials to attempt to limit the outrage that was expected. The video's release occurred strategically, with the officers involved being fired and arrested prior to the video to show that the officers were being punished for the murder. The video was said to be released on January 27th, 2023, in the evening, and protests started to form right after the video's release throughout the country. The incident happened on January 7th, 2023, 20 days prior to the release of the video (Yearwood, 2023).

The release of the BWC video of the Nichols killing helped give the prosecutor legitimate evidence to charge the officers with murder which is rare when officers kill civilians. There have been multiple other instances in recent events that gave the public a view of police brutality and death with the release of the BWC video. This video has been crucial to holding certain officers accountable and to be used for trials and lawsuits against officers who have violated their duties and the law. For the death of Nichols, his family had filed a $550 million federal lawsuit against the City of Memphis and the Memphis Police Department. Their claims include that the police officers were unqualified, untrained, and unsupervised (Valencia et al., 2023).

It is not always the police agencies to blame for delays in the footage. There can be other actors involved in delaying footage. For example, in the death of Nichols, the judge delayed the release of the footage, along with various judges in other situations and states blocking the release of the footage. Judges could do this for several reasons, including the potential for the release of the video to impact a criminal trial.

Lawsuits and problems with BWCs and the release of footage continue to be an issue well into 2023. In April, the Alaska Black Caucus filed a lawsuit against Anchorage municipality because of delays in equipping BWCs (Samuels, 2023).

Editing BWC footage without permission can be a significant issue in departments. The Metro Nashville Police Department had recently run into this issue within their department (Crescencio, 2022). Two employees were reprimanded after they had been found to have edited out curse words from the video footage. This tampering of evidence can seriously impact the charges filed, criminal trials, and civil trials.

The NYPD has also had issues in releasing their video footage with allegations of breaking policy. In 2021, New York State Judge Eileen Rakower accused the NYPD of illegally withholding footage in the police-involved shootings of Kawaski Trawick in 2019. The judge stated in a hearing that the NYPD had operated in bad faith during this incident (Umansky, 2021).

During the killing of Sylville Smith in Milwaukee, the Attorney General moved to postpone the release of the video (Wood, 2017). The community was upset with this decision. This led to a group that organized and protested at the city hall, interrupting a meeting to pressure the city leaders to release the video. The government argued that the video needed to be held while the investigation was going on and deciding on charges against the police officer.

As videos of police officers using unnecessary force and corruption from BWC videos become more common, it gives a perception of accountability to police. The arrest of the firing of an officer who was planting drugs could have gone undiscovered without the use of BWC footage. Police have been accused of planting drugs on civilians for decades, but there was often little evidence ever to prove these accusations. With BWC footage, more officers than ever have been arrested and convicted for planting drugs on innocent people. Zachary Wester was one of those officers who was sentenced to 12 years for planting drugs during a traffic stop (Gaub et al., 2022).

Abuse of power can create a serious distrust of police from victims (McCarthy et al., 2020). Victims of police abuse related to planting evidence are often found guilty because the testimony of a police officer is held to a higher standard than a defendant's testimony. This type of corruption may be significantly reduced with proper investigation and utilization of BWCs. This also causes a genuine issue as many of the former arrests and convictions that were due to the officer's arrests are now questionable as it is likely that an officer had only planted evidence once ever in their career.

In Fairfax County, prosecutors learned about a racially biased officer who was consistently planting drugs on innocent people. The scandal led to prosecutors attempting to throw out four hundred convictions that were based on the former officer Jonathan Freitag (Dunkle, 2021). There were people in prison that they knew were innocent, and they were now moving to exonerate these wrongly convicted citizens like Elon Wilson, who was a former District of Columbia firefighter incarcerated for 21 months. Wilson received 390,000$ for the wrongful arrest. For the investigation of this corruption, the Federal Bureau of Investigation was even investigating Freitag for the accusation of planting drugs and stealing drugs, including cocaine and marijuana, from the evidence of crimes, and creating false police records. These injustices are now made visible to the public, governmental officials, and anyone else to help provide the right accountability and changes to make a more just police force and society. Without video footage of such actions, the proof of wrongdoing is often a lot more difficult to prove in these cases.

OUTSIDE OF THE US

Looking outside the US can help provide important perspectives that may not be widely available in the US. A main barrier can be the cost of the technology, including the cameras themselves and the necessary data storage and management systems, especially for many developing nations. A large police department, like the Los Angeles Police Department, spent over 57 million dollars on BWCs in 2016, with only about four million dollars spent on the actual cameras (Mather & Zahniser, 2016).

Police departments must invest in training officers on how to use the cameras, as well as developing policies and procedures for their use. The cameras must also be regularly maintained and calibrated to ensure that they are functioning properly (Braga et al., 2017). Addressing these challenges will require a commitment to transparency and accountability in law enforcement, as well as a willingness to invest in technology and training to ensure that BWCs are used appropriately and effectively.

The use of BWCs by law enforcement agencies has been gaining traction globally as a way to improve police accountability and transparency, but the implementation has brought a lot of criticism (Al-Shehhi, 2018). However, the delay in releasing footage captured by BWCs has become a common issue in many countries, including Europe (Maskaly et al., 2017), Canada (Saulnier et al.,2021), Japan, China (Zhang, 2022), and Australia (Sivasubramaniam et al., 2021).

One of the main reasons for delays in releasing BWC footage is related to data protection laws. Many countries have strict data protection regulations that govern the collection, storage, and sharing of personal information (Salbu, 2002). These regulations often require that footage captured by BWCs be reviewed and redacted before it can be released to the public, which can be a time-consuming process. In addition, there may be worries about violating the privacy of individuals who are captured on camera, principally if they are not involved in a criminal investigation.

Another reason for delays in releasing BWC footage is related to the investigative process. Police investigations often involve multiple agencies, especially in serious transnational cases, and the release of footage can potentially compromise ongoing investigations or interfere with the rights of suspects. In some cases, the release of footage could also compromise the safety of police officers or witnesses involved in the investigation. If the footage is not released in a timely manner, there is a risk that the public may lose faith in the ability of BWCs to hold police officers accountable for their actions, especially in countries where the people already have a poor perception of the police.

In Canada, there have been instances where police have delayed releasing BWC footage, leading to public criticism. The Toronto Police Service (TPS) addressed this criticism by updating its policy that outlines when BWC footage can be released and provides clear timelines for doing (Brown, 2020). Under the new policy, footage must be released within 60 days of the incident, or within 30 days if there is significant public interest. Other regions of Canada have also adopted similar policies to regulate BWC footage (Saulnier et al., 2021).

The delay in releasing BWC footage is a common issue faced by law enforcement agencies around the world. While data protection laws and the investigative process can pose significant obstacles to the timely release of the footage, delays can undermine the effectiveness of BWCs in improving police accountability and transparency. To address this issue, law enforcement agencies must develop clear policies and procedures that balance the need for transparency and accountability with the need to protect privacy and maintain the integrity of ongoing investigations. Many countries have already taken steps to address this issue by implementing clear guidelines for the timely release of BWC footage.

RECOMMENDATIONS FOR IMPROVEMENT

There is a serious disconnect between some communities and law enforcement. It is essential that law enforcement agencies evaluate how their policies impact community-police relations to build trust (Hemmer, 2017). A serious effort needs to be made to bring the community and police together to ensure that the tenants of community policing are active, especially active partnerships and trust. The responsibility for change is needed throughout the government and society to limit the problems associated with BWC footage and community satisfaction with the release. If police are not held accountable by other parts of the government, they may not have the pressure or incentive to change. The mayor, city council, Attorney General, and other government officials can help ensure that the police act in efficient and proper steps when serious events happen and are caught on BWC cameras.

As police often want to protect their own and the release of BWC footage can compromise an officer's life and career, it is important to remind law enforcement agencies of their responsibilities and the cost of an agency losing the trust of a community. The loss of trust in a community can put police officers in more danger and make their lives, and their family lives stressful and difficult. The police are to protect and serve the community first, and when the public does not perceive that, it can become a downward spiral. As police culture is difficult to change, it will likely take more than just written policies but changes in recruitment, leaders, training, educational curriculum, and support from outside agencies.

Portland police and the Portland Police Union were scrutinized by a federal judge over their BWC policies and practices. The federal judge had wondered why the union had insisted that officers view the BWC footage before writing reports, especially when using deadly force (Bernstein, 2023). The Portland Bureau has been known to be the largest municipal police force in the country without BWC. The judge recommended that the officers write a statement before watching the footage and then follow up with a supplemental report.

BWC policies, or the lack thereof, can have serious legal implications in the courtroom. As BWC footage is often used in criminal and civil trials, those agencies that do not have sufficient policies can lead to some of the footage being challenged by admissibility and reliability of evidence issues (Coudert et al., 2015).

More research is needed on how BWC footage should and should not be released, and the impact certain types of policies has how community satisfaction. The perspective of the victim and or the victim's family is an important view that is overlooked in the research. Another important aspect of BWC that is under-researched is the impact of releasing BWC video when the victim or suspect is underage and if it differs from other BWC footage releases.

CONCLUSION

With the mass protests and dissatisfaction that some communities in the US have with police, it is essential that police agencies review and modify their policies to increase legitimacy, transparency, and trust with the public. The protests that have erupted have led to deaths, many injuries, millions of dollars in damage, and brought attention to the injustices. These protests may continue if serious changes are not made by police agencies. An important step is to ensure proper policies surrounding BWCs and the release of the footage to the public when appropriate.

With sound policies, it is important that police administrators and agencies ensure that the policies are followed and practiced how they are intended. The police can start a process to improve police-community relations and help with collective strategies of engagement. There is a delicate balance that needs to be followed to ensure that the community, family, victims, and others are respected and listened to with the release and sharing of BWC footage to ensure an equitable policy.

The research shows that it is important for law enforcement agencies to create clear policies for BWC and the footage that they collect. These policies need to be transparent and provide accountability for law enforcement while protecting a certain level of privacy and due process rights of individuals. The implementation of proper and clear guidelines for BWCs can cause constant use of the BWCs and limit abuse. When different officers are using BWCs in significantly different ways, it can cause a perception of bias or differential treatment.

REFERENCES

Al-Shehhi, M. (2018). *A criminological critique of body worn cameras in policing: the case of the United Arab Emirates*. University of Salford.

Ariel, B. (2016). Police body cameras in large police departments. *The Journal of Criminal Law & Criminology, 106*(4), 729–768.

Ariel, B., Farrar, W. A., & Sutherland, A. (2015). The effect of police body-worn cameras on use of force and citizens' complaints against the police: A randomized controlled trial. *Journal of Quantitative Criminology, 31*(3), 509–535. doi:10.1007/s10940-014-9236-3

Artwohl, A. (2002). Perceptual and memory distortion during officer-involved shootings. *FBI L. Enforcement Bull., 71*, 18.

Berdjis, N. (2016). *A descriptive study on police body cameras and civil liability cases* [Master's thesis]. University of Colorado.

Bernstein, M. (2023). Disputed Portland police body camera policy draws questions from federal judge. *The Oregonian*.

Boivin, R., & Gendron, A. (2022). An experimental study of the impact of body-worn cameras on police report writing. *Journal of Experimental Criminology, 18*(4), 747–764. doi:10.1007/s11292-021-09469-8

Brooks, C. (2022). *Federal Law Enforcement Officers, 2020-Statistical Tables*. Academic Press.

Brown, G. R. (2020). Police body-worn cameras in the Canadian context: Policing's new visibility and today's expectations for police accountability. In *Police on Camera* (pp. 122–148). Routledge. doi:10.4324/9780429439759-8

Bush, C. L. (2020). *Public Perceptions of Delays in the Release of Police Body-Worn Camera Footage* [Doctoral dissertation]. Walden University.

Cao, L. (2015). Differentiating confidence in the police, trust in the police, and satisfaction with the police. *Policing; Bradford, 38*(2), 239-249.

Coudert, F., Butin, D., & Le Métayer, D. (2015). Body-worn cameras for police accountability: Opportunities and risks. *Computer Law & Security Report, 31*(6), 749–762. doi:10.1016/j.clsr.2015.09.002

Crescencio, A. (2022). Metro Nashville Police employees altered body camera footage without authorization, officials said. *News Channel 5 Nashville.*

Delaney, N. (2019). *Strong, Cheap, and Ready Access to Body-worn Camera Footage under New Jersey's Open Public Records Act (OPRA).* Will Promote Police Accountability and Transparency.

Dunkle, S. (2021). The air was blue with perjury: Police lies and the case for abolition. *NYUL Rev., 96*, 2048.

Ellison, K. (2021). The Death of George Floyd, the Trial of Derek Chauvin, and Deadly- Force Encounters with Police: Have We Finally Reached an Inflection Point? Or Will the Cycle of Inaction Continue? *Ann. Rev. Crim. Proc., 50*, i.

Escutia, X. (2016). *Body-worn cameras, procedural justice, and police legitimacy.* California State University.

Fallik, S. W., Deuchar, R., & Crichlow, V. J. (2020). Body-worn cameras in the post- Ferguson era: An exploration of law enforcement perspectives. *Journal of Police and Criminal Psychology, 35*(3), 263–273. doi:10.1007/s11896-018-9300-2

Farmer, A. (2016). *Copwatchers: citizen journalism and the changing police-community dynamic* [Doctoral dissertation]. University of Delaware.

Farrar, W., & Ariel, B. (2013). *Self-awareness to being watched and socially desirable behavior: A field experiment on the effect of body-worn cameras and police use of force.* Police Foundation.

Gaines, L. K., & Kappeler, V. E. (2011). *Policing in America.* Routledge.

Gaub, J. E., White, M., Malm, A., Watts, S., & Brown, K. L. (2022). Investigating the prevalence and utility of police body-worn cameras in the George Floyd protests. *Policing: An International Journal.*

Grabiner, G. (2016). Who polices the police? *Social Justice (San Francisco, Calif.)*, 58–79.

Hemmer, J. W. (2017). *Exploring Police Beliefs in Community Oriented Policing and Community Trust: A Multiple Case Study* [Doctoral dissertation]. Northcentral University.

Licht, I. H. (2018). How body cameras may result in a more proactive and community-engaged police force. *Chicago Policy Review*.

Maskaly, J., Donner, C., Jennings, W. G., Ariel, B., & Sutherland, A. (2017). The effects of body-worn cameras (BWCs) on police and citizen outcomes: A state-of-the-art review. *Policing*, *40*(4), 672–688. doi:10.1108/PIJPSM-03-2017-0032

Mastrofski, S. D., Reisig, M. D., & McCluskey, J. D. (2002). Police disrespect toward the public: An encounter-based analysis. *Criminology*, *40*(3), 519–552. doi:10.1111/j.1745-9125.2002.tb00965.x

Mateescu, A., Rosenblat, A., & Boyd, D. (2016). Dreams of accountability, guaranteed surveillance: The promises and costs of body-worn cameras. *Surveillance & Society*, *14*(1), 122–127. doi:10.24908/ss.v14i1.6282

Mather, K., & Zahniser, D. (2016). Deal to spend $57.6 million on LAPD body cameras clears key hurdle. *Los Angeles Times*.

Maury, K. J. (2016). Police body-worn camera policy: Balancing the tension between privacy and public access in state laws. *The Notre Dame Law Review*, *92*, 479.

McCarthy, B., Hagan, J., & Herda, D. (2020). Neighborhood climates of legal cynicism and complaints about abuse of police power. *Criminology*, *58*(3), 510–536. doi:10.1111/1745-9125.12246

Mullinax, B. J. (2016). Silent Witness-Reconstruction from Body Worn Camera Videos. *Accident Reconstruction Journal, 26*(5).

National Conference of State Legislatures (NCSL). (2021). Body-Worn Camera Laws Database. *April Report*.

Parry, M. M. (2017). *Watching the Watchmen: How Videos of Police-Citizen Encounters Influence Individuals' Perceptions of the Police*. Arizona State University.

Paternoster, R., Brame, R., Bachman, R., & Sherman, L. W. (1997). Do fair procedures matter? The effect of procedural justice on spouse assault. *Law & Society Review*, *31*(1), 163–204. doi:10.2307/3054098

Paulsen, D. (2016). *Public opinion about police use of body-worn cameras* [Dissertation]. Retrieved from ProQuest Dissertations & Theses Global. (UMI No. 10163614).

Roy, A. (2014). *On-officer video cameras: Examining the effects of police department policy and assignment on camera use and activation*. Arizona State University.

Salbu, S. R. (2002). The European Union Data Privacy Directive and International Relations. *Vand. J. Transnat'l L.*, *35*, 655.

Saulnier, A., Bagg, J., & Thompson, B. (2021). Canadian policing and body-worn cameras: Factors to contemplate in developing body-worn camera policy. *Canadian Public Policy*, *47*(2), 131–157. doi:10.3138/cpp.2020-096

Sivasubramaniam, D., Burke, K. C., Saulnier, A., Szabo, R., Agius, E. J., & Bottoms, B. L. (2021). International perspectives on procedural justice: Trust and respect matter even when body-worn cameras are present. *Law and Human Behavior*, *45*(5), 440–455. doi:10.1037/lhb0000454 PMID:34871016

Skogan, W. G. (2005). Citizen satisfaction with police encounters. *Police Quarterly*, *8*(3), 298–321. doi:10.1177/1098611104271086

Skogan, W. G. (2006). Asymmetry in the impact of encounters with police. *Policing and Society*, *16*(02), 99–126. doi:10.1080/10439460600662098

Smith, J. J. (2019). To adopt or not to adopt: Contextualizing police body-worn cameras through structural contingency and institutional theoretical perspectives. *Criminal Justice Review*, *44*(3), 369–385. doi:10.1177/0734016819847267

Smykla, J. O., Crow, M. S., Crichlow, V. J., & Snyder, J. A. (2016). Police body-worn cameras: Perceptions of law enforcement leadership. *American Journal of Criminal Justice*, *41*(3), 424–443. doi:10.1007/s12103-015-9316-4

Sterling, G. (2013, June 5). *Marketing Land*. Retrieved October 3, 2013, from Pew: 61 Percent In US Now Have Smartphones: http://marketingland.com/pew-61percent-in-us-now-have-smartphones-46966

Taylor, E., & Lee, M. (2020). The camera never lies?: Police body-worn cameras and operational discretion. In *Police on Camera* (pp. 80–94). Routledge. doi:10.4324/9780429439759-6

Thomas, E. (2016). The privacy case for body cameras: The need for a privacy-centric approach to body camera policymaking. *Colum. JL & Soc. Probs.*, *50*, 191.

Toor, M. (2018). *PBA Sues City Over 'Illegal' Releasing Of Body-Camera Footage*. New York City Police Benevolent Association.

Tyler, T. R. (1990). *Why people obey the law: Procedural justice, legitimacy, and compliance*. Yale University Press.

Tyler, T. R. (2003). Procedural justice, legitimacy, and the effective rule of law. In M. Tonry (Ed.), *Crime and Justice Chicago*. University of Chicago Press. doi:10.1086/652233

Umansky, E. (2021). *Judge Says NYPD Illegally Withheld Footage in Police Shootings*. Pro Publica News.

Valencia, N., Sanchez, R., Kirkland, P., & Tamsett, M. (2023). Tyre Nichols' family files federal $550 million civil lawsuit against Memphis and police officers. *CNN*. https://www.cnn.com/2023/04/19/us/tyre-nichols-death-lawsuit-memphis-police/index.html

Voigt, R., Camp, N. P., Prabhakaran, V., Hamilton, W. L., Hetey, R. C., Griffiths, C. M., Jurgens, D., Jurafsky, D., & Eberhardt, J. L. (2017). Language from police body camera footage shows racial disparities in officer respect. *Proceedings of the National Academy of Sciences of the United States of America*, *114*(25), 6521–6526. doi:10.1073/pnas.1702413114 PMID:28584085

White House. (2015). *Remarks by the President after Meeting with Task Force on 21st Century Policing*. Office of the Press Secretary Speech Transcript.

White, M. D., Todak, N., & Gaub, J. E. (2017). Assessing citizen perceptions of body-worn cameras after encounters with police. *Policing*, *40*(4), 689–703. doi:10.1108/PIJPSM-07-2016-0105

White House. (2022). *FACT SHEET: President Biden to Sign Historic Executive Order to Advance Effective, Accountable Policing and Strengthen Public Safety*. https://www.whitehouse.gov/briefing-room/statements-releases/2022/05/25/fact-sheet-president-biden-to-sign-historic-executive-order-to-advance-effective-accountable-policing-and-strengthen-public-safety/

Wood, S. E. (2017). Police body cameras and professional responsibility: Public records and private evidence. *Preservation. Digital Technology & Culture*, *46*(1), 41–51. doi:10.1515/pdtc-2016-0030

Yearwood, E. L. (2023). His name this time was Tyre Nichols. *Archives of Psychiatric Nursing*, *43*, A1–A2. doi:10.1016/j.apnu.2023.02.001 PMID:37032025

Zhang, J. (2022, December). Body-worn cameras in China: a survey. In *Third International Conference on Computer Science and Communication Technology (ICCSCT 2022)* (Vol. 12506, pp. 943-950). SPIE.

Chapter 3
Best Practices for the Reintegration of Offenders Into the Community

Evelyn Lorraine Anderson
https://orcid.org/0000-0002-5801-1250
National University, USA

Ana M. Gamez
California Baptist University, USA

ABSTRACT

This chapter provides a discussion on the best practices for the reintegration of offenders into the community. More than one approach is necessary to address the emerging needs of this population. This chapter discusses some of the most prevalent barriers to reintegration and the stigmas ex-offenders face as they reintegrate into the community. This chapter also evaluates recidivism reduction strategies and community corrections strategies to facilitate the transition of offenders into the community. It then discusses the need for relationship building between law enforcement and the community to assist in reintegration strategies for justice-involved people. The chapter concludes with best practices for reintegrating offenders into the community and a review of reintegration strategies in California, Florida, and Texas state prisons.

INTRODUCTION

More than two million people are incarcerated in the United States (Prison Policy Initiative [PPI], United States, [U.S.], 2020). The vast majority of those jailed were in state prisons (1,047,000), local jails (514,000), and federal prisons (209,000)

DOI: 10.4018/978-1-6684-8569-9.ch003

(PPI, US, 2020). Black people represented the largest population of offenders per 100,000 at 2,306 followed by American Indians/ Alaska Natives at 895, Hispanics at 831, and Whites at 450. Thousands of other Americans are under community supervision or community corrections such as parole or probation, local jails, and halfway houses (PPI, U.S., 2020). According to Carson (2021), the incarceration rate for U.S. residents across all race/ethnic groups decreased by 12% to 16% from 2019 and 2020. The Federal and state prison population incarceration rate decreased by 15% compared to 2019 (Carson, 2021). The Bureau of Prisons (BOP) population increased by 5,200 admissions in that same period, representing only a 3% increase (Carson, 2021). Even with decreases in incarceration rates, the U.S. continues to have the highest incarceration rate in the world (World Population Review, 2023).

The National Institute of Justice (NIJ) defines recidivism as the rearrest, reconviction, or reincarceration within the first 3 years of release (NIJ, 2022). The rate of recidivism is a common measure used to determine the reasons why prison populations change (Berry & Wiener, 2020; National Institute of Justice [NIJ], 2022). The percentage of offenders convicted of an offense 1 year post-release was 22%, two years was 38%, and three years was 45% (CDCR, 2023). Meitl (2021) reported that as many as 83% of ex-offenders were rearrested on a new offense. Males are more likely to reoffend than women (CDCR, 2023). The three largest race/ethnicity groups released from prison during the fiscal year 2017–18 were Hispanic (n = 15,821), White (n = 9,101), and Black/African American (n = 8,475). Of those released, the conviction rate was 46% for Hispanics and Whites and 43% for Black/African Americans over a 3-year period(CDCR, 2023).

This chapter examines barriers to reintegrating offenders into the community. These barriers include the lack of transportation and housing as well as challenges in obtaining employment. Other barriers offenders face include insufficient medical, mental health, and substance abuse/addiction care. This chapter also evaluates recidivism reduction strategies and community-based organizations' role in helping offenders transition into the community. Finally, this chapter provides recommendations on the best practices for reintegrating offenders.

Barriers to Reintegration

Many barriers to the successful reintegration of offenders into the community have been identified in the literature (Gonzalez, 2021; Leverentz, 2011; Razali et al., 2021; Salem et al., 2021; Stewart et al., 2017). Newly released offenders often have limited resources and access to services they need to survive in the community (Salem et al., 2021). Some of the more prevalent barriers discussed in the literature include inadequate medical care (Vail et al., 2017), limited employment opportunities (Brown, 2018; Graffam et al., 2004; Harley et al., 2014), mental health and substance abuse issues (Grann et al., 2008; Sveinsdottir & Bond, 2020), and a lack of transportation and housing (Beeble & Hampton, 2021; Brown, 2018).

Researchers have examined the extent to which certain groups experience barriers following release from a correctional institution. Paat et al. (2017) examined perceptions of Hispanic ex-offenders' reintegration challenges. They reported that Hispanic ex-offenders perceived discrimination and stereotypes, which hindered their access to needed services and resources.. Homeless females formally incarcerated and on parole or probation experienced barriers as they transitioned into community settings (Salem et al., 2021). According to Salem et al. (2021), some of the challenges experienced by newly released females during the transition into the community include limited availability of resources, an inability to reconnect with their family and children, to care for themselves, and high rates of trauma.

Perceived challenges in reintegrating into the community can become risk factors for recidivism. Stewart et al. (2017) examined parolees' perceptions of barriers to reentry into society. Early exposure to substance abuse, crime, and substance use increased the likelihood of recidivism. Many parolees believed that society had negative expectations of them reoffending. Thus, some acted in ways to confirm the expectations (Stewart et al., 2017). According to Razali et al. (2021), some of the challenges experienced by ex-offenders when they reintegrate into the community include negative self-perceptions, low self-esteem, relationship and family difficulties, and the inability to secure stable housing and employment to access community services and resources.

- **Access to Resources.** The lack of essential resources makes transitioning from a correctional institutution to civilian life difficult. Common barriers encountered by newly released offenders include housing, money, employment, and medical insurance (Salem et al., 2021). A lack of resources such as housing, food, and money makes it difficult to survive in the community after being released from a correctional institution. Furthermore, many offenders do not know where to connect to resources and lack access to technology. Gonzalez (2021) underscored the need to provide life skills training for newly released offenders.
- **Medical.** Access to medical resources such as emergency medical care, treatment, follow-up care, specialty care, and prescription medication are necessary to maintain wellness upon release from prison or jail. Researchers have found that ex-offenders negatively perceive the quality of medical care they receive while incarcerated (Vail et al., 2017). For example, some experienced an inability to access quality medical care, a lack of trust in providers, delays in receiving a diagnosis of severe and chronic medical conditions, substandard medical coordination with community hospitals, and

inadequate medical and mental healthcare. Vail et al. concluded that some of the medical barriers faced by ex-offenders post release include difficulty in managing chronic medical conditions and paying for medical care. High costs associated with medical care, health insurance coverage, and emergency room visits are severe barriers as ex-offenders attempt to reintegrate into the community. Some researchers have found that ex-offenders have disproportionately high risk of death and severe illness immediately after release (Vail et al., 2017). Another barrier is the limited availability of medical care for chronic conditions involving the heart, liver, and diabetes. Patients who lack the requisite financial resources or medical insurance coverage to receive those services do not receive proper medical treatment and follow-up care for chronic illnesses. It is necessary to implement community-based care for chronic illnesses and behavior disorders (Vail et al., 2017).

- **Employment.** Researchers have found that finding and keeping employment is challenging for many ex-offenders (Beeble & Hampton, 2021; Brown, 2018). According to Meitl (2021), ex-offenders may lack the requisite education to secure viable employment. Financial instability is a risk factor in reintegrating into the community (Graffam et al., 2004). The inability to find stable employment and financial instability contribute to recidivism (Brown, 2011). Harley et al. (2014) studied the barriers to employment among ex-offenders. Harley et al.found that ex-offenders with disabilities had an increased risk of experiencing marginalization, discrimination, and social neglect as they attempted to reintegrate into the community and obtain employment. Ex-offenders lack human capital, are vulnerable to workplace discrimination, and have the stigma of being ex-offenders (Harley et al., 2014). Researchers who have examined employment and earnings in ex-offenders with disabilities have found that while African Americans with disabilities have higher employment rates than White and Hispanic ex-offenders, they tend to earn less than individuals from those racial groups (Ethridge et al., 2020).

Successful community transition necessitates using rehabilitation counselors and employment specialists to work with employers to increase employment opportunities for ex-offenders (Harley et al., 2014). According to Goodstein (2019), the hiring practices in firms restrict opportunities for ex-offenders to obtain meaningful work. Changing the hiring practices to support ex-offenders positively impacts the organization and the employee. Some of the ways to expand employment opportunities for ex-offenders include (a) changing the ex-offender hiring practices by removing questions about prior criminal history, (b) recruiting ex-offenders directly into the workplace, (c) improving the capabilities and dignity of ex-offenders such that they do not experience discrimination, and (d) increasing community stakeholders' role and involvement in the employment process (Goodstein, 2019).

- **Housing.** Many ex-offenders have difficulty finding housing (Brown, 2018). The inability to find housing puts ex-offenders at risk of recidivism. Housing is one of the most essential needs upon ex-offenders' reentry from prison into the community (Bowman & Ely, 2020). Housing is more than four walls and a structure; it is a means through which ex-offenders establish social, relational, and familial context make meaning of their life. Bowman and Ely (2020) conducted a study investigating the impact of a supportive housing program for ex-offenders and the positive outcomes for those that went through the program. Participants made positive transformative changes to decrease future criminal behavior and showed hope, self-worth, and independence. Researchers who have examined ex-offender housing stigmas and discrimination have found that stereotypes and stigmatization of ex-offenders negatively affected landlords' willingness to rent to ex-offenders (Berry & Wiener, 2020). Lutze et al. (2014) conducted a longitudinal study wherein they investigated the ability of a Reentry Housing Pilot Program to provide housing to high-risk and high-need offenders who were released from prison and had no place to live. They concluded that the Reentry Housing Pilot Program reduced ex-offenders' inclination to reoffend and return to prison.
- **Substance Use and Addiction.** Successful reintegration requires addressing substance abuse problems and addiction. Substance abuse involves the excessive use of alcohol, illicit drugs, prescription medication, or a combination of substances. Substance abuse causes impairment in a person's level of functioning in physical, emotional, cognitive, and behavioral areas. A high rate of substance abuse and addiction exists among those who are incarcerated. Substance addiction is a chronic problem that negatively affects individuals cognitively and physiologically. Addiction is a chronic disorder that requires treatment to address cravings, tolerance, withdrawal symptoms, and potential triggers). Factors that are important in the reintegration process to address substance abuse and addiction include the "desire to change, self-esteem, institutional treatment, family support, and continuity of care" (Razali et al., 2021, p. 568). Substance abuse is a significant risk factor in successfully reintegrating into the community and it was rated the third main barrier to securing employment for ex-offenders (Sveinsdottir & Bond, 2020). Doherty et al. (2014) evaluated the barriers to successfully reintegrating female offenders into the community. They found substance abuse and unresolved traumas were barriers to the reintegration process. The treatment

of substance abuse has yielded positive effects. Miller et al. (2016) examined reentry programming for female offenders who used opioids. They evaluated the effectiveness of the Second Chance Act reentry program amongfemale offenders diagnosed with a substance abuse disorder . Miller et al. found that females participating in the program were less likely to receive a probation revocation or be arrested on a new criminal charge. According to Whipple et al. (2016), ex-offenders must navigate barriers to reintegrate into the community successfully. Whipple et al. investigated housing and abstinence self-efficacy among ex-offenders and reported positive effects for stable or recovery-oriented housing. Specifically, they found that the more days ex-offenders spent in stable or recovery-oriented housing (e.g., independent living or recovery situations), the more their levels of abstinence self-efficacy increased; conversely, the more they engaged in risky behaviors, the lower their levels of abstinence and self-efficacy were.

- **Mental Health and Reintegration**. Mental illness is a risk factor for incarceration and bouts with recidivism, and many offenders have poor mental health. Many newly released ex-offenders have difficulty obtaining mental health treatment for chronic mental health conditions. The barriers ex-offenders encounter include a lack of understanding as to where to find support and the limited availability or lack of access to mental health professionals, Successful reintegration of ex-offenders involves addressing their mental health issues while they are incarcerated and upon their release. The risk of recidivism increases and the cycle of incarceration continues when ex-offenders do not have the resources to address their mental health issues. According to Grann et al. (2008), substance use disorders and personality disorders are associated with an increased risk of violent reoffending among ex-offenders. Treating mental illness promotes wellness and is a protective factor against recidivism. Stewart et al. (2017) examined the impact of a community mental health initiative on outcomes for offenders diagnosed with a mental health disorder. They found that men who had received treatment in a community mental health program had a lower risk of reoffending and being reincarcerated than men who only had received discharge planning. Mentally ill ex-offenders encounter barriers in finding sustainable employment. Sveinsdottir and Bond (2020) examined barriers to employment in individuals with severe mental illness who were justice-involved. They concluded that the most common barriers among those with severe mental illness were failure to engage in vocational opportunities and disengagement from vocational services. Thus, a comprehensive approach is needed to address the needs of ex-offenders with mental illness as they reintegrate into their communities.

- **Stigmas of Incarceration and Institutionalization.** Overt negative attitudes, beliefs, and stereotypes by the community against ex-offenders who are released into the community may hinder their successful reintegration. Ex-offenders may have negative psychological experiences as a result of being incarcerated. It is not uncommon for ex-offenders to have trouble finding employment and housing. Ex-offenders have completed their sentence but may remain supervised by law enforcement entities by way of probation or parole. Many ex-offenders internalize stigmas and experience negative feelings, low self-esteem or self-worth, and shame. Reintegration strategies are weakened because of the burden the stigma of incarceration puts on the offender (Clear et al., 2001). Having a criminal record is another stigma former offenders face (Brown, 2011). Binnall et al. (2022) conducted a study in which they investigated college students' perceptions of classmates who were formally incarcerated. They found that students' negative views and stigmas were mitigated by frequent, close contact with formally incarcerated classmates; thus, they were more likely to have positive views of those who were formally incarcerated. Some employers and landlords may also have preconceived notions about offering employment or housing to individuals with a criminal record, especially if the individual is under supervised release.

RECIDIVISM REDUCTION STRATEGIES

An estimated 93% of incarcerated offenders are eventually released into the community; thus, reintegration programs need support and funding (Berghuis, 2018). Berghuis (2018) noted that many successful programs capitalize on the ex-offenders' strengths that empower and help them engage. Factors that influence the successful reintegration of ex-offenders have been identified (Graffam et al., 2004). According to Graffam et al. (2004), the factors ex-offenders believed they needed to make a positive change were readiness to change, motivation, social networks (e.g., family contact and decreased social isolation), housing, rehabilitation services, counseling, and employment. Family support is vital to the successful reintegration of ex-offenders. Simonds et al. (2021) reported that ex-offenders who lacked social capital (e.g., relationships, support) had difficulty effectively transitioning back into the community. They further noted that family members felt obligated to help ex-offenders as they reintegrated into the community. According to Vail et al. (2017), one way to improve reintegration into the community from an ex-offender's perspective is to offer transitional care and medical services to newly released ex-offenders, including identifying who needs services and providing regular follow-ups and social services. Overall, people that experience incarceration lack various resources needed to thrive in society like housing, rehabilitation services, counseling, and employment (Graffam et al., 2004). Government officials recognized that a balance or counteractive measure may need to be included in their funding schemes that addressed the need for employment resources, like better educational opportunities, for citizens from poorer communities.

Representative Carl D. Perkins called the counteractive measure "Educational Equality" (Perkins, 1976). Perkins believed in "Educational Equality," which includes educational opportunities for all and a belief that the education system should develop serviceable skills in students and give them the requisite training to procure "honest" employment (Perkins, 1976, p. 1). He envisioned education becoming a true partnership between government entities. By 1991, Representative Perkin's vision evolved into the Carl D. Perkins Vocational and Applied Technology Education Act (Ed.gov, 2023). This legislation provided financial backing to entities that supported the implementation and management of educational and vocational programs. In 1991, the federal government allocated 1.6 billion dollars to this legislation (Ed. gov, 2023). States received allotted funding and detailed organizational and planning responsibilities. They also received funding specifications for community-based organizations and programs, tech-prep education, facilities and equipment costs, community education and employment centers, lighthouse schools, and tribally controlled postsecondary vocational institutions (Ed.gov, 2023). In fiscal year 2022, the federal government allocated $1.35 billion in Perkin's Plan funds to the states; the most significant allocations went to California, Texas, and Florida. The distribution amounts were calculated based on the 2020 income and population estimates from the Bureau of the Census (Perkin's Collaborative Network, [PCRN], 2020), a practice aligned with Representative Perkin's goal to fill the gaps in poorer areas. California received approximately $137 million, of which $475,000 were allocated to correctional institutions; Texas received $123 million, of which $1.36 million went to correctional institutions; Florida received approximately $80 million, of which $120,000 went to correctional institutions (PCRN, State Profiles, 2020.).

State Allocations of Carl D. Perkins Funding Between 2011-2020

This section describes the situation involving incarceration in the states who received the largest funding allocations from the Carl D. Perkins Vocational and Applied Technology Education Act between 2011 and 2018.

- **California.** In 2020, there were 191,000 Californians locked up in local jails (78,000), state prisons (101,000), and federal prisons (12,000), and California prisons released approximately 37,000 male offenders (Prisoner

> Policy Initiative [PPI], 50 States, 2020). This data illustrates that about 5% of the population in California are incarcerated. Black people represented the largest population of offenders per 100,000 at 3,036 followed by American Indians/ Alaska Natives at 996, Hispanics at 757, and White at 453 per 100,000 people. An additional 258,000 Californians were under community supervision or community corrections, such as parole or probation, local jails, and halfway houses (PPI, 50 States, 2020). The recidivism rate in California is around 44% (California Department of Corrections Rehabilitation [CDCR], Recidivism Report, 2020). This illustrates that about 50% of those released from incarceration will likely return to jail. The CDCR hosts the Office of Correctional Education, which offers academic and education programs at state prisons. These programs are designed to increase public safety and reduce recidivism (CDCR, Office of Correctional Education, 2023). The CDCR offers several career and technical education (CTE) educational and vocational programs to improve offenders' access to employment opportunities post-release. CDCR offers programs in basic education, adult secondary education, post-secondary education, and student support services. Additionally, they offer the following CTE courses: Automotive and Body Repair, Carpentry, Barbering, and Painting (CDCR, Office of Correctional Education, 2023). The CDCR Office of Research examines the outcomes of offenders post-release to improve the processes of rehabilitation and to reduce recidivism. California's recidivism definition aligns with the National Institute of Justice's definition. Although California uses a 3-year conviction rate to measure recidivism, "they also offer arrests and returns to custody as supplemental measures" (CDCR, Office of Research, 2023, p. 1).

The CDCR Office of Research data from 2011–2012 to 2017–2018 showed a decrease in each recidivism rating area, including arrests, convictions, and return rates. Arrest rates dropped from 75.3% in 2011–2012 to 68.4% in 2017–2018; conviction rates dropped from 54.3% in 2011–2012 to 44.65 in 2017–2018, and return rates dropped from 25% in 2011–2012 to 19.8% in 2017–2018 (CDCR, Recidivism Report, 2020). The decrease in release rates is partly attributed to the realignment of jail populations (implemented in 2011). This measure shifted low-level offender housing (low-level includes drug arrests and some property crimes), supervision, monitoring, and tracking from state prisons to county jails (Board of State and Community Corrections, 2023). Additionally, in November 2014, voters passed Proposition 47; this measure reduced the penalties for certain low-level offenses and intended to reserve prison jail space for high-level offenses. Another measure that contributed to reducing recidivism rates was the implementation of Proposition 57, which California voters passed in November 2016. Proposition 57 incentivized specific programs and encouraged offenders to take responsibility for their rehabilitation by participating in credit-earning programs and demonstrating good behavior while incarcerated (CDCR, In-Prison Credit-Earning Opportunities, 2023).

Propositions 47 and 57 are examples of how changes in legislation and pre- and post-trial practices can impact the recidivism rate for offenders. Researchers found no evidence that Proposition 47 contributed to an increase in violent crime (Bird et al., 2018). However, there was some evidence of an increase in property crimes but no increase in burglaries and auto thefts compared to other states (Bird et al., 2018). Recidivism rates decreased by male offenders in 12 California counties; the arrest rates were 1.8% lower than for similar male offenders prior to the measure, and the 2-year reconviction rate decreased for the same population of male offenders (Bird et al., 2018). Researchers concluded that the declines in recidivism rates, between 10.3% and 11.3%, were directly attributable to the passage of Proposition 47 (Bird et al., 2018). After Proposition 47 law enforcement arrest rates and convictions by district attorneys were reduced (Bird et al., 2018). It was noteworthy that Proposition 47 redirected monies not spent on incarceration to treatment intervention programs. Researchers could not substantiate whether the shift in funding directly impacted the recidivism rate (Bird et al., 2018).

The CDCR released two reports on recidivism rates of offenders between 2016–2017 and 2017–2018 in which it examined the impact of Proposition 57. Secretary Jeff Macomber stated, "Our focus has been and continues to be on creating an environment in prison that provides vital resources to the incarcerated population so that they can become better citizens upon release" (Anonymous, 2023, p. 1). The preliminary findings suggested that recidivism rates were reduced because of the passage of Proposition 57 (Anonymous, 2023). Anonymous (2023) utilized the national standard for measuring recidivism rates by examining arrests, convictions, and returns to prison three years following incarceration and tracking demographics, discovered that an average of 53% of offenders did not recidivate. In 2016–2017, 52.4% successfully reentered society, a 3% increase from the prior year. In 2017–2018, the percentage of offenders who did not recidivate increased to 55.4%, a 3% increase from the prior year. Of those who did recidivate, their crimes were low-level misdemeanor convictions for alcohol or drug-related offenses. Fifty percent of the group that successfully reentered society earned some form of enhanced credit, and those who earned enhanced credit based on Educational Merit Credit or Rehabilitative Credit had even lower conviction rates at 28.9% and 22.5% (Anonymous, 2023).

- **Florida.** In 2020, there were approximately 157,000 Floridians locked up in local jails (60,000), state prisons (80,000), and federal prisons (13,000), and Florida released approximately 30,000 male offenders (PPI, 50 States,

2020). Black people represented the largest population of offenders per 100,000 at 2,555 followed by White at 626 and Hispanics at 536 per 100,000 people. An additional 183,000 Floridians were under community supervision or community corrections, including parole or probation, local jails, and halfway houses (PPI, 50 States, 2020). The recidivism rate in Florida hovers around 20%-23% (Florida Department of Corrections [FDC], Recidivism Report, 2022).

The FDC hosts the Office of Programs and Reentry, which offers academic and education programs at adult state prisons. The Office of Programs and Reentry's goals are to reduce recidivism and increase public safety (FDC, Bureau of Education, 2022). The Bureau of Education offers several CTE and vocational programs, including academic education, library services, and transition programs. Academic instruction includes traditional coursework like math, science, and English, and students work toward earning their high school diploma or high school equivalency. Additionally, the FDC offers numerous vocational CTE courses that include 11 career clusters aligned with in-demand professions. They use a combination of Inmate Welfare Funds and Carl D. Perkins Grant monies to fund masonry skills, culinary, carpentry, and plumbing programs (FDC, Bureau of Education, 2022). The FDC also has a structured Community Transition Team that creates action plans for offenders and links them to community-based partners. The partners include industry employers, reentry service providers, education providers, trade and professional associations, and the Workforce Development Department (FDC, Community Transition Services, 2022). These programs are designed to increase public safety and reduce recidivism (FDC, Office of Programs and Reentry, 2022).

The FDC defines recidivism using the nationally accepted definition that states an act of recidivism occurs when an ex-offender is convicted of a new felony or misdemeanor committed within 3 years of release from custody or committed within 3years of placement on supervision for a previous criminal conviction (FDC, Recidivism Report, 2022). Additional measures of recidivism include arrests, criminal filings, and supervision violations (FDC, Recidivism Report, 2022). The FDC analyzed recidivism rates over a 10-year period and determined that between 2008 and 2018, the recidivism rate decreased from 27.7% in 2008 to 21.2% in 2018. The FDC also concluded that recidivism rates over the prior 5 years ranged from 24% - 25%. Recidivism rates when referencing rearrest rates over 60 months decreased from 61.4% in 2013 to 60.5% in 2018 (FDC, Recidivism Report, 2022). The FDC reported that one-third of the offenders returned to prison within 5 years of release. However, they determined that the overall return rate decreased from 36.1% in 2008 to 21.2% in 2018. Additionally, the FDCconcluded that most of the returns to prison happened in the first 3 years because only 3% to 4% happened in

Year 4 and Year 5 and 5 andthat males (22.5%) were more likely to recidivate than females (11.5%) (FDC, Recidivism Report, 2022).

The FDC research illustrated that poverty is the number one predictor of recidivism. Additionally, the FDCdetermined that if an offender gains employment post-release, their recidivism rates decrease up to 40% in some cases (FDC, Recidivism Report, 2022). Regardless of the prior offense, the recidivism rate for ex-offenders was significantly lower when they obtained employment within 1 year of their release (FDC, Community Transition Services, 2023). The FDC used this data-driven information to shape its approach to reintegration. It partnered with 75 second chance employers throughout the state of Florida to connect offenders to employment post-release. During the fiscal year 2021/2022, the FDC connected approximately 800 offenders to employment. The FDC attributes its success to employing a mandatory 100-hour employability/life skills program wherein offenders are introduced to employment readiness and retention training. The training includes career exploration, job searching, job application and resume writing, interviewing, negotiation, personal finance management, and personal development (e.g., goal setting and life skills) (FDC, Community Transition Unit, 2023). The FDC has utilized employment-specific technologies to further the engagement process for offenders. Specifically, the FDC used Zoom monitors to connect ex-offenders with employers, community-based organizations, and programs for job interviews and service referrals. The FDC plans to enhance its technology usage by explaining the federal bonding process, creating an electronic portfolio, linking to government resources like food subsidies and financial support, and exploring the workforce system (FDC, Community Transition Unit, 2023).

- **Texas.** In 2020, there were approximately 219,000 Texans locked up in local jails (58,000), state prisons (134,000), and federal prisons (22,000), and Texas released approximately 78,119 male offenders (PPI, 50 States, 2020). Black people represented the largest population of offenders per 100,000 at 2,855 followed by Hispanics at 972 and White at 768 per 100,000 people. An additional 438,000 Texans are under community supervision or community corrections, which includes parole or probation, local jails, and halfway houses (PPI, 50 States, 2020). The recidivism rate in Texas hovers around 20% (Texas Department of Criminal Justice, [TDCJ], Biennial Reentry and Reintegration Service Report [BRRSR], 2022).

The Texas Department of Criminal Justice (TDCJ) offers academic and vocational programs at state prisons. These programs are designed to increase public safety and reduce recidivism (TDCJ, BRRSR, 2022). The TDCJ hosts a reentry task force working group model and includes statewide councils. The councils that support the reentry process include behavioral health, forensic services, veterans, homeless, and employment services. Each of these groups works collaboratively to ensure Veterans are linked to the Veteran's Administration pre- and post-incarceration; offenders who have physical or behavioral health concerns have a strategic plan upon release; those who are in danger of becoming homeless or need employment resources are connected to the statewide community-based programs, which provide these services pre- and post-incarceration (TDCJ, BRRSR, 2022). The TDCJ case managers begin the case management process during the initial offender classification, where severe medical and mental health issues are identified. Each offender is given an individualized reentry case plan that addresses goals, next steps in custody, and community case plans. Upon release, the case plan transitions to the parole office and/or community case manager to ensure continuity (TDCJ, BRRSR, 2022). The TDCJ manages a partnership with the Texas Department of State Health Services to ensure all offenders have a certified birth certificate and state-issued identification card before release. A vital component of this collaborative process is issuing an identification card with the offender's proposed home address and removing the need for a Social Security card to obtain the identification card (TDCJ, BRRSR, 2022).

The Pre-Release Reentry Services process is deployed in three phases. In Phase 1, the offenders receive identification documents, including a replacement Social Security card, certified birth certificate, military records, identification cards, resumes, and certification certificates earned in CTE programs. These can include renewal driver's licenses and commercial driver's licenses. These items are essential for employment post-incarceration (TDCJ, BRRSR, 2022). In Phase 2, a risk assessment is conducted to assess the likelihood of reoffending. A case plan is completed to address mitigating re-offense factors (TDCJ, BRRSR, 2022). Medical benefit linkages are also created in this phase. Reentry case managers completed 925 health benefit applications between September 2020 and July 2022 (TDCJ, BRRSR, 2022). Phase 3 occurs primarily post-release. In this phase, community-based partners provide employment-related services pre- and post-release. The services include job preparation classes and basic needs like housing and food resources. Reentry staff members coordinate job fairs and hiring events. They also assist with application preparation and resume writing (TDCJ, BRRSR, 2022).

The TDCJ defines recidivism using the nationally accepted definition that states an act of recidivism occurs when an ex-offender is convicted of a new felony or misdemeanor committed within 3years of release from custody or committed within 3 years of placement on supervision for a previous criminal conviction (TDCJ, BRRSR, 2022). Additional measures of recidivism include arrests, returns to custody, criminal filings, and supervision violations (TDCJ, BRRSR, 2022). The TDCJ recidivism rate is among the lowest in the United States at 20.3%. Researchers examined the recidivism rate from 2007 to 2017 and found that the rate had decreased from 23.9%

in 2007 to 20.3% in 2017. The TDCJ determined that the reentry process requires a coordinated, collaborative process focused on obtaining self-sufficiency for the reentering individual (TDCJ, BRRSR, 2022).

According to Hudson (2014), the Workforce Innovation Opportunity Act (WIOA) of 2014 is considered a major legislative reform of the job-training system. The Obama-Biden Administration sought to improve the training and job skills, ensure the training matched in-demand professions, and promote better collaboration and partnerships between educational and workforce institutions (Hudson, 2014). WIOA orchestrated strategic partnerships with the U.S. Department of Labor, Education, and Health and Human Services. WIOA prioritized employment services for economically disadvantaged youth and adults, including those who were homeless, had criminal records, and possessed limited basic skills and work experience (Council of State Governments, 2017). The programs were data-driven and built on proven measures (Hudson, 2014). The states implemented WIOA in 2016, and WIOA funding provided the primary source of federal funding for workforce development. WIOA provided funding directly to the states, and the states decided whether to allow their department of corrections or community colleges to receive the funding or to participate in grant processes (Council of State Governments, 2017).

States Use of Workforce Innovation Opportunity Act Funding Between 2011-2018

This section describes incarceration in the states that received the most funding from the Carl D. Perkins Vocational and Applied Technology Education Act and implemented Workforce Innovation and Opportunity Act provisions between 2011 and 2018.

- **California.** California's approach to reducing prison recidivism utilizing the guidelines outlined in WIOA, which include bringing together the California Department of Corrections and Rehabilitation, California Prison Industry Authority, and the California Workforce Association (CDCR, Workforce Partnership Agreement, 2022). California established three objectives in this collaboration: ensuring that the workforce and education programs incorporated the state's industry needs and the content was tailored to fit in-demand professions; upskilling the existing workforce; ensuring the programs were accessible to all Californians. Additionally California WIOA guidelines were intended to guarantee that the offenders unique needs and skill potential were aligned, and the programs were coordinated and integrated to guarantee they were presented economically (CDCR, Workforce Partnership Agreement, 2022). In 2018, the California legislature created the Prison to Employment program. This program offered entities a chance to integrate workforce, reentry services, and supportive services to improve employment outcomes while reducing recidivism for formerly incarcerated and justice-involved people (California Workforce Development Board, 2023). As of April 2022, "Prison to Employment funds served over 5,730 formerly incarcerated and justice-involved individuals statewide" (California Workforce Development Board, 2023, p. 4).

- **Florida.** Florida's approach to reducing recidivism in the prisons utilizing the guidelines outlined in WIOA includes bringing together the CareerSource, Florida Department of Education's Divisions of Career and Adult Education, Department of Economic Opportunity, Division of Blind Services, and the Division of Vocational Rehabilitation (Florida Career Source [FCS], WIOA, 2022). They focused on "streamlining services, empowering individuals, universal access, and increased accountability" (FCS, WIOA, 2022, p. 2). The Florida Department of Education authorized grant funding opportunities for correctional facilities, combining funding from Carl D. Perkins and the WIOA funding (Florida Department of Education [FDE], Funding Opportunities, 2022). The funding was intended to improve the academic and technical skills of offenders in correctional institutions participating in career and technical education programs (Florida Department of Education, Funding Opportunities, 2022).
- **Texas.** Texas's approach to reducing prison recidivism utilizing the guidelines outlined in the WIOA includes bringing offenders and employers together through job fairs and its Website for Work program. This collaboration incorporated the Texas Workforce Commission, the Reentry and Integration Division, and the Workforce Development Board. The Website for Work program contains steps for offenders to follow to obtain education or training and vital information for employers (TDCJ, Website for Work, 2022). Offenders are linked with vocational training and certifications pre- and post-release. Some offenders are also enrolled in college level education designed to help them earn an associate's, bachelor's, or graduate degree (TDCJ, Website for Work, 2022). The Website for Work also provides employers with vital information (TDCJ, Website for Work, 2022). Employers are provided with vital information about the hiring of ex-offenders and potential liabilities, the fidelity bonding process where employers can obtain a bond for $5,000, and the 6-month bond buyout process. Employers are also informed of hiring restrictions (TDCJ, Website to Work, 2022). In 2018, the Texas Reentry and Integration Division hosted 15 job fairs, which resulted in positive interactions between employers and ex-offenders; of the 885 ex-offenders who attended,

43% received job offers and 59% obtained employment (TDCJ, Website for Work, 2022).

- **FAFSA.** The Free Application for Federal Student Aid (FAFSA) Simplification Act was passed in 2020. This legislation significantly changed the criteria for specific populations to apply for and receive financial aid under the Pell Grant system. The changes included the reinstatement of eligibility for people without Selective Service registration, people with drug convictions, unaccompanied homeless youth, foster care youth who received lifetime eligibility, and the ban on Pell Grant eligibility for imprisoned or incarcerated individuals was removed (FAFSA Simplification Act, 2023). At the time of this legislation, approximately 41% of the 2 million plus incarcerated individuals in the U. S. did not have a high school diploma. An estimated 50% of formally incarcerated offenders are rearrested within eight years of release, and the risk of recidivism increases when offenders lack an education. The U.S. Department of Education conducted a pilot project with incarcerated individuals entitled the Second Chance Pell Experiment. The pilot project propelled the legislation for the FAFSA Simplification Act that helped remove the ban on incarcerated individuals receiving Pell Grants. The U.S. Department of Education estimates that with the full reinstatement of the Pell Grant program to confined or incarcerated people, approximately 760,000 individuals will become eligible for the program (U.S. Department of Education, Press Office, 2023). The Pell Grant program will be available to offenders in prisons nationwide in the fiscal year 2024–25.

COMMUNITY CORRECTIONS

Community Corrections encompasses approximately 30% of the supervised ex-offenders or justice-involved individuals in the United States; the supervision occurs while they are on probation or parole, in work-release programs, or halfway houses (PPI, US, 2020). Whether these community-based program strategies are effective depends on how recidivism is measured (Christian, 2022). Justice-related organizations measure recidivism with a focus on arrests, convictions, and rearrest rates (National Institute of Justice, 2022). Transitioning from incarceration into the community can present common barriers, including mental and physical health obstacles, financial struggles, housing instability, difficulty finding employment, and family disruptions (Harding et al., 2019; Western, 2018). Christian (2022) suggested that without a wraparound service model incorporating cognitive therapeutic intervention techniques, the offender may struggle with the typical barriers to reintegration into the community.

A higher prevalence of mental illness exists among incarcerated individuals than it does among the general population (Hicks et al., 2020). Untreated mental illness is a barrier to successful reintegration (Jaegers et al., 2020). This concept was reiterated when the CDCR listed mental health as a risk factor that can contribute to the recidivism rate (CDCR, Office of Research, 2023). The TDCJ allotted substantial resources to ensure that an offender's mental health is diagnosed at the inception of incarceration, a transitional case plan is arranged, and the plan includes a transitional process ensuring the continuity of mental health services post-incarceration (TDCJ, BRRSR, 2022). The recidivism rate of offenders who engage in mental health programs pre- and post-release was lower than those who did not. The reduction in recidivism is attributable to jails and community-based service providers having significant treatment interaction and a continuum of care thereby reducing the risk and likelihood of rearrest when they engage offenders in transitional services pre- and post-incarceration (Hicks et al., 2020). In their review of the Fresh Start Prisoner Reentry Program, Hunter et al. (2016) determined that case management for offenders should occur while they are incarcerated and continue upon release. The CDCR (2023), the FDC (2022), and the TDCJ (2022) designed components of their in-custody program model to include transitional services, and those components were designed to reduce recidivism and enhance public safety.

Other barriers to successful transition into the community exist for ex-offenders (Divakran et al., 2023). Formerly incarcerated individuals experience higher instances of poor physical health and substance use disorders, crises, and obstacles as they transition into the community. Incarcerated individuals who encounter those barriers are at increased risk of recidivism (Divakaran et al., 2023). To mitigate increases in recidivism rates for that population, governmental and community-based nonprofit organizations and programs should work together, embrace policy and research, and consider the contributions of community-based and nonprofit organizations (Christian, 2023). One example of different entities working together occurred in California with the passage of Propositions 47 and 57. Those laws impacted how local law enforcement officers and district attorneys addressed legal matters and resulted decreases inarrest and conviction rates (Bird et al., 2018). The purpose of Propositions 47 and 57 was to reduce arrests for low-level offenses and prosecutions and decrease prison overcrowding. The collateral effect was that the ex-offender with a substance abuse problem was diverted into a community-based treatment program instead of returning to prison for a low-level offense (Bird et al., 2018). Collaboration among legislators working alongside the CDCR had a positive impact on recidivism.

Transitional services like health care and social services are essential in reentry. Their effectiveness in the reduction of recidivism of offenders is an area of concern. Wright et al. (2014) examined 29 different community-based prisoner reentry programs and determined that life skills training and substance use prevention were the most prevalent. Unlike Christian (2022), Wright et al. (2014) believed that cognitive behavioral therapies were necessary. Wright et al. concluded that these therapies were the least effective or had the least favorable outcomes for offenders. Similar to Christian (2022) and Divakaran et al. (2023), Wright et al. (2014) concluded that the inclusion of an aftercare or transitional service component had the most significant positive effect or outcome on the offender's life. The standard components utilized in correctional settings across the United States include in-custody academic and vocational programs, transitional services, and linkages to employment-related programs post-release (CDCR, 2023; FDC, 2022; TDCJ, 2022). The TDCJ incorporated a more intentional reentry process, which resulted in TDCJ gaining one of the lowest recidivism rates in the nation at 20.3%, approximately 5% lower than the recidivism rate in California and Florida. By allotting $1.3 million to its integration program, the TDCJ made a greater investment when compared to California ($475,000) and Florida ($120,000) (PCRN, State Profiles, 2020). The reentry process in TDCJ included an initial classification process where mental and medical health screening began. This process led to facility placements and case plans that traveled with the offender through incarceration. A second assessment determined the likelihood of a re-offense, and the data were used to mitigate re-offense factors. Lastly, housing, employment, substance use, and other contributing factors to incarceration were integrated into the case plan. There was a deliberate effort and process used to ensure the pre-release case plan transitioned to the Texas Department of Parole, the community corrections entity, or the community-based network partner who would ensure a continuity of care persisted for the ex-offender post-release (TDCJ, BRRSR, 2022).

ROLE OF LAW ENFORCEMENT IN REINTEGRATION OF OFFENDERS

Officers play a vital role in the reintegration of offenders into the community. The job of police has been evolving over the past 3-4 decades. Police officers enforce local, city, county, state, and federal laws. Crime prevention (e.g., detention, arrests) is one of the many essential functions of police officers. Policing high-crime areas helps prevent crime and protects vulnerable populations. However, an officer's job functions go beyond crime prevention. Officers are first responders during emergencies and major disasters (e.g., natural or manufactured), assist in preserving life, property, personal and home safety education, and serve as liaisons between government and city entities. According to the IACP (2007), to build trust within the communities served, law enforcement agencies must maintain integrity, honesty, and ethical conduct and conduct police work unbiasedly. As trust becomes robust, law enforcement agencies will enhance the quality of their relationships with the community, its people, and its organizations.

Law enforcement plays a vital role in relationship-building with the community to address major social issues such as substance abuse. Establishing a collaborative relationship between law enforcement and community partners is essential. Collaborative relationships can be accomplished through the following:

1. Building relationships between law enforcement and the community through effective communication, dialogue, and rapport building.
2. Active police involvement and engagement with the community and community-based organizations help build trust and destigmatize the negative aspects of policing.
3. Educating law enforcement and the community about each other's values, beliefs, attitudes, goals, and needs can help decrease stigmas and biases.
4. Collaboration between the community and law enforcement can help achieve goals that promote successful reintegration strategies.
5. Rethinking law enforcement's role beyond the arrest and detection phase to address the community's needs.

A substantial level of mistrust exists in the community towards law enforcement. Graffam et al. (2004) reported that offenders believed there was variability in how officers treated offenders; some were professional, while others were unprofessional. Building trust and relationships with the community is vital to understand the community being served and to support diversity and inclusion efforts. Building a sense of community fosters a sense of belongingness among individuals. Healthy communication and relationship building between law enforcement and the community foster psychological safety. Community members can trust law enforcement's legitimacy when they feel safe. It not only positively reinforces healthy behaviors but also helps ex-offenders begin to have a true sense of belonging in their communities and develop a sense of pride.

- ***Crisis Intervention Strategies***. In many agencies, law enforcement officers receive specialized training in crisis intervention techniques to diffuse and de-escalate volatile situations involving the community (Hill et al., 2004; Miller, 2007). According to Hill et al. (2004), crisis intervention teams (CIT) provide officers with needed skills to safely de-escalate situations in which community members are mentally ill and in crisis. Officers are first responders to many situations and may frequently encounter community members who are mentally ill and in crisis. Officers must know how to handle those situations without using excessive force. Crisis intervention strategies help officers to defuse situations that could result in an escalation of force in a manner that maintains the respect and dignity of the community member. For example, de-escalation strategies are beneficial in police contact with a community member who is having a psychotic episode and is hallucinating. Training on de-escalation strategies with individuals who are mentally ill or have disabilities promotes community trust, partnership, and a reduction of the use of force. The collaboration between law enforcement and mental health crisis response providers helps address the needs of mentally ill community members in crises (Wellborn, 1999). Community policing also plays a role in preventing crimes involving vulnerable populations such women and children. According to Murray (2006), community policing fosters relationships and partnerships and works best when information is shared between stakeholders. Interagency collaborations and partnerships positively contribute to reintegration efforts. Kim et al. (2010) examined partnerships between law enforcement and probation departments. They found that partnerships have increased in recent years. Those relationships helped officers better understand the function of probation departments and positively influence views on crime reduction strategies.

Recommendations and Best Practices

More than 2 million people are incarcerated in the United States. Of those, over one-third are in community correctional settings. The population of incarcerated people in the United States is the largest prison population in the world (PPI, 2020). Support for ex-offenders encompasses early intervention, responsiveness, comprehensiveness, and long-term commitment (Graffam et al., 2004). Active interventions help address problems before they worsen. Early intervention is necessary prior to the release of the offender to help address barriers to reintegration and anticipate issues that may arise. Some of the more prevalent barriers to the reintegration of ex-offenders include housing, medical, substance abuse, mental health treatment and support, employment, and finances. Graffam et al. (2004) concluded that preparing and supporting offenders and equipping them to handle issues in the community help strengthen their likelihood of success. One approach to the reintegration of ex-offenders into the community is insufficient. It is necessary to consider a multidimensional and multidisciplinary approach. Multi-level interventions at various levels and gender-sensitive perspectives for women transitioning to community reentry must be incorporated into reintegrative approaches (Salem et al., 2021). Enhancing community partnerships and relationships with law enforcement can positively help reintegration efforts.

Evidence-based recidivism reduction strategies must be employed to change the trajectory of incarceration and recidivism. Strategies include offering educational and vocational programs that cross the custodial environment's threshold. Research-based techniques must be used to determine the actionable targets of intervention efforts. Case management professionals must be adequately trained in working with offenders and assisting them with overcoming the barriers that lead to incarceration and reoffending. Members of the legislature, prison managers, community-based organizations and programs, employers, health and wellness entities, and city, county, state, and federal government officials must work together to create bridges that lead to streamlined access to the vital services ex-offenders need to reintegrate into the community successfully.

Summary

This chapter examined barriers to the reintegration of offenders, the stigma of incarceration, the essential need for relationship building between law enforcement and the community, recidivism reduction strategies, and best practices for reintegrating offenders into the local community. The chapter reviewed how California, Florida, and Texas state prison managers utilized the funding allotted under Carl D. Perkin's (Perkin's) Vocational and Applied Technology Education Act and the WIOA. California ($137 million), Florida ($80 million), and Texas ($123 million) were the states in the union with the most significant allocations of Perkins and WIOA funds (PCRN, State Profiles, 2020). These allotments were based on population and income variables (Bureau of the Census, 2020). All three states included recidivism reduction strategies that ensured the offenders had access to education, training, and supportive services designed to elevate their access to employment opportunities. The programs were linked to in-demand professions and aligned with the offenders' skills. Each state established comprehensive partnerships with the workforce development entity in their state, the department of corrections or state prison entity, the department of education, and several employers (CDCR, 2023; FDC, 2022; TDCJ, 2022).

REFERENCES

Anonymous. (2023, May 5). *CDCR issues recidivism report.* Correctional News. https://correctionalnews.com/2023/05/05/cdcr-issues-recidivism-reports/

Barnert, E. S., Lopez, N., & Chung, P. J. (2020). Barriers to health care for Latino youths during community reentry after incarceration: Los Angeles County, California, 2016–2018. *American Journal of Public Health, 110*(S1), S63–S70. doi:10.2105/AJPH.2019.305374 PMID:31967868

Beeble, M. L., & Hampton, C. (2021). Community reintegration of repeat female offenders in county jails. *Women & Criminal Justice, 31*(6), 518–535. doi:10.1080/08974454.2021.1947441

Bender, K. (2018). Education Opportunities in Prison Are Key to Reducing Crime. *Advancing Racial Equity and Justice, Criminal Justice Reform, Education*. https://www.americanprogress.org/article/education-opportunities-prison-key-reducing-crime/

Berghuis, M. (2018). Reentry programs for adult male offender recidivism and reintegration: A systematic review and meta-analysis. *International Journal of Offender Therapy and Comparative Criminology, 62*(13), 4655–4676. doi:10.1177/0306624X18778448 PMID:29890873

Berry, M. C., & Wiener, R. L. (2020). Exoffender housing stigma and discrimination. *Psychology, Public Policy, and Law, 26*(2), 213–232. doi:10.1037/law0000225

Binnall, J. M., Scott-Hayward, C. S., Petersen, N., & Gonzalez, R. M. (2022). Taking roll: College students' views of their formerly incarcerated classmates. *Journal of Criminal Justice Education, 33*(3), 347–367. doi:10.1080/10511253.2021.1962932

Bird, M., Lofstron, M., Martin, B., Raphael, S., & Nguyen, V. (2018), *The impact of Proposition 47 on crime and recidivism*. https://www.ppic.org/wp-content/uploads/r_0618mbr.pdf

Board of State and Community Corrections. (2022). *Realignment.* https://www.bscc.ca.gov/m_realignment/

Bowman, E. I., & Ely, K. (2020). Voices of returning citizens: A qualitative study of a supportive housing program for ex-offenders in a rural community. *The Prison Journal, 100*(4), 423–446. doi:10.1177/0032885520939273

Brown, C. (2011). Vocational psychology and ex-offenders' reintegration: A call for action. *Journal of Career Assessment, 19*(3), 333–342. doi:10.1177/1069072710395539

Brown, K. (2018). *A life-history approach to community reintegration: Female ex-offenders & experiences of facilitators and barriers of successful community reintegration.* https://www.academia.edu/98834039/A_Life_History_Approach_to_Community_Reintegration_Female_Ex_Offenders_Experiences_of_Facilitators_and_Barriers_of_Successful_Community_Reintegration

California Department Corrections Rehabilitation. (2023). *Corrections, and workforce partnership agreement.* https://cwdb.ca.gov/wp-content/uploads/sites/43/2018/02/Corrections-Workforce-Partnership-for-the-Prison-to-Employment-Initiative_.pdf

California Department of Corrections and Rehabilitation. (2023). *Office of Correctional Education.* https://www.cdcr.ca.gov/rehabilitation/oce/

California Department of Corrections and Rehabilitation. (2023). *Office of Research.Offender recidivism.* https://www.cdcr.ca.gov/research/offender-outcomes-characteristics/

California Department of Corrections and Rehabilitation. (2023). *Recidivism report.* https://www.cdcr.ca.gov/research/wp-content/uploads/sites/174/2023/04/Recidivism-Report-for-Offenders-Released-in-Fiscal-Year-2017-18.pdf

California Workforce Development Board. (2023). *Prison to employment.* https://cwdb.ca.gov/wp-content/uploads/sites/43/2021/10/P2E-Interim-Report_ACCESSIBLE.pdf

Carson, E. A. (2021). *Prisoners in 2021 – statistical tables.* United States Department of Justice. Office of Justice Programs. Bureau of Justice Statistics.

Christian, J. (2022). The promise and challenge of local initiatives that support reentry and reintegration. *The Annals of the American Academy of Political and Social Science*, *701*(1), 191–203. doi:10.1177/00027162221115380

Clear, T. R., Rose, D. R., & Ryder, J. A. (2001). Incarceration and the community: The problem of removing and returning offenders. *Crime and Delinquency*, *47*(3), 335–351. doi:10.1177/0011128701047003003

Council of State Governments Justice Center and the National Reentry Resource Center. (2017). *Workforce Innovation and Opportunity Act.* https://csgjusticecenter.org/wp-content/uploads/2020/02/6.13.17_WIOA_What-Corrections-and-Reentry-Agencies-Need-to-Know.pdf

Divakaran, B., Bloch, N., Sinha, M., Steiner, A., & Shavit, S. (2023). The reentry health care hub: Creating a California-based referral system to link chronically ill people leaving prison to primary care. *International Journal of Environmental Research and Public Health, 20*(10), 5806. doi:10.3390/ijerph20105806 PMID:37239534

Doherty, S., Forrester, P., Brazil, A., & Matheson, F. (2014). Finding their way: Conditions for successful reintegration among women offenders. *Journal of Offender Rehabilitation, 53*(7), 562–586. doi:10.1080/10509674.2014.944740

Ed.gov. (1991). *Institute of Educational Sciences.* https://files.eric.ed.gov/fulltext/ED330818.pdf

Ethridge, G., Dowden, A. R., Brooks, M., Kwan, N., & Harley, D. (2020). Employment and earnings among ex-offenders with disabilities: A multivariate analysis of RSA-911 data. *Journal of Vocational Rehabilitation, 52*(3), 279–289. doi:10.3233/JVR-201077

Florida Career Source. (2022). *Workforce Innovation Opportunities Act Unified Plan.* https://careersourceflorida.com/about-us/policies-and-initiatives/wioa/

Florida Department of Corrections. (2022). *Bureau of Education, Community Transition Unit.* https://fdc.myflorida.com/development/programs.html

Florida Department of Corrections. (2022). *Bureau of Program Development.* https://fdc.myflorida.com/development/applied.html

Florida Department of Corrections. (2022). *Recidivism Report.* https://fdc.myflorida.com/pub/recidivism/FDC%20Recidivism%20Report%202018%20Cohort.pdf

Florida Department of Education. (2018-2019). *Funding opportunities, Carl D. Perkins Career and Technical Education, Department of Corrections.* https://www.fldoe.org/academics/career-adult-edu/funding-opportunities/2023-2024-funding-opportunities/perkins.stml

Gonzalez, A. (2021). Successful transition to life after incarceration: A pilot program. *The American Journal of Occupational Therapy, 75*(Supplement_2), 1–1. doi:10.5014/ajot.2021.75S2-RP222

Goodstein, J. (2019). Firms, ex-offenders, and communities: A stakeholder capability enhancement perspective. *Business Ethics Quarterly, 29*(4), 491–518. doi:10.1017/beq.2018.48

Graffam, J., Shinkfield, A., Lavelle, B., & Mcpherson, W. (2004). Variables affecting successful reintegration as perceived by offenders and professionals. *Journal of Offender Rehabilitation, 40*(1/2), 147–171. doi:10.1300/J076v40n01_08

Grann, M., Danesh, J., & Fazel, S. (2008). The association between psychiatric diagnosis and violent reoffending in adult offenders in the community. *BMC Psychiatry*, *8*(1), 92. Advance online publication. doi:10.1186/1471-244X-8-92 PMID:19032787

Harding, D. J., Morenoff, J. D., & Wyse, J. B. (2019). *On the outside:Prisoner reentry and reintegration*. University of Chicago Press. doi:10.7208/chicago/9780226607788.001.0001

Harley, D. A., Cabe, B., Woolums, R., & Turner-Whittaker, T. (2014). Vulnerability and marginalization of adult ex-offenders with disabilities in community and employment reintegration. *Journal of Applied Rehabilitation Counseling*, *45*(4), 4–14. doi:10.1891/0047-2220.45.4.4

Hicks, D. L., Comartin, E. B., & Kubiak, S. (2022). Transition planning from jail: Treatment engagement, continuity of care, and rearrest. *Community Mental Health Journal*, *58*(2), 288–299. doi:10.1007/s10597-021-00820-x PMID:33835278

Hill, R., Quill, G., & Ellis, K. (2004). The Montgomery County CIT model: Interacting with people with mental illness. *FBI Law Enforcement Bulletin*, *73*(7), 18–25.

Hudson, D. (2014). *The first significant legislative reform of our job-training system in a number of years: The White House President Barack Obama*. https://obamawhitehouse.archives.gov/blog/2014/07/22/first-significant-legislative-reform-our-job-training-system-number-years

Hunter, B. A., Lanza, A. S., Lawlor, M., Dyson, W., & Gordon, D. M. (2016). A strengths-based approach to prisoner reentry: The fresh start prisoner reentry program. *International Journal of Offender Therapy and Comparative Criminology*, *60*(11), 1298–1314. doi:10.1177/0306624X15576501 PMID:25805715

IACP. (2007). Building trust between the police and the citizens they serve: An internal affairs promising practices guide for local law enforcement. *International Association of Chiefs of Police*. https://www.theiacp.org/sites/default/files/all/b/BuildingTrust.pdf

Jaegers, L. A., Skinner, E., Conners, B., Hayes, C., West-Bruce, S., Vaughn, M. G., Smith, D. L., & Barney, K. F. (2020). Evaluation of the jail-based occupational therapy transition and integration services program for community reentry. *AJOT: American Journal of Occupational Therapy*, *74*(3). https://link.gale.com/apps/doc/A623794160/HWRC?u=nu_main&sid=bookmark-HWRC&xid=0bccfcdf

Kim, B., Gerber, J., & Beto, D. R. (2010). Listening to law enforcement officers: The promises and problems of police-adult probation partnerships. *Journal of Criminal Justice, 38*(4), 625–632. doi:10.1016/j.jcrimjus.2010.04.035

Leverentz, A. (2011). Barriers to reintegration. In L. Gideon & H.-E. Sung (Eds.), *Rethinking corrections: Rehabilitation, reentry, and reintegration* (pp. 359–381). Sage Publications, Inc. doi:10.4135/9781452230474.n14

Lutze, F. E., Rosky, J. W., & Hamilton, Z. K. (2014). Homelessness and reentry: A multisite outcome evaluation of Washington State's reentry housing program for high-risk offenders. *Criminal Justice and Behavior, 41*(4), 471–491. doi:10.1177/0093854813510164

Meitl, M. B. (2021). Four thousand voices: Self-reported barriers to reentry. *Federal Probation, 85*(2), 16–21.

Miller, H. V., Miller, J. M., & Barnes, J. C. (2016). Reentry programming for opioid and opiate involved female offenders: Findings from a mixed methods evaluation. *Journal of Criminal Justice, 46*, 129–136. doi:10.1016/j.jcrimjus.2016.04.001

Miller, L. (2007). Crisis intervention strategies for treating law enforcement and mental health professionals. In F. M. Dattilio & A. Freeman (Eds.), *Cognitive-behavioral strategies in crisis intervention* (3rd ed., pp. 93–121). The Guilford Press.

Murray, J. (2006). Criminal exploitation of women and children and the important role of community policing. *Police Practice and Research, 7*(2), 125–134. doi:10.1080/15614260600676791

National Institute of Justice. (2022). *Recidivism.* https://www2.ed.gov/about/offices/list/ovae/pi/AdultEd/correctional-education.html

Paat, Y.-F., Hope, T. L., Lopez, L. C., Zamora, H. Jr, & Salas, C. M. (2017). Hispanic exconvicts' perceptions of challenges and reintegration. *Journal of Offender Rehabilitation, 56*(2), 87–109. doi:10.1080/10509674.2016.1268233

Perkins, C. D. (1976). Educational equality. *Journal of Teacher Education, 27*(4), 296–296. doi:10.1177/002248717602700406

Perkins Collaborative Resource Network. (2020). *State profiles.* https://cte.ed.gov/profiles/national-summary

Perkins Collaborative Resource Network. (2022). *State allocations, estimated fiscal year (FY) (2022).* https://cte.ed.gov/grants/state-allocations

Poulin, L. I. L., Colibaba, A., Skinner, M. W., Balfour, G., Byrne, D., & Dieleman, C. (2023). Lost in transition? Community residential facility staff and stakeholder perspectives on previously incarcerated older adults' transitions into long-term care. *BMC Geriatrics*, *23*(1), 180. doi:10.1186/s12877-023-03807-3 PMID:36978019

Prison Policy Initiative. (2020). *50 state profiles.* https://www.prisonpolicy.org/profiles/CA.html

Prison Policy Initiative. (2020). *United States profile.* https://www.prisonpolicy.org/profiles/

Razali, A., Mustaffa, J., & Kamsani, S. R. (2021). Reducing recidivism among former offenders: Strategies to increase success in social reintegration. *Turkish Online Journal of Qualitative Inquiry*, *12*(3), 5672–5685.

Salem, B. E., Kwon, J., Ekstrand, M. L., Hall, E., Turner, S. F., Faucette, M., & Slaughter, R. (2021). Transitioning into the community: Perceptions of barriers and facilitators experienced by formerly incarcerated, homeless women during reentry—a qualitative study. *Community Mental Health Journal*, *57*(4), 609–621. doi:10.1007/s10597-020-00748-8 PMID:33387178

Simonds, R., Reisig, M. D., Trinkner, R., & Holtfreter, K. (2021). The effect of prior incarceration on trust and social support: Results from two factorial vignette studies. *Journal of Offender Rehabilitation*, *60*(7), 464–484. doi:10.1080/10509674.2021.1966154

Simplification ActF. A. F. S. A. (2023). https://fsapartners.ed.gov/knowledge-center/library/dear-colleague-letters/2023-08-04/fafsa-simplification-act-changes-implementation-2024-25

Stewart, L. A., Farrell-MacDonald, S., & Feeley, S. (2017). The impact of a community mental health initiative on outcomes for offenders with a serious mental disorder. *Criminal Behaviour and Mental Health*, *27*(4), 371–384. doi:10.1002/cbm.2005 PMID:27272741

Sveinsdottir, V., & Bond, G. R. (2020). Barriers to employment for people with severe mental illness and criminal justice involvement. *Journal of Mental Health (Abingdon, England)*, *29*(6), 692–700. doi:10.1080/09638237.2017.1417556 PMID:29265941

Texas Department of Criminal Justice. (2022). *Biennial reentry and reintegration services report.* https://www.tdcj.texas.gov/documents/rid/RID_Reentry_Biennial_Report_09_2022.pdf

Texas Department of Criminal Justice. (2022a). *Website to work, how it works.* https://reentry.tdcj.texas.gov/index.php/how-it-works/

Texas Department of Criminal Justice. (2022b). *Website to work, success stories.* https://reentry.tdcj.texas.gov/index.php/success-stories/

Texas Workforce Commission. (2018). *Workforce Innovation and Opportunity Act Report.* https://www.twc.texas.gov/files/partners/wioa-annual-report-2018-twc.pdf

United States Department of Education. (2022). *Office of Career Technical, and Adult Education (OCTAE). Correctional education.* https://www2.ed.gov/about/offices/list/ovae/pi/AdultEd/correctional-education.html

United States Department of Education. (2023). *Press Office. U.S. Department of Education to Launch Application Process to Expand Federal Pell Grant Access for Individuals Who Are Confined or Incarcerated.* https://www.ed.gov/news/press-releases/us-department-education-launch-application-process-expand-federal-pell-grant-access-individuals-who-are-confined-or-incarcerated

United States Department of Labor. (2022). *Workforce Innovation and Opportunity Act.* https://www.dol.gov/agencies/eta/wioa/

Vail, W. L., Niyogi, A., Henderson, N., & Wennerstrom, A. (2017). Bringing it all back home: Understanding the medical difficulties encountered by newly released prisoners in New Orleans, Louisiana - a qualitative study. *Health & Social Care in the Community, 25*(4), 1448–1458. doi:10.1111/hsc.12445 PMID:28370837

Wellborn, J. (1999). Responding to individuals with mental illness. *FBI Law Enforcement Bulletin, 68*(11), 6–8.

Western, B. (2018). *Homeward: Life in the year after prison.* Russell Sage Foundation. doi:10.7758/9781610448710

Whipple, C. R., Jason, L. A., & Robinson, W. L. (2016). Housing and abstinence self-efficacy in formerly incarcerated individuals. *Journal of Offender Rehabilitation, 55*(8), 548–563. doi:10.1080/10509674.2016.1229713 PMID:28603403

World Population Review. (2023). *Incarceration Rates by Country 2023.* https://worldpopulationreview.com/country-rankings/incarceration-rates-by-country

Wright, B. J., Zhang, S. X., Farabee, D., & Braatz, R. (2014). Prisoner reentry research from 2000 to 2010: Results of a narrative review. *Criminal Justice Review, 39*(1), 37–57. doi:10.1177/0734016813501192

Chapter 4
Levers of Heightening Trust and Certainty in Communication:
The Relevance of Communication in Building Trust

Anna Rostomyan
Berlin School of Business and Innovation, Germany

ABSTRACT

In today's modern world, trust between the interactants is shrinking, since while communicating with each other, there is almost always the fear of being misled by means of disinformation or miscommunication. The chapter discusses the necessity of the application of five expression management techniques formerly proposed by Andersen and Guerrero, namely 1) intensification, 2) de-intensification, 3) simulation, 4) inhabitation, and 5) masking, which, according to the studies of the authors of this chapter, have the potential of raising the level of emotional connection between the speaking partners, who then gain the ultimate chance of influencing each other's viewpoint by means of heightening the trust level through the application of these emotion expression management techniques for the benefit of both parties both in the business field and in our everyday lives. To elucidate this, extracts from contemporary English fiction are discussed by the author that show the impact of emotion management to achieve emotive impact on the listener(s).

DOI: 10.4018/978-1-6684-8569-9.ch004

INTRODUCTION

While communicating with one another a lot of our presuppositions and assumptions are based on the level of confidence of our speaking partners speaks with. To a high degree, their confidence depends on their self-awareness, as well as the level of trust between the interactants and the level of certainty in which the speaks with about a certain subject that he or she is certainly and undoubtedly sure about.

Nonetheless, merely being sure about something does not necessarily presuppose the ability to speak about it with certainty. For this, one has to be very self-aware and self-confident to be able to deliver his/her speech accordingly in order to have the desired influence on the interlocutor.

Moreover, the trust level between the interactants highly depends on the emotive bonds between them for which the emotional intelligence (EQ) skills of the speaking partners may be of great utility to build genuine connection between the latters for them to communicate and cooperate harmoniously, fruitfully and peacefully with one another.

In this respect it is notable that currently trust seems to be shrinking in highly developed, democratic countries. There seems to be an increasing common fear that audiences are being manipulated by the mass media, companies, services and individuals. At the same time, people in developed countries increasingly turn to alternative information sources, like social networks, blogs and other forms of online communication where they seek for the right evaluation of the offered products (Quandt, 2012, p. 7).

In fact, trust is an essential social and communicative notion, which is mainly aimed at a specific connection between two or more social interactants. Therefore, the present chapter will elucidate the importance of trust in social interaction, as well as highlighting its significance in communicative interaction by means of discussing five expression management techniques that can be used to enhance emotional bonds between the communicative interactants.

The Importance of Trust in Human Interaction

Numerous definitions of trust can be found in diverse disciplines: e.g., in sociology (e.g., Coleman, 1990), social psychology (Deutsch, 1958), political science (Miller, 1974), economics (Williamson, 1993), communication studies (Kohring & Matthes, 2007), as well as some other related disciplines.

According to Kohring and Matthes (2007), the theoretical basis for the concept of trust in news media is based on selectivity, that is to say trust in news media means trust in their specific selectivity rather than in objectivity or truth.

Despite great efforts made by scholars, trust seems to remain an intractable concept. Trust has been defined in many ways and little consensus has been achieved among scholars. Some examples: "Trust is defined as a willingness to rely on an exchange partner in whom one has confidence." (Moorman, Deshpande & Zaltman, 1993, p. 82) According to another definition, "We define trust in terms of confident positive expectations regarding another's conduct" (Lewicki & Bies, 1998, p. 439). Moreover, "An individual may be said to have trust in the occurrence of an event if he expects its occurrence and his expectations lead to behavior which he perceives to have greater negative consequences if the expectation is not confirmed than positive motivational consequences if it is confirmed" (Deutsch, 1958, p. 266).

Despite the existing contradictory viewpoints and subsequent definitions of the term, there is a certain consensus on then basic and most important meaning of trust, i.e., it is necessary and present when the actors (the trustors) cannot or do not want to control the actions of their interactants, expecting a certain action on the part of these alteri (trustees) (Quandt, 2012, p. 8).

As we may guess, these expectations are primarily based on a past experience(s), which can be based on both a former personal experience and any other experience connected with the same or similar actors under the same and/or similar circumstances and situations. Here, the emotional background knowledge comes to the fore and plays an irreplaceable role in guiding the communicators throughout the whole speech event (Rostomyan, 2012). Here, cooperation of the interactants, especially a communicative interaction, becomes possible based on a mutually shared background knowledge that makes fluent and flawless interaction possible.

Moreover, it is generally believed that the expected actions of the trustees will not have an emotional negative impact on the trustors later on; moreover, the effects and consequences are supposed to be beneficial for both parts.

In social communication especially, there is always a certain need for trust because of the problem of societal complexity and contingency of events in social constellations (Quandt, 2012, p. 8), where there should be mutual expectation of the parties involved that would be beneficial for both of them. As everyday events cannot be fully foreseen or predicated, there is always a certain need of trust between the interactants to develop safely grounded expectations upon the outcome of the events which serves a secure basis for successful social action and interaction. Hence, trust is, undoubtedly, a crucial characteristic feature of the societal communication irrespective from logical or emotional reasons, since the lack of it can bring to the malfunctioning of the society. This fact leads to the observation that for building successful relationships within the frames of this or that cultural or sub-cultural society, there is an urgent need of firstly building trust between the interactants which sometimes seems to be dwindling nowadays.

According to Thorsten Quandt (2012), there are various types of trustees: trust in people one knows quite well based on their close relationship status when the interactants possess a large amount of information on each other concerning different fields which accompanies both sides of the interlocutors during the whole speech event makes their actions mutually to a greater degree predictable, and there is trust in people whom we do not know well. Although a lot of scientists consider the first type of the aforementioned trustees as irrelevant as there is always a natural propensity in trusting in people who stand close to us, yet we do consider it as relevant since a lot of what happens in the process of communication occurs on the basis of emotional background knowledge which makes the act of any joint communication possible the basis of which should be trust.

Especially in the business field, there should be trust and certainty between the partners, the CEOs and the managers, as well as the employees of the company to operate successfully and effectively, which will resultantly lead to better work output and better results.

Speaking about our everyday lives, we can also state that trust and certainty between the interactants are of utmost importance, since all interaction is based on these two. Furthermore, in case we manage to communicate these two through our verbal and non-verbal communication, we will stand a better chance of having a positive influence on our interlocutors (see more in Rostomyan, 2022a).

In this connection, it should be noted that since we human beings are also emotional beings and not only rational ones, to build a genuine and long-lasting trust and bond between the speaking partners, we should also be able to convey our internal states, our emotions and feelings, desires and aspirations accordingly in order to reach to the hearts of our interactants. For this, different communication emotion management techniques can be applied, which will be discussed in our next section.

The Application of Emotion Expression Management Techniques Based on Trust

When discussing the complexity of human emotions Andersen and Guerrero speak about five expression management techniques of emotions: 1) intensification, 2) de-intensification, 3) simulation, 4) inhibition, and 5) masking, with the help of which people try to handle the expression of their emotions (Andersen & Guerrero, 1998, pp.49-96).

1) ***Intensification*** (or *maximization*) refers to creating the appearance that emotions are felt more strongly than they are. It is important to note that intensification involves the display of an emotion that is genuinely felt; its display is simply exaggerated (see Andersen and Guerrero, 1998).

In fact, people sometimes when feeling an emotion express it more strongly than they actually feel it. For instance, if a person is slightly surprised, he/she may act as if the surprise is exceedingly high. Likewise, if someone feels somewhat sad, he/she may express an overwhelming portion of grief. Other examples of intensification include laughing generously at something which is only slightly amusing, etc. It is also noteworthy that intensification seems to be used both with positive and negative emotions. Via intensification the speaker may basically have an emotive influence on the interlocutors, subtly suggesting to them what emotions they should feel (Rostomyan, 2020a, p. 98). It is also worth mentioning that by means of using a case or cases of intensification in your speech, you may sound more certain about what you are speaking about, which will resultantly raise the level of trust in your interlocutor's mind.

To elucidate this, let us examine the following pair of examples: the first one represents a case of intensification bearing positive implication, whereas the second one carries overall negative implication:

Example 1*: She sat down rather stiffly in the straight-backed armchair beside the fire.*

'How pretty the fire is,' she said.

'Jeanne, I think I'm **crazily** *in love with you,' said* **Andrews in an excited voice**.

(Dos Passos, 1921, p. 360)

Example 2: *'A big society party.'*

'Which raises money for charity.'

'Which you **don't give a damn** *about. It's just another step up the Highland Park social ladder for you. You're social climbing and Boo's being raised by Consuela!'*

(Gimenez, 2007, p. 67)

In the first example Andrews is experiencing rather positive emotions towards his interlocutor. As we know, there are a number of intensifying adverbs which amplify the positive meaning of the word they are attached to, i.e. *completely, greatly, entirely, fully, totally, extremely, tremendously, crazily, terrifically, really, truly,* etc. As a matter of fact, intensification of speech is a permanent and highly important feature of colloquial style. There are different ways and means of giving emotive force to a whole sentence or any part of it. Apart from the emphasis given by information theme and rheme, language provides a great number of other means of giving a sentence or a clause, or any unit of the sentence purely emotive emphasis. Here belong: stress, various kinds of intensifiers, exclamations, the emphatic *do* in declarative and imperative sentences, reduplication, emphatic syntactic structures, interjections, vocatives, expletive words, etc. (Buzarov, 1969, p. 66). In this case, the speaker uses the intensifying adverb *crazily* to reinforce the actual positive implication of his expressive speech act and to stress his inner positive emotional state of being in love. By means of using these tiny tricks, the speaker momentarily raises the chances of creating an emotional bond between him and his speaking partner, which in its turn raises the level of trust between them. His positive emotions are not only manifested on the verbal level, but also on the vocal level: *said Andrews in an excited voice* (Rostomyan, 2013, p. 144). Here, we can state that by means of intensifying our speech, we subtly suggest on the verbal level to our listeners that we are sure about what we are talking about and also convey our emotions accordingly, which helps us build trust between our interlocutors and interactants. It follows, that in case of intensifying our emotions through the emotion expression management technique intensification, we stand a better chance of raising the emotional impact on our speaking partners, at the same time heightening the trust level.

In the second example, we observe a case of negative emotional intensification. In familiar conversation between equals a few somewhat vulgar intensifiers often occur as premodifiers of adjectives or adverbs, such as *darn(ed), damn(ed), goddamn(ed), goldarn(ed)/goldurn(ed)* (a euphemistic substitution for goddamn), *bloody, hellish, all-fired(ly)* (meaning extremely) and a few others, which can also be used for both positive and negative evaluations. In the adduced extract, the intensifying adjective *damn* attaches negative emotive emphasis to the act of reproach: the conversation occurs between spouses; the husband is dissatisfied with his wife's addiction to being a renowned person in the social circles of Highland Park; hence, we may guess that he undergoes emotions belonging to the negative scale, such as resentment, anger, annoyance and the like, which are being expressed in his speech act when he reproaches his wife for not taking care of their child, Boo, and leaving the maintenance of the child only to their housemaid (Rostomyan, 2013, p. 144). These kinds of intensifying adverbs can be used to display negative emotions that can be applied in case of the experience of emotions belonging rather to the negative scale and in case of shrinking trust to reproach our communicative interactants. This is done not only to express our negative emotions, but also instead to show dissatisfaction for the sake of rebuilding emotional connection and making our speaking partners revise their actions, words, and strategies that will become beneficial for all the parties involved.

In this connection, it is of paramount importance to denote that in the process of decoding any intensified utterance the felicity condition of sincerity (Searle, 1969,

p. 66) is by all means to be taken into consideration as illustrated in the passage below, since without the sincerity condition, the trust may be on a superficial and fluctuating level and sometimes some people may use it to reach trust between the interactants for the benefit of themselves and not for the sake of the other person and/or for the society in general:

Example 3: *'Mr. Fenney,' Rob said, 'your speech at the bar luncheon, it was* **truly** *inspiring.'*

First day on the job and the boy was already brown-nosing like an experienced associate. Could he possibly be sincere?

'Thanks, Bob.'

Missy ***winked****. Scott didn't know if the wink was because she knew his speech was bullshit or if she was flirting again. (Gimenez, 2007, p. 14)*

In the aforementioned example, Mr. Scott Fenney, who has just performed an important speech at the bar luncheon, does not actually know how to decode the intensified expressive speech act uttered by Rob, who seems to be amazed by Fenney's speech. Rob attaches extra positive emotive emphasis to his expressive speech act by applying the intensifying adverb truly which preceding the adjective inspiring gives positive emotive emphasis to it; thus, intensifying the overall positive meaning of the speech act. However, as Rob is Fenney's subordinate, the latter does not really believe in the sincerity condition of the performed speech act. As for Missy, she converses with Scott via non-verbal means of communication, i.e. she winks at him. In this case Scott does not know either how to process the received information; according to the author's remarks, it can embody diverse implicit meanings, such as flirting or just subtly pointing out to the fact that Scott does not have to believe in Rob's words (Rostomyan, 2020a, p. 100). This kind of communicative action can be encoded and decoded in case of some mutually shared common knowledge between the communicative interactants, which is conducted based on the level of trust between the latters (Rostomyan, 2012).

2) ***De-intensification*** (or minimization) refers to giving the impression that emotions are felt less strongly than they are. However, it should by all means be mentioned that only part of the felt emotion is hidden, while some portion of it is being displayed. As with intensification, de-intensification involves the display of an emotion which is genuinely felt; its display is merely softened. Actually, sometimes people feel a certain emotion and display it on the outside,

> without being able to suppress the expression of the felt emotion, yet they express it not as strongly as they feel it. This is where the emotion expression management technique de-intensification come to the fore. For instance, if a person is angry with someone, he/she may simply exhibit mild irritation rather than revealing all of his/her anger in order not to damage their interpersonal relations formerly based on trust (Rostomyan, 2020a, pp. 100-101).

To illustrate this phenomenon, let us examine a situation, in which a man tries to hide his actual emotions by minimizing the degree of the experienced emotions:

Example 4: *'Look,* **honey**, *I'm* **kind of** *busy, so if everything's under control there, I need to get back to work.' (Gimenez, 2007, p. 35)*

It is truly obvious that the speaker feels irritated and embarrassed because of being disturbed and interrupted while working. This is the reason why he quite probably undergoes rather negative emotions at the moment of speech production. Nevertheless, he does not explicitly manifest those very negative emotions not to upset the interlocutor, who obviously is a close person to the speaker, as the latter, when addressing his interlocutor, uses the noun *honey* as a vocative expression, which is generally used to denote close rapport between equals. Besides, he uses the approximator *kind of* to minimize the degree of his categoricity and, thus, tries to minimize the overall negative emotive emphasis of the act of reproach (Rostomyan, 2013, p. 145). De-intensification can very often be applied in communication when one or both of the speaking partners cherish each other so much that they do not want the other to bother about some existing problems and want to create the appearance that everything is under control, mutually trusting one another. For this very reason, they tend to de-intensify their truly felt emotions and on the basis of trust between the interactants the other person can decode the intended meaning accordingly that the speaker tries to convey not showing all of the portion of the truly felt emotions not to cause harm or damage to the other person. This includes instances of not displaying the overall degree of sadness, grief, hesitation, anxiety or nervousness connected with a certain occasion and/or event.

The next extract from contemporary English fiction again illustrates another instance of de-intensification:

Example 5: '**Kind of** *funny, ain't it, Scotty?'*

'What?'

'Back in school, we used to talk about working together. After all this time, we are.' He shrugged. **'Kind of** *funny.' (Gimenez, 2007, p. 126)*

This extract represents a stretch of discourse between former best friends (undoubtedly formerly having trust towards one another), who used to study together and had dreamed of working as a team in the future. However, the reality turned out to be quite different from their expectations: Scott became a renowned corporate lawyer with a very high income, whereas Bobby did not manage to find a good job after graduating from the university. However, because of certain circumstances, Scott currently faces financial difficulties and cannot afford to hire a better lawyer to help him with a certain case he has been appointed to handle by the Judge. So, Bobby uses he approximator *kind of* to de-intensify the degree of his being content that they finally come to work together. Yet, the adjective *funny,* to which the approximator kind of is attached, points out to the fact that there is some irony in his speech act. Besides, he also uses a non-verbal means of communication, i.e. he *shrugs*, which also indicates that Bobby implicitly hints to that fact that life is a ladder during which we may either rise or fall, and on this very occasion the former best friends, who have been isolated from each other because of the former status gap between them, happen to be on the same stage again. Here, we can see that not to damage the existing trust between the speaking partners, one of them uses the emotion expression management technique de-intensification and tries not to display his negative emotions fully at the strongest level so that not to ruin and damage their relationship based on former trust. This comes to suggest that de-intensification can often be applied for keeping trust between the communicative interactants.

3) ***Simulation*** refers to displaying an emotion which is not genuinely felt. Such efforts seem to be misleading. Buller and Burgoon (1998) suggest that here deception is embodied in intentionally encoding a message by a sender to foster a false deduction by the receiver (Buller & Burgoon, 1998, pp. 381-402). However, in contrary to its reputation, deception can be viewed as a behavioural competent in interpersonal relations. Knapp and Comadena (1979) suggest the notion of '*collaborative deception*', which is recognized by all the parties involved and is being practiced to maintain a presumably shared desire for the smooth flow of interaction and co-operation (Knapp & Comadena, 1979, pp. 270-285). One form of the so-called collaborative deception occurs *'when lies are used to mutually benefit the self-esteem of the participants'* (O'Hair & Cody 1994, p. 186).

Collaborative deception seems especially related to the display rules that foster predictable social encounters. Simulation, in particular, seems likely to be used for this purpose, as it is the only management technique, which involves no genuine experience of emotion. The most frequently cited example of this emotion management technique is smiling when one does not experience such positive emotions as: gladness, happiness, joy, delight, and the like, but for collaborative peaceful interaction displays it (Rostomyan, 2013, p. 145).

From the positive perspective, this management technique can be applied in case of not willing to lose social bonds. Yet, one has to be very careful here not to be misled based on trust with this very emotion expression management technique, since the expression of emotions in this case does not presuppose the existence of such. Nonetheless, if applied for good causes it can save relationships and keep the level of trust between the interactants.

Let us consider an illustration of simulation by adducing the following situation:

Example 6: *As the applause grew louder, the corporate tax lawyer whom Scott was campaigning to succeed as the next state bar president leaned in close and whispered, 'You know, Scotty, you've got an impressive line of bullshit. Now I see why half the coeds at SMU dropped their drawers for you.'*

Scott squeezed the knot of his silk tie, smoothed his $ 2000 suit, and whispered back through brilliant white teeth, *'Henry, you don't get laid or elected telling the truth.' (Gimenez, 2007, p. 10)*

As it can be concluded from the given passage above, the speaker displays emotions, which are not genuinely felt: according to the description of the author, he smiles a big smile showing his brilliant white teeth, displaying falsified positive emotions, such as happiness, gladness, cheerfulness and other related positive emotions, yet not genuinely feeling them on the inside. As he himself explains to the corporate tax lawyer, whom he was campaigning for, he merely plays sincerity in front of the audience to acquire their positive disposition towards him, since by telling the truth he would not be elected. Here, Scott adheres to the display rule of vocational requirements of displaying positive emotions in accordance with his occupation (Hochschild, 1983), where one has to act in a certain way depending on the vocational requirements, since to simulate his emotions is a part-and-parcel of his profession as a lawyer. Here, it should also be noted that based on the vocational requirements, the appearance of Scott as a lawyer is also flawless, i.e. "*Scott squeezed the knot of his silk tie, smoothed his $ 2000 suit, and whispered back through brilliant white teeth*", which also shows that he approaches the campaign professionally by means of also dressing accordingly.

The next example again illustrates another case of simulation:

Example 7: *Sid* **smiled** *at Bobby. 'Do all the work, like I do for Scott on Dibrell matters.'*

Sid's **smile disappeared** *when he turned to Scott and saw that Scott wasn't smiling.*

'Yeah, Sid, only difference is, I need Bobby. You can be replaced.'

Sid **squirmed and forced a sheepish grin**. *(Gimenez, 2007, p. 123)*

In this case, Sid simulates his truly felt emotions by displaying a *smile* on his face, which is generally considered to be a non-verbal means of communicating and transmitting positive emotions. Yet, as we may guess from the context, in reality he does not feel such positive emotions as happiness, gladness, cheerfulness and the like. His smile disappears, when he understands that Scott does not buy his falsified positive disposition towards them. Then, he again displays a "*grin*", which, according to the words of the author, is a "*sheepish*" one, as his truly felt negative emotions have actually been revealed by his interlocutors, which comes to suggest that the simulation of emotions failed, since the felicity condition of sincerity was most presumably lacking.

As we have mentioned, the phenomenon of simulating the emotions besides its "bad" reputation may have a "collaborative" function and, in this case, it can be regarded as a very useful tool for handling the process of communicative interaction, as it can be revealed in the next stretch of discourse, where the shop assistant simulates positive emotions to satisfy the needs of the consumers based on the requirements of her profession in customer service:

Example 8: *Darcy tells her that I will need a complementary shade, as the maid of honor.*

'How nice. Sisters?' **The woman smiles.** *Her big, square teeth remind me of Chiclets.*

'No,' I say.

'But she's like my sister,' Darcy says, **simply and sincerely**. *(Giffin, 2011, p. 143)*

In the given extract above, Darcy wants to buy a definite shade of lipstick for herself for her wedding, as well as for her maid of honour. To attract their attention and to exhibit a pleasant appearance, the shop assistant displays positive emotions with a non-verbal marker, i.e. she *smiles*. Thus, the woman's smile in this case is expressed for a positive purpose, which is a true and indispensable part of her vocation (Hochschild, 1983). As we can see from the development of affairs, the shop assistant manages to build a trust bond between her and the customers, since Darcy in response to the question of the latter replies quite "*simply and sincerely*".

4) ***Inhibition*** involves exposing the appearance of no emotion when in reality one is feeling a definite sort of emotion. Sometimes people feel an emotion, but do not express it for some reason. Prime examples of inhibition include keeping a straight face when something seems funny, hiding attraction towards someone, keeping a seemingly calm voice when feeling angry, agitated or irritated, etc.

It has been proven by diverse linguists and psychologists that people learn to exhibit the expression of certain emotions in due course of time (Brannigan & Humphries, 1969, pp. 406-408). This phenomenon is evidenced by the fact that often children's interactions are generally uninhibited as compared with adult interactions, as can be observed in the stretch of discourse elucidated below:

Example 9: *But Boo was quiet. Then, without looking at him, she said: 'You secretly loved my mother, but she married A. Scott. You've never gotten over it. You've always wondered what your life would've been like if she had married you instead.'*

Bobby hadn't figured on that. He had **to take a deep breath**. *He pushed himself up but looked down at her.*

'**How***?'*

'I saw how you looked at her when you got here. Your eyes went all over the crowd, kind of **frantic** *like, until you saw her. Then you just looked at her for a long time. Like, forever.'*

Bobby walked directly to the beer cooler. (Gimenez, 2007, p. 172)

Here, Boo speaks to Bobby, a friend of her father. Decoding the meaning of Booby's non-verbal behaviour, i.e. his *frantic like* look across the crowd searching for the mother of Boo, she understands that Bobby has been infatuated by her mother for already quite a long time. She does not strive towards inhibiting her subsequent emotions and thoughts. On the contrary, she freely and honestly expresses them on the outward in her speech. Bobby is astonished by the frankness of the child. Moreover, he does not know how to react. As we may guess from the context, at the moment of speech production Booby's felt emotions rather belong to the negative scale, such as irritation, nervousness, uneasiness, shame, and the like. So, he utters an elliptical sentence, i.e. *how*, leaving out a great deal of information and wondering how a small girl could come up with such a precise conclusion. Hearing the child's response, Bobby feels that he is no longer capable to manage to inhibit the display of his emotions, since as we know people, when undergoing too strong emotions, do not manage to have a cognitive control over them which are consequently being manifested through verbal and/or non-verbal means of emotion expressions (Rostomyan, 2022a). Thus, not to give himself away he merely remains silent and walks directly to the beer cooler. As we may reveal from the adduced extract above, the openness of displaying the emotions of the child builds a trust link between the speaking partners and Bobby does no longer hide his emotions and asks a question to learn how Boo had revealed them by herself.

In contrast to child communication, while observing adult communication, we can very often reveal that in certain circumstances adults deliberately inhibit their genuine emotions as can be detected in the following illustration, which depicts an incident when one of the interactants has to hide his truly felt emotions:

Example 10: *The judge was* **eyeing** *Scott over his reading glasses;* **a wry smile** *crossed his face.*

'Didn't really want to be another Atticus Finch **after all**, *huh, Mr. Fenney?'*

Scott knew better than to respond. The judge's smile dissolved into a look of disappointment that, for some odd reason bothered Scott.

(Gimenez, 2007, p. 107)

In the present stretch of discourse, we can truly observe that the Judge is very dissatisfied with the work of Mr. Scott Fenney and, thus, he scolds him by an indirect act of reproach for not being really devoted to his lawyer's duties as Atticus Finch, the hero of Harper Lee's novel *To Kill a Mockingbird*, was, who preferred to be the lawyer of an Afro-American woman, which was out of question in those times, and to fight for justice rather than to follow the society's acknowledged norms and principles of the era. The author also implicitly hints to the Judge's discontent pointing out to his *wry* smile; the smile, being a universal sign of transmitting positive emotions, in this case is used for negative implications, hence the use of the adjective wry. He expresses an indirect act of reproach, at the end of which he intensifies his speech by means of adding the phrase "*after all*", thus reinforcing the overall negative implicit meaning (Rostomyan, 2012, p. 287). Scott feels embarrassed and bothered, but being conscious of the fact that he does not have to exhibit those very negative emotions in the presence of the Judge; he inhibits his genuinely felt emotions and simply remains silent to avoid subsequent tense relations with the Judge. As we may guess, there is a prior trust between the interactants and Scott understands the meaning of the wry smile of the Judge as a sign of the discontent of his. In this case we again witness an instance of emotion management according to vocational requirements.

5) ***Masking*** differs drastically from the other management techniques in the way that it involves showing a particular emotion when one is feeling a completely *different* emotion. For instance, in certain circumstances a person may express happiness, when he/she feels anger or sadness. Likewise, someone may show hatred towards another person, when he/she truly loves that person. Masking is believed to be much more difficult to apply than any other emotion management technique '*probably because it is easier to moderate an existing emotion than to express an emotion that is very different from what one is feeling*' (Andersen & Guerrero, 1998, p. 56). This includes cases when people do not display worry and anxiety when one of their close friends or relatives has, for example, to undergo surgery. Instead, they display such emotions as felicity, hope, faith, and the like, to encourage the sick person. As it can be observed in the following example, Rachel has to mask her really felt emotions because of the existing obstacles:

Example 11: *We should hang up now. This is going in a bad direction.*

'Rach?' **His voice is low and intimate.**

I feel breathless, hearing him say my name like this. The one syllable is familiar, warm. 'Yeah?'

'You still there?' he whispers.

I manage to say, 'Yes, I'm still here.'

'What are you thinking?'

'Nothing,' I lie.

I have to lie. Because what I am thinking is; maybe you are my type just a little bit more than I once thought. (Giffin, 2011, p. 67)

In the aforementioned piece of contemporary English discourse, the interlocutors have previously been merely close friends. Dex is now engaged to Rachel's best friend Darcy. Thus, it bothers Rachel that her former best friend addresses her so warmly, tenderly and intimately; by only using the first syllable of her name, i.e. *Rach*, even pronouncing it in a low, intimate and cherished tone. As a result, she realizes that he has developed tender emotions towards her. Since there is trust and certainty between the speaking partners, Dex does not intend to hide his truly felt emotions, which are revealed on the vocative level. Yet, Rachel does not know how to respond properly to the expressed speech act since although she undergoes similar delicate positive emotions towards him, analyzing her emotions rationally and not letting the emotional part of her brain overrule the rational one, she masks her truly felt positive emotions, giving the appearance that she is cool, chilly, serene, since she is well-aware of the fact that she is not allowed to express her attraction towards the fiancé of her best friend, Darcy. This is the very reason why she intentionally hampers the encoding process of her real emotions not to ruin their friendship (Rostomyan, 2013a, pp. 147-148). As we can conclude, masking can also be used to save trust and connection with the interactants based on some mutually shared prior knowledge.

In the next example, we may again observe a case of masking the emotions for the sake of keeping the trust and positive relationship between the speaking partners:

Example 12: *'This won't affect your position in the firm?'*

Upon retiring to the master suite, that was Rebecca's first and only question, her way of asking, **Will this affect your income***?*

'No, of course not. I'm still Tom Dibrell's lawyer.'

Her expression said she wasn't buying it.

'Rebecca, look, I've got Bobby working the case. He'll get me through it, she'll get convicted, and things will go back to normal. Don't worry.'

But Scott was worried. *That feeling of impending doom had grown stronger. (Gimenez, 2007, p. 128)*

As we can see from the extract above taken from contemporary crime fiction, the wife of Scott, Rebecca, is worried about the probable reduction of her husband's income and their reputation. As a matter of fact, Scott himself is also worried about the same issue, as the author's remark indicates, i.e. in the description of Scott's internal state of worry: "*But Scott was worried*". In fact, the state of affairs is such that Scott has been appointed to handle a case, which may very possibly harm his career as a successful corporate lawyer. Yet, he tries to mask his emotions, striving towards displaying a seemingly unworried description of the situation not to give ground for his wife to worry more than she does. As we may guess, he does so to keep his face and to keep the trust between them. Nonetheless, it is visible that it is very hard for him to mask his real emotions as, notwithstanding his efforts to mask his emotions, "*the feeling of impending doom grows stronger*". However, according to the author's remark, on the non-verbal level the wife shows via her facial expression that she did not believe in his words, maybe by means of analyzing the behaviour of her husband. Here, the emotion expression management technique of masking is used not to cause negative emotions in the interlocutor on the part of Scott, who though being uncertain about the current state of affairs tried to convince his wife that everything will be good and they will not fail. Hence, he made her believe the best based on the trust between the latters. Nonetheless, though having trust in her husband, realizing the current state of affairs, the wife did not relax and was further worried about the present situation. As we can see, in this case, masking of emotions and to showing them as they are on the outward, is done for the sake of their mutually shared trust not to cause reasons for worry for the wife, which is an act of care.

To sum up with, the application of the emotion expression techniques discussed above, may not always but often solve the emerged emotionally tense situation and by means of applying them appropriately and accordingly for the benefit of both of the parties involved the speaker has the potential of positively influencing them and keeping the trust level, sometimes even heightening it. Thus, we do firmly believe that these emotion expression management techniques can be considered as efficient levers for sounding certain, resultantly saving the relationships and even reinforcing the trust level between the communicative interactants.

Case Study

To reveal the awareness of people on the importance of trust and certainty between the interactants in the process of communication we have carried out a quantitative analysis based on probability sampling with 30 participants.

The results of the quantitative analysis survey based on probability are depicted in the **Figure 1** depicted below:

The findings of our survey come to prove that the majority of the interviewees believe that trust and certainty are essential and important in communication, which

Figure 1. Awareness on the significance of trust and certainty in communication
Source: *Dr. Anna Rostomyan survey*

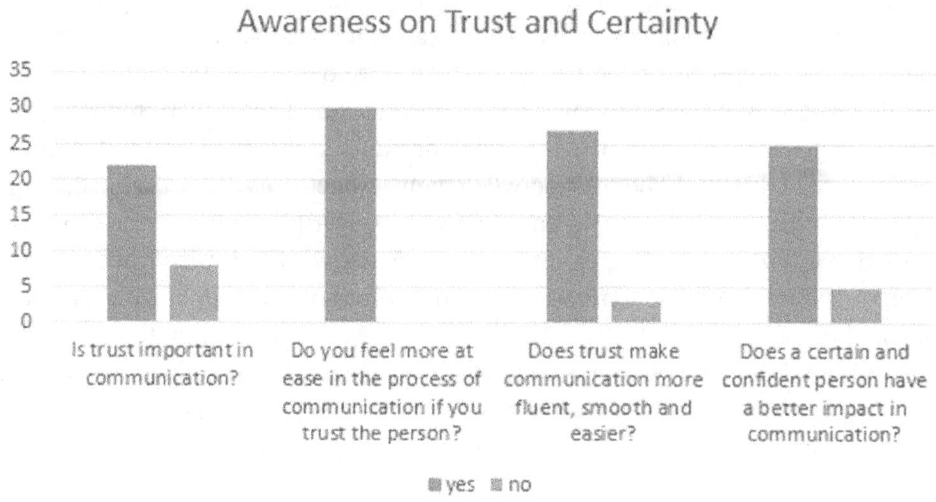

foster harmonious and flawless communicative interaction between the speaking partners.

Besides, as for the qualitative analysis, respondents have to replied that they feel more bound to trust a person with whom they have an emotional connection. It follows that in case the speakers use the emotion expression management techniques in the process of interpersonal communication, they will stand a better chance of keeping and even heightening the trust level.

This brings us to the assumption that in case we manage to strengthen and heighten the trust and certainty in the process of communication with the help of the discussed emotion expression management techniques, we will have better results in fruitful interaction.

DISCUSSION

It is noteworthy that emotion expression management techniques are applied differently according to the culture, family, vocational and personal preferences.

Our research through years has also shown that these can also be governed by some previous emotional experiences and largely according to some certain pre-learnt patterns, which are acquired early in life.

Therefore, if we are aware of these in the process of communication, we can interact more efficiently with our speaking partners and understand their speaker meaning accordingly, which will also help us in building and keeping trust with the latters.

All in all, when we acquire and possess emotion management techniques, we stand a better chance in cross-questioning the witnesses and the accused in the quest for justice.

CONCLUSION

In the process of communicative interaction with our speaking partners we far too often not only exchange ideas or code and decode information, but also express our emotions and feelings towards them, as well as displaying our internal states depending on very different extralinguistic factors.

Here, the desire of a harmonious interaction is carried out based on the concept of trust and the level of certainty of the communicators, which makes our peaceful interaction possible.

Our studies have truly proven that by means of applying the discussed emotion expression management techniques at hand accordingly in the process interpersonal communication, the speakers stand a better chance of sounding more certain and building trust between their interactants. Nonetheless, one has to be very careful in dealing with trust since it can be misleading in unveiling the required information, especially in criminal cases. Yet, the trust between the defense and the accused, the prosecution and pleading party should be strong and unshakable in order to win the case.

In case both of the interacting parties are aware of these emotion expression management techniques both of them may greatly benefit from the process of communication, since being not only rational, but also emotional beings, in case of managing emotional bonds with our speaking partners, we will resultantly also enhance our trust level with the latters.

REFERENCES

Andersen, P., & Guerrero, L. (1998). Principles of Communication and Emotion in Social Interaction. In P. A. Andersen & L. K. Guerrero (Eds.), *Handbook of Communication and Emotion* (pp. 49–96). Academic Press.

Arnold, M. B. (1960). *'Emotion and Personality'. Psychological Aspects, 1.* Columbia University Press.

Buller, D., & Burgoon, J. (1998). Emotional Expression in the Deception Process. In P. A. Andersen & L. K. Guerrero (Eds.), *Handbook of Communication and Emotion* (pp. 381–402). Academic Press.

Burgoon, J. (1993). Interpersonal Expectations, Expectancy Violations, and Emotional Communication. *Journal of Language and Social Psychology, 12*(1-2), 30–48. doi:10.1177/0261927X93121003

Buzarov, V. V. (1998). *Essentials of Conversational English Syntax.* Crone-press.

Coleman, J. S. (1990). Foundations on Social Theory. The Belknap Press and Harvard University Press.

Deutsch, M. (1958). Trust and suspicion. *The Journal of Conflict Resolution, 2*(4), 265–279. doi:10.1177/002200275800200401

Dos Passos, J. (1921). *Three Soldiers.* Modern Library.

Ekman, P. (1979). About Brows: Emotional and Conversational Signals. In M. von Cranach, K. Foppa, W. Lepenies, & D. Ploog (Eds.), *Human Ethology: Claims and Limits of a New Discipline: Contributions to the Colloquium* (pp. 169–248). Cambridge University Press.

Ekman, P. (2004). *Emotions Revealed: Recognizing Faces and Feelings to Improve Communication.* Henry Holt and Company. doi:10.1136/sbmj.0405184

Ekman, P., & Friesen, W. (1975). *Unmasking the Face: A Guide to Recognizing Emotions from Facial Clues.* Prentice-Hall.

Fineman, S. (Ed.). (2000). *Emotion in Organizations.* Sage. doi:10.4135/9781446219850

Fineman, S. (Ed.). (2008). *The Emotional Organization: Passions and Power.* Blackwell.

Giffin, E. (2011). *Something Borrowed.* Arrow Books.

Gimenez, M. (2007). *The Colour of Law.* Sphere.

Goleman, D. (1995). *Emotional Intelligence.* Bantam Books.

Grice, P. (1969). *Utterer's Meaning and Intentions: Philosophical Review.* Academic Press.

Hochschild, A. R. (1983). *The Managed Heart: Commercialization of Human Feeling*. University of California Press.

Knapp, M., & Comadena, M. (1979). Telling It Like It Isn't: A Review of Theory and Research on Deceptive Communications. *Human Communication Research*, *5*, 270–285. doi:10.1111/j.1468-2958.1979.tb00640.x

Kohring, M., & Matthes, J. (2007). Trust in news media: Development and validation of a multidimensional scale. *Communication Research*, *34*(2), 231–252. doi:10.1177/0093650206298071

Lewicki, R. J., & Bunker, B. B. (1995). Trust in Relationships: A Model of Development and Decline. In B. B. Bunker, J. Z. Rubin, & ... (Eds.), *Conflict, Cooperation, and Justice*. Jossey-Bass Publishers.

Lews, J. (1985). Trust as a Social Reality. *Social Forces*, *53*(4), 967–985. doi:10.2307/2578601

Miller, A. H. (1974). Political issues and trust in government, 1964-1970. *The American Political Science Review*, *68*(3), 951–972. doi:10.2307/1959140

Moorman, Ch., Deshpande, R., & Zaltman, G. (1993, August). Factors Affecting Trust in Market Research Relationships. *Journal of Marketing*, *57*(1), 81–101. doi:10.1177/002224299305700106

O'Hair, D., & Cody, M. (1994). Deception. In W. R. Cupach & B. H. Spitzberg (Eds.), *The Dark Side of Interpersonal Communication* (pp. 181–213). Lawrence Erlbaum. doi:10.4324/9781315807010-8

Quandt, T. (2012). What's Lest of Trust in a Network Society? An Evolutionary Model and Critical Discussion of Trust and Societal Communication. *European Journal of Communication, 27(1), 7-21.*

Rostomyan, A. (2009). *Means of Expressing Emotive Emphasis in Conversational English. Foreign Languages in Armenia, 10.*

Rostomyan, A. (2012). *'The Vitality of Emotional Background Knowledge in Court', Italian Association for the Study of Law and Literature. Polemos, 6(2).*

Rostomyan, A. (2013a). Management Techniques of Emotions in Communicative Conflict Reduction. In Communication and Management, Communication: Breakdowns and Breakthroughs, Probing the Boundaries. Inter-disciplinary Press.

Rostomyan, A. (2020a). *Business Communication Management: The Key to Emotional Intelligence*. Tredition.

Rostomyan, A. (2020b). *Your Guide to Becoming a Successful Leader*. Tredition.

Rostomyan, A. (2022a). *The Ultimate Force of Emotions in Communication: A linguo-cognitive Analysis of Verbal and Non-verbal Expressions of Emotions (on the material of English)*. Dissertation (Yerevan State University). Düren: Shaker Verlag.

Rostomyan, A. (2022b). *Emotional Intelligence as a Keystone towards Success*. Generis Publishing.

Searle, J. R. (1969). *Speech Acts: An Essay in The Philosophy of Language*. Cambridge University Press. doi:10.1017/CBO9781139173438

Williams, M. (2007). Building Genuine Trust through Interpersonal Emotion Management: A Threat Regulation Model of Trust and Collaboration across Boundaries. *Academy of Management Review*, *2*(2), 595–621. doi:10.5465/amr.2007.24351867

Williamson, O. E. (1993). Calculativeness, Trust, and Economic Organization. *The Journal of Law & Economics*, *36*(1), 453–486. doi:10.1086/467284

Chapter 5
Community Policing Practices in Egypt:
Descriptive Analytical Study

Ramy Metwally El-Kady
https://orcid.org/0000-0003-2208-7576
Police Academy, Egypt

ABSTRACT

This chapter aims to shed light on the practices of community policing in Egypt, show its most prominent forms, and highlight its social role in solving and settling social and criminal problems in Egyptian society. The chapter will rely on the descriptive analytical approach to identify the practices of community policing in Egypt. The chapter plans to introduce community policing and its theoretical framework by addressing its definition, components, goals, and requirements and reviews the most prominent applications of community policing in Egypt, the most important of which are community participation committees in police departments, police reconciliation committees, and community participation committees in police stations. Reform and rehabilitation, and finally, the societal role of the police in community initiatives aimed at reducing the living burdens on citizens. The chapter concluded with the importance of the community policing model in enhancing public participation in maintaining security and combating crime and its reflection on building confidence in the police.

DOI: 10.4018/978-1-6684-8569-9.ch005

INTRODUCTION

The police service in Egypt and most countries of the world specialize in maintaining security and combating and controlling crime as one of its mandates; this traditional approach is applicable through the criminal justice system (Rosenbaum, 1994), whether by taking all procedures and measures that prevent the occurrence of crime or by arresting the perpetrators of crimes and bringing them to justice (Remington, 1965). The police in Egypt specialize in undertaking two functions: The first is administrative, which maintains security and public order, prevents crimes, and protects lives and property; this function is preventive. It aims to take all procedures and measures to avoid and prevent accidents and crimes. The second function is judicial: to detect crimes, arrest their perpetrators, and bring them to trial. This function is characterized by being therapeutic (El-Kady, 2020). It addresses the consequences of the occurrence of the crime, such as disturbing security and social peace, and then prohibits all forms of violation of the existing law. So, it maintains its strength to carry out its mission with respect for the law (Al-Shawa, 1997).

Many police systems in many countries have tended to evolve their police strategies from a traditional to a professional model, depending on community policing as a professional model of policing (Cordner, 2014). It evolved, in part, from a growing dissatisfaction with traditional police practices and a recognition of their shortcomings (Rosenbaum & Lurigio, 1994). Community policing means rooting citizens' participation in security work to ensure adequate participation between citizens and the police to maintain community security in various areas because by knowing the tasks assigned to this security segment, it is possible to arrive at a specific or appropriate definition for community policing, so the Community Policing could be defined as "a process where police officers work closely with community members to identify, prevent, and investigate criminal justice matters." (Hassan, 2005).

Community policing is a police system based on strengthening the partnership between the police and government agencies, active civil society institutions in the field of community service, in confronting crime and reducing its rates of commission and achieving community satisfaction with police work by following a work mechanism, based on several work principles that are distinct from the areas of traditional police work, or they mean the distribution of traditional police tasks in preventing and controlling crime between official police agencies and volunteer groups from the local community (Shaaban, 2009).

This approach to policing involves organizational decentralization (Skogan & Hartnett, 2019), new channels of effective communication and transparency with the public, a commitment to responding to the community's priorities, and adopting a broad problem-solving approach to neighborhood issues. Police departments that adopt this new stance have an entirely different relationship with the public they serve (Skogan & Hartnett, 1999).

Community policing is often regarded as an Anglo-American policing method in origin, but it is now found across the world and is growing in influence (O'Neill, 2023). Community policing has now become a global term to express a police model that is widely used and widespread by the majority of police agencies in the world, from the specifics of problem-solving by the local officers to the grand philosophy of policing that is community-sensitive, accountable, and transparent (Brogden, 2013). Community policing is almost universally accepted as the most effective method for improving police-community relations, and proponents also believe it will ultimately be an effective crime control strategy (Cordner, 1997).

Objectives of the Study

This study aims to shed light on the numerous practices of community policing in Egypt, show its most prominent forms, including community participation committees in police stations, police reconciliation committees, community participation committees in correctional and rehabilitation centers, and police-community initiatives, and highlight its social role in solving and settling social and criminal problems in Egyptian society.

Study Questions

The study aims to answer several questions, most notably:

1- What are the practices of community policing in Egypt?
2- What are the most prominent forms of these practices and their impact on Egyptian society?
3- What is the ideal scenario for activating community policing practices in Egypt?

Study Methodology

The study will rely on the descriptive analytical approach to identify the practices of community policing in Egypt. The descriptive analytical approach is "studying the phenomenon as it exists in reality, describing it closely and expressing it qualitatively or quantitatively to reach conclusions that contribute to understanding and developing this reality" (Obaidat et al., 1996, p.220). This approach aims to research and analyze community policing practices. The study tools that the researcher will use in writing this chapter are the Arab and foreign legal literature related to the research topic in the field of police sciences and criminal law, as well as the relevant specialized literature, whether they are books, doctoral dissertations, or legal articles published on the research topic, in addition to Articles and news published in various media and the Internet.

The Chapter Plan

The chapter plan is based on two parts: The first introduces community policing and its theoretical framework by addressing its definition, components, goals, and requirements. The second reviews the most prominent applications of community policing in Egypt, the most important of which are community participation committees in police stations, police reconciliation committees, and community participation committees in police stations. Reform and rehabilitation, and finally, the societal role of the police in community initiatives aimed at reducing the living burdens on citizens.

INTRODUCTION TO COMMUNITY POLICING

In this part of the chapter, we will discuss the definition of community policing, explaining its origins, theories, components, goals, requirements in comparative systems, and obstacles to its application in Egypt. In the beginning, many countries have known applications for community policing, including Australia, Canada, Denmark, France, Japan, the Netherlands, the United Kingdom, and the United States of America. Among the Arab countries, we mention Bahrain, the Emirates, Jordan, Libya, Saudi Arabia, Sudan, and Egypt (Hassan, 2005).

It is essential to point out the multiplicity of experiences and models of community policing from one society to another, according to the customs and nature of the societal fabric in each country. Therefore, we find some successful applications in some countries, which may not receive similar success in other countries. We want to point out that there is a difference between community partnership and community policing. Community partnership often expands its scope to include all areas of community development, not just security. On the other hand, community police represent one of the means of activating community participation in police work. Therefore, community police are a form of community partnership. However, this form of partnership is characterized by a unique nature that varies from one society to another according to the customs and nature of these societies (Skogan, 1995).

Definition of Community Policing

Many terms refer to community policing or community-oriented policing (COP). In Arab systems, there are several terms, including "community policing," "community police," and "public security" (Hassan, 2005). Many definitions have been said about community policing in many countries. Some show Community policing as a strategy and philosophy and define it as "a strategy of policing that focuses on developing relationships with community members. It is a philosophy of full-service policing that is highly personal, where an officer patrols the same area for an extended time and develops a partnership with citizens to identify and solve problems collaboratively" (Bertus, 1996, p. 139; Cox & Fitzgerald 1992, p. 159). Others define community policing - given its essence - as "a policy and strategy aimed at achieving control of crime, reducing fear of it, improving the quality of life, improving police services, and improving police performance effectively and efficiently" (Friedmann, 1992, p.9; Na, 2016, p. 4).

Add to that others define it as: "the collaboration and integration of the roles of all sects and categories of society, including individuals, governmental and non-governmental institutions, in an integrated social security system - functionally and voluntarily - to eliminate the problems that plague society and lead to the commission of criminal behavior, compared with the security institution and under its supervision" (Al-Attar, 2011, p.60). Some jurisprudence defined it as: "a philosophy of security management based on a full partnership between police agencies and members of society and its various institutions to prevent crime and achieving security and stability for society in the face of everything that disturbs public security" (Shaaban, 2009, p.17).

The community police work to devote the concept of comprehensive security in its idea and responsibilities, and the participation of all sections of society with the security institution in preventive measures and activating their role in combating crime. It also includes the openness of the traditional police to the various elements of society and achieving effective participation between the police and society in reducing crime in fulfillment of the slogan "security is everyone's responsibility" (Al-Ashmawy, 2012, p.2).

The Community Policing Consortium published a statement in 1994 to enhance law enforcement agencies' comprehension and use of community policing. They defined community policing as "a collaboration between the police and the community that identifies and solves community problems" (Community Policing Consortium, 1994, p. vii). Another definition of Community policing was developed by the COPS Office, in partnership with ICF International and the Police Executive

Research Forum (PERF), is "a philosophy that promotes organizational strategies, which support the systematic use of partnerships and problem-solving techniques, to proactively address the immediate conditions that give rise to public safety issues, such as crime, social disorder, and fear of crime." (Scheider et al., 2009). Community policing operates on the premise that crime reduction cannot solely rely on the efforts of the police and other criminal justice organizations. Nevertheless, for crime prevention to yield optimal outcomes in combating criminal activities, it is imperative to integrate the endeavors of politicians, the courts, civil society groups, public and private entities, and individuals (Shaaban, 2009). Finally, The Council of Arab Interior Ministers defined the community police as a police force that seeks to communicate and interact with the various elements of society and its activities to establish the concept of participation between police officers and the various groups of society and to solve problems through this constructive partnership and to seek to achieve social security, reduce crime, and confront it through awareness and educational programs (El-Kady, 2020).

Critics of community policing argue that the term "community" is vague and its political aim is questionable (Correia, 2000). Some believe that community policing is a return to the "bobby on the beat" concept, while others believe it is unlikely to change police officers' work significantly. Some argue that community policing advocates a fundamental shift to policing, but it would be difficult to achieve due to the progressive and democratic attitude of shared governance (Herbert, 2006).

Critics also question the potential efficacy of community policing, arguing that it may lead to reduced crime control effectiveness, increased bureaucratic and governmental power, unequal treatment, and erosion of constitutional rights. Additionally, police personnel may become overly involved in implementing particularistic community normative standards, which could invite corruption or vigilantism (Skolnick, 1998). Some see that community policing is not a single concept. It may mean a contrast to rapid response and enforcement-oriented policing so that constables are closer to the community and can represent its norms; a process by which crime control is shared with the public, as in neighborhood watch; or a means of developing communication with the public and interest groups (Fielding, 1995). (see: Figure 1)

History of the Community Policing in the US

The scholars refer to Community policing roots in Sir Robert Peel's 1829 Peelian Principles (Alderson, 1984), emphasizing the importance of community cooperation and crime prevention. The term "community policing" emerged in the late 20th century as a response to the concept of police organization (Stenson, 1993). The growth of automobiles, telecommunications, and suburbanization in the early 20th

Figure 1. Parties of community policing

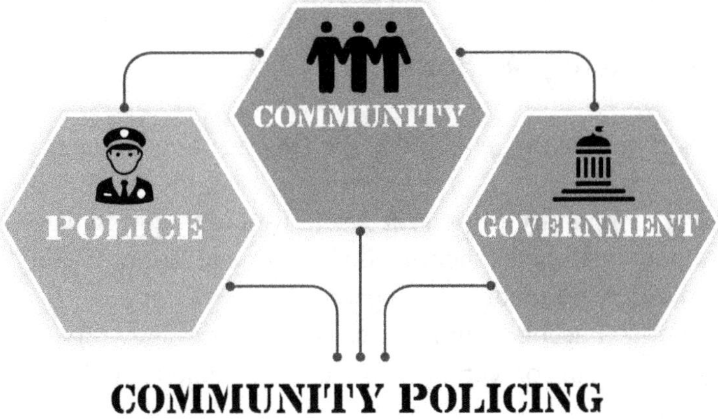

century led to a shift towards reactive techniques, such as answering emergency calls swiftly and relying on motor vehicle patrols (Gau, 2010). Some police forces, like the Chicago Police Station, began rotating personnel between neighborhoods to prevent corruption, resulting in a decrease in foot patrols (Skogan, 2000).

Contemporary ideas about community policing arose from reconsidering police strategies and practices in the 1960s and 1970s (Skolnick & Bayley, 1988). By the 1960s, countries like the United States worked to restore relationships between police forces and black people. In 1967, President Lyndon B. Johnson created a Blue Ribbon group to address perceived distrust of the police by community members, particularly along racial lines.

The President's Commission on Law Enforcement and Administration of Justice recommended introducing a new type of police officer as a community liaison and building ties between law enforcement and minority populations (Ray, 1963). The Kansas City preventative patrol experiment and a study by the US-based Police Foundation also highlighted the challenges police personnel face in their neighborhoods (Chriss, 2016).

The inception of the US Department of Justice, Office of Community Oriented Policing Services (COPS Office) in 1994 provided a significant impetus to the community policing movement in the USA. The COPS Office has allocated over 13 billion dollars, primarily through grants, to about 13,000 out of the 18,000 law enforcement agencies in the United States. The main objective of these awards is to promote the advancement of community policing. This objective was intended to be achieved by allocating funds towards the recruitment of community police officers, acquiring time-efficient technology to enhance the amount of time dedicated to community policing, creating and disseminating knowledge resource materials, and implementing a range of pioneering pilot programs aimed at exploring different policing advancements (Scheider et al., 2009).

Community Policing Methods

Common ways of community policing in the US and eastern countries include:

- Creating a community to prevent crime by providing guidance, talking to students, and creating neighborhood watch organizations.
- Increased usage of foot or bicycle patrols.
- Increased officer accountability to the communities they serve.
- Creating teams of officers to conduct community policing in defined neighborhoods.
- Clear and effective communication and transparency between the police and the communities regarding their objectives and strategies.
- Partnerships with other groups such as government agencies, community members, nonprofit service providers, commercial corporations, and the media.
- Moving toward decentralizing the police authority, allowing more discretion among lower-ranking officers and more initiative expected from them (Watson, 1998).

Components of Community Policing

Applying the concept of community policing requires adherence to the following elements (see Figure 2)

Expansion of Community Participation

Community policing is regarded as a strategy for improving relations between the police and the public while strengthening police effectiveness in preventing and controlling crime (Skolnick & Bayley, 1988). The extent of the success of community policing is measured by the extent of public participation and the extent of success in reducing rates of fear of crime and the number of its victims through broad positive participation from all sectors of society and its institutions (Trojanowicz & Bucqueroux, 1990).

The four elements of community policing are the organization of community-based crime prevention, the reorientation of patrol activities to emphasize nonemergency servicing, increased police accountability to local communities,

Figure 2. Components of community policing

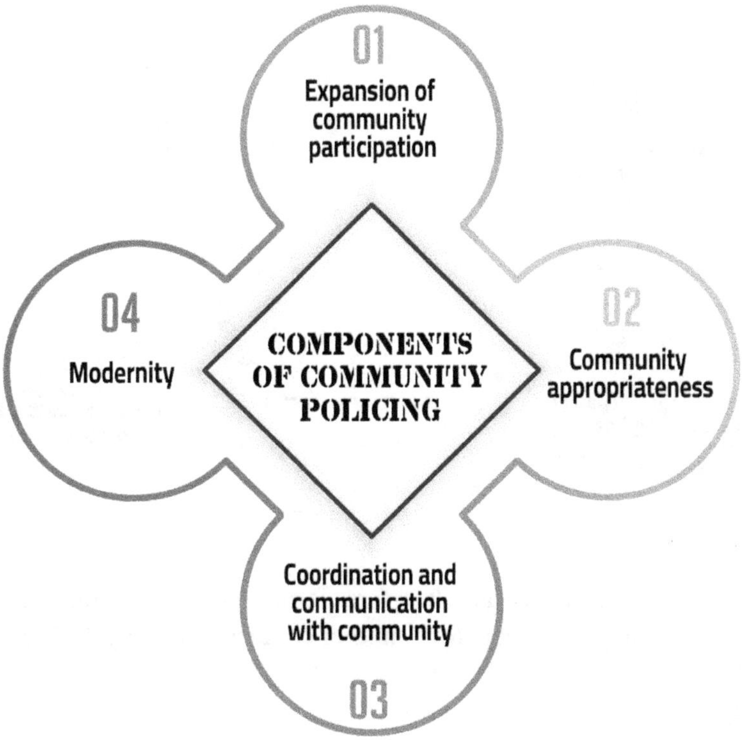

and the decentralization of command. It thus involves significant changes in the customary roles of the police (Skolnick & Bayley, 1988) (see Figure 3).

Obstacles to the advancement of community policing encompass established norms based on conventional perceptions of the police's responsibilities, the necessity for police to respond to urgent situations, constraints on resources, long-standing assumptions about patrol tactics, difficulties in evaluating effectiveness, customary public expectations of the police's duties, and the bureaucratic separation of community programs within the police department (Stenson, 1993). Despite the challenges, the community-policing movement is expected to expand due to its advantages to the public, such as improved crime prevention and police accountability. Additionally, the police force benefits from increased legitimacy through consensus building with the public, higher morale, and enhanced career prospects (Mastrofski et al., 2007).

Community Appropriateness

Community policing should be compatible with the circumstances and needs of the community and be used as a framework for building an effective relationship

Figure 3. Elements of community policing

between the police and the public. Therefore, community police practices vary from one local community to another from another country (El-Kady, 2020).

Modernity

Community policing is considered a new method of policing that strengthens mutual trust between society and security agencies away from the traditional methods used in police work (Cordner, 2014).

Effective Communication and Transparency With Community Institutions

Police officers deal with the local community's needs and problems with citizens' participation (Wilson, 2013) to confront their problems and combat and prevent crime through coordination with other civil agencies and figures with influential positions in the local community through constant communication (Shaaban, 2009). Some scholars see that Community policing succeeded in achieving Effective communication and transparency when residents have a more favorable view of their local police department, improved trust between law enforcement and residents, more accurate information from residents regarding criminal activity in their community, and a better understanding of the needs of citizens and their expectations of the police (Lortz, 2016).

Objectives of Community Policing

Community policing seeks to achieve many goals, the most important of which are (see Figure 4):

Figure 4 Objectives of community policing

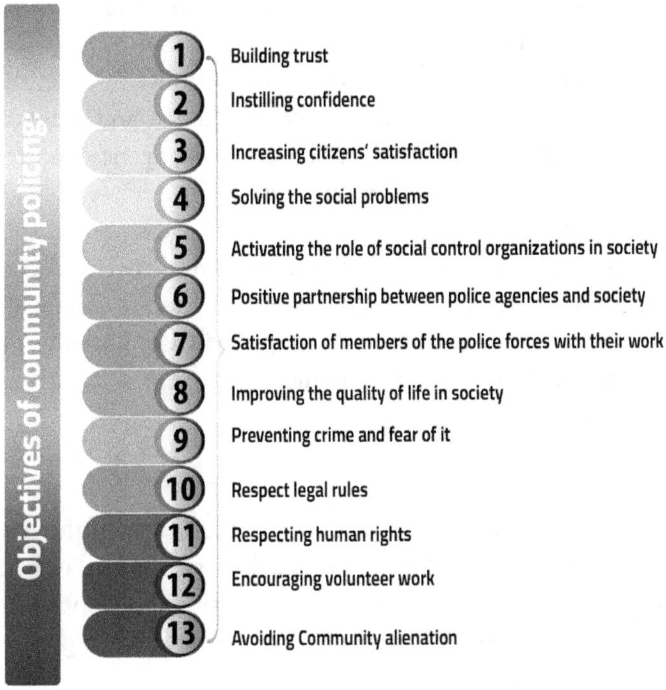

Trust Building

Trust forms the foundation of any successful relationship between a public service and citizens. Individuals who distrust law enforcement are less inclined to report criminal activities and engage in collaborative efforts to address societal issues. Furthermore, they are more inclined to attribute the rise in crime only to the police and hold them accountable. Community policing promotes the development of trust and positive relationships inside agencies, which can be relied upon during times of crisis. Trust is essential for ensuring equitable and efficient law enforcement. In a democratic society, the authority and influence of the police are derived from the confidence bestowed upon them by the population (Scheider et al., 2009).

Trust building between the police and the community is a crucial objective of community policing. This philosophy aims to enhance the collaboration between the police and society, a goal that cannot be accomplished without mutual trust. Trust is a fundamental prerequisite for the efficacy of this ideology in the realm of law enforcement. Establishing trust between the police and the public is complex due to the numerous factors influencing this connection. There are several reasons why the general public distrusts the police. Firstly, the traditional perception of the police as enforcers of the law, regardless of whether individuals have violated it, contributes to this distrust (El-Kady, 2020).

Additionally, the public's negative perception of the police is sometimes influenced by instances where officers misuse force, engage in violence, and abuse their authority. Undoubtedly, establishing trust between law enforcement agencies and the public and enhancing their relationship is a fundamental concern in security policies worldwide. This is due to the significant benefits that arise from public cooperation with the police, which significantly facilitates their role in maintaining security and apprehending criminals. Consequently, the police employ several methods to establish trust among residents and accurately portray themselves to the public, dispelling any misconceptions arising from cultural, social, theatrical, and media influences.

Instilling Confidence

Community policing aims to instill confidence in the hearts of the masses towards the police services by breaking the psychological barrier and fear of police officers among members of society (Brown, 1987) by performing police tasks without discrimination between members of society who benefit from police services for any reason (Abdel Qader et al., 2007).

Increasing Citizens' Satisfaction

One of the objectives of community policing is to increase citizens' satisfaction with police services by responding quickly to the needs of community members and providing them with flexible support from police agencies without violating existing laws in society (Hassan, 2007). A field study conducted in 2020 proved that increasing the local community's satisfaction with the police was one of the goals of implementing community policing in Egypt by a police sample consisting of several policemen (Mahran, 2020).

Solving Problems

Problem-solving is a methodical and analytical approach used to identify community issues, gather and analyze information about these issues, create and execute strategies that can eliminate or minimize the issues, and assess the effectiveness of these strategies. Problem-solving entails surpassing conventional law enforcement approaches to crime to actively tackle issues that communities find concerning (Scheider et al., 2009).

Solving societal problems that drain society's resources and threaten its stability is also one of the community policing objectives, especially the social problems that lead to the commission of crimes (Bullock, 2013). There are many applications to activate the community police to deal with social problems, such as drug addiction (Hunt, 2000), violent extremism (Silk, 2012), and urban violence. Despite this, the findings indicate that community policing had little effect on the control of or the decline in violent crime (McDonald, 2002).

The community police solve the problems that lead to crime by building a comprehensive information base about the local community in which it works, including information about criminal phenomena, people at risk of committing crimes, and people targeted by criminal acts, and analyzing that information down to develop solutions that lead to solving existing problems in the local community and reducing crime rates (Fouad, 2007).

Problem-solving and community policing are strategic concepts that aim to alter the objectives and methods of law enforcement. Problem-solving policing directs police focus on the underlying problems that contribute to occurrences rather than solely on the incidents. Community policing prioritizes forming collaborative alliances between law enforcement and communities to diminish crime and bolster security.

The dominant paradigm that prioritizes professional law enforcement has proven ineffective in managing or preempting criminal activities, has failed to establish policing as a respected occupation, and has contributed to an undesirable disconnect between the police and the communities they are meant to serve. While there are dangers associated with adopting these new organizational tactics, such as politicization, reduced crime-fighting efficacy, and increased police powers, the potential benefits of creating more robust and safer communities justify taking these risks (Moore, 1992).

Community policing prioritizes the requirement for law enforcement to engage actively in systematic and regular problem-solving initiatives. Problem-solving should be incorporated into all police operations and serve as a guiding principle for decision-making. Agencies are advised to adopt a creative approach to addressing problems rather than just concentrating on occurrences and consider apprehending offenders as only one of many possible remedies (Scheider et al., 2009).

The Scanning, Analysis, Response, and Assessment (SARA) model, created by Eck and Spelman (1987) during collaboration with the Newport News, Virginia, Police Department, is a conceptual framework officers and agencies employ to tackle problems systematically (see Figure 5).

Figure 5. SARA Model of solving problems

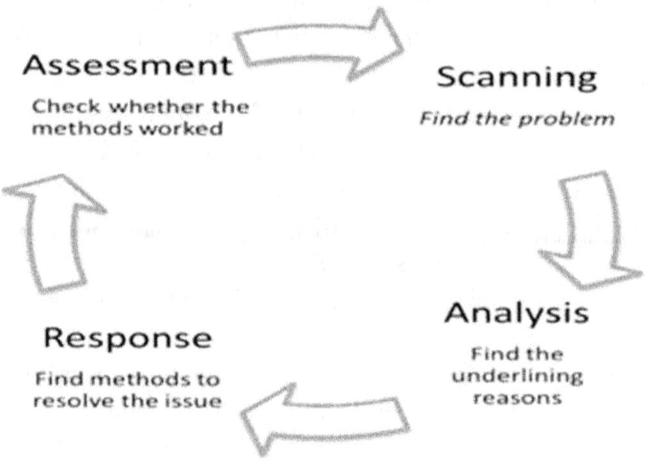

The scanning phase entails the identification of problems. This endeavor aims to identify a fundamental issue, ascertain the nature of that issue, evaluate the extent of its severity, and establish first benchmarks. Identifying stakeholders for the given challenge is usually done comprehensively at this phase (Schmerler et al., 1998).

Analysis is the core component of the problem-solving process. The analysis aims to cultivate comprehension of the intricacies of the problem, ascertain the constraints of existing solutions, discover correlations, and foster comprehension of causality. During the analysis phase, it is crucial to gather extensive information about each element of the crime triangle by inquiring about the "Who?", "What?", "When?", "Where?", "How?", "Why?", and "Why not?" aspects related to the victim, offender, and crime location (Spelman & Eck, 1989).

In the SARA paradigm, the response phase entails creating and executing plans to resolve a recognized problem. This is achieved by seeking strategic solutions that are comprehensive and unrestricted. The solution should be a logical extension of the knowledge acquired during the analysis and be customized to address the unique situation. The objectives of the reaction can vary from complete eradication of the problem to significant reduction of the problem, minimizing the harm caused by the problem, or enhancing the quality of community cohesion (Schmerler et al., 1998).

The assessment phase aims to ascertain the effectiveness of the response strategies. This information not only aids the present endeavor but also accumulates data that enhances knowledge for the future. Strategies and programs can be evaluated for their processes, outcomes, or both. If the implemented responses prove ineffective, it is necessary to analyze the information collected during the analysis. Before developing and testing novel solutions, it may be necessary to gather additional information (Sampson, 1994). The process should be perceived as cyclical rather than sequential (Clarke & Eck, 2005).

Law enforcement agencies should actively participate in SARA problem-solving procedures with relevant stakeholders who have a vested interest in addressing specific issues and can contribute significantly to establishing creative solutions. Ultimately, the police should evaluate if they are most suitable to serve as members or advisors, notwithstanding their inherent leadership role in convening collaborative problem-solving groups. Whenever feasible, law enforcement should aim to transfer and distribute the duty for addressing public safety issues to other organizations (Scott & Goldstein, 2005).

Activating the Role of Social Control Organizations

Activating the role of social control organizations in society that work to preserve the values and culture of society, and lead to the individual self-regulating his behavior towards others and society, and highlights the role of community police in confronting the phenomenon of violence and the spread of values, ideas and behavioral patterns as a result of the communications revolution by controlling those Changes, especially in the hearts of young people, to conform with our Arab, Islamic, and Eastern societies (Ahmed, 2007).

The Partnership Between Police and Society

Community Policing depends on the idea that Security is everyone's responsibility (Mahran, 2020). So, it is based on positive partnerships between police agencies and society to spread security and stability through committees to solve problems and raise awareness of security objectives and their importance for the advancement and prosperity of society (Badran, 2007). Recent research in the United States, Europe, Asia, and Australia indicates that community policing is a coherent concept grounded on the notion that, together, police and the public are more effective and more humane coproducers of safety and public order than are the police alone (Stenson, 1993).

Community policing acknowledges that police alone can seldom resolve public safety issues and instead promotes collaborative collaborations with relevant groups. The prospective partners include government agencies, businesses, non-profits, service providers, individual community members, community groups, and the media. Community policing promotes collaborations with individuals or groups who have a vested interest in addressing public safety issues and possess the means to contribute resources towards the creation and execution of solutions. These partnerships aim to achieve two interconnected objectives: generating solutions through collaborative problem-solving and enhancing public confidence in the police through community engagement. Community policing prioritizes regularly integrating these collaborations into police operations (Scheider et al., 2009). (see Figure 6).

Figure 6. Goals of partnership between police and society

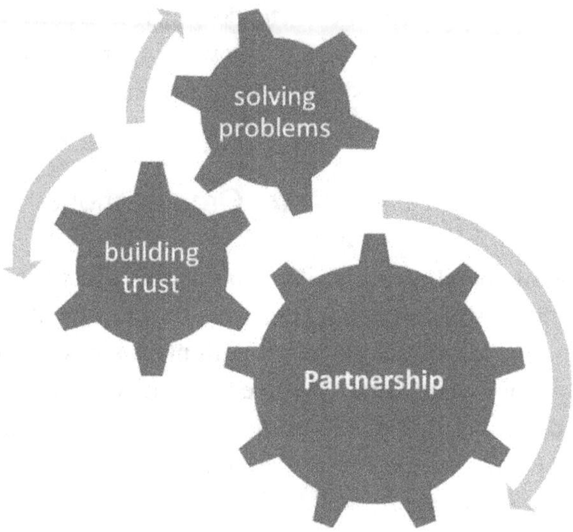

Satisfaction of Members of the Police Forces With Their Work

The satisfaction of members of the police forces with the work of civil society comes when the assistance leads to the success of the security efforts, as well as when they adopt the provision of health and social care for them by the official authorities and through the cooperation of community members with them in performing their work (Hassan, 2007).

Improving the Quality of life in Society

Improving the quality of life in society is achieved when confidence is generated in police agencies and citizens by solving social problems that lead to the commission of crimes; thus, this leads to achieving community development and improving the quality of life (adds, 2007). An ecological analysis found that police-community collaboration is associated with higher aggregate quality of life assessments, and community policing as a form of public social control mediates the adverse effects of concentrated disadvantage (Reisig & Parks, 2004).

Prevention of Crime

Preventing crime and its fear is one of the community policing objectives (Goldstein, 1990); educating the community about the concept of the police, its role, and its importance in eliminating crime by solving the problems that lead to it contributes to the public's cooperation with the police agencies in eliminating crime by reporting it and coming forward to testify, or by giving the police agencies the information necessary to track and arrest the perpetrators of crimes, as well as contributing to Treating the consequences of crimes and dealing with dangerous criminal situations without fear of being exposed to criminal acts (Al-Dardiri, 2007).

Community policing acknowledges that the police should prioritize addressing social disturbance and the fear of crime. Both factors have a substantial impact on the overall well-being of individuals and have been demonstrated to play a significant role in the occurrence of criminal activities. The police must communicate with the community regarding their primary mission and objectives. Public engagement is crucial in determining the role of law enforcement and establishing priorities for addressing public safety concerns (Scheider et al., 2009).

Respect Legal Rules and Human Rights

Respect legal rules and human rights is one of community policing objectives by making society aware of the existing laws and their purpose, urging them to respect them, and educating police personnel about human rights and the necessity of respecting them through monitoring and documenting, studying and analyzing abuses and violations that occur by police personnel, and developing the necessary solutions to eliminate them, as well as through educating the masses about their rights and obligations towards others. And society (Dowidar, 2007).

Encouraging Volunteer Work

Community policing depends on and encourage volunteer work in the security field and encouraging volunteer work in the security field by forming groups and associations of friends of the police and civil society associations with security goals and supervising the solution of problems of an individual nature and family conflicts and disputes (Al-Attar, 2011).

Avoiding Community Alienation

Community policing aims to avoid Community alienation among police officers, negatively impacting their sense of mastery and decision-making abilities. It treats the lack of community support as leading to increased alienation, apathy, and inactivity. This, combined with working in a highly populated community, increases negative sentiments and tiredness among officers (Wilson, 1989).

Community Policing Requirements

Establishing an effective community policing system requires the following (see Figure 7):

Figure 7. Community policing requirements

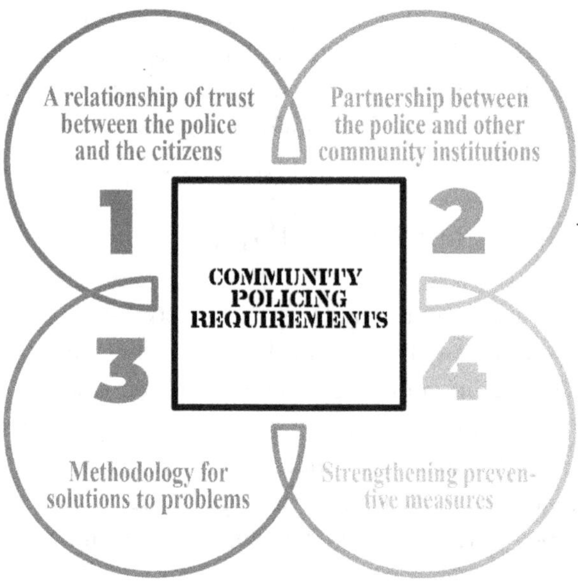

A Relationship of Trust Between the Police and the Citizens

Applying the concept of community policing requires the necessity of establishing a relationship of trust between the citizens and the police, which can be achieved by achieving rapprochement between the police and citizens by reorganizing the work of the police force by achieving security presence by redeploying police personnel in their work areas. They are alternatively working to stabilize them in their jobs for an extended period or through increasing foot patrols while ensuring the implementation of decentralized management and decision-making by delegating the authority to police officers in dealing with various security situations in a way that enables them to move quickly and efficiently to deal with problems and quarrels and confront criminal acts, which falls within the limits of his jurisdiction.

There is no doubt that the police officer's interaction with the citizens and the establishment of a mutually cooperative relationship between them makes them feel secure and confident in the agencies concerned with them. The increased confidence in the security officer leads to a reduction in his burden and a greater degree of cooperation. In the long run, it leads to a decrease in the number of crimes and an increase in the efficiency of the police force: the police and their control of security (Shaaban, 2009).

Partnership Between the Police and Other Community Institutions

The concept of community policing is based on the ability of the police agency to establish a genuine partnership relationship between it and other institutions related to the concept of public security, as it is characterized by working together in close cooperation. Therefore, it has become feasible for the police agency to resort to other community institutions, to groups of citizens, and to specialists from various professions in the government and private sectors who are present in the local community, which requires the existence of mechanisms for exchanging information between them and community institutions in a way that reduces the isolation of the police from society (Shaaban, 2009).

Methodology for Solutions to Problems

This curriculum requires developing a system to analyze incidents that occur to diagnose the state of security in society. This requires a system for collecting data on various incidents and problems and carefully analyzing them to find out the similar factors that cause them and to arrive at solutions planned scientifically and implemented. Appropriately, applying this approach leads to reducing the number of incidents and rationalizing the use of police resources more efficiently.

On the other hand, following a problem-solving approach is considered the appropriate approach in the community policing system and a tool for confronting forms of crime, which requires a change in the work procedures of the police apparatus, the most important of which is activating cooperation between police officers working in the field of public security and criminal investigation, and focusing on the use of data and developing mechanisms—fixed exchange of information between different security agencies (El-Kady, 2013).

Strengthening Preventive Measures

As the police function aims to prevent crime, it requires addressing the causes of accidents, crimes, deviations, and associated factors. The police force plays a vital role in crime prevention by identifying opportunities that allow crime to be committed and preventing its existence (Shaaban, 2009).

Obstacles to Implementing Community Policing in Egypt

Some have argued that some obstacles are limiting the success of implementing community policing, including some general obstacles on the part of community members, Such as the negativity of citizens towards crime prevention, the disintegration of society and technology, the mental image of the police officer, the heterogeneity of the population, and the legal nature of community policing, weak communication between the police and the public, lack of security awareness among citizens, the reluctance of many community members to cooperate with the police, and the ambiguity of the idea of community policing in their minds (Mahran, 2020). There are also other obstacles to implementation by the police, which include a misunderstanding of the program, fear of the impact of community policing on their role, and some negative actions of some police officers (Mahmoud, 2015) (See Figure 8).

Figure 8. Obstacles to implementing community policing

THE MOST PROMINENT COMMUNITY POLICING PRACTICES IN EGYPT

In this part of the chapter, we will discuss the most prominent community policing practices in Egypt, which include community participation committees in police stations, police reconciliation committees, police conciliation mechanisms in police stations, community participation councils to support prisoners, community awareness programs, and the use of social media to communicate with the public (see Figure 9).

Figure 9. The most prominent community policing practices in Egypt

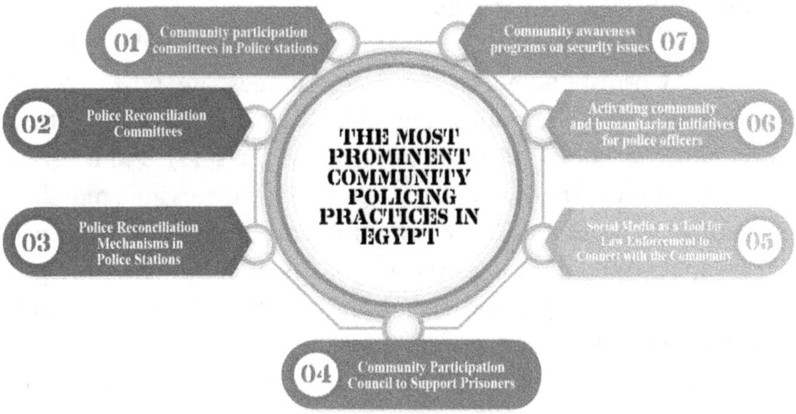

Community Participation Committees in Police Stations

The Ministry of Interior has introduced the experience of community participation committees in some police stations since June 15, 2011, to achieve effective communication with the community through these committees' application of the concept of community policing, which is based on the idea of a security partnership between the police and the community to reach a solution to security problems and to deviate from the traditional approach to managing security work in police stations.

The experience of community participation committees aims to achieve citizen satisfaction with the security services provided by police stations and stations, identify deficiencies, and treat them with some cooperation and coordination, in addition to changing some of the concepts associated with the relationship of the security man with the citizen, through the efforts of those in charge of working in police stations and stations to identify the problems. Local security and improving the sense of security in society, prompting it to achieve fruitful cooperation with security, which reflects the extent of security awareness among members of society and that security is everyone's responsibility.

The application of the experience of the police community participation committees was initially extended to four security directorates (Cairo - Giza - Alexandria - Assiut) to be applied in ten police stations in the directorates above. This experience was expanded to reach (25) police stations in the scope of seven security directorates at the republic level by establishing committees within the police stations. The members of these committees are chosen from citizens (from 5-7) among those residing in the district of the police station. They are chosen through civil committees from among persons known for their excellent conduct and behavior, considering the representation of all sectors of society.

The duration of the committee's work is from (6 -12) months, with the change of its members. Corresponding to these committees are other committees of police officers, including the police station commander, the head of the criminal investigation unit, the public relations officer, and the service unit officer, if any (civil status - passports...) (El-Kady,2012). These committees hold monthly or semi-monthly meetings to present all collective problems, such as the presence of drug trafficking hotspots, schools being exposed to acts of bullying, or the presence of street vendors. All previous problems are discussed, provided that they are resolved with the knowledge of the security committee.

As for problems that cannot be solved, the committee selects one of its members to participate in the community participation committees, whose meetings are held at the Security Directorate's headquarters periodically to present the problems to the Director of Security, the Director of Investigations, the Director of Public Relations, or whomever the Director of Security deems appropriate to attend the committee.

This experiment aims to remove any harmful residue between the police and citizens and achieve integration in policing through community partnership, where monthly meetings are held between members of the two councils to identify the social and security problems existing within the scope of the police stations, and to discuss proposed solutions to confront them in partnership between the community and the police.

Practical observations indicate that the community participation committees in police stations have achieved remarkable success in achieving their goals of improving the relationship between the police and the public and increasing the level of satisfaction of citizens residing in the areas of the police stations with the work of police officers and their understanding of their essential role in maintaining security and achieving social peace. It was noticed that the experience of community participation committees had a good impact on activating public participation in achieving security and improving the relationship between the police and the public.

This model was among the forms of community policing that Egypt has known. It represented an absolute beginning in improving the relationship between the police and the public, a commendable initiative by the Ministry of Interior after January 2011. However, the results of applying this model were not evident in light of the many challenges that Egypt faced after that, most notably facing a massive wave of terrorist operations.

Police Reconciliation Committees

There are many applications of police conciliation in Egyptian law and comparative legislation between police conciliation mechanisms that take place within the framework of a criminal case and police conciliation committees that take place outside this framework. The reconciliation system began working in the Ministry of the Interior in 1940 by establishing the Arab Affairs Office, which was the first entity to look into disputes between families and families. Then, a ministerial decision was issued in 1958 to establish the Reconciliation Office, which specialized in combating crimes of self-aggression committed due to disputes. Revenge between families, and then the matter developed in 1965 to forming reconciliation committees at the republic level by Ministerial Resolution No. (160) of 1965, which Ministerial Resolution No then amended. (579) of 1978 (Khaled,2010).

The model of reconciliation committees applied in the Ministry of Interior is represented by the responsibility of police stations and stations at various levels through committees formed at the village, sheikhdom, center, division, and governorate levels. Police reconciliation committees specialize in settling disputes between citizens that result in a breach of public security, such as revenge disputes in Upper Egypt. Police reconciliation is one of the most prominent and critical social roles undertaken by the police in Egyptian society, as the police work through conciliation and mediation mechanisms to intervene to settle disputes and disputes existing between individuals to achieve social peace through reconciliation that is agreed upon between the parties to the dispute (El-Kady, 2020).

On the other hand, police reconciliations are considered one of the proactive approaches followed by the security services, as a security initiative to solve criminal problems and as an appreciation by the police of the situation and the existing security situation in the Egyptian street through its role and administrative function in preventing the occurrence of crimes and reducing their rates, as police reconciliations are among the most successful means of preventing crime, or at least preventing its increase. From a social point of view, crime represents a difference or conflict of interests between two parties, the victim and the perpetrator. Police reconciliation is the intervention of a police officer in an existing dispute between two or more parties, where the police officer sees, according to the circumstances of the incident before him or the parties' desire, that it is not essential to proceed with the matter. Judicial procedures. In this case, the policeman turns into a conciliator or conciliator policeman. He settles disputes between the two parties by applying the principle of consent and preserving the interests of the parties and their social relations (El-Kady,2013).

The importance of police reconciliations is due to the achievement of security and social peace among citizens, in addition to reducing the burden on the judicial bodies, including prosecution offices and courts. Not all cases and reports that come to the attention of the police are brought before the investigating authorities, and such a procedure is through what is done by the settlement of these disputes - allows the investigating authorities to devote themselves to looking into the most severe and essential cases. It is essential to mention that the policeman's role as a conciliator between opponents in criminal disputes is, in most cases, due to the social status and respect that citizens have for the policeman through his job, which helps him through his good dealings with citizens, to carry out this conciliatory function and intervene to settle the dispute—disputes between opponents. The importance and feasibility of reconciliation committees are due to their preventive role. If some civil, family, or sectarian disputes were left without police intervention, the dispute would turn into a criminal crime in the form of beating or murder. Police reconciliation is one of the essential tasks a policeman carries out through daily work to reconcile Disputants or opponents to reach reconciliation between the parties to the dispute or conflict (El-Kady, 2020).

The Purpose of Establishing Police Reconciliation Committees

Police reconciliation committees aim to achieve social peace and prevent crime through mediation between conflicting parties in sectarian disputes and revenge crimes in a way that leads to calming the souls of the victims and their families and suppressing the desire for revenge within them. However, the purposes of these committees do not extend to compensating the victim. Reforming the social disorder resulting from crime and social rehabilitation of offenders are the purposes criminal justice seeks to achieve in comparative legislation (El-Kady, 2020).

The Social Dimension of Police Reconciliations

Many simple disputes often arise between individuals, whether those with permanent ties of family relationship, kinship relationship, neighborly relationship, fellowship, work...etc. Exacerbating these disputes may bring the matter before police stations. If the police finish solving these problems between the parties, they will end irreversibly; otherwise, the parties will return months later to the police in the form of continuing social tension between them in the form of a crime of beating or murder (El-Kady, 2023).

There is no doubt that the police's interest in achieving reconciliation between individual disputes and disputes between families in retaliatory disputes makes it the police force finds it challenging to search, investigate, and monitor the security situation in retaliatory crimes that are characterized by violence and all of their perpetrators are predominant in the desire for revenge (El-Kady, 2020).

On the other hand, to activate the police reconciliation system, problems and disputes must be solved by police officers qualified in the art of dealing with the public and resolving problems amicably through peaceful methods of negotiation, arbitration, conciliation, etc. In addition to the necessity of a complete understanding of the nature of society and the problem that must be addressed. This solution can be based on a complete understanding of the problem and how to solve it, and this requires the policeman to have a sense of justice and the right way to perform it.

The police officer in the Egyptian street serves as a representative of the state and is responsible for enforcing the law. They embody the state's authority among the people, ensuring the protection of citizens and upholding the societal systems designed for security and reassurance. Additionally, they can peacefully resolve disputes without resorting to the judiciary if these resolutions are based on mutually agreed-upon practices (Al-Hakim et al., 2002). The effectiveness of police activity relies on effective communication with citizens, which in turn is contingent upon the citizens' prompt and cooperative response.

For this to occur, the public must see a sense of mutual trust between themselves and the police force and a strong connection and affection towards the police officers. Furthermore, it is interconnected, cohesive, and efficient (Badr, 1996). Undoubtedly, establishing a direct connection with the public and recognizing the positive outcomes of police officers' interventions greatly motivates the public to work with the police force, resulting in the most substantial impact on society. This emphasizes the crucial and impactful significance of effectively engaging with individuals and introducing the police function. Effective communication fosters a sense of mutual trust between citizens and law enforcement authorities (Al-Alam,2000).

Some researchers have argued that police reconciliation committees, such as community policing practices, are considered to be based on the social role they play in conflict and social peace, as well as one form of public participation in security work by contributing to reconciliation or as forms of community participation between the police and citizens, through the intervention of members of these committees to resolve social problems and conflicts between the parties to the conflict (Hassan, 2005). So, it is undoubtedly considered one of the most essential local practices for community policing in Egypt.

In this direction, reconciliation is one of the essential forms of police-people cooperation in combating crime and establishing trust in the police system, as it plays a role in reducing revenge crime and is one of the crucial hubs of crime prevention in its broad context (El-Shorbagy, 2005). Some consider that, although the reconciliation committees are geographically and qualitatively limited in scope, they can be used to develop an operational strategy for community policing, bearing in mind that the community security system covers all aspects of community security and is mainstreamed in all urban and rural areas according to the circumstances of each community (Abdel Aziz, 2010).

The police reconciliation committees have significantly contributed to maintaining security in many of the areas in which they are located and have contributed significantly to reducing the phenomenon of revenge spreading in some areas of

Upper Egypt, which has contributed to achieving citizen satisfaction and security stability due to the security efforts made to resolve the criminal problems and disputes occurring in these areas (El-Kady, 2020).

Police Reconciliation Mechanisms in Police Stations

There was a query on the involvement of the police in Victim-offender mediation: Is it possible for representatives of the police authority to initiate mediation? Indeed, the answer to this question is yes. Police officers working at police stations and stations begin reconciling adversaries through what is known as the "Conciliation Notes" mechanism, which is established by the case book. Police officers reconcile adversaries with permanent ties and relationships, such as family and neighborhood disputes. Police officers often resort to reconciling adversaries.

It should be noted that practical practices have shown the extent to which this mechanism has been applied in such a way as to say that, in comparison between conciliatory practices in some police stations and police reports written daily, it is clear that the reconciliation notes in the cases book may converge with the police reports that are written daily in the police station, and that sometimes even compromise practices may go beyond the preparation of police reports that are written daily in these police stations (El-Kady, 2020).

In addition to the central role played by police officers in the Customary Judicial Councils in the feuds in Upper Egypt and the Police Reconciliation Committees in many urban police stations, it is essential to note that the police officer's role as a reformer between parties in criminal disputes is often due to the social standing and respect that citizens have for the police officer by his job, which helps him through his good dealings with the citizens to perform this function.

It should be noted that the case book mechanism is well-known in many countries. One study of the work of the Poitier Police station in France showed that nearly a quarter of cases of petty altercation and riot had been completed (24%) (Through police mediation, since French police officers tended to resolve family disputes, even if they were accompanied by abuse through mediation. According to the study, more than half of cases of family disputes, which included battery offenses (55%), were resolved through mediation (83%). When acts of battery did not accompany such disputes, the mediation of family disputes was reduced when such disputes were of some gravity since the police officer rarely concealed cases of destruction of public property or theft from a car (El-Kady, 2013).

This mechanism was able to reduce the burden on the judiciary. The Paris Office had directed the police stations to cease mediation and to refer communications and complaints without discrimination, but direct referral of communications - on instructions. In addition to the widespread use of this mechanism in Italy, Italian police often offer parties an amicable settlement in the area of crimes of little gravity. In Belgium, the Belgian police were often able to reconcile in treating certain crimes of little gravity from their point of view (El-Kady, 2023).

It is noted that the reconciliatory practices carried out by policemen within the police station were welcomed by both parties of the crime, given the attempts made by the policeman to reconcile the two sides while explaining to them the legal procedures to be followed to the case, as both sides often prefer to accept Settlement of the case is far from completing the prescribed legal procedures. Some may believe that the exercise of this task by the police may lead to putting pressure on the parties to impose reconciliation on one party. However, this fear can be answered by saying that accepting the settlement by one of the parties does not prevent him from submitting his complaint before the Public Prosecution to take the prescribed legal measures. Additionally, these practices may be the reason for criminal, administrative, and civil accountability for police officers on the grounds of exploiting power and influence to force a party to accept an amicable settlement (El-Kady, 2020).

The Complaint Against an Unknown Person

Police conciliation practices are diverse and disparate; in addition to the previous practices, the police in some countries know some similar conciliation practices, the most important of which is the complaint against an unknown person, which is among the mechanisms used by police stations in Paris to resolve criminal disputes, where the police officer takes the initiative to mediate between the two parties in minor crimes, which often have no relationship or ties between the parties, and which do not deserve to be referred to the Public Prosecution. The police officer, after the completion of the reconciliation work between the two parties, proposes to the victim to amend his statements in the minutes of gathering evidence by not accusing the perpetrator or by acknowledging that the perpetrator is someone other than the perpetrator, in exchange for the perpetrator repairing the damage he sustained. Thus, the Public Prosecution dismissed the case because the perpetrator was unknown (El-Kady, 2013).

The police officer motivates both parties to accept the settlement by explaining the advantages of the complaint against an unknown person: the accused will not be able to file a complaint against the complainant if released. Suppose the complainant is reassured by the police officer's advice and suggestions and agrees to the form of the complaint against an unknown person. In that case, this allows the police officer to limit his investigations in the report to the impossibility of identifying the suspect. If the complainant agrees to the police's proposal, the latter will notify the complainant of this. Some have considered this a form of hidden consent because the policeman and the victim know that the complaint against an unknown person is only one form of preservation. In contrast, a second opinion has considered it a form of indirect mediation, aiming to reduce the number of victims—cases referred to the Public Prosecution (El-Kady, 2010).

Activating the Police Commissions in Egyptian Law

Police reconciliation is one of the proactive approaches of security services as a security initiative to solve criminal problems, and the police appreciate the situation and the security situation on Egyptian streets through its role and administrative function in preventing crime and reducing crime rates (El-Kady, 2023).

It is proposed that a bill to amend the Code of Criminal Procedure should be introduced to give effect to the role of police commissions, which would allow judicial enforcement officers and prosecutors to refer criminal cases that can be resolved amicably to police commissions, with the result that the termination of such disputes would have the effect of keeping papers or ordering those proceedings should not be brought.

Article 18 bis" a" Criminal Procedures Code added some paragraphs at the end of the article, which states: "The Department of Public Prosecutions or the Superintendent of Judicial Control may - if, by the circumstances of the case, the parties consider it possible to resolve the dispute amicably - refer the parties to the police commissions within their jurisdiction to reach a friendly settlement between the adversaries.

When notified to the Public Prosecutor's Office, the Superintendent of the Department or his or her Deputy is competent to refer the dispute to the competent committee at the village or village level. Suppose the Committee is competent at the district or town level. In that case, it may invite the parties to the dispute and the members of the Committee within 48 hours to attend the reconciliation session at the headquarters of the section, town, or other designated place.

The reconciliation committees at the village, village, or district level operate under the supervision of their President. The meeting proceedings are established in a record of the proceedings. They are submitted to the competent department no later than two weeks from the date of notification to the Public Prosecutor's Office. The report of the Commissions of Reconciliation must include the determination of the causes of the conflict, the solutions proposed by the members of the Commission, and the position of the adversaries thereon. The report submitted to the Office of the Prosecutor may include a request for an extension of the legal period established to resolve the dispute for a further week, which the Chairman of the Commission causes.

Suppose a Reconciliation agreement is reached between the parties. In that case, the Chairman of the Commission shall prove it in a record of the peace, sign it by the parties to the dispute, and send it to the Office of the Public Prosecutor with the opinion on the conduct of the case. The assessment of this report and the conciliation agreement between the parties shall be subject to the authority of the Public Prosecutor's Office to ensure that criminal proceedings are brought or filed based on such proceedings. In the event of a failure to reach reconciliation between the parties, the Chairperson of the Reconciliation Committees shall prove this, accompanied by a statement of the Commission's efforts to bring the conflicting parties closer to the solutions presented by it and the parties' position on attempts at reconciliation" (El-Kady, 2020).

Distinctions Between Police Reconciliation Committees and Community Participation Committees

Below, we review the distinctions between police reconciliation committees and community participation committees by addressing the areas of agreement and differences between them, as follows:

a. **Areas of agreement**: Police reconciliation committees agree with community participation committees in their keenness to solve social problems, whether they are related to disputes between individuals or related to the security situation of the Egyptian street, in addition to considering police reconciliation committees and community participation committees among the applications of community policing in Egypt. On the other hand, the community participation committees agree with the police reconciliation committees in that they are based on solving the social problems of citizens, considering that these social problems are among the causes of crimes in society (El-Kady, 2020).
b. **Differences**: Police reconciliation committees differ from community participation committees in some matters, the most important of which are the following:

Essence

Community participation committees are one means of implementing community policing. It is a new police philosophy based on social communication between the police and citizens, unlike police reconciliation committees, which are one of the means of administrative control in reducing and preventing crimes through solving problems. And the existing disputes between citizens.

Legal Nature

Community participation committees have a social nature that is neither judicial nor administrative, given their formation from citizens residing in the police stations. In contrast, police reconciliation committees - as we previously indicated - are administrative committees.

Scope of Application

The scope of community participation committees is limited to security problems, such as criminal hotspots in the district or center; their basis is to achieve effective communication and transparency between citizens and the police in confronting these security problems, unlike police reconciliation committees, which specialize in reconciling the parties to existing disputes among citizens (El-Kady, 2020).

Community Participation Council to Support Prisoners

The Community Participation Council was established to support prisoners, those released, and their families under Prime Minister's Decision No. 2904 of 2010. This Council is an advisory body for the Community Protection Sector, one of the sectors affiliated with the Ministry of Interior, which supervises correctional and rehabilitation centers. The Council includes several state ministries in its membership, led by the Ministries of Media, Health, Social Solidarity, and Manpower. From the national councils: At its forefront are the National Council for Human Rights, the National Council for Women, the National Council for Childhood and Motherhood, the General Union of Civil Associations, and several civil associations and institutions (El-Kady, 2020).

The Council also includes entities of the Ministry of Interior that work in the care and rehabilitation of inmates in correctional and rehabilitation centers, assisting their families and reintegrating those released. About them in society. This council meets monthly and issues its recommendations by an absolute majority to activate cooperation and coordination paths with various government agencies and correctional and rehabilitation centers in the areas of training, awareness, culture, vocational rehabilitation, and production for inmates of correctional and rehabilitation centers, those released and their families. In addition to developing areas of cooperation in line with modern penal policy, it proposes ways to cooperate with bodies, associations, and civil society institutions. It coordinates its efforts and activities to benefit prisoners, those released, and their families.

As well as preparing scientific and applied studies and research related to inmates in correctional and rehabilitation centers and those released, in coordination with specialized scientific institutions and investing in the efforts of international and regional organizations in this field and supporting the capabilities and developing the skills of correctional and rehabilitation center employees in the task of rehabilitating inmates by the concepts of modern penal policy, and improving the policies of education, social and psychological services in correctional and rehabilitation centers of various types (El-Kady, 2020).

This will be in coordination with the relevant authorities to confirm the complementary role of state agencies in this field, and to support correctional and rehabilitation centers with material and technical capabilities to ensure their continued development and provide the necessary funding sources for that, and to propose programs that ensure the gradual integration of inmates into society through preparatory programs for release that begin organizationally within the correction and rehabilitation centers or after his release.

The participation of released persons who have previously benefited from rehabilitation programs in correctional and rehabilitation centers in the efforts of civil society organizations to rehabilitate inmates socially, culturally, and professionally and to change society's view of those released by establishing and consolidating a community culture aimed at calling for the care of the families of inmates in correctional and rehabilitation centers during the implementation of the sentence, and working To provide job opportunities for those released.

The Community Participation Council to support inmates in correctional and rehabilitation centers represents a unique model of community policing models applied in Egypt in light of the specializations entrusted to it and its integrated formation, which includes the majority of government agencies and institutions active in supporting and assisting these inmates, civil society organizations and concerned police agencies, and its advisory role assisting the punitive administration. It aims to study the problems of punitive implementation and present solutions and assistance available to rehabilitate inmates and reintegrate them into society as good individuals (El-Kady, 2020).

Community Awareness Programs on Security Issues

The Ministry of the Interior worked to activate the mechanisms for implementing the concept of community police through coordination with the directors of the education directorates in the governorates to celebrate the start of the new academic year with the faculty members and students at all educational levels. It directed several officers to several schools at the beginning of the academic year in the various educational levels to deliver lectures or brief presentations on cooperation with police officers to achieve security and stability in society during the morning assembly (El-Kady, 2020).

They are additionally organizing visits for school students at various levels to some of the police agencies affiliated with the directorate (Rescue - Traffic - Civil Protection - one of the police stations) and hosting them in the police clubs in each directorate to familiarize the students with the nature of the work and tasks of police officers and to develop their loyalty and love for the police force. In addition to allocating one of the classes on one of the days of the first week of the academic year in various academic levels to talk about the national role of the police force throughout history and the heroism and sacrifices of police officers to protect the security of the homeland and the citizen, in addition to organizing visits for university students (governmental and private) to the Police Academy.

The Ministry of Interior was keen to launch awareness initiatives and campaigns for citizens, aiming to restore traffic discipline on Egyptian streets (El-Kady, 2020) and to emphasize that traffic is a message in which the police and citizens participate and reflects the Ministry of Interior's interest in the traffic problem and coordination with the concerned authorities to remove everything that obstructs traffic, and mobilize all security efforts with the participation of Civil society organizations to correct traffic behavior on the street, considering that traffic is a societal problem.

This is done by organizing field visits to several schools at various educational levels, organizing several meetings with university youth and popular meetings with associations of taxi, transport, and microbus drivers, holding seminars with youth from community organizations, publishing several working groups daily for traffic awareness at the level of the governorates of the Republic, and holding seminars. Educational for officers and forces of traffic departments, lectures are given by professors of social sciences, traffic leaders, and human resources.

The initiative program also includes coordination with the Ministry of Housing and Utilities to carry out quick repairs to several traffic hotspots that have been monitored, activate the plan to repair and replace traffic lights, cameras, and directional signs, activate the plan to re-plan axes and squares and create outlets in all car licensing units to facilitate licensing procedures for the driver of a vehicle that has not been installed.

Traffic violations will be imposed on him, and consideration will be given to implementing a distinguished driving license for a vehicle driver who has not committed violations for three consecutive years, in addition to developing an intelligent system that includes large screens at the bridges and important squares that display the road condition and the acceleration time between two points, and coordinating with the Ministry of Petroleum to oblige gas stations not to supply any motorcycles without metal plates, and distinguishing and clarifying the places for pedestrian crossings to oblige pedestrians to cross them (El-Kady, 2020).

Activating Community and Humanitarian Initiatives for Police Officers

The Ministry of Interior was interested in activating humanitarian initiatives as one of the ways to strengthen the relationship between the police and citizens. The most prominent of these humanitarian initiatives is coordination with care homes and civil society organizations concerned with orphan care in the governorates to participate in the celebration of Orphan Day by hosting several orphan children in police clubs during the first week of April and providing lunch. Moreover, some symbolic gifts for them, in addition to organizing festivals for several disabled children and those with special needs in police clubs in coordination with the Specific Federation of Disability Associations under the slogan (I Can).

In addition to participating in humanitarian activities related to blood donation work, visiting patients in hospitals, and other humanitarian initiatives, there is no doubt about the importance of these initiatives in improving the mental image of the police force and rebuilding bridges of trust with citizens, which will lead positively to improving the mental image of the police force. This policy is reflected in activating citizens' participation and support for the police in achieving security (El-Kady, 2020).

Social Media as a Tool to Communicate With the Community

The use of technology has had significant effects in developing security work, and one of these areas is the use of technology and social networking sites to enhance the concept of community policing. Electronic Community-Oriented Policing (E-COP) is a police strategy that integrates mass communication, individual behavior, and social behavior theories into everyday tasks (Uricska, 2023). It uses push, pull, and networking strategies to carry out community-focused policing online without referring to actual geographic locales (Hu et al., 2020). Social networking platforms have allowed police stations to communicate with the people they protect and serve without using traditional mainstream media. E-COP uses digital technologies, crime mapping, Geographic Information System (GIS), fingerprints, DNA analysis, Integrated Automated Fingerprint Identification System (IAFIS), Combined DNA Index System (CODIS), hotspot policing, cameras, smartphones, body-worn cameras, and dash-mounted cameras (Hu et al., 2020).

A crucial element of community policing is enhancing communication and transparency between the police and the public. A program like E-COP provides a new opportunity for the police to inform the public while giving residents a new avenue to engage with the agency (Earle, 1970). Mass media is growing into ever-new forms and platforms, and the best thing the police can do to retain and grow public faith in them is to develop their public image with tact and care for both professional standards and existing public expectations. Image management initiatives can significantly impact police legitimacy, and the police routinely deploy image management to uphold and strengthen their validity (Hu et al., 2020).

The mainstream media act believes that the mass media itself partially distorts the public's view of facts about criminal attitudes. It informs the public about crimes being perpetrated and the demand for vigilance and self-protection, encouraging crime prevention but also heightening public dread of crimes by promoting a moral panic based on false perceptions of crime threats from media themes rather than genuine incidents of violent crimes (Hu et al., 2020).

In Egypt, the Ministry of the Interior was keen to employ information technology and social media in the field of effective communication with citizens and provide public security services in a way that facilitates the procedures for obtaining them by launching the official page of the Ministry on the Internet, which contains windows for all public security sectors and allows to request services for the citizens remotely. The Ministry of the Interior was keen to launch a developed portal on the Internet and mobile phones as an integrated site that combines citizen security concerns, examining complaints, and providing public security services, including civil status and traffic services, work permits, criminal evidence, immigration, nationality, Hajj, and Umrah, joining the police academy, reporting missing persons, absentees, and stolen cars, and announcing... Those wanted by security forces and renewing driver's licenses, cars, identification papers, and passports remotely, as the number of people dealing with and following the Ministry's official pages on the Internet is approximately 29 million people (see: Speech of the Minister of Interior at the "Story of a Homeland" conference, dated 2/10/20, published at: https://www.albawabhnews.com/4883107).

CONCLUSION

The chapter produced a set of results and recommendations, the most prominent of which are:

Results

1- The importance of the community policing model in enhancing public participation in maintaining security and combating crime and its reflection on building confidence and citizens' satisfaction with the performance of the Police.
2- Community policing faces obstacles like negative attitudes, societal disintegration, technological advancements, diverse population, legal framework, inadequate

communication, low-security awareness, reluctance to cooperate, and ambiguous understanding. Law enforcement agencies also face confusion, apprehension, and misconduct.

3- Diversity and disparity of community policing models in Egypt include community participation committees in police stations, police reconciliation committees, police conciliation mechanisms, community participation councils to support prisoners, community security awareness programs, and community and humanitarian initiatives in which police officers participate to reduce the living burdens of citizens, which reflects positively on the societal role of the police.

4- The Egyptian police expanded the concept of community policing by activating the role of community participation committees and councils in various areas of security work to enhance the participation of governmental and non-governmental state institutions and civil society institutions in serving the citizens.

5- The Ministry of the Interior was keen to employ information technology and social media in effective communication with citizens and provide public security services to facilitate the procedures for obtaining them in a way that supports the concept of community policing.

Recommendations

1- The significance of surmounting the barriers to implementing community policing lies in the technical and training readiness of community policing participants, specifically regarding their roles. It is crucial to address the evolving perceptions of law enforcement officers and enhance their operational frameworks. Additionally, establishing comprehensive systems and regulations that outline the fundamental principles governing the interaction between the police and individuals engaged in community policing is imperative.

2- The importance of officially recognizing the concept of community policing by calling on legislators to establish a legal framework regulating community policing practices and establishing formal organizational structures to implement them.

3- Improving the personal capabilities of police officers in community policing by continuing to teach introductory curricula to community policing and holding training courses to introduce police officers to pioneering security experiences in community policing.

4- There is a necessity to adopt awareness programs in all media about the importance of strengthening community policing and the role of community members in its success.

5- Call on national research centers and all researchers to continue conducting more research and field studies on mechanisms for activating and strengthening community policing in society.
6- Pay more attention to community policing models applied locally and examine ways to support and continue them.
7- Paying more official attention to community policing models applied locally, examining ways to support and continue them, and highlighting best practices in this field.

REFERENCES

Abdel Aziz, A. (2010). *Community Policing and Activating Security Performance*. Ph.D. Thesis, College of Graduate Studies, Cairo.

Abdel Qader et al. (2007). *Towards Applying the Concept of Community Policing in Egypt. Community Policing Symposium*. Police Research Center.

Adds, E. (2007). *Contemporary Concepts of Community Policing*. *Community Policing Symposium*. Police Research Center.

Ahmed, H. M. (2007). *Community policing - a contemporary scientific vision*. Community policing symposium. Police Academy. Police Research Center.

Al-Alam, S. (2000). Security media and its role in influencing public opinion trends. *Journal of the College of Training and Development*.

Al-Ashmawy, M. (2012). Community policing and its applications in Egypt. Police Research Center Review.

Al-Attar, B. (2011). *Community policing and its impact on reducing crime*. Ph.D. Thesis. College of Graduate Studies.

Al-Dardiri, O. (2007). *Community policing - a contemporary scientific vision. Community Policing Symposium*. Police Research Center.

Al-Hakim. (2002). Police Reconciliation Strategy, Leadership Institute for Police Officers. College of Training and Development. Police Academy.

Al-Shawa, M. S. (1997). *Mediation and Criminal Justice*. Dar Al-Nahda Al-Arabiya.

Alderson, J. (1984). Law and disorder. H. Hamilton, OCLC 12216164.

Badr, A. M. M. (1996). The Policeman, the Citizen, and Alienation. Alfikr AlShurti Periodical.

Badran, H. M. (2007). *The concept of community policing.* Community policing symposium. Police Research Center.

Bertus, F. (1996). *The Use and Effectiveness of Community Policing in a Democracy.* National Institute of Justice.

Brogden, M., & Nijhar, P. (2013). *Community policing.* Routledge. doi:10.4324/9781843925798

Brown, L. and Wycoff, M.D. (1978). Policing Houston: Reducing fear and improving services. *Crime and Delinquency*, 71–89.

Bullock, K. (2013). Community, intelligence-led policing and crime control. *Policing and Society*, *23*(2), 125–144. doi:10.1080/10439463.2012.671822

Chriss, J. J. (2016). Beyond community policing: from early American beginnings to the 21st century. Routledge. OCLC 931534901.

Clarke, R. V., & Eck, J. E. (2005). Crime Analysis for Problem Solvers: 60 Small Steps. Office of Community Oriented Policing Services, US Department of Justice.

Community Policing Consortium. (1994). Understanding Community Policing: A Framework for Action, Monograph, NCJ 148457, Bureau of Justice Assistance.

Cordner, G. (2014). Community policing. The Oxford Handbook of police and policing, 148–171.

Cordner, G. W. (1997). Community policing: Elements and effects. *Critical issues in policing: Contemporary readings, 5*, 401-418.

Correia, M. E. (2000). The conceptual ambiguity of community in community policing – Filtering the muddy waters. *Policing*, *23*(2), 218–233. doi:10.1108/13639510010333840

Cox, S. M., & Fitzgerald, J. D. (1996). *Police in Community relations: Critical issues*. Brown & Benchmark.

Dowidar, S. N. (2007). *Police and Society: Towards a New Concept of Security. Community Policing Symposium*. Police Research Center.

Earle, H. H. (1970). *Police-Community Relations: Crisis in Our Time.* Charles C Thomas Publisher, Ltd.

El-Kady, R. (2010). *Mediation as an alternative to Criminal proceedings - A comparative study*. PhD thesis. Faculty of Law. Cairo University.

El-Kady, R. (2012). Community partnership in confronting the phenomenon of bullying. A symposium on (security, media, and society shared responsibility). Police Academy.

El-Kady, R. (2013). *Police conciliations - An analytical study of the role of the police in resolving criminal disputes*. Dar Al-Nahda Al-Arabiya.

El-Kady, R. (2013). Police reconciliations and ways to activate their role in achieving security. *Police Research Center Review*, (44).

El-Kady, R. (2020). *Criminal Mediation in Comparative Legislation*. Center for Arab Studies for Printing and Publishing.

El-Kady, R. (2023). The Role of the Police in Criminal Mediation. *International Journal of Police Science*. https://doi.org/ doi:10.56331/19122023/ijps

El-Shorbagy, A. (2005). *The efforts of the public security sector in preventing criminal crime*. Symposium on the role of civil society in preventing crime. Police Research Center.

Fielding, N. (1995). *Community policing, Clarendon Studies in Criminology*. Oxford University Press.

Fouad, M. A. (2007). *The Community Policing Experience. Community Policing Symposium*. Police Research Center.

Friedman, R. R., & Clark, M. (1992). *Community policing*. doi:10.1007/978-1-137-07200-9

Gau, J. M. (2010). *Wilson, James Q., and George L. Kelling: Broken Windows Theory. In Encyclopedia of Criminological Theory*. SAGE Publications, Inc. doi:10.4135/9781412959193.n281

Goldstein, H. (1990). *Problem-Oriented Policing*. McGraw-Hill Publishing.

Hassan, A. (2005). *The Community Policing System and the Role of Voluntary Work in Achieving It*. Symposium organized by Naif Arab University for Security Sciences & Dubai Police Academy on The Concept of Community Policing.

Hassan, Y. (2007). *Community policing - a contemporary scientific vision*. Community policing symposium. Police Research Center.

Herbert, S. K. (2006). *Citizens, cops, and power: recognizing the limits of community*. University of Chicago Press. doi:10.7208/chicago/9780226327358.001.0001

Hu, X. (2020). Electronic Community-Oriented Policing: Theories, Contemporary Efforts, and Future Directions. Lexington Books.

Hunt, S. R. (2000). *Drug addiction and alcoholism as qualifying impairments for Social Security disability benefits: The history, controversies, and congressional response*. Brandeis University, The Heller School for Social Policy and Management.

Khaled, A. A. A. M. (2010). *Community policing and activating security performance*. PhD thesis, College of Graduate Studies.

Lortz, M. (2016). *What is Community Policing?* Everbridge.

MacDonald, J. M. (2002). The effectiveness of community policing in reducing urban violence. *Crime and Delinquency*, *48*(4), 592–618. doi:10.1177/001112802237131

Mahmoud, M. M. A. (2015). *Mechanisms for implementing community policing* (Vol. 24). Alfikr AlShurti Periodical.

Mahran, A. J. A. (2020). Community transformations towards community partnership, the community police approach - a field study of the repercussions of the June 30 Revolution. *Journal of the Faculty of Arts*, *80*(3).

Mastrofski, S. D., Willis, J. J., & Kochel, T. R. (2007). The challenges of implementing community policing in the United States. *Policing. Journal of Policy Practice*, *1*(2), 223–234.

Moore, M. H. (1992). Problem-solving and community policing. *Crime and Justice*, *15*, 99–158. doi:10.1086/449194

NA. N. (2016). Community policing: Comparative perspectives and prospects. Springer.

O'Neill, M., van der Giessen, M., Bayerl, P. S., Hail, Y., Aston, E., & Houston, J. (2023). Conditions, Actions, and Purposes (CAP): A dynamic model for community policing in Europe. Policing. *Journal of Policy Practice*, *17*, paad014.

Obaidat. (1996). *Scientific Research Methods and Techniques*. Sanaa Publishing House.

Ray, J. M. (1963). Rethinking community policing. OCLC 892799678.

Reisig, M. D., & Parks, R. B. (2004). Can community policing help the truly disadvantaged? *Crime and Delinquency*, *50*(2), 139–167. doi:10.1177/0011128703253157

Remington, F. J. (1965). The role of police in a democratic society. *The Journal of Criminal Law, Criminology, and Police Science*, *56*(3), 361–365. doi:10.2307/1141253

Rosenbaum, D. P. (1994). The challenge of community policing. *Sage (Atlanta, Ga.)*.

Rosenbaum, D. P., & Lurigio, A. J. (1994). An inside look at community policing reform: Definitions, organizational changes, and evaluation findings. *Crime and Delinquency*, *40*(3), 299–314. doi:10.1177/0011128794040003001

Sampson, R. (1994). *Problem Solving, Neighborhood-oriented Policing in Rural Communities: A Program Planning Guide*. Bureau of Justice Assistance, Office of Justice Programs, US Department of Justice.

Scheider, M. C., Chapman, R., & Schapiro, A. (2009). Towards the unification of policing innovations under community policing. *Policing*, *32*(4), 694–718. doi:10.1108/13639510911000777

Schmerler, K., Perkins, M., Phillips, S., Rinehart, T., & Townsend, M. (1998). Problem-solving Tips: A Guide to Reducing Crime and Disorder through Problem-solving Partnerships. Office of Community Oriented Policing Services, US Department of Justice.

Scott, M., & Goldstein, H. (2005). Shifting and Sharing Responsibility for Public Safety Problems. Office of Community Oriented Policing Services, US Department of Justice.

Shaaban, H. (2009). Community Police (Reality and Expectations). *Security Studies Journal*.

Silk, D. (2012). Community policing to prevent violent extremism. *FBI L. Enforcement Bull.*, *81*, 1.

Skogan, W. G. (1995). *Community participation and community policing*. Center for Urban Affairs and Policy Research, Northwestern University.

Skogan, W. G. (2000). Community policing: Chicago style. Oxford University Press. OCLC 490662808.

Skogan, W. G., & Hartnett, S. M. (1999, December 2). *Community Policing, Chicago Style*. Oxford University Press.

Skogan, W. G., & Hartnett, S. M. (2019). Community policing. *Police innovation: Contrasting perspectives*, 27-44.

Skolnick, J. H., & Bayley, D. H. (1988). Theme and Variation in Community Policing. *Crime and Justice*, *10*, 1–37. doi:10.1086/449142

Skolnick, J. H., & Bayley, D. H. (1988). *Community policing: Issues and practices around the world*. US Department of Justice, National Institute of Justice, Office of Communication and Research Utilization.

Spelman, W., & Eck, J. E. (1989). Sitting ducks, ravenous wolves, and helping hands: new approaches to urban policing. Public Affairs Comment, School of Public Affairs, University of Texas.

Stenson, K. (1993). Community policing as a governmental technology. *Economy and Society*, *22*(3), 373–389. doi:10.1080/03085149300000025

Trojanowicz, R. C., & Bucqueroux, B. (1990). *Community policing: A contemporary perspective*. Anderson Publishing Company.

Uricska, E. (2023). *The Relationship between the Framing of Speeding Messages and Changes*. .S2CID 260399463 doi:10.32577/mr.2023.1.16

Watson, E. M., & Alfred, R. (1998). Strategies for Community Policing. Prentice-Hall Inc.

Wilson, J. M. (2013). *Community policing in America*. Routledge. doi:10.4324/9780203830512

Wilson, L. (1989). *Family structure and dynamics in the Caribbean*. Doctoral Dissertation, University of Michigan.

Chapter 6
The Invisible MENA Population in Dearborn, Michigan:
Diversity-Blind Police Traffic and Arrest Data

Robbya Reneea Green-Weir
Florida Agricultural and Mechanical University, USA

ABSTRACT

Dearborn, MI is the enclave of Arab Americans in the United States. Arabs migrated to Dearborn, MI, many as refugees of war, seeking prosperity. The Arab American experience is invisible because this population is classified as "White'" according to the U.S. Census. However, many Arab Americans do not identify as "White." Therefore, interpretations using "White" statistics may be flawed. It is imperative that the Office of Management and Budget include a Middle Eastern North African (MENA) category to separate the "White" data and disaggregate MENA data. The Obama and Biden Administrations have submitted proposals on collecting MENA population data. It is unknown if the 2030 U.S. Census will include MENA categories. Law enforcement and other organizations can incorporate both quantitative and qualitative data collection methods to capture MENA population statistics and their lived experiences. Until then, the MENA population and their needs will remain invisible to the general population and justice may be elusive.

The history of Dearborn, MI leadership includes mayors and police chiefs with staunch segregationist views and attitudes resulting in strained relationships between the Dearborn's MENA community and the Dearborn Police Department. That type

DOI: 10.4018/978-1-6684-8569-9.ch006

of leadership in Dearborn resulted in incidences of discrimination, and harassment of MENA residents and students in school, hostile work environment of officers in the Dearborn Police Department, and lawsuits of MENA residents against the Dearborn Police Department. Microdata of the MENA population is lacking which leads to the assumptions that information on this subject is under reported. The absence of this data has serious implications regarding building trust, transparency of law enforcement activity, understanding the social determinants of crime or criminal behavior, access to community resources, and allowing law enforcement agencies to fully serve every community. The availability and accuracy of MENA data in the Dearborn Police Department, the limitations in the existing Dearborn Police Department data, and quality improvement opportunities are the focus of this chapter.

Dearborn and Dearborn Heights, MI, boasts of having the largest and most diverse Arab community in the US (Leech, 2017). Wayne County, MI, where Dearborn and Dearborn Heights are located rank second in the U.S. behind California (Harjanto & Batalova, 2022). Self-reported data show persons of Arab ancestry in Dearborn as 44.3% of the Dearborn population and 27.6% of the Dearborn Heights population (Statistical Atlas, n.d.). Microdata such as this is only a fraction of the data made available publicly (Ekhator-Mobayode & Hoogeveen, 2022). Census data on the MENA population in Dearborn is lacking because the federal government classifies MENA as White (Maghboulen, et al., 2022). It is unclear if the 2030 Census will or will not revise race and ethnicity standards to include this as a distinct population in the survey (Dameka Reese, Assistant Division Chief of Data Collection for the America Community Survey, Census Bureau, personal communication, December 14, 2022).

Microdata dealing with ethnicity and the MENA population is not collected by the Dearborn Police Department (Ronald Haddad, Police Chief, personal communication, March 20,2021; Issa Shahim, Police Chief, personal communication, February 22, 2022) for traffic and arrest violations. Dearborn's city administration currently lacks direction regarding the measurement of the MENA population. In 2014, the Department of Justice updated its Guidance for Federal Law Enforcement Agencies Regarding the Use of Race, Ethnicity, Gender, National Origin, Religion, Sexual Orientation, or Gender Identity, but it does not apply to law enforcement agencies (United States Department of Justice, 2023). Specifically,

In making routine or spontaneous law enforcement decisions, such as ordinary traffic stops, Federal law enforcement officers may not use race, ethnicity, gender, national origin, religion, sexual orientation, or gender identity to any degree, except that officers may rely on the listed characteristics in a specific suspect description. This prohibition applies even where the use of a listed characteristic might otherwise be lawful (p.4)

HISTORY OF ETHNIC AND CULTURAL CHANGE IN DEARBORN, MI

The history of Dearborn and Arab migration into the city is discussed to understand the importance of collecting MENA data. Major changes to the federal immigration laws and policies saw a large influx of Middle Eastern residents in Detroit. Detroit's exploding auto industry drew immigrants world-wide. Ford Motor Company Highland Park Plant opened in 1910, advertising $5 per day pay. Ford's policies at the time excluded African American people from employment in the auto plants, opening the doors for new immigrant jobs. The Ford Motor Company's River Rouge plant opened in the late 1920s in the South End part of Dearborn and is the largest single industrial complex in the world. The largest number of Arab immigrants arrived in Dearborn and settled in the South End part of the city. War refugees from the Lebanese Civil War, Gulf War, Iraq War, and Syrian War also settled in Dearborn. The timeline of the Arab American arrival in Detroit and Dearborn are as follows:

Late 1880s

- Syrian and Lebanese immigrated to Detroit, MI and worked on the east side in close proximity to Ford Motor Company's Jefferson auto plant.

Early 1900s

- Some Yemenis arrived in Detroit area as early as 1900
- The first Palestinians settled in Highland Park, MI near the Ford Motor Company Model T plant.
- Chaldeans first came to Detroit between 1910 and 1912

Late 1920s

- Ford Motors opened the River Rouge plant in Dearborn, MI, many Arab-Americans followed and settled in the South End of the city.
- Yemeni Sunni Muslims, Palestinians, and Jordanians, primarily Orthodox Christians but also Sunni Muslims immigrated to Dearborn.

1967 – Arab-Israeli War resulted in many Palestinians being displaced. This set the stage for another war in 1973.

1975 – Immigrants from Yemen and Lebanon settled in the South End of Dearborn due to the civil war in Lebanon.

1991 – Large numbers of Iraqi Shi'a immigrants came to Dearborn for political reasons being expelled from Iraq at the end of the Gulf War.

2003 – Iraqi refugees arrived in a second wave following the U.S. invasion to disarm Iraq of weapons of mass destruction and to end Saddam Hussein's support for terrorism (Apel, 2020; Jouppi, 2017; Kumaus, n.d.).

The South End community profile as of 2015 is described as high unemployment, prevalent poverty, low educational attainment, and more than 50% of the housing is renter-occupied (Chen, et al., 2015). Conditions had not changed much by 2018, with a reported 70% low income in the area (Matheny & Laitner, 2018). The residents are also exposed to elevated levels of air and water pollution (University of Michigan, n.d.). Contrast this community with the more affluent West Dearborn, where the median income is $72,000 to $78,000 (City Data, 2021).

ORIGIN OF RACIAL AND ETHNIC TENSION IN DEARBORN

The discussion begins with Henry Ford, founder of Ford Motor Company. Henry Ford was a confirmed racist against African American people and people of Jewish decent such that they were not allowed in the community. Recall previously, Ford Motor Company policies excluded African American people from employment in the early years of operation. When Henry Ford began hiring African American people, believing African American people were inferior, African American people worked in the foundry and forge, which were the most dangerous places to work in the auto company. African American people also could not rise to executive levels (Little, 2021). African American people still were not allowed to live in the community. At least two Dearborn mayors furthered the racist climate against African American and then other people of color. Those mayors are Orville Hubbard and Michael Guido. Table 1. Lists the mayors and police chiefs chronologically by years in office.

Table 1. History of Dearborn administration mayors and police chiefs

Mayor	Police Chief
Clyde Ford (1929-1936	
John Carey (1936-1942)	
Orville Hubbard (1942 – 1978)	John O'Reilly, Sr. (1966 -1977)
John O'Reilly, Sr. (1978 – 1985)	
Michael Guido (1986 – 2006)	Michael Celeski (2005 – 2008)
John O'Reilly, Jr. (2007 – 2022)	Ronald Haddad (2008 – 2022)
Abdullah Hammoud (Current Administration)	Issa Shahin (Current Administration)

Orville Hubbard, well known for his views on segregation and non-White people, served as Mayor of Dearborn, MI, from 1942 to 1978. Mayor Orville Hubbard told the *Montgomery* (Alabama) *Advertiser* on March 26, 1956, that he was "for complete segregation, one million percent. Mayor Orville Hubbard stated publicly and in advertising as saying, "Keep Dearborn Clean," which was widely understood to mean keep Dearborn White (Detroit Historical Society, para. 4, n.d.). Mayor Hubbard's statement "Keep Dearborn Clean" was carried forward from John Carey's campaign platform, alleging that Clyde Ford was responsible for the existence of disorderly behavior and gambling houses in the east and south sections of Dearborn (Dearborn Historical Commission, p. 11, 1979). However, during his tenure Mayor Hubbard's comments and actions translated to the understanding that "Keep Dearborn Clean" meant keeping African American people out of Dearborn. Mayor Hubbard's campaign promise was "keep the niggers out" (Wheeler, p. 323, 2016). As Middle Easterners began moving into Dearborn, Mayor Hubbard was also quoted as saying, "Syrians are even worse than the niggers" (Warikoo, para. 9, 2020). David Good, a member of the Dearborn Historical Commission, and the former editor of The Dearborn Historian, says that Hubbard was an unregenerate racist who enacted numerous city policies exacerbating segregation and racial tensions in Dearborn over the course of his 36-year tenure as mayor (Good, 1989, as cited in Audet, 2020, para. 3).

Dearborn is located on the southwest edge of Detroit. Detroit has been predominantly African American since the 1980 Census (Office of Policy Development and Research, n.d.). In fact, "White Flight" began before the 1967 uprising in Detroit, MI, due to racial tensions. White flight is a phenomenon whereby White Americans move when neighborhoods diversify due to their fears and stereotypical beliefs (American Psychological Association, 2021). Figure 1 is a graphic of the Detroit-Dearborn and Dearborn Heights city borders.

Dearborn was also a "Sundown Town." Sundown towns are all White municipalities or neighborhoods in the United States that practice a form of racial segregation by excluding non-"Whites" from day-to-day activities, services, and rights through the use of discriminatory laws, intimidation, or violence. The consequences of African American people being found in a sundown town after dark could vary between being harmed, forced out of town, or killed (Cohen, 2020).

Dearborn continues to struggle to shed itself of its racist history. Police Chief, Ronald Haddad has been quotes as saying "We've been revamping our policies for years to try to better serve the public — but I've learned by experience that no matter what we do, some people harbor the same old feelings about Dearborn" (Hunter, para. 4, 2021).

Michael Guido was the Mayor of Dearborn from 1986-2006 and promoted an anti-Arab campaign. Figure 2 is a graphic of the front page of a 12-page pamphlet

Figure 1. Map of Detroit-Dearborn border

Figure 2. Mayor Guido's anti-Arab flyer

distributed to largely White Dearborn residents during his political campaign for mayor (Taleb-Agha, 2020).

Dearborn currently has a mayor, Abdullah Hammoud, and a police chief, Issa Shahin, who are Arab American. The previous police chief, Ronald Haddad, was also Arab American. The Dearborn Police Department boasts of increased hiring of African and Arab American officers. Dearborn has made strides to remove the stigma of its racial past. One might assume that a city with the largest concentration of Arab American citizens in the U.S. would not have concerns centering on marginalization and discrimination. According to Warikoo (2021), the Yemeni community has experienced greater levels of marginalization and systemic discrimination in development, recreation, representation, and environmental protection which they attribute to their darker skin color or being characterized as the brownest of Arab Americans. The Yemeni community is concentrated more in lower income areas in southeastern Dearborn. The Lebanese American community is the largest ethnic group in Dearborn and the most influential among the city's Arab American groups. Below are four examples of discrimination in Dearborn toward Arab Americans. The first two examples are from the U.S. Commission on Civil Rights (2021), followed by two from the Dearborn News.

U.S. Commission on Civil Rights

Understand that when one sues a policeman or a police station, many Arab Americans feel they are taking their lives in their hands and that it is a very dangerous thing to do. So, most of these do not get reported (para. 16).

Arab Americans, the minute they get arrested in the city of Dearborn, they are called names. I can cite at least five cases where similar crimes are committed and non-Arab people get slapped on the hands with a fine, while Arab Americans spend time in jail. That happened to an Arab American woman. She is spending 60 days in jail for discharging arms supposedly on New Year's Eve. She has four children and is living on welfare (para. 18).

Dearborn News

Leaders of the Arab Community filed a civil rights claim on behalf of 14 teens who were injured and arrested while celebrating in the parking lot of Fordson High School, Dearborn. MI after graduation. Reports state the teens were spraying shaving cream and throwing eggs. The FBI investigated, and the Dearborn Police conducted an internal investigation on claims that police officers physically and verbally abused (face burned by Mace, leg wound, and ethnic comments) the teens and a parent during the arrest. All but one of the students arrested were of Arabic descent (Geddes, 1990).

In the case of Ali Beydoun v. The City of Dearborn, Police Chief Haddad, and eight other officers, Beydoun was riding his bike home from work around 4 AM. He worked at a local hookah lounge in east Dearborn that closed at 3 AM. Beydoun stopped on a side street to fix the chain on his bicycle when a police car approached him and asked for his identification. Beydoun, who was not fluent in English, had a panic attack. Within minutes, eight officer were at the scene using excessive force on him to arrest him. The officers cuffed Beydoun and placed him in the back of the police vehicle. Beydoun was never arrested and taken to jail but instead dropped off at Oakwood Hospital to be treated for injuries (back and face) sustained from the altercation with Dearborn Police (Hijazi, 2016).

Four Arab American police officers that have resigned from the Dearborn Police Department. Their complaints included anti-Arab sentiments, deliberate alienation, and insults in front of colleagues. When these police officers were asked if the rough treatment could be a part of the training process, the response was White recruits were treated better overall and held to a different standard. One officer said "I'm not a sensitive person … But I couldn't deal with this hostile environment for the next 25 years of my life" (Harb, 2016).

THE LABRINTH TO MENA RECOGNITION

Arabs in America had to identify as White to gain American citizenship. The earliest court case found in the literature dates back to 1909. However, the final ruling by the federal government occurred in 1944 when all Arabs and North Africans were deemed White. During this period, the federal courts were inconsistent in defining Arabs as "White," granting some and denying others eligibility for citizenship. The 1977 Office of Management and Budget (OMB) Directive 15 included MENA in the definition of White (Haney-Lopez, 2006; Gualtie, 2009; Tehranian, 2009). White was defined as "a person having origins in any of the original peoples of Europe, the Middle East, or North Africa" (United States Census Bureau· 2020). However, research shows that many MENA Americans do not identify as White and have been advocating to include a MENA category in federal standards for gathering data on race and ethnicity for more than 30 years (Wang, 2023). The answer to why MENA Americans do not identify as White begins with a brief discussion about identity.

There are several definitions and theories about identity (e.g., psychology, sociology, biblically, etc.). The commonalities among them refer to a sense of self. Racial identity is defined as individuals attributing their membership to a racial group (Sellers, et al., 1998, p. 23). The privilege of the White racial category has not matched the discrimination in housing, at work, and other parts of daily life that many Arab Americans have faced (Wang, 2022). Therefore, the OMB's category for White can be insufficient.

Ethnic identity is based on the culture of one's ancestors' national or tribal group (Helms, 1994, p. 293). However, the OMB categories included in the 2020 Census require two minimum categories for ethnicity – Hispanic or Latino and Not Hispanic (U.S. Census Bureau, 2020). Again, the OMB categories for ethnicity are insufficient for MENA Americans.

Arab American communities are not monoliths and MENA data should be disaggregated.

For example, Assyrians and Chaldeans have origins in Arabic-speaking countries but do not identify as Arab. The MENA region is comprised of diverse religious groups such as Christian, Copts, Druze, Shi's, and Sunni Muslims. Chaldeans, who are Christians from Iraq, speak Arabic, but given Muslim extremists in the East may not identify as Arabs. In the United States, where White and Christian identities are closely linked, Christian Arabs are more likely than Muslim Arab Americans to self-identify as White. Lebanese and Syrian residents, regardless of whether they are Muslim or Christian, might define themselves as "White." Some members of the Sudanese may identify as both African American and Arab (Naber, 2000; Janmohamed, 2019).

Maghbouleh, et al. (2022), investigated how MENA individuals identify themselves and how non-MENA and MENA individuals perceive racial status of MENA traits (ancestry, cultural traits, skin color, generation, and religion). Researchers administered two online surveys in a randomized controlled research design with 421 non-Hispanic White adults, 333 pre-identified Middle Eastern adults, 329 adults who reported as having at least one grandparent born in the MENA region, and 121 individuals reported at least one grandparent born in North Africa. Results for self-identification show (a) when MENA are not offered a MENA option, 80% choose to identify as White, (b) when MENA is offered, only 10% continue to choose White, (c) second-generation immigrants, MENA Muslims and nonreligious MENAs, those with idle Eastern (versus North African), and those who perceive more discrimination against MENA people chose the MENA option, (d) individuals with MENA ancestry identify as both White and "MENA", and (e) offering MENA as an option reduced the percentage of respondents choosing "Some Other Race" from 15 to 0 (Conclusion and Discussion, para. 4-6). Previous research conducted by the U.S. Census Bureau showed similar findings (Buchanan, et al., 2016). The reduction of MENA respondents choosing "Some Other Race" may be a function of the Arab American campaign "Check it right; you ain't White" to define themselves on the 2010 U.S. (Maghbouleh, et al., 2022). A decade later the slogan "I am Arab, I am American, I matter" was to get Arab Americans to check 'other' for the 2020 U.S. Census (Chaplin, 2020). "Yalla Count MENA In!" is one of the slogans for the 2030 U.S. Census (yallacountmenain, n.d.).

The Obama Administration proposed changes to the 2020 Census that was stalled by the Trump Administration. The Biden Administration's proposed changes to the 2030 Census are in Figure 1 below. Public comment on proposed changed to the 2020 Census closed on April 27, 2023. The OMB is expected to make its decision in the summer of 2024 (Wang, 2023). Figure 3 is a replica excerpt of the proposed race-ethnicity question.

Figure 3. Example of initial proposal of a combined race-ethnicity questions for updating OMB's race and ethnicity statistical standards

What is your race or ethnicity?

Select all that apply AND enter additional details in the spaces below.

Note, you may report more than one group.

__ **MIDDLE EASTERN OR NORTH AFRICAN** – Provide details below.

__ Lebanese __ Iranian __ Egyptian

__ Syrian __ Moroccan __ Israeli

Enter, for example Algerian, Iraqi, Kurdish, etc.

The availability to enter additional details is necessary. Depending on the agency and programs of the United Nations, the number of MENA countries ranges from 15 to 24. These agencies include the World Bank, Food and Agricultural Organization, United Nations, and International Monetary Fund. However, MENA individuals are generally defined as having heritage from one of the 22 Arab League Nations and a few non-Arabic speaking countries such as Iran, Turkey, and Israel.

Historically, the first Census in 1790 only had three categories – free Whites, "all other free persons", and "slaves" (Pratt, et al., n.d.). There have been several attempts to expand the Census to include other race and ethnicity categories. The "Some other race" box was approved in 2000 and became the second most common answer in the 2020 Census (U.S. Department of Congress, 1960, 2000).

The White category may continue to be preferred by members of immigrant generations which could be attributed to perceived discrimination, racial profiling, micro-aggressions; data misuse and confidentiality or fear of surveillance in the name of national security interests (Abdel-Moneim, 2018; Maghboulen, et al., 2022). In fact, Immigration and Custom Enforcement (ICE) inadvertently posted more than 6,000 names and personal information during a routine update of the website late November 2022 (Aleaziz, 2023).

The United States Census Bureau administers the American Community Survey (ACS) annually to collect more information about the nation and its people. The ACS asks topics not on the decennial Census about education, employment, internet access, and transportation. The ACS provides current information to communities annually that helps determine how to distribute billions of federal spending for economic development, emergency management, and understanding local issues and conditions. The ACS asks participants about ancestry (U.S. Census Bureau, 2008). Ancestry is defined geographically, genealogically, or genetically. Geographic ancestry refers to ancestors originating from similar geographic regions. Genealogical ancestry refers to one's ancestral pedigree, and genetic ancestry refers to ancestors from whom one is biologically descended (Lu, et al., 2022) . The ancestry question in combination with the topics mentioned above, help governments and communities enforce laws, regulations, and policies against discrimination based on national origin. Excerpts from the Census below provides examples of Federal and other uses from the data on the ACS (U.S. Census, n.d.).

Examples of Federal Uses

- Required to identify vulnerable populations that may be at disproportionate risk of experiencing limitations in health care access, poor health quality, and suboptimal health outcomes.
- Required to enforce against discrimination in education, employment, voting, financial assistance, and housing.
- Used in many reporting and research tasks to investigate whether there are differences by ancestry in education, employment, home ownership, health, income and many other areas of interest to policymakers.

Examples of Other Uses

State and local agencies use these statistics to understand the needs of all the groups in their communities over time. Some social, economic, or housing trends may have different impacts for different ancestry groups; understanding these changes may highlight future social and economic challenges. Advocacy groups use statistics about specific ancestry groups to understand current and future challenges and to advocate for policies that benefit their groups (para. 3-4)

Figure 4 below illustrates the wording for the ancestry question on the ACS form.

Conceptual and logistic issues regarding whether MENA should be considered a racial group, or an ethnic group was the debate for the 2020 Census. Other reasons have not been fully articulated in the literature. Until the OMB categories are refined, the ACS is a source where MENA Americans have the option to self-identify. While the ACS is the largest household survey administered annually by the Census Bureau, the ACS should not be considered a solution to fix the problem as it is sent to a small percentage of the population on a rotating basis throughout the decade and no household will receive the survey more often than once every five years.

Figure 4. The American community survey ancestry question

What is this person's ancestry or ethnic origin?

____

____

(For example, Italian, Jamaican, African Am., Cambodian, Cape Verdean, Norwegian, Dominican, French Canadian, Haitian, Korean, Lebanese, Polish, Nigerian, Mexican, Taiwanese, Ukrainian, and so on.)

There are several terms and concepts that support disaggregating MENA data. While the literature on these terms is plentiful, there will not be an in-depth discussion of these terms as this is not the focus of the chapter.

TERMINOLOGY AND CONCEPTS

Intersectionality

Intersectionality is a theoretical framework that posits that multiple social categories (e.g., race, ethnicity, gender, socioeconomic status, [religion]) intersect at the micro level of individual experience to reflect multiple interlocking systems of privilege and oppression at the macro, social-structural level (racism, sexism, heterosexism, ethnocentrism) (Bowleg, 2012). According to Zahkari (2021),

Having accurate racial and ethnic identification options available helps… recognition of more types of biases that often conflate ethnicity, religion, national origin for many of MENA descent. Misidentification of one's identity has been shown to produce negative health outcomes, likewise, overlooking bias-motivated crimes also limits the effectiveness of programs intended to mitigate further incidents. (p. 5)

Colorism

Colorism is discrimination based on skin tone "… where lighter skin tones, straight hair, etc. are preferred over darker skin tones, kinky hair, etc. … Individuals belonging to the same ethnoracial category may face differential treatment due to their varying skins tones … as darkness increases and Afrocentric appearance increases, so does the probability of being perceived as dangerous, incompetent, ugly, and much more" (Monk, 2021, para. 5, 6). As such, skin color disadvantages people with darker skin while privileging those with lighter skin. Khalifeh (2017) quotes a Yemeni person employed in Dearborn as saying, "Being Yemini in Dearborn is like being Black in America." (The rift, para. 23). Harb (2016) quotes Professor Zahr, an adjunct law professor at the University of Detroit, "For black people, their skin color is their blackness … for us, our names are our blackness" (A transactional relationship, para. 19).

Discrimination

Discrimination refers to the treatment of, in favor or against, a person based on the group or class to which that person belongs rather than on individual merit (USLegal, n.d.). Al-Sheemary (2015) states, "Lebanese homeowners discriminate and refuse to rent to Iraqis, to exclude them from majority Lebanese neighborhoods." Another quote from Professor Zahr, "Some of the anti-Black bigotry in the Arab American community stems from [the White designation on the US Census] … One of the main characteristics of whiteness in this country has been anti-blackness … so if you try to be White, you manifest that through racism".

Hierarchy Within Races

Hierarchy within races is the belief that certain ethnic groups within a race are superior or inferior to others within the same race. Hierarchy is a social status with dominant and non-dominant groups (National Museum of African American History and Culture). According to Khalifeh (2017) about Dearborn, MI, "We do have a hierarchy in the community," referring to the Lebanese ranking higher than Yemini. According to Al-Sheemary (2015),

The ability of many Lebanese to pass as white is prized and used for political and economic gain in a world in which being Arab or Muslim carries negative notoriety. To distance Lebanese-ness from Arab-ness is to try to achieve white middle-class acceptability at the expense of marginalizing other Arab ethnic groups. (para. 8)

ANTI-RACISM RESEARCH METHODS

Positive practices in anti-racism research includes (a) using appropriate comparison groups to contextualize findings, (b) employing mixed method approaches in conjunction with quantitative administrative data to better understand the lived experience of clients, (c) disaggregating data and analyzing intersectional experiences, and (d) empowering professionals and community to use the data to create and improve community-based solutions (University of Minnesota Libraries).

Comparison Groups

Internal comparison groups come from the same population. In a non-experimental research design or when random assignment is not possible or feasible an internal comparison group consists of exposed and non-exposed groups of study participants. The group not exposed to an intervention/treatment in a non-experimental research design is not a control group. Control groups are associated with experimental research involving random assignment of study participants. If the unit of analysis is Dearborn, MI, internal comparison groups would be challenging to define for the MENA population without micro-data (disaggregation).

Mixed Method Approaches

Mixed method approaches include qualitative data collection methods (e.g., interviews, focus groups, observation, etc.) followed by or in conjunction with quantitative data collection methods discussed in the next section. Qualitative research approaches are best used to understand or explain lived experiences of groups with police, healthcare, social services, etc. Understanding the lived experiences of the MENA population can be accomplished if microdata (disaggregated) existed for the MENA population.

Quantitative Administrative Data

While there are several types of quantitative or numerical data (e.g., discrete and continuous), this chapter focuses on the value of disaggregating MENA ethnicity data. President Biden's proposal for the 2030 Census should be implemented for the reasons previously stated and subsequently discussed. In the meantime, organizations can design and implement data collection on the ethnicity of the MENA population to better understand and address their needs. A major healthcare system in Metropolitan Detroit collected ethnicity data on the MENA population absent from the Census. The benefits of which is discussed later in the chapter.

Analyzing Intersectional Experiences

The availability of micro (disaggregated) data will enable Intra-MENA population analysis. Both individual MENA groups -Yemeni, Lebanese, Syrian, Iraqi, etc.; and a combination of experiences can be explored (e.g., MENA group by religion, gender, age, socioeconomic status). Any differences in intersectionality research are useful for theme development or categorization of common experiences of groups. Identifying common experiences can point to actionable solutions, as it is discussed in the next section.

Empowering Professionals and Community

Thematic analyses can facilitate open communication with community organizers and lay leaders; direct community engagement, foster collaborations with organizations to leverage resources, and create community-based solutions to better address the needs of populations. Research is replete with examples of how data empowers communities. Below is an overview of three examples.

Data-Informed Community Engagement (DICE) Framework involved other stakeholders to share the burden of crime prevention. The DICE Framework in Atlantic City included the City's Planning and Development Department regarding the remediation of vacant properties and the local electric utility company for installing of new LED streetlights. Other cities using the DICE Framework include Kansas City, MO, Newark, NJ, and Dallas, TX (Santana, Caplan, and Kennedy, n.d.) .

Brownsville In Violence Out is an anti-gun violence initiative whereby a group of well-respected community members in the 73rd District, Brooklyn, NY respond to low-level 911 calls shadowed by plain-clothed officers. Brownsville In Violence Out is part of The Mayor's Office of Criminal Justice Crisis Management System, established in 2015. Outcomes include a reduction in shootings, homicides, shoplifting, robberies, and assaults. Several times a year, members of the Brownsville Safety Alliance stand sentry on two blocks for five days. Comparable models are underway in Oregon and Denver (Jilani, 2023).

RESEARCH USING MICRO DATA ON THE MENA POPULATION

A task force was assembled at one of the top three health systems in Metropolitan Detroit, MI in the late 2000s to better understand the population they served. The primary charge of the task force was to collect quantitative data on race, ethnicity, primary language, and religion that included the MENA population. The self-reported survey question at that time was "Are you of Arab/Chaldean descent?" It has since changed to "Are you "Middle Eastern / North African descent?" because the former did not resonate with some groups.

The four-year initiative to expand ethnicity to include MENA patients improved the IT infrastructure, customer service, policies and procedures, training, translated health information, and evaluation. The findings validated the creation of a website dedicated to the Arab ancestry population, and two health centers – first in Detroit that closed and one in Dearborn - to tailor healthcare delivery to serve that population. The results also allowed analysis of risk events by race to improve the quality of healthcare delivery to groups of MENA patients.

The MENA Box Knowledge Community, a subgroup of the Islamophobia Working Group on the University of Michigan campus aimed to make MENA box a standard category as for other categories for people of color. Effective fall 2019, the Rackham Graduate School included MENA identity options on their applications (Syed, 2019; University of Michigan, n.d.).

In a recent Dearborn Police study, 24 one-on-one interviews were conducted by phone or Zoom from Fall 2021 to Summer 2022 with African Americans that live, work, attend the universities, or drive through Dearborn or Dearborn Heights. The average duration of interviews averaged 35 minutes. The purpose of the study was to capture the lived experiences about their interactions with the Dearborn Police. It was during this research that the lack of MENA police data was discovered. The findings of this research discussed below have implications for community safety.

Common themes emerged in the interviews with African Americans who live, work, and play in Dearborn, MI, regarding their interactions with the Dearborn Police. These comments fell within 3 domains and 12 sub-themes in Table 2 below. The majority of the oral stories were about traffic violations from 1963 to 2022. The participants were 80% male, aged 29 – 86 years old, with varied levels of education, employment, and income.

Table 2. Thematic analysis of African American oral stories

Domains	Bias	Abuse of Power	Consequences
Sub-Themes	Class	Disrespect	Mental trauma
	Racial Profiling	Fear	Material costs
	Feeling Targeted	Inappropriate Discretion	Trust
	Stereotyped		Long-term opinion and relationship with Dearborn

Since this research, the Dearborn Police Department stopped using defective vehicle equipment (e.g., broken taillight, etc.) of commuters to and through Dearborn, MI, as a cause to pull drivers over. It must also be noted that in 2020 Michigan Governor Whitmer issued executive orders 2020-47 and 2020-78 instructing police departments to stop enforcing certain plate violations (Michigan.gov, 2020). Table 3 and 4 below shows a reduction in citations discovered after being pulled over

Table 3. Reduction in the number of citations reported by the Dearborn Police Department

Citations	2021 (Number)	2022 (Number)
No proof of or no insurance	3,251	1,711
Drove while license suspended/revoked/denied	2,146	929
No proof of registration	1,243	847

Table 4. Race breakdown of citations reported by the Dearborn Police Department

Race	2021 (Percent)	2022 (Percent)
African American	28.25	21.26
White	67.06	72.2

because of defective equipment from 2021 and 2022 by race (Dearborn Police Department, n.d.).

The statistic for White is flawed. It is not known what percentage of the White population consists of "MENA" groups. An opportunity for future research is to duplicate this research with the MENA population. Quantitative data alone does not reveal the lived experiences of the MENA population with law enforcement in Dearborn. Qualitative research methods (focus groups, interviews, observations) in conjunction with quantitative research methods can offer the MENA American a voice and provide greater depth and understanding of the hidden aspects of the MENA experience (e.g., categorization of common experiences of groups, better understand their needs, etc.).

OPPORTUNITY FOR IMPROVEMENT IN POLICE DEPARTMENTS

Police departments, like the health system and university briefly discussed above, can design, and implement collection of race and ethnicity data tailored to the people in the communities they serve. Benefits of collecting MENA data are (a) measuring police effectiveness and efficiency, (b) assessing disparities or equity in the group and sub-group populations, (c) assessing if the group and sub-groups are disproportionately affected, (d) assessing officer behaviors (Pryor, et al., 2020). According to the authors, excerpts of the gold standard for each benefit is in Table 5 below.

Table 5. Available information from micro-level data collection

Police Effectiveness	Disparities	Group Proportions	Officer Behaviors
Crime rates	Use of force	Are there disparities in the number of pedestrian and vehicle stops compared to the representation in the population?	Are some officers responsible for a disproportionate number of stops?
Complaints of racial or identity profiling	Yield rates of contraband	What is the proportion of the number of citizen complaints to the number of police?	What are common factors among officers with the highest rate of use of force?
Calls for service	De-escalation techniques	What is the proportion of number of citizen complaints alleging racial or identity profiling to the number of police stops?	What are common factors among officers with the highest number of citizen complaints?

(pp. 9-12)

This guidebook for law enforcement agencies is an excellent resource regarding how to engage the community to collect this type of data, data integrity, officer training, auditing the data, analyzing the data, and communicating data results.

IMPLICATIONS OF CHANGE OR STATUS QUO

Status Quo

There are at least two false assumptions in aggregating MENA in the White race: (a) that race categories are discrete, and (b) race categories are meaningful in analysis. There is an inability to measure variables appropriately with the discrepancies in the existing data. Race is not biological. Race is a social construct formed during the second half of the 17th century based on the economic and social conditions during that time. According to Carmichael (2010),

Race is a notoriously inaccurate proxy for genetics since it's such an imprecise way of describing people. Looking at a patient's full genetic analysis would give you much more information than race does, but the era of personalized medicine is still years away. (para. 5)

Collecting ethnicity data has the potential of small sample sizes and opportunities for misclassifications, but this level of data gets closer to understanding and addressing the needs of ethnic groups.

Aggregating the MENA population as White mask variation within racial and ethnic categories and erase the experiences of certain communities. Any findings from aggregating MENA data with White may is not applicable to the MENA population. There are inherent difficulties in making multilevel inferences based on one variable or a single level of analysis.

Change

Disaggregating MENA will secure representation for a historically statistically invisible community. The benefit of having more information is a better understanding of the social determinants of crime and criminal behavior, address the determinants, and connect the community to the right resources. The potential for more inclusive data and resulting benefits outweigh the administrative costs of changes to systems and forms.

BUILDING COMMUNITY TRUST

The Dearborn Police can build trust in the Dearborn and Dearborn Heights communities by prioritizing transparency, accountability, and community engagement. Implement community policing strategies that foster positive interactions. Establish civilian review boards to ensure accountability for police actions. Provide cultural competency training for officers. Actively listen to community concerns and address them promptly. Foster partnerships with local organizations to create joint initiatives. Emphasize fair and unbiased policing, and regularly assess and communicate progress. Below is a brief summary of Dearborn's progress and areas of improvement toward building trust in residents.

Implement Community Policing Strategies That Foster Positive Interactions

In 2000, community leaders and local, state, and federal law enforcement agencies formed an organization called Advocates and Leaders for Police and Community Trust (ALPACT) in partnership with the Michigan Department of Civil Rights to work on issues such as racial profiling that had high potential of damaging police-community relations. The Dearborn Police avoided active involvement with federal investigations of terrorists in the aftermath of 9/11 and actively patrolled to protect its MENA residents (Sun & Wu, 2015). Dearborn elected their first Arab Police Chief, Ronald Haddad, in 2008. Dearborn elected their first Muslim Police Chief, Issa Shahim in 2022. The Dearborn Police Department has also implemented a Transparency Dashboard on their website that include arrest and traffic violation data. As previous discussed, however, the data for White is flawed because of the lack of microdata for the MENA population.

Establish Civilian Review Boards to Ensure Accountability for Police Actions

Accountability for Dearborn (A4D), a non-Dearborn Police Department organization, started a petition for a civilian review board February 2022. To date A4D has not met their petition goal. A4D's purpose is to require transparency and accountability from the Police Department among other goals.

Cultural Competency Training for Officers

The impact of police perception of a group of people on policing behaviors remains a subject of research (Carmichael, et al., 2021). The Dearborn Police Department provides police academy training for recruit officers and mandatory internal training on various topics to include implicit bias. To date, there is only one study regarding outcomes of implicit bias training conducted with the NYPD. That study found "no evidence that implicit bias training impacted policing outcomes of greatest public policy concern … further evidence is needed" (Fineberg, et al., 2021, p. 5). The Urban Institute's evaluation of interventions developed through the National Initiative for Building Community Trust and Justice found that, "after implicit bias trainings, officers tended to have greater understanding of the potential for implicit biases and situational factors to influence their decisions. … the evaluation did not examine whether these understandings led to changes in officers' behaviors in the field" (Jannetta et al., 2019, pp. 9-10).

Foster Partnerships With Local Organizations to Create Joint Initiatives

The Dearborn Police Department partners with ACCESS in substance abuse prevention. ACCESS or the Arab Community Center for Economic and Social Services, is a non-profit organization to assist the Aram immigrant population adapt to life in metropolitan Detroit. The Dearborn Police Department has partnered with the Arab American and Chaldean Council, Byblos Banquet Center, and Forgotten Harvest to assist flood victims. This information is not available on the Dearborn Police Department website. The Dearborn Police Department website is not current on providing information on other local partnerships or joint initiatives.

Accountability, Fair, and Unbiased Policing

A4D reportedly has police officer-level data. This data is not available on the Dearborn Police Department website. Without transparency of this level of data, the public will not know which Dearborn Police officers are responsible for a disproportionate number of stops, officers with the highest rate of use of force, officers with the highest number of citizen complaints, for example, and how issues are addressed. Police officer-level data could facilitate a better understanding of the population's needs, foster community engagement, and develop community-based solutions for equity and justice.

To further build trust, the Dearborn Police Department must begin by creating a MENA box for traffic and arrest violations, and complaints. Dearborn Police have at least two resources to improve the quality of data collection on MENA Americans – one resource is the University of Dearborn, Dearborn, MI, and another resource is Henry Ford Health System, in the neighboring city of Detroit, MI. Additionally, Pryor et al. (2020), published a guidebook on collection of race/ethnic data for law enforcement. The question is, do the Dearborn police and other law enforcement agencies have the motivation to incur the administrative costs to improve the quality of data collection procedures for MENA Americans absent changes to the OMB and Census categories?

"Injustice anywhere is a threat to justice everywhere. We are caught in an inescapable network of mutuality, tied in a single garment of destiny. Whatever affects one directly, affects all indirectly."

— Martin Luther King Jr., Letter from the Birmingham Jail, April 16, 1963 (Bill of Rights Institute, n.d.)

REFERENCES

Adbel-Moneim, M.E. (2018, Spring). Reporting identity: Social and political implications of adding a MENA category to the U.S. Census. *Bard digital Commons*. 1-72.

Al-Sheemary, B. (2015, March 1). Intra-Arab discrimination in Dearborn. *Open Democracy*.

Aleaziz, H. (2023, January 19). ICE releases thousands of migrants affected by data breach. *Los Angeles times*. https://www.latimes.com/world-nation/story/2023-01-19/ice-leak-personal-information-immigrants-asylum

American Psychological Association (n.d.). *White flight may still enforce segregation*. Author.

Apel, D. (2020, January). *Between two worlds: Arab Americans in Detroit*. Academic Press.

Audet, A. (2020, July 7). The racist, segregationist history behind Dearborn's Orville Hubbard status. Retrieved. *WDET 101.9*.

Bill of Rights Institute. (n.d.). *Letter from the Birmingham Jail*. Letter from Birmingham Jail - Bill of Rights Institute.

Bowleg, L. (2012, July). The problem with the phrase women and minorities: Intersectionality—an important theoretical framework for public health. *American Journal of Public Health, 107*(7), 1267–1273. doi:10.2105/AJPH.2012.300750 PMID:22594719

Buchanan, A., Marks, R., & Figueroa, M. A. (2016, September). 2015 forum on ethnic groups from the Middle East and North Africa. *U.S. Census Bureau, Population Division*. https://www.census.gov/content/dam/Census/library/working-papers/2015/demo/MENA-Forum-Summary-and-Appendices.pdf

Carmichael, J., David, J., Helou, A., & Pererira, C. (2020). Déterminante of citizen's perceptions of police behavior during traffic and pedestrian stops. *Criminal Justice Review*, *46*(1), 99–118. Advance online publication. doi:10.1177/0734016820952523

Carmichael, M. (2010, February 14). Why racial disparities in health care persist. *Newsweek*.

Champlin, C. (2020, April 10). I am Arab, I am American, I matter. *LAist*. https://laist.com/news/2020-census-arab-americans

Chen, Y., Ignasiak, C., Nieske, M., & Whipp (n.d.). *The Southend District: Vision plan and economic development strategy* [Presentation]. Academic Press.

Dearborn Police Department. (n.d.). *The Dearborn Police Department transparency dashboard*. Author.

Detroit Historical Society. (n.d.). *Encyclopedia of Detroit*. Academic Press.

Ekhator-Mobayode, U. E., & Hoogeveen, J. (2002, January 13). *Microdata collection and openness in the Middle East and North African (MENA): Introducing the MENA microdata access indicator*. Academic Press.

Executive Order 2020-47 (2020). Executive Orders (michigan.gov)

Executive Order 2020-78 (2020). Executive Orders (michigan.gov)

Feigenberg, B., Glaser, J., Packis, E. (2021). Implicit bias training for police. *UChicago Urban Labs.*

Gualtieri, S. (2009). *Between Arab and White: Race and ethnicity in early Syrian-American diaspora*. University of California Press.

Haney-Lopez, I. (2006). White by law: The legal construction of race (Rev. and updated 10th anniversary ed.). New York, NY: New York University Press.

Harb, A. (2016). Arab American cops leaving Dearborn police force. *The Arab American News*.

Harb, A. (2017). *Arabs and African Americans: A complicated relationship*. Academic Press.

Harjanto, L. & Batalova, J. (2022, January 13). Middle Eastern and North Africa immigrants in the United States. *Migration Policy Institute*.

Helms, J. E. (1994). The conceptualization of racial identity and other "racial" constructs. In E. J. Trickett & R. J. Watts (Eds.), *Human diversity: Perspectives on people in context* (pp. 285–311). Jossey-Bass.

Hunter, G. (2021, February 3). *Dearborn police confront city's racist past, critics*. detroitnews.com

Janmohamed, Z. (2019, January 10). *The divisiveness that permeates Detroit's communities of color*. https://www.theguardian.com/us-news/2019/jan/09/detroit-arab-african-american-discrimination-race

Jannetta, J., Esthappan, S., Fontaine, J., Lynch, M., & La Vigne, N. (2019). *Learning to Build Police-Community Trust*. The Urban Institute.

Jilani, Z. (2023, June 6). New York City community policed itself for five days [news report]. Chicago, IL: NewsNation.

Jouppi, S. (2017, August 8*). CuriosiD: How did Detroit become a center for Arabs in the United States*. Academic Press.

Khalifeh, H. (2017, July 7). Local Yemenis feel marginalized as Lebanese brethren gain momentum. *The Arab American News*.

Kumaus, T. (n.d.). *Historical timeline of the Arab community of Dearborn, MI*. Academic Press.

Leech, N. (2017, July 5). How Dearborn, Michigan became the heart of the Arab America. *The National News*. https://www.thenationalnews.com/arts/how-dearborn-michigan-became-the-heart-of-arab-america-1.117177

Little, B. (2021, June 4). *How American icon Henry Ford fostered anti-semitism*. Academic Press.

Lu, C., Ahmed, R., Lamri, A., & Anand, S. S. (2022, September 15). Use of race, ethnicity, and ancestry data in health research. *PLOS Global Public Health*, *2*(9). Advance online publication. doi:10.1371/journal.pgph.0001060 PMID:36962630

Maghbouleh, N., Schachter, A., & Flores, R. D. (2022, February 15). Middle Eastern and North African Americans may not be perceived, not perceive themselves, to be White. *Proceedings of the National Academy of Sciences of the United States of America*, *119*(7), e2117940119. Advance online publication. doi:10.1073/pnas.2117940119 PMID:35131945

Matheny, K., & Laitner, B. (2018, January 18). Utility wants to add 1,000-plus tons of air pollutants to Dearborn's skies. *Detroit Free* Press. https://www.freep.com/story/news/local/michigan/wayne/2018/01/16/utility-wants-add-1-000-plus-tons-air-pollutants-dearborns-skies/1029332001/

Monk, E. P. Jr. (2021). The unceasing significance of colorism: Skin tone stratification in the United States. *Daedalus*, *150*(2), 76–90. doi:10.1162/daed_a_01847

Naber, N. (2000). Ambiguous insiders: An investigation of Arab American invisibility. *Ethnic and Racial Studies*, *23*(1), 37–61. doi:10.1080/014198700329123

National Museum of African American History & Culture (n.d.). *Social identities and systems of oppression*. Author.

Office of Policy Development and Research, State of the Cities Data Systems (n.d.). *SOCDS Census data: Output for Detroit city, MI*. Academic Press.

Pratt, B. M., Hixson, L., & Jones, N. A. (n.d.). Measuring race and ethnicity across the decades: 1970-2010 mapped to 1997 U.S. Office of Management and Budget Classification Standards. The United States Census Bureau.

Pryor, M., Heydari, F., Goff, P.A., & Friedman, B. (n.d.). *Collecting, analyzing, and responding to stop data: A guidebook for law enforcement agencies, government, and communities*. Academic Press.

Santana, A. G., Caplan, J. & Kennedy, L. (n.d.). *Data-informed community engagement: the Newark Public Safety Collaborative*. Academic Press.

Sellers, R. M., Smith, M. A., Shelton, J. N., Rowley, S. A., & Chavous, T. M. (1998). Multidimensional model of racial identity: A reconceptualization of African American racial identity. *Personality and Social Psychology Review*, *2*(1), 18–39. doi:10.1207/s15327957pspr0201_2 PMID:15647149

Statistical Atlas. (n.d.). *Ancestry in Dearborn*. The Demographic Statistical Atlas of the United States - Statistical Atlas.

Sun, I. Y., & Wu, Y. (2018). From invisibility to unwanted spotlight: Arab Americans' perception of the police. Race, Immigration, and Social Control. In C. Cunneen, K. Russell-Brown, S. L. Gabbidon, & S. Garner (Eds.), *Race, immigration, and social control. Palgrave studies in race, ethnicity, indigeneity and criminal justice*. Palgrave Macmillan. doi:10.1057/978-1-349-95807-8_6

Syed, Z. (2019, January 10). ME/NA identify boxes now included in Rackham applications. *The Michigan Daily*. https://www.michigandaily.com/news/academics/mena-identity-boxes-now-included-rackham-applications/

Taleb-Agha, K. (2020, December). *History of Arab Americans in Dearborn (1975-)*. Academic Press.

Tehranian, J. (2009). *Whitewashed: America's invisible Middle Eastern minority*. New York University Press.

The Dearborn Historical Commission (1979, Winter). *The Dearborn History, 1*(1), 1-35.

United States Census Bureau. (2008, December 8). *American Community Survey 5-year data (2009 – 2021)*. Author.

United States Census Bureau. (2020). *2020 Census frequently asked questions about race and ethnicity*. Author.

United States Census Bureau. (n.d.). *Why we ask questions about ancestry*. Author.

University of Michigan. (n.d.). *Environmental justice case study: the Dearborn, Michigan Arab American community and industrial air pollution*. websites.umich.edu/~snre492/berry.html

University of Michigan National Center for Institutional Diversity. (n.d.). *ME/NA box knowledge community*. https://lsa.umich.edu/ncid/engagement-opportunities/knowledge-communities/mena-box.html

University of Minnesota Libraries. (n.d.). *Conducting research through an anti-racism lens*. https://libguides.umn.edu/antiracismlens

University of Minnesota Libraries (n.d.). *Conducting research through an anti-racism lens*. Author.

U.S. Commission on Civil Rights (2001, May). *Civil rights issues facing Arab Americans in Michigan*. Author.

U.S. Department of Congress, Bureau of Census (1960). *Notice of required information for the 1960 Census of Population and Housing*. Academic Press.

U.S. Department of Congress, Bureau of Census (2000). *Informational Census Form*. Academic Press.

U.S. Department of Justice (2023, May). *Guidance for federal law enforcement agencies regarding the use of race, ethnicity, gender, national origin, religion, sexual orientation, gender identity, and disability*. Academic Press.

USLegal (n.d.). *Discrimination law and legal definition*. Academic Press.

Wang, H.L. (2018, January 29). No Middle Eastern or North African category on 2020 Census, Bureau says. *NPR*.

Wang, H. L. (2022, February 17). The U.S. Census see Middle Eastern and North African people as white. Many don't. *NPR*. https://www.npr.org/2022/02/17/1079181478/us-census-middle-eastern-white-north-african-mena

Wang, H.L. (2023, April 7). New 'Latino" and 'Middle Eastern or North African' checkboxes proposed for U.S. forms. *NPR*.

Warikoo, N. (2020). Statute of former Dearborn Mayor Orville Hubbard taken down. *Detroit Free Press*.

Warikoo, N. (2021, August). Yemeni Americans in Dearborn struggle to be included in city government. *Detroit Free Press*.

Wheeler, R. E. (2016). About microaggressions. *Boston University School of Law Library Journal, 108*(2), 321–329.

Yalla Count MENA In. (n.d.). https://yallacountmenain.org/

Zakhari, N. K. (2021, December). *Count MENA: Clarifying the impact of U.S. hate crimes on the Middle Eastern and NorAfrican Community*. Master of Science Capstone Project. https://jscholarship.library.jhu.edu/bitstream/handle/1774.2/66668/Zakhari-Capstone%20Project-2021.pdf?sequence=1

Chapter 7
The Italian Reform of Criminal Justice:
An Important Change Through Technological Progress

Maria Anastasia Arcuri
https://orcid.org/0009-0002-8256-0724
University of Rome "Tor Vergata", Italy

ABSTRACT

In the age of the internet, the criminal trial, while respecting constitution guarantees, cannot be insensitive to technological innovation which by now concerns every sector of human activity and every public service, which is also justice. The use of technology is able to redesign the new process of security and forensics, to improve government and law. The advanced technology in the application of the law provides efficiency. The Italian criminal justice system is currently under an important transformation by means Cartabia reform. The aim of the Italian reform is modernizing and simplifying the criminal process as well as increasing its efficiency and transparency. The chapter aims to explore the items relating to the Italian reform of criminal justice focusing to technology making changes. The work also intends to reflect on the role of technology in generating the self-reinforcing trust of criminal justice.

INTRODUCTION

Over the last decade, technological innovation has become increasingly important, leading to the development of a variety of areas including, not only computer science and information technology, but also medical, healthcare, and life areas: of business

DOI: 10.4018/978-1-6684-8569-9.ch007

and management; of environmental, agricultural, and physical; of education. The technological advancement is viewed as necessary in all fields.

In the age of the internet, the criminal trial, while respecting constitutional guarantees, cannot be insensitive to technological innovation which, by now, it concerns every sector of human activity and every public service, which is also justice. The use of technology is able to redesign the new process of security and forensics, to improve government and law. The use of advanced technological tools does not simply mark an extension of existing practices. The advanced technology in the application of the law provides efficiency.

On the other hand, the rapid increase in the use of new technologies, without a clear legal framework to ensure transparency and trust, could cause injustice, and the rule of law could be damaged. The rapid deployment of new technologies entails clear benefits if the law is reformed.

The potential of new technologies could increase the efficiency of the criminal justice system more generally.

The Italian criminal justice system is currently undergoing an important transformation by means of the Cartabia reform. The aim of the Italian reform is to modernize and simplifying the criminal process as well as increasing its efficiency and transparency. One of the most relevant aspects of the reform is the increase in digitalization in the criminal proceeding, which should reduce the duration of the trial by 25%, as envisaged by the National Recovery and Resilience Plan (PNRR) by 2026.

The PNRR is an Italian project to recover and promote the country's development after the COVID-19 pandemic. It's part of the Next Generation EU (NGEU) program to respond the economically and socially crisis by promoting digitalization and innovation in Europe.

The reform of criminal justice follows a pandemic phenomenon that has contributed to revolutionizing of the judicial system and, consequently, the way of understanding and carrying out the legal profession: the technological knowledge has significantly and rapidly increased by the necessity of the current and new coming professionals in the field into the community of justice system. This will facilitate the application of the reform, also for the increasingly pervasive use of information technology in investigations on smartphones, tablets and personal computers.

The chapter aims to explore the items relating to the Italian reform of criminal justice focusing to technology making changes. The work also intends to reflect on a role of technology in generating the self-reinforcing trust of criminal justice.

The chapter is divided into three principal parts.

The first part is about the Italian reform of criminal justice and analyzes its content. Main objective of the Italian reform is the efficiency. Efficiency of the process and, with it, of justice, to have by the use of advanced technology. If used appropriately, the technology has the potential to increase trust in the rule of law. The technological development raises efficiency rate of justice and reduces its times according the objectives of PNRR. This part defines the efficiency of the justice system not in the meaning of corporate "competitiveness" but aimed either or at eliminating the backlog, or at accelerating it of proceedings, as well as, and above all, in the role of engine and producer of "public value". Efficiency for greater transparency in the exercise of jurisdiction and in its accessibility and, therefore, as an exaltation (and certainly not a debasement) of its qualitative standard. The Italian reform of criminal justice sets out to identify the necessary safeguards to ensure the potential of new technologies.

In the second part, on the other hand, all the technological innovations that lead to the reduction of justice times are first of all analyzed: both in the rules of the criminal trial and in the penal system. The interventions inspired by the needs of technological innovation concern: 1. digitalization and the electronic criminal process; 2. notifications and electronic communications; 3. audiovisual recordings and remote processing. The second part of the chapter also deals with the interaction between offices, lawyers and magistrates, which can only take place through high levels of digitalization and which contributes considerably to the reduction of trial times. To this end, the Process Office (PO) has been set up, whose employees work to ensure that the process is reasonable in length. The realization of this objective can be pursued both through the innovation of personnel organizational models and through a more efficient use of information and communication technologies.

Finally, in the last part the study is focused on the role of technology like better practice to reinforce trust on criminal justice. The work asses the trust to be an indispensable element for each need by criminal justice. Major theme that is described into the chapter is he need to leverage advanced technologies to improve information-sharing and transparency across the criminal justice system. More specifically, the use of advanced technology courts of justice for better, faster results with a highly reduced margin of error. The application of new technology has the potential to make justice system more effective and fairer. Innovative technology, through structured online tools and more flexible, could radically expand citizens' access to justice too. The planned adoption of technology has the potential to make the criminal justice system quicker and more accessible. This part discuss how the criminal justice system can take advantage (and reduce the risks) from the emerging technologies. The use of new technologies is becoming routine, the Italian reform ensures maximizing their potential while minimizing the associated risks (Cartabia Reform" - legislative decree no. 150 of 10 October 2022).

THE NEED FOR AN ITALIAN REFORM OF CRIMINAL JUSTICE

Incipit

Over the years, the need for a reform of criminal justice in Italy has involved more and more scholars and legal practitioners.

Italian criminal justice is going through a serious crisis of efficiency, effectiveness and authority, which puts citizens' trust at risk.

International attention on the performance of a country's judicial system is high.

In this regard, the EU Justice Scoreboard of 2021 and 2022 set the benchmarks for a judicial system in efficiency, quality and independence, which are monitored by the European Rule of Law Mechanism, in order to measure the ethical and democratic dimension together with the economic and financial sustainability of a country[1].

Specifically, the following are evaluated:

a. the duration of judicial proceedings;
b. the amount of arrears and outstanding debts;
c. the quality of justice outcomes.

Italy, following the latest assessments conducted by the European Judicial Systems of the European Commission for the effectiveness of justice of the Council of Europe (CEPEJ)[2], has not given any signs of recovery either in procedures, let alone pending and arrears, showing limitations in organizational factors and office management.

The critical factor of justice "over time" emerges both in the Country Specific Recommendations addressed to our country by the European Commission[3], and in the Doing Business data of the World Bank and WJP Rule of Law Index, processed by the World Justice Project and promoted by the American Bar Association[4].

The vision, which leads to reform, takes the form of strong concerns dictated by the spread of a profound crisis of citizens' trust in justice, in the rule of law and in constitutional democracy, and Italy is showing strong tensions in maintaining the rule of law (Canzio, G., 2021).

An overall reform project of the justice system has become decisive in dealing with dysfunctions and anomalies. This overall reform project comes with the so-called "Cartabia Reform" - legislative decree no. 150 of 10 October 2022 - which takes the name of the Minister of Justice, Marta Cartabia, who proposed it in 2021 and which entered into force on 30 December 2022.

The reform is part of a particular historical moment, following the Covid_19 pandemic, which has - in part - contributed to revolutionizing the functioning of the judicial system and, consequently, how to understand and carry out the legal profession.

In recent years, the rapid and significant development of technological knowledge and skills leads to radically modify the way of operating in judicial systems, through the increasingly pervasive use of information technology in investigations on smartphones, tablets and personal computers.

This innovation is functional to the almost natural transition to a reform process that is capable of implementing an innovative organic design of justice.

This design intends to increase the efficiency of the judicial system, combining the pragmatic approach of the European matrix and the relaunch of constitutional constructs (Marandola, A., 2022).

In fact, the reform is important for Italy, but it is important for the entire European Union (EU).

The EU financially supports the reform project of the Italian criminal justice system, as we will see in the next paragraph. Its success becomes crucial, both for the credibility of the reform projects and for the credibility of the EU itself.

The interest is also high for Italian citizens, to regain confidence in the criminal justice system but also for the economic growth of their country (Ippolito, F., 2018).

Goals

The main goal of the Italian reform is efficiency (Gatta, G. L., 2021).

The realization of the goal of making the process and justice efficient must be achieved through the use of advanced technologies.

When used appropriately, technology has the potential to increase trust in the rule of law.

The Cartabia Reform has set itself the goal of achieving greater respect for constitutional law, for victims of crimes and for defendants, guaranteeing a reasonable duration of the trial and the achievement of the goal established with the PNRR (National Recovery and Resilience Plan), i.e. reducing the average length of criminal trials by 25% by 2026 (Curzio, P., 2022).

According to the goals of the PNRR, technological development raises the rate of efficiency of justice and reduces its time[5].

The PNRR identifies a project, approved in Italy, to recover and promote the country's development after the COVID-19 pandemic. This is an initiative, agreed at the European level, which is part of the Next Generation EU Program (NGEU), which has a duration of six years, from 2021 to 2026, to respond to the crisis generated by the global health emergency. It intends to recover the harmful consequences brought about by the pandemic both economically and socially, by promoting digitalization and innovation.

Specifically, in order to achieve the goals of the PNRR, once the work of the Lattanzi Commission (named after President Giorgio Lattanzi, President Emeritus of the Constitutional Court and President of the Scuola Superiore della Magistratura in Italy, and established by Minister Cartabia) was completed, the enabling law no. 134 of 27 September 2021 was approved first, with the "purpose of simplification, speed and rationalization of the criminal trial, in compliance with the defense guarantees" (Graziano, N., 2021), and then the Legislative Decree no. 150 of 10 October 2022 and the Legislative Decree no. 151 on the Process Office (PO), which identifies the organizational structure to "guarantee the reasonable duration of the process, through the innovation of organizational models and ensuring a more efficient use of information and communication technologies" (Civinini, M. G., 2021; Pagni, I., 2021).

The goal of the reform is to achieve the simplification and rationalization of the procedural justice system, starting from the preliminary investigation phase up to the first instance hearing and the appeal judgments, defining the maximum terms of duration, according to an overall decongesting of the justice' demand and of the number of proceedings (Padovani, T., 2021).

In particular, through the use of technologies, the reform aims to achieve accelerations and simplifications of:

- deeds and documents (which would be digitized),
- communications and notifications (which would become telematics),
- procedures for physical and/or paper attestations and verbalizations (which would be replaced by audiovisual recording and remote processing).

The guideline of the reform - to be found in the reduction of procedural times - would be obtained with "the digitalization of criminal justice" and "the development of the telematic criminal process" (Cananzi, F., 2022).

These goals must be achieved in order to reach an efficient level of justice capable of also contributing to obtaining a "fair trial" (articles 111 of the Constitution[6] and 6 of the ECHR[7]).

The conquest of these goals, with the reform of the regulatory framework of the Italian judicial system, allows participation in the PNRR, through which substantial European funds enter the Italian public economy to facilitate the achievement of the goals of the plan itself.

The Italian criminal justice reform aims to identify the safeguards necessary to ensure the potential of new technologies.

It does not only pass through the "review" of the procedural rules but above all in the organizational arrangement of the work of the judge and the judicial offices (with the introduction of the PO). Through European funding, investments can be made in staff, structures and technologically advanced equipment to improve know-how, and construction and promote digitalization.

Certainly the modernization of the structures and technological innovation reduces the times of justice (Sottani, S., 2021).

In particular, in Italy, digitalization in the criminal process is at a greater level of backwardness than in the civil process. Digitalization alone can contribute significantly to reducing process times. It is no coincidence that it is one of the "central points" of the reform of the criminal trial (Gatta, G. L., 2021).

It is a reform which, in the history of Italian legislative drafting, poses - for the first time - the relationship between technique and criminal procedural law.

The ultimate goal is to achieve the efficiency of the judicial system not in the sense of corporate "competitiveness", but aimed either at eliminating the backlog, speeding up proceedings, as well as, and above all, in the role of the engine and producer of "public value". It is necessary to achieve the efficiency of the judicial system to obtain greater transparency in the exercise of jurisdiction and in its accessibility and, therefore, to raise its quality standard.

The Potential of Technology

Criminal justice in the "digital and telematic field" is the main goal of the Italian reform so that technology demonstrates that it is the means of excellence at the service of man.

This takes place in the basic awareness that technology represents, if properly implemented, an added value. The result of a design and prudent use of the technological means becomes the support par excellence for a human activity to be made easier.

The reform project intends to develop new relationships between criminal procedure and technology, characterized by a stable and organic synergy between them.

The intersection between these two areas, in fact, represents one of the turning points for tackling the streamlining of process times.

Technological development now involves more and more sectors and institutions of our societies, becoming a constant of the entire functioning system of our civil life[8].

Evolution and human progress, dictated by the intensification of applications of advanced technologies, cannot refer to specific sectors.

More modern societies increasingly define an "ecosystem", composed of a connection of elements that make up an organic and functionally unitary whole.

All expressions of law must be considered as elements of a much broader organic and functional entity: our society.

The law cannot remain closed to technological progress.

Even more so when it comes to criminal law: a law that draws the goods worthy of protection from society and that changes with the change of this (Cesari, C., 2019).

The need to combine technology with criminal law arises from the strong awareness that our daily life is permeated by the broadest technological applications. Due to their instrumental nature, all the various applications of advanced technology cannot be traced back to a certain sector but, precisely, to the system of our civil life.

Of course, each sector has its specificities, which must be taken into account. Indeed, the challenge is precisely that of being able to achieve a unitary reform, avoiding the temptation to apply the schemes that belong to one sector or another.

We must not fall into general expressions that would call into question the value attributed, however, to technology, to its potential, to which no area can close the doors, not even the law.

Through the Italian reform, "a dialogue" is sought between law and technology in the name of "doing justice" through every auxiliary tool that can contribute to the end.

The world historically runs towards progress... and historically the progress of science and technology has also coincided with the progress of ethical and social thought, as Benedetto Croce claimed, since the 1940s (Croce, B., 1947).

It is necessary to move away from "a closed world of law", which risks becoming anachronistic, to go so far as to think "of a technology that embodies and is the bearer of the values and guarantees that animate the law and even more so the criminal law, in compliance with the man and technological evolution, which remains the result of the intellectual work of man himself" (Amisano, M., 2022).

REFORM INTERVENTIONS "IN THE FIELD TECHNOLOGY" IN ITALY

The interventions brought about by the Italian reform, as we will see in the paragraph, will produce their effects on the penal procedure.

The ultimate goal is to reduce the time needed for justice by seeking the cornerstone of the reform process in technological innovation.

The aim is to rationalize the digital criminal discipline, in the same way as a more modern procedure, capable of making use of the significant advantages given by technological innovation in terms of efficiency (Gatta, G. L., 2021).

More specifically, the reform will achieve two results in terms of:

1. digitalization of criminal proceedings;
2. interaction between offices, lawyers and judges.

These are two closely connected results, since only in the presence of high levels of digitalization will it be possible to obtain greater communication between individual offices and between them and the lawyers, together with the magistrates. The trial times will benefit from all this.

To this end, a technical-scientific committee for the digitalization of the process is set up at the Italian Ministry of Justice, chaired by the Minister of Justice or his delegate, with consultancy and support functions for technical decisions related to the digitalization of the process.

The reform plan makes use of a three-year plan for the digital transition, which ensures the completion of the transition to digitalization of the criminal process, through the necessary technological equipment of the technical and IT services by the Ministry of Justice, the infrastructural strengthening of the judicial offices as well as the adequate training and professional updating of judicial administration staff, magistrates and lawyers.

In particular, the PO is established, in order to achieve the objective of a reasonable duration, to be pursued both through the innovation of the staff organizational models and through a more efficient use of information and communication technologies. The PO represents the modernization and digitalization of judicial activity, in which interdisciplinary skills are put to good use.

The plan has the ultimate goal of coordinating and planning the unitary management of the necessary interventions in terms of technological resources, infrastructural equipment and training needs, in order to implement innovative technological interventions connected to the digitalization of the process.

Furthermore, the reform provides for the subsidiary value of the analogue in the event of malfunctioning of the IT systems.

This is a key provision, designed to deal with problems of malfunctioning of computer systems, the essential nature of which has been well highlighted by the pandemic experience with the emergency discipline from Covid_19.

Two hypotheses of malfunctioning of the computer systems are envisaged.

The first, which has a general nature, concerns the malfunctions of the domains of the Ministry of Justice, while the second, which has a sectoral nature, concerns those malfunctions that can occur in a single office or, in any case, at a local level.

In both hypotheses, during the entire period of malfunctioning of the computer systems, the reform, in order to overcome the dysfunction, provides for the non-telematic filing of deeds and documents drafted, exceptionally, in the form of an analogical document, postponing the obligation to provide for the rapid conversion of the documents into digital form when the computer systems will resume operation.

In the Criminal Process

Surely the main innovation brought about by the reform is represented by the implementation of the telematic criminal process; in fact, there is a tendency for a greater use of digitalization and information technology for the entire duration of the proceeding (Galgani, B., 2022).

Specifically, in the field of criminal procedure, the interventions involved the entire procedural process: from the preliminary investigations, to the hearing, to the alternative rites, to the trial, to the appeal judgments, up to the criminal execution.

The maximum duration terms for preliminary investigations have been changed and a notification mechanism has been introduced, which always guarantees the safeguarding of investigative secrecy, but which avoids the file stalling, in the interest of victims and suspects.

The notifications must take place electronically, as also happens for the transmission of files between the judicial offices, in order to reduce the so-called crossing times between the procedural phases, which can last for months or years.

The filters for the celebration of the processes are increased, as happens, for example, by allowing the use of audio and visual recordings, which allow remote participation in the proceedings or the hearing. Furthermore, in the case of past events, audiovisual recordings and remote processing can always be used, in place of paper reports and documents that come from paper archives, which are cumbersome to retrieve and reproduce quickly and functionally.

Specifically, as regards the criminal trial, the interventions inspired by the needs of technological innovation concern:

1. digitalization and the electronic criminal process;
2. notifications and telematic communications;
3. audiovisual recordings and remote processing.

Digitalization and Telematic Criminal Process

The first intervention aims to make a digital and telematic transition of the criminal process to drastically reduce the times.

The law that allows the entry of technological innovation into justice gives rise to the unfolding of the opportunity that technology itself represents.

The insufficient level of digitalization of documents and computerization of procedures is one of the causes of the slowness of the Italian criminal process.

The procedural process still provides for the physical transfer of large folders from one office to another.

With touch-only digitalization on the screen, the transfer would take place electronically, avoiding movement of paper files and giving the individual magistrate and chancellery staff the opportunity to view the documents by accessing the system from their workstation.

It would also increase the communication capacity between individual offices.

To do this, both investments (which can be achieved with the PNRR) in technologically advanced tools and technically trained staff are required, as well as regulatory interventions that must consider the preparation and conservation of procedural deeds and documents in digital format together with telematic methods for the filing of deeds and documents, for communications and notifications, in every state and degree of the proceeding (as well as of particularly relevant aspects such as the guarantees relating to the certainty of the filing and notification of the documents, their secrecy, and the possible malfunctioning of the IT systems).

From the reform we recall the exemplary steps of the applications of advanced technologies:

a. the digitized criminal procedural document;
b. electronic filing;
c. the electronic file.

First of all, the criminal procedural act emerges and this must originate and be kept in digital mode, as an "ICT document".

Then, the reform provides for the use of electronic methods for the electronic filing of deeds, briefs, requests and documents at every stage and level of the proceeding.

Finally, the training, conservation, updating and transmission of IT files is considered.

Where possible (due to their nature or for specific procedural needs), the conversion without delay of the residual analogical deeds and documents into digital form is also envisaged.

The digitalization of the documents of the criminal proceeding is necessary in all phases of the proceeding, starting from the registration of the crime report up to the executive phase.

Telematic Notifications and Communications

The second intervention concerns the notifications and communications that must be made electronically.

The use of advanced technologies in the modernization of the discipline of notifications reduces the significant waste of time for the effective knowledge of the process documents.

Thanks to the reform, telematic procedures become the ordinary means which the secretariat or chancellery must use to proceed with the notifications and communications of the documents.

From the first contact with the prosecuting authority, there is an obligation for the defendant who is not detained, to also indicate the telephone and electronic numbers available to him.

Furthermore, it is envisaged that he has the right to declare domicile for the purposes of notifications also at a suitable electronic address.

Furthermore, it is envisaged that all notifications to the defendant who are not detained, which are subsequent to the first and different to the one with which he was summoned for trial, are normally carried out by delivery to the defender, also by certified e-mail. The reform, without prejudice to the priority accorded to the electronic notification method, admits subsidiary forms of notification corresponding to the traditional ones in absolutely foreseen hypotheses (in the digital transition regime).

Audiovisual Recordings and Remote Processing

The third area of interventions recovers the audio and visual recordings, as forms of technological innovation, allowing remote participation in the proceedings or in the hearing (as solutions to the impediments, for example, caused by the past pandemic emergency).

Key values of the criminal process, such as orality and immediacy, can be preserved by audio and video recordings which can also ensure significant time savings. For example, in the event of a postponement of the hearing for the examination of a witness, who is a resident of hundreds of kilometers from the court, the testimony could be taken remotely. Or, instead of examining a witness years later, authorizing the reading of the summary information of the witnesses, included in the deeds, it would be much more effective to save time to listen to or see the recordings made at the time.

Furthermore, the use of audiovisual recordings and remote processing ensure a more accurate representation of the act than what happens with writing.

Specifically, two results can be achieved.

On the one hand, it is possible to guarantee control over the respect of the fundamental rights of the subjects involved in the act (especially in the case of acts carried out during investigations and interrogations outside the hearing).

On the other hand, it is possible to allow that procedural document to be listened to or reviewed again in all cases in which repetition is not possible (which is relevant both for investigative acts and for investigative acts carried out in a probative incident or trial).

The reform provides for the necessary adaptation of the judicial infrastructures to this end through, on the one hand, the acquisition and provision of technologically advanced equipment in the judicial offices, on the other, a regulatory intervention which:

a. allows audiovisual recording as a further form of documentation of the interrogation, except for the contingent unavailability of the necessary tools or technical auxiliaries;
b. recognizes the cases in which at least the audio recording of the statements made by the people informed on the facts must be provided, without the obligation of transcription;
c. identifies the cases in which, with the consent of the parties, participation in the proceedings or in the hearing can take place remotely.

In practice, the use of audiovisual recordings in the process, with an appropriate investment program, will be essential to modernize procedural communication, in order to encourage "direct and continuous personal contact" to better understand each other during the process. To this end, the orality of the process can be completely revitalized by the simplicity and practicality of remote audiovisual communication systems.

THE ROLE OF TECHNOLOGY FOR ITALIAN CRIMINAL JUSTICE

The Italian reform of criminal justice pursues the aim of modernizing the criminal procedure, through the enhancement of technologies at the service of carrying out more effective and accurate acts.

There are three lines of intervention that demonstrate the role played by technology in achieving the goals of transparency, trust, effectiveness and efficiency.

The first focuses on the "flagship" of the telematic criminal process, reviewing the formal and communicative requirements of the criminal act and finally assigning it a dimension of privileged digital birth (Delvecchio, F., 2022).

The importance of the transition from the physical-paper dimension to the digital one is irrefutable: the replacement of paper folders with telematic files can really take place if the criminal act is born digital (Galgani, B., 2021).

The creation and conservation of procedural documents in digital format guarantee their authenticity and integrity, legibility, easy availability and, where required by law, secrecy.

The reform, with this intervention, promotes a solid regulation, which considers the new technological tools, in order to revisit the formal requirements of the deed in a technological key.

The jurist will have to work hand in hand with technicians, computer scientists and management engineers, so that "the digital model" fits perfectly "with the legal model", so as to always be an expression of the "rule of law".

"The digital model" could be expressed through an "IT scheme of the deed", to be clear, concise and standardized, according to uniform editorial criteria, so as to make the combination of IT technologies and the judicial function truly virtuous.

Digitalization would thus allow, not only the elevation of the quality of documents in general, but also a better "computer processing" of the same, with significant repercussions, for example, in terms of functionality of OCR systems (Optical Character Recognition) and database search.

In this sense, the Council of Europe, with the Saturn Guidelines for Judicial Time Management (2021) and the Concept note on the preparation of a backlog reduction tool (2022), recommend a generalized use of new technologies "within the courts " and, specifically, they clearly invite the elaboration of "standard electronic templates", which are functional to the drafting of decisions by both the magistrate and his collaborators[9].

Procedural documents in digital format would help cross-border judicial cooperation, because they can be easily translated and classified in interoperable computer archives[10].

The reform provides for the use of electronic methods also for the filing of deeds and documents and for notifications and communications. However in a transitional adjustment regime, the use of non-telematic methods is limited to completely exceptional cases. This means that the transition to digital, in its broadest sense, must be governed with extreme care, in order not to prejudge the unity of the ritual, as happened in Italy in the first period of the COVID-19 health emergency (Ruggieri, F., 2020).

The reform aspires to a corpus of legislation capable of fully regulating the telematic criminal process, in order to allow rapid adaptation to the technological standards gradually established at a supranational level.

The second line of action concerns the regulation of telematic notifications, which provide for providing the proceeding authority with the mobile phone number and email address available from the first contact, as well as the option to declare domicile at a suitable electronic address.

Finally, the third line of intervention of the reforming project questions the documentary procedure of the deeds which takes place through the drafting of the minutes, proposing the use of more reliable documentation techniques from the point of view of representative fidelity, such as phonographic and audiovisual reproduction.

Remote processing allows, through videoconferencing systems and IT platforms, to carry out procedural activities with subjects who co-participate from different physical places (as in virtual hearing, in which none of the procedural protagonists share a common physical space). The higher aim is to seek, with the help of technology, the possibility of representing "other" spaces (compared to the physical ones), capable of giving disposition to reality and transmitting the essential values of the jurisdiction through different icons (Garapon, A., 2021).

The Cartabia reform, on these assumptions for intervention, lays the foundations for a transition of the penal rite on technologically oriented tracks.

The main idea is to exploit the potential offered by our life, characterized and pervaded by all the different forms and modalities of advanced technology.

The Italian reform intends to guarantee the maximization of the technological potential, minimizing the risks associated with it.

On the other hand, Richard Susskind has long supported the undisputed importance of the use of new technologies in the process, going so far as to assert that with them all the problems related to access to justice at a global level would be solved (Susskind, R., 2019).

For Transparency

The main theme of the chapter is the need to leverage advanced technologies to improve information sharing and transparency throughout the criminal justice system.

Digitalization, on which the most robust assumption of change in the criminal procedure is based, lays its foundations in digital writing. Digital writing is mathematical writing and, as such, allows the dematerialization of documents, whether textual, audio or video. Not only.

It gives rise to a fast, almost impromptu communication between sender and recipient. It is also the premise of remote communication and remote work.

With digitalization, it is possible to structure archives of unlimited scope on memories and servers that occupy ever smaller and smaller spaces.

The digitized data collected can be shared promptly and become accessible to a plurality of users (the data on the cloud or via a network can be used further and give rise to various applications).

The creation of digital platforms should be understood as an institutional action designed for the future.

In the justice sector, all processes and mechanisms of participation, inclusiveness and transparency must be integrated from the outset.

In the context of criminal justice, these characteristics offer solutions in more than one field. They optimize document management.

Overall, they respond to the need to make the law transparent and accessible and to recover margins for its certainty.

Fort Trust

This chapter focuses on the role of technology as a best practice in building trust in criminal justice.

Trust is an indispensable element for every requirement of criminal justice.

We need justice accessible to all, so that no one is left out.

The digitalization of the criminal process and the strong interaction between offices, lawyers and magistrates determine the effectiveness and efficiency of the public governance systems.

In particular, the efficiency of the justice system allows the citizen to be animated by a feeling of trust in the institutions and government apparatuses of the State, fueling the awareness that the rights of each of them can receive rapid, efficient and as effective protection as possible.

The changes that are caused by technological progress and that are adopted in criminal justice create the certainty that the institutions and apparatuses of the country's government are always well prepared for changes and improvements in their quality standards.

The transition from a perspective centered on digital technology, as a rewriting of existing procedures in a context of dematerialization, to a perspective that makes digital technology a means through which to transform work processes and to increase the connection between operational units of institutions and between the latter and the citizen and businesses, represents the turning point.

The "transformation" here must be taken in a literal and profound sense.

In fact, the term "transformation" refers to the possibility of enhancing an idea of sustainable quality which includes efficiency and which at the same time considers the effectiveness of the protection of rights and the provision of services as a fundamental element.

It is a "transformation" designed not only to recover trust, but above all to increase it, because the quality of justice is achieved not only in a sectoral sense, but also in the sense of overarching function in the way in which the rules that decline rights and prerogatives are effectively implemented and protected on the territory.

For Effectiveness and Efficiency

The use of advanced technologies guarantees better and faster results with an extremely small margin of error and has the potential to make the criminal justice system faster and more accessible, in order to be more effective and fair.

Innovative technology, through structured and more flexible online tools, radically expands citizens' access to justice.

On the side of the citizen, technology promotes human progress. Digital is seen as a tool that multiplies devices in the hands of citizens to assert their rights.

These potentials are often accompanied by advantages in terms of efficiency, i.e. improvement of the cost-benefit ratio in various procedural areas.

The use of technologically advanced instrumentation in criminal proceedings, in fact, guarantees a significant saving of resources, which originates from two different points of view.

On the one hand, technology is increasingly widespread and accessible, even economically, which ensures the presence on the market of highly advanced products at low or in any case reasonable costs, which favor their use even if the state budget is suffering.

On the other hand, the use of technology can significantly reduce process costs, as happens, for example, if the hearings are held remotely, electronically.

The remote celebration of trials makes it possible to avoid not only the risks, but also the costs of transferring the defendants from the place of detention to the venue where the trial is being held.

The same is true in the case of electronic surveillance, which is useful for guaranteeing the best control over the territory of subjects subjected to custody measures, also supporting the reduction of prison overcrowding, which involves excessive maintenance costs, as well as controversial conditions for expiating the sentence.

Certainly, a further reflection to be made concerns the positive implications deriving from the transition to digital, both in terms of efficiency and effectiveness.

For example, a positive implication concerns the ease and the speed of searching and consulting the virtual file compared to the paper file, determined by the possibility of access through a folder available on the computer desktop, organized into specific sub-folders - depending on the procedural acts performed - and which can also be found using the "text search" function.

The advantages of making work easier for justice officials are beyond any doubt, but there are also advantages for private citizens, who could easily and quickly find and dispose of documents in their name as well as their lawyers, in representing their rights.

The benefits in terms of saving time would also be enjoyed by the magistrate, who, in drafting his own provisions, could easily find entire portions of deeds that would not need to be transcribed again.

Alongside this last aspect, digitalization would allow the magistrate to operate at any time and in any place, having only to connect to a telematic station, which would allow for multiple files to be consulted even simultaneously. This latter function would benefit not only the study of files made up of multiple folders, but would also represent, at the same time, a significant novelty in allowing a panel of judges to work simultaneously on the same file, which would otherwise be impracticable if on paper.

Furthermore, the technological equipment would limit physical access to judicial offices to cases of strict necessity, thanks to the potential of a "virtual counter", capable of conveying the requests of the lawyers, who could also connect via a special app installed on their mobile devices (smartphones, tablets, etc.).

The work of computerization of the workflow (Delvecchio, F., 2021), therefore, would produce greater efficiency in the dialogue with users, confirming the principle whereby the increase in digitalization levels results in more efficient interaction between individuals, offices and lawyers, as well as undoubted advantages organizational structures for the judicial offices themselves.

The strength of modest and simple digital innovations, such as those exemplified, would significantly improve the work and communication processes of judicial offices, revealing the results in terms of efficiency that a virtual organization of communication is capable of producing.

Ultimately, the criminal justice system would be more effective and efficient in functioning with the aid of adequate computerized equipment, in compliance with a more correct allocation of resources, because they are to the advantage of the system as a whole.

CONCLUSION

The reform of the Italian justice system falls within those reforms whose impact is not only that of investing in a sectoral sense but rather that of catalyzing technological progress to improve all the structures that are necessary for carrying out the functions of the country's governance.

In fact, Italy has reformed the criminal justice system to create a virtuous link between technological innovations, at the service of public governance, and the evolution of society.

The Italian justice policy is part of the EU justice policy, of which Italy is a part, which is a young policy and, as such, is more inclined to all programs of modernization and innovation.

Europe was born as an economic entity: the European Economic Community.

Within the recommendations on justice policy and the rule of law, which the European Commission is providing to the Member States, the recommendations made to Italy on the reforms of the judicial system are recommendations that come from economic policy and refer to the potential economic growth of the countries and the great economic potential of Italy[11].

The issue of effectiveness is at the heart of these recommendations. The quality of justice, in this context, is seen as a factor of economic growth.

This explains many of the recommendations that have been made to Italy and also the self-obligations of the Italian government related to the recovery plan through the use of the most advanced technologies.

Italy's recovery plan reflects an operational program that exploits the applications of advanced technology also in the Italian judicial system.

It is probably correct to say that justice reform in Italy is the largest justice reform program that Europe has ever seen, and perhaps the world has ever seen, in terms of amounts of EU funding.

The challenge is accomplished with the help of technologies to achieve "public value": judicial resources are used effectively to innovate, recovering and strengthening the conditions of trust of citizens in the criminal justice system.

REFERENCES

Amisano, M., (2022). Prevedere -e non predire- attraverso gli algoritmi e le loro insidie. *Archivio Penale, 2.*

Cananzi, F. (2022). Dall'emergenza alla legge delega al governo: verso un processo penale veramente telematico? *Sistema penale, 3.* https://www.sistemapenale.it/pdf_contenuti/1648540299_cananzi-2022a-processo-penale-telematico-emergenza-legge-delega.pdf

Canzio, G. (2021). *Le linee del modello "Cartabia"*. Una prima lettura, in Sistema penale. https://www.sistemapenale.it/it/opinioni/canzio-riforma-cartabia-prima-lettura?out=print

Cesari, C., (2019). *L'impatto delle nuove tecnologie sulla giustizia penale – un orizzonte denso di incognite.* file:///C:/Users/Laptop02%20Unical/Downloads/Dialnet-Editoriale-7169241%20(1).pdf

Civinini, M. G. (2021). *Il "nuovo ufficio per il processo" tra riforma della giustizia e PNRR. Che sia la volta buona!* Questione Giustizia. www.questionegiustizia.it/rivista/articolo/il-nuovo-ufficio-per-il-processo-tra-riforma-della-giustizia-e-pnrr-che-sia-la-volta-buona

Communication from the Commission to the European Parliament. (n.d.). *2030 Digital Compass: the European way for the Digital Decade*. https://eur-lex.europa.eu/legal-content/EN/TXT/HTML/?uri=CELEX:52021DC0118&rid=4

Council Recommendation on the 2020 National Reform Programme of Italy and delivering a Council opinion on the 2020 Stability Programme of Italy, COM (2020) 512 final, del 20 maggio 2020, cons. 24.

Croce, B. (1947). Progresso tecnico e morale, Corriere della Sera, 21 settembre

Curzio, P. (2022). Relazione sull'amministrazione della giustizia nell'anno 2021. Considerazioni finali, Corte Suprema di Cassazione, Roma, 21 gennaio, https://www.cortedicassazione.it/cassazione-resources/resources/cms/documents/Cassazione_Relazione_2022.pdf

Delvecchio, F., (2021). L'informatizzazione della giustizia penale, in Diritto penale contemporáneo. *Rivista trimestrale, 2.*

Delvecchio, F., (2022). Prospettive e tempi della digitalizzazione del proceso. *Processo penale e giustizia, Fascicolo, 1.*

European judicial systems – CEPEJ Evaluation report. (2022). https://www.coe.int/en/web/cepej/special-file-report-european-judicial-systems-cepej-evaluation-report-2022-evaluation-cycle-2020-data-?p_p_id=56_INSTANCE_Pec933yX8xS5&p_p_lifecycle=0&p_p_state=normal&p_p_mode=view&p_p_col_id=column-4&p_p_col_pos=1&p_p_col_count=2

European Parliamentary Research Service. (2022). *Digitalising cross-border judicial cooperation.* https://www.europarl.europa.eu/RegData/etudes/BRIE/2022/739256/EPRS_BRI(2022)739256_EN.pdf

Galgani, B. (2021). *Digitalizzazione e processo penale: riflessioni sul dover essere di una nuova "cartografia".* disCRIMEN, fascicolo 2. https://discrimen.it/wp-content/uploads/disCrimen-2-2021.pdf

Galgani, B. (2022). *Il processo penale in "ambiente" digitale: ragioni e (ragionevoli) speranze.* Questione Giustizia. https://www.questionegiustizia.it/articolo/il-processo-penale-in-ambiente-digitale-ragioni-e-ragionevoli-speranze

Garapon, A. (2021). *La despazializzazione della giustizia.* Mimesis.

Gatta, G. L. (2021). *Riforma della giustizia penale: contesto, obiettivi e linee di fondo della "legge Cartabia".* Sistema penale. https://www.sistemapenale.it/it/scheda/gatta-legge-2021-134-delega-riforma-giustizia-penale-cartabia

Graziano, N., (2021). Investimenti e riforme indirizzate a "tagliare" la durata dei giudizi. L'Ufficio del processo, in Guida al Diritto, 26 giugno, n. 25.

Ippolito, F. (2018). *Recuperare la fiducia e non rincorrere il consenso*. Questione giustizia. https://www.questionegiustizia.it/rivista/articolo/recuperare-la-fiducia-e-non-rincorrere-il-consenso_597.php

Marandola, A. (2022). "Riforma Cartabia" e rito penale. La Legge Delega tra impegni europei e scelte valoriali, Cedam, Padova.

Ministry of Justice. (n.d.). *Implementation of PNRR measures.* file:///C:/Users/Laptop02%20Unical/Downloads/12_PNRR_Giustizia.pdf

Padovani, T., (2021). La "sottile linea rossa" della riforma condizionata dai nodi organizzativi. *Guida al Diritto, 40.*

Pagni, I. (2021). *L'Ufficio per il processo: l'occasione per una (ulteriore) osmosi virtuosa tra teoria e pratica, con uno sguardo alle riforme processuali in cantiere.* Questione Giustizia. www.questionegiustizia.it/articolo/l-ufficio-per-il-processo

Ruggieri, F. (2020). *Il processo penale al tempo del Covid-19: modelli alternativi di gestione della crisi*. La legislazione penale. https://www.lalegislazionepenale.eu/wp-content/uploads/2020/05/Ruggieri-sistema-delle-fonti-1.pdf

Sottani, S. (2021). *Le norme del PNRR in tema di giustizia: opportunità e nuovi problema*. Questione Giustizia. www.questionegiustizia.it/articolo/le-norme-del-pnrr-in-tema-di-giustizia-opportunita-e-nuovi-problemi

Susskind, R. (2019). Online court and the future of Justice. Oxford University Press.

ENDNOTES

1 The 2021 EU justice scoreboard in https://commission.europa.eu/system/files/2021-07/eu_justice_scoreboard_2021.pdf; The 2022 EU justice scoreboard in https://commission.europa.eu/system/files/2022-05/eu_justice_scoreboard_2022.pdf

2 European judicial systems – CEPEJ Evaluation report – 2022 in https://www.coe.int/en/web/cepej/special-file-report-european-judicial-systems-cepej-evaluation-report-2022-evaluation-cycle-2020-data-?p_p_id=56_INSTANCE_Pec933yX8xS5&p_p_lifecycle=0&p_p_state=normal&p_p_mode=view&p_p_col_id=column-4&p_p_col_pos=1&p_p_col_count=2

3 Country specific recommendations in https://ec.europa.eu/economy_finance/country-specific-recommendations-database/

4 Doing business 2008 in https://www.doingbusiness.org/content/dam/doingBusiness/media/Annual-Reports/English/DB08-FullReport.pdf

5 Ministry of justice. Implementation of PNRR measures, in file:///C:/Users/Laptop02%20Unical/Downloads/12_PNRR_Giustizia.pdf

6 The art. 111 of the Italian Constitution in the 1st paragraph states that the exercise of jurisdiction miust take place in compliance with the principles of due process regulated by law.

7 The art. 6 of the ECHR (European Convention for the Protection of Human Rights and Foundamental Freedoms) in § 1 deals with the iussue of a fair trial and a reasonable duration.

8 Communication from the Commission to the European parliament. The council, the European economic and social committee and the committee of the regions. 2030 Digital Compass: the European way for the Digital Decade in https://eur-lex.europa.eu/legal-content/EN/TXT/HTML/?uri=CELEX:52021DC0118&rid=4

9 Revised Saturn Guidelines for judicial time management (4th revision) il cui testo è reperibile all'indirizzo https://rm.coe.int/cepej-2021-13-en-revised-saturn-guidelines-4th-revision/1680a4cf81 (lett. A, punto 3, p. 8).

10 European Parliamentary Research Service, Digitalising cross-border judicial cooperationc, December 2022, https://www.europarl.europa.eu/RegData/etudes/BRIE/2022/739256/EPRS_BRI(2022)739256_EN.pdf

11 Council Recommendation on the 2020 National Reform Programme of Italy and delivering a Council opinion on the 2020 Stability Programme of Italy, COM(2020) 512 final, del 20 maggio 2020, cons. 24.

Chapter 8
Creating a Data and Technology-Enhanced Approach to Police Social Service Issues:
A Planning Model

Caroline Conrad Ban
https://orcid.org/0000-0002-2377-8072
Valparaiso University, USA

John G. McNutt
https://orcid.org/0000-0002-5172-9163
University of Delaware, USA

ABSTRACT

The landscape of law enforcement is changing. Mental health needs are on the rise, and the vast majority of law enforcement calls for service are already related to social issues. Public safety today requires greater attention to justice, innovation, and new technology. It also requires additional professionals, like social workers, for social service delivery. The future of public safety is clearly a serious situation for police and emergency services organizations and their professional employees. This chapter will (1) discuss the situation that communities and organizations face, (2) identify some of the alternative strategies that can be employed, and (3) provide a process planning model for creating new approaches on the ground in communities. This model emphasizes a data-informed and collaborative approach to the issue.

DOI: 10.4018/978-1-6684-8569-9.ch008

Public safety organizations face a challenging environment as we enter the third decade of the millennium. While these organizations face new criminal activity challenges, the social service caseload of police departments has grown dramatically (Patterson, 2008; Lane, 2019; Marsden, Nigam, Lemetyinen & Edge, 2020; Shore & Lavoie, 2019). This happens at a time when pressure on public organizations of all stripes is under intense scrutiny.

In June of 2023, the bipartisan United States Conference of Mayors published a report entitled, *The Mental Health Crisis in American Cities and Their Responses to It,* showing an overwhelming rise in mental health needs and insufficient resources in 117 cities across 36 states. Of those cities surveyed, "97 percent said requests for mental health services increased in their city over the last two years," and "88 percent said they do not have adequate access to the mental health resources needed to address this crisis" (p. 3). Additionally, 71% of cities reported that residents lacked access to sufficient mental health resources (The United States Conference of Mayors, 2023). The majority of cities cited substance use, homelessness, housing, and economic needs as chief concerns, all of which have been further exacerbated by the COVID-19 pandemic. This reflects a national and global crisis in mental health (Gramlich, 2023; Pinals, et al., 2020).

Although the Conference of Mayors' report is new, the idea that police officers are often tasked with social needs is not; Patterson (2008) reported that up to 80% of police calls are related to social service needs, not active crimes. This has long been true, especially in smaller cities where resources are scarce and rarely available on a 24/7 basis. This makes the police the social agency of last resort. Police officers are often faced with the prospect of dealing with poverty or social needs situations as criminal matters. An arrest is a more likely option when insufficient community resources are available. This is not often an ideal response and one that adds to the burden on local correctional institutions. Even in situations where the police decide to handle the situation without an arrest, the options are limited.

Increased mental health needs require new innovations in public service delivery, and social workers are now part of the response (Lamin & Teboh, 2016; Patterson & Swan, 2019; Toft et al., 2021). According to the United States Conference of Mayors's report (2023), cities reported that "79 percent are using co-responder teams composed of police officers and mental health [professionals] or social workers" and "43 percent are routing calls only to mental health or social workers in certain situations" (p. 20). Further, a majority of cities reported that they transport people with behavioral health crises to mental health or social services facilities other than jails.

Police Social Work is one intervention that can address this situation (Giwa, 2018; Lamin & Teboh, 2016; Leipsiger & Hillman 2020; Patterson, 2008; Patterson & Swan, 2019; Treger, 1975, 1980). This intervention involves adding trained social workers to law enforcement organizations. Police social workers since the early 20th

century have sought to address social needs in lieu of arrest (Wells, 1915), and the field grew in the 1970s with the development of Harvey Treger's (1980) Police-Social Work Model (Patterson, 2021). There is a substantial body of research that documents the effectiveness of social work interventions in many settings, including crisis intervention, mental health, family violence, and so forth (see O'Hare, 2020; 2019; Drisko & Grady, 2019. Wike et al 2016; Thyer & Myers, 2011).

In addition to police social work, various interdisciplinary mental health interventions have emerged, including co-response teams, Crisis Intervention Teams, and Mobile Crisis Response Teams.

While these mental health interventions will help ease the issues that police departments face, they cannot be effective unless the relationships between police departments and their communities are functional (Lamin & Teboh, 2016 DeVylder, 2022). There are a number of trust-building interventions that can help in that regard, and these are prerequisites for police social work and other mental health interventions. These include accreditation, accountability dashboards, body-worn cameras, and review committees.

The landscape of law enforcement is changing. Public safety today requires greater attention to social justice, new technology, and skills for social service interaction in the face of rising mental health needs. This is clearly a serious situation for police and emergency services organizations and their professional employees. The social and political environment is also changing.

This chapter will (1) discuss the situation that communities and organizations face, (2) identify some of the alternative strategies that can be employed and (3) provide a process planning model for creating new approaches on the ground in communities. Our approach emphasizes a data-informed and collaborative approach to the issue.

ISSUES AND PERSPECTIVES: THE SITUATION WE FACE

The COVID-19 pandemic certainly has contributed to higher mental health needs (Gramlich, 2023), but ongoing community and law-enforcement conflicts and new technologies are also spurring changes. Law enforcement was created to protect and serve, a necessary function of modern society, but who and how it protects has created conflict since its inception, especially for different populations (Wilson et al. 2023; Lamin & Teboh, 2016). Members of BIPOC groups experience disproportionately high rates of police contact and higher rates of excessive use of force with police compared with their White counterparts (DeVylder, 2022; Machado & Lugo, 2021). African American men especially experience negative phenomenological impacts after the shooting of unarmed Black men by police (Matthews & Lyons, 2015). Additionally, an estimated fifty percent of people killed by police are people with mental health issues who pose no immediate threat (Ellsworth et al., 2020; National Association of Social Workers, 2018). Not all populations have the same lived experience.

The wide availability of Smartphone cameras, social media, and Body-Worn Cameras are now more readily able to highlight gross abuses (Toft et al., 2021). Increased technology has improved transparency, but in the case of body cameras, that is only if it is released and uncensored, a major criticism (Umansky & Farooq, 2023).

The rising mental health crises facing people, combined with the ongoing law enforcement-community conflict, have increased pressure on individual officers. Policing has always been a stressful job (Syed et al., 2020: Drew & Martin, 2021), but current conditions have greatly aggravated the situation; one example is that police officers are more likely to die by suicide than in the line of duty (Miller, 2005). President Obama's Task Force on 21st Century Policing (2015) identified officer wellness as one of its six pillars for police reform, but awareness is not the same as acceptance. Mental health issues among police are still highly stigmatized.

To address concerns, there are practical needs for both strategies and a new model to address justice issues and mental health needs. With the right partnerships, there is an opportunity for social workers and other mental health professionals to provide services to community members and officers. Increased data, technology, and assessment in law enforcement and social services can improve transparency and efficiency. Community context, self-determination, and the optimal size of police agencies are worth exploring. Embedded social workers and increasing mobile mental health crisis response teams are necessary to respond to higher mental health needs. Citizen engagement and responsiveness are also essential. Together, these changes support a new policing model for communities and practitioners.

ALTERNATIVE STRATEGIES: EMPLOYING DATA, TECHNOLOGY, AND OVERSIGHT IN LAW ENFORCEMENT AND SOCIAL SERVICES

This section is divided into two parts. The first part will discuss current trends in mental health interventions, police social workers, mobile crisis response teams, and training for police officers. The second part will discuss community-based policing strategies and techniques to build relationships and trust with the community as a prerequisite for successful mental health intervention.

EMBEDDED POLICE SOCIAL WORKERS AND MOBILE CRISIS RESPONSE TEAMS

The use of embedded Police Social Workers (PSWs) and social workers outside of the police system is recently increasing and is an important trend for the future of policing (Lamin & Teboh, 2016; Patterson, 2008; Patterson & Swan, 2019; Ban & Riordan, 2023; U.S. Mayor's Conference of Cities, 2023). The scope of the role and impact of embedded police social workers is still being explored but provides a promising approach for micro and macro community intervention (Lamin & Teboh, 2016; Patterson, 2004; Patterson & Swan, 2019; Treger 1975, 1980, Ban & Riordan, 2023). Mobile Crisis Response Teams (MCRTs), external to the police departments, also present another opportunity for increased mental health resources available to people experiencing a mental health crisis outside of the police department (Ghelani, 2022). Relationships, technology, ethics, and interactions between Police Social Workers, MCRTs, police, and the community are also important for future exploration as this field of practice grows.

Mobile Crisis Response Teams (MCRTs) employ social workers or mental health professionals outside a police department and often coordinate with a police department (Balfour et al., 2022; Ghelani, 2022). There are pros and cons to MCRTs. These teams are usually seen as more independent because they do not work for the police department. In some locations, this level of separation may add another level of legitimacy for the community. In some places like Crisis Assistance Helping Out on The Streets (CAHOOTS) in Oregon, mental health crisis calls coming through dispatch are routed directly to social workers and mental health professionals, bypassing the police department (Balfour et al., 2022). This kind of system, of course, requires an increased level of training for dispatchers to know how to divert crisis calls correctly. This is a need that seems to be recognized by municipal leaders as well, as 69% of cities reported that they are ". . . improving how 911 dispatchers respond to and direct behavioral crisis calls" (The United States Conference of Mayors, 2023, p. 20).

Further research is needed on MCRTs, and there are limitations to this model. First, strong communication and collaboration are needed between teams and law enforcement, especially since these entities are not housed in the same location (Ghelani, 2022). Cases that fall ambiguously between law enforcement and social services, such as domestic violence calls, must receive appropriate response and care. Secondly, while MCRTs must have legitimacy with the community, they must also be accepted by law enforcement so that officers are willing to transfer appropriate cases to them. Law enforcement may be reluctant to seek help if MCRTs are not fully staffed or there is a lack of understanding between the two entities (Lamin & Teboh, 2016). In Lamin and Teboh's (2016) qualitative study with officers from 40 police departments in Minnesota, several respondents hesitated about being required to be paired with a social worker. Relationships between police and hospitals are important to prevent clients from falling through the cracks or avoid unnecessary repeat contact with police (Ban & Riordan, 2023).

While Toft and colleagues (2021) highlight many of the complex challenges between social work and policing, a growing number of police departments and communities are supportive of Police Social Workers (PSWs) (Lamin & Teboh, 2016; Giwa, 2018; Leipsiger & Hillman 2020; Logan et al., 2023; Patterson & Swan, 2019; Ban & Riordan, 2023; Sherraden, 2020, U.S. Mayor's Conference of Cities, 2023). PSWs have been widespread since the early 1900s (Roberts, 2007; Lamin & Teboh, 2016; Patterson & Swan, 2019; Wells, 1915) and received a resurgence in the 1970s-80s when the Police-Social Work Model was developed by Treger (1980). In this model, social workers are hired by police departments and as second responders to provide case management during or after an incident. Police-Social Workers need strong clinical skills and must be involved in group (mezzo) and community, organization, or policy-level (macro) work (Giwa, 2018; Ban & Riordan, 2023; Balfour et al., 2022; Burgett & Ban, 2022).

While community context and history may determine that a police social work model may not be right for every community, this approach has several advantages. First, by location, PSWs have more access to law enforcement and, thus, are more likely to interface with clients at the edge of the criminal justice system. Secondly, by working more closely with law enforcement, Police-Social Workers have a fuller picture of broader patterns of community needs or issues for reform within the law enforcement system (Burgett & Ban, 2022). The Police-Social Workers will also likely have more readily available access to police department data, technology, and police leadership.

Police Social Workers show some preliminary positive outcomes. Lamin and Teboh (2016) found that 69% of study participants thought that Police-Social Workers would reduce fatalities and increase police-community trust, and they argue that the role of Police-Social Workers has been unnecessarily minimized. In a case study, Ban and Riordan (2023) found that the Police-Social Worker was almost twice as efficient in dealing with mental health calls than police officers (compared to Short et al., 2014), diverted clients from the criminal justice system, and contributed to a shift in culture (Burgett & Ban, 2022). Police Social Workers also carry the clout of the police, which can be used strategically and skillfully for organizing social service agencies (McNutt & Ban, 2023; Ban & Riordan, 2023). This access helps Police Social Workers deliver better preventative services on a micro and macro level.

Police Social Workers are strategically positioned to help create or promote "Continuum of Care" systems designed to share case management data across public and private/non-profit agencies for better client services (Ban & Riordan, 2023). Housing, mental health, and substance use issues are often at the center of 911 calls (The United States Conference of Mayors, 2023; Ban & Riordan, 2023).

There are, of course, considerations in the Police-Social Worker hiring and placement process including, (1) ensuring that the worker maintains professional memberships and a solid grounding in social work values and ethics (Logan et al., 2023; Ban & Riordan, 2023), (2) prioritizing adequate professional continuing education (Logan et al., 2023) and (3) making available social work supervision (Logan et al., 2023). Differences in practice situations should be considered. Case records, for example, should be kept in locked and confidential files outside the usual police record. Social workers also need policy protection. Finally, PSWs need to navigate a potential clash of ethics, professional nomenclature, and practices (Logan et al., 2023). This is not easy work, but the results of interprofessional collaboration, if done well, can have rich and life-changing impacts on clients.

An ideal approach might be one that employs both Police-Social Workers and MCRTs, but more research is needed to determine the efficiency and effectiveness of this model in meeting community needs. Dispatch training also needs to be a part of any collaborative Police-Social Worker and MCRT approach. This would involve training police dispatchers about which type of personnel or units to send to a given call.

Training as Intervention

Training is a traditional, yet important, intervention for officers. This would involve both training in how to handle different types of mental health emergencies and how to support officer mental health.

Training and Consultation for Police Officers

Training and education have been important parts of policing dating back to San Francisco's Police Chief, August Vollmer, in the early 20th century (Dunham et al., 2021), but rising mental health needs in cities coupled with mental health stresses on officers (Miller, 2005; Balfour et al., 2022) provide new reasons for additional training focused on mental health and wellness for all members of the law enforcement system.

Training for Officers in Dealing With Mental Health Crisis

Providing training for law enforcement officers in handling mental health emergencies is critical (Fiske et al., 2020; Balfour et al., 2022). This can include recognizing potential mental health emergencies, crisis intervention training and strategies, referral resources, and so forth. While these types of exercises have long been a part of police academy training, they can be added to department procedures. A comprehensive review of police departments from 2020 suggests that while a specialized crisis response is improving, there are still significant gaps (Fiske et al., 2020). The recent United States Conferences of Mayor's Mental Health Report (2023) provides some cause for optimism since the vast majority of their 117 cities provide Crisis Intervention Training to officers and dispatchers, as well as wellness programs for officers. Still, officers only receive roughly 20% of their training on service-related calls, even though Patterson (2008) found that non-criminal calls for service amount to roughly 80% of patrol work (Ellsworth et al., 2020; Patterson, 2008). This means there is room for improvement.

Bias training is another part of police training that promises to have benefits for mental health (Balfour et al., 2022). It goes without saying that training must be a continuous process, not a "one-and-done" situation.

Training for Officer Mental Health and Resiliency

Suicide rates continue to be high for officers, as officers are more likely to die by suicide than in the line of duty (President's Task Force on 21st Century Policing, 2015; Miller, 2005). The website https://bluehelp.org compiles the list of first responder suicides and provides resources for officers and families. Mental Health training should include dispatch and civilian officers as well.

Some agencies may have access to a mental health professional to help officers debrief from emotionally and mentally taxing situations (Burgett & Ban, 2022). In other cases, PSWs may provide some mental health services to officers. Police mental health responses appear to be improving (The United States Conference of Mayors' Report on Mental Health, 2023):

93% percent (99) of the cities reported that they had improved their emergency response to people experiencing a behavioral health crisis. When asked how they had done that: 92 percent said they provided crisis intervention training to first responders.... Ninety-four percent (99) of the cities reported that their police department provides mental health and wellness programs to their officers. Of these, 96 percent are providing counseling as needed and particularly after critical incidents. (p. 20)

This is good news for officer wellness. Anything that can help police officers deal with the stresses of a very complex and stressful job will have multiple benefits for the future of law enforcement.

Telemedicine, Telepsychiatry, and Other Possibilities

The growth of telemedicine and telepsychiatry offers substantial new possibilities for assisting police officers in dealing with mental health emergencies (Schlief et al., 2022). This can be through consultation with the police officer or intervention via some type of telemedicine system. While training police officers to deal with mental health issues is important, having a clinician available as a backup is immensely valuable.

The development of helplines is also a positive step and one that can move many cases away from law enforcement's already full plate (Balfour et al., 2022).

Enriched community directories of mental health and social services, available online, are also good possibilities for many communities. These could help police officers make referrals.

Collaboration between the agencies dealing with mental health and those dealing with public safety is crucial (Balfour et al., 2022). This includes partnerships at the local, state and national levels.

The Broader Crisis of the Mental Health System

While providing mental health services through public safety organizations is important, we must acknowledge that the mental health system in the United States is facing a crisis of its own (Carroll & Hayes, 2023). While this is a situation that has been developing for a long time, the COVID-19 pandemic has greatly aggravated the problem. Shortages of clinicians (Kuehn, 2022), facilities, and funding plague many areas of the United States (Balfour et al., 2022).

This crisis has real implications for law enforcement organizations and police officers dealing with issues in communities (Wood et al., 2021). This is a policy-level issue but one that has immediate ramifications for practitioners. While resources have always been an issue in mental health, there is general recognition that the situation has reached crisis proportions (Gramlich, 2023).

Building Trust With Communities: A Prerequisite for Mental Health Intervention

Building a baseline of police and community trust is a prerequisite for other mental health inventions (Toft et al., 2021). Data, technology, and assessment increase trust.

There cannot be successful community mental health interventions without a level of trust and transparency.

Body-Worn Cameras and Accountability Dashboards

Body-worn cameras (BWCs) may be used to monitor community interactions. Some earlier studies of this technology showed a significant reduction in the use of force by 50%, complaints by 88%, and arrests, and encouraged officers to use less dangerous restraints (Headley et al., 2017; Ariel et al., 2015). However, more recently, this is complicated by the fact that videos are often delayed and censored if released (Umansky & Farooq, 2023; Bush, 2020; Miller & Chillar, 2022; White & Malm, 2020). While it appears that cameras may initially make communities feel safer (Miller & Chillar, 2021, Subramanian, & Skrzypiec, 2017; Koen, et al., 2018; White & Malm, 2020), cities need better policies about how to disseminate footage if it is to increase community trust.

Another approach is the creation of Accountability Dashboards. Such dashboards use technology to visually represent progress on police reform (Ray, 2023). Using technology to publicly communicate areas for improvement and progress is necessary for establishing, improving, and rebuilding trust.

Accreditation

National accreditation through the Commission on Accreditation for Law Enforcement Agencies (CALEA) (CALEA, n.d.) is another way law enforcement agencies can increase transparency. CALEA was created by four major police organizations: the International Association of Chiefs of Police (IACP), the National Organization of Black Law Enforcement Executives (NOBLE), the National Sheriffs' Association (NSA) and the Police Executive Research Forum (PERF) to certify the adoption of standards by local law enforcement. There are roughly 2,000 police agencies out of 18,000 that are accredited (CALEA, n.d.).

There is disagreement about CALEA's effectiveness (Hougland & Wolf, 2016). Rodriguez (2021) argues that it may have an impact on officer misconduct, and Feys et al. (2018) comment on the need for more empirical studies. Anecdotally, CALEA may increase community trust. After Michael Brown was killed, seven police departments directly south of Ferguson, MO, voluntarily consolidated to seek CALEA accreditation and focus on community-oriented policing (North County Police Cooperative, n.d.). (This is likely the largest consolidation of police departments in U.S. history.) CALEA is not part of our model as the literature is still being developed but warrants further exploration.

Successful Mental Health Intervention Requires Community Trust

There is a difference between community trust and mental health. Trust issues make mental health interventions by police more problematic. Community members who do not trust law enforcement will be reluctant to refer and may even obstruct police efforts to deal with a mental health issue. Thus, police departments must consider ways to establish trusting and transparent relationships with communities. Trust is a prerequisite for successful mental health intervention.

Citizen engagement is critical to building stronger relationships with government (McNutt & Ban, 2023). Community boards are elected or appointed and advise or oversee the local law enforcement agency. Boards may hold considerable influence, are informed by the public, and are recommended to increase trust (Reece & Macy, 2015). The structure and enforcement capacity of such boards should reflect the desires of the community and consider the community's needs for transparency, current community relationships, history of law enforcement and community conflict, and demographic makeup. Community leaders can work with elected leaders and law enforcement to create a model that is best suited.

Community-Based Policing Strategies

Police departments have embraced Community Oriented Policing (COP) (Giwa, 2018; Lamin & Teboh, 2016), and Problem Oriented Policing, including the Scanning, Analysis, Response, and Assessment (S.A.R.A.) Model (Arizona State University Center for Problem-Oriented Policing, n.d.). These are complementary models for mental health interventions.

Community-oriented policing, involving policing-based community activities and other forms of engagement between law enforcement and citizens, also builds trust before crises occur (Giwa, 2018). Giwa (2018) links the ideas of community-oriented policing and the need for Police-Social Workers in racialized communities.

In general, law enforcement must pay attention to underrepresented or high-risk groups and neighborhoods in the municipality and attempt to build relationships with key community leaders (Giwa, 2018). Citizens may also provide helpful feedback on policies, especially around grievances or opportunities for new programs. Paying attention to social service agencies in the community as well as gaps in community needs, such as housing, also can help law enforcement build preventative relationships to improve social service delivery.

BUILDING A DATA AND TECHNOLOGY-ENHANCED APPROACH TO LAW ENFORCEMENT SOCIAL SERVICES ISSUES

The goal of providing a system to meet mental health and social services needs within a public safety context is important, possible, and realistic for most communities. The approach advocated here proposes that communities make use of the totality of community information (or an Information Ecosystem) and use it to create a planning structure that will support a planning process.

Creating a Community Information Ecosystem for Public Safety

Communities have always been rich stores of information about residents, businesses, groups, organizations and other populations. Some of that information is easy to access, while other aspects require effort to extract. Knowledge about the community is the foundation of intelligent planning and policy making. Traditionally, information resources for criminal justice planning came from standard statistical series (Census of Population and Housing, Uniform Crime Reports and so forth), survey results and focus groups/community meetings and local data sources. While these are indispensable resources, new data sources and the means to analyze and present them offer truly wonderful possibilities.

The intersection of technology and ever-larger amounts of data creates an enormous resource. They allow criminal justice planners the ability to make decisions based on a deep understanding of communities, the people who live there, and the problems that they face.

These new resources create an ecosystem for public safety planning. An Information Ecosystem is defined by Goldkind and McNutt (2019) as:

Information ecosystems or environments are composed of data generated from client interactions, individuals, organizations, and private corporate data and public data sources such as government agencies at the city, state, and federal levels. (p. 271)

This allows planners to see communities more holistically. Much of this data is quantitative in nature. This is data from survey research, administrative records, sensor data, and social media data. This is complemented by qualitative data, including crowdsourced data, focus groups, and observational data.

Traditional Government Data

Government organizations collect vast amounts of data in both their normal operation and in the research efforts they conduct. There are many data sources that local government collects and makes available to internal stakeholders.

External sources of data from the federal and state governments and independent sources are important resources to encourage accountability and transparency across police agencies. The Police Scorecard, Department of Justice (DOJ), Federal Bureau of Investigation (FBI) Use of Force Database, Police Executive Research Forum (PERF), and independent reporting sources like the *Guardian's* Use of Force Database provide another layer of open data that are important for facilitating community trust.

Government data in the United States is generally of excellent quality, but it occasionally has limitations. Some datasets are incomplete and many do not cover the time researchers might be interested in examining. Some data is not released or released at a level of aggregation that is unusable for some research. Freedom of Information requests can help researchers have access to data that government organizations would prefer not to make public. Some organizations collect their own data to supplement data that does not exist or is inaccessible. The availability of open public data is an important step that governments could take to resolve not only this issue but many challenges facing the modern world (Balfour et al., 2022).

New Sources of Data

The traditional sources of government data will continue to be useful. Data from the Census, Uniform Crime Reports, Victimization Survey, offender processing results, and other sources are the bedrock of current planning. The movement toward open government and open civic data has made available a wide range of previously unavailable data (McNutt, 2018). In addition, data from systems such as 311 and 991 are adding to our understanding of the psychosocial aspects of public safety. Data from sensors, including license plate readers, CATV cameras, smartphones, and a variety of other sources, can also be useful. The use of this data source is really in the early days as the potential sensor availability is immense and frequently untapped.

In addition to government data, nonprofit organizations, and commercial enterprises also have data that can be helpful. These organizations collect data during their day-to-day operations that can be useful to public agencies. The ridesharing firm Uber provides utilization data to transportation planners, Yelp makes data on user experiences available to health departments, and Linked In partners with labor organizations to spot trends in the job markets. Data from social media (Won, et al., 2013) and web searches (Boland & McNutt, 2016) can be used to identify disease outbreaks, overdoses, and mental health emergencies. Commercial organizations are often willing to share the data that they collect through data philanthropy efforts (McKeever, et al., 2018). Data Collaboratives (Susha, Janssen & Verhulst, 2017) are agreements that allow this sharing to go forward, although some commercial interests allow this sharing directly.

Nonprofit organizations often have data that is unavailable to the public sector. This data can give a more complete picture of the situation, and the involvement of nonprofit organizations can provide more on-the-ground domain understanding than is available otherwise. Nonprofit think tanks, research centers, and institutions can assist with other types of data collection.

Citizen-crowdsourced data (Noveck, 2021) is an emerging source of data that can supplement existing data systems. These approaches include citizen science methods that involve citizens and community members in the collection of data. This practice has a long history in astronomy and biology. A related, although different approach is participatory action research that involves community members in all aspects of the research. These data sources are often underutilized in contemporary planning but represent a way to obtain data that is otherwise unavailable.

The substantial expansion of data and processing power has brought new possibilities to police and emergency services organizations. The development of programs such as 3-1-1 (Li, et al., 2020) provides a range of additional data points that illuminate important factors around social needs. Other sources of Open Data and data-based government, as well as technology in government and technology in social services, provide new opportunities for more responsive public safety. The need to share data cannot be overemphasized.

New Tools for Analysis and Visualization:

The creation of vast amounts of new data has led to the development of an arsenal of new tools to conduct data analysis and data visualization. This toolset, often referred to as Data Science, promises many wonderful capabilities for public managers. While many studies are conducted with traditional statistical software and even spreadsheets like Excel, some datasets exceed the capacity of traditional systems. More advanced statistical languages, such as R and Python, and Machine Learning/Artificial Intelligence applications, address these emerging needs. Tools such as Geographic Information Systems have grown ever more sophisticated and have evolved additional capacities. New methodologies for presenting and visualizing data are emerging and are incorporated into practice.

This data ecosystem can support evidence-informed policymaking in new and profoundly more substantial ways. Some of this data is sensitive and can endanger privacy and human rights. Algorithms incorporated into these systems can be biased and can lead to decisions that perpetuate oppression and injustice. Care must be taken to build the safeguards that will protect human rights in a new digital age.

The engagement of the community information ecosystem requires an effort that can be facilitated by the creation of a structure. This structure can facilitate using the fruits of that set of relationships and can also support a planning process.

Building a Structure

A set of interactive components aimed at extracting and managing the data from the Community Information Ecosystem is critical to the overall success of the effort. This structure includes data collaboration agreements, community member involvement, Local Learning and Innovation Labs, Hackathons, Citizen Action Groups, and a panel to ensure the ethical use of the data. These elements create the facility necessary to process the data and guarantee its ethical use. They also provide a means of creating and evaluating new interventions.

Figure 1. A structure to support public service planning

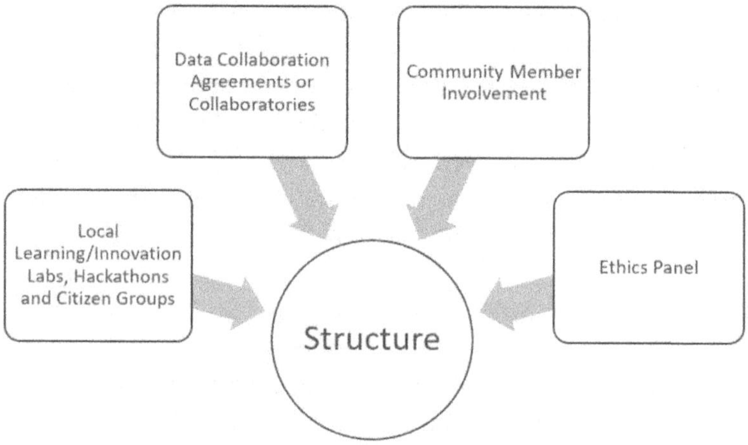

Community Member Involvement

Mechanisms for community members to become involved can include a variety of formal and informal vectors, including task groups, consultations, participatory budgeting, and so forth (Noveck, 2021). These must be meaningful opportunities to participate rather than public relations efforts.

Data Collaboration Agreements

Also called Collaboratories, these agreements create formal relationships around the exchange of data (Verhulst & Young, 2017). This agreement protects user privacy, trade secrets, and other rights. They permit the exchange of data with nongovernmental actors.

Local Learning and Innovation Labs, Hackathons, and Citizen Action Groups

These structural elements create new program elements or entire new programs. They are agile elements that can work outside the structure of government using the power of citizen coproduction and co-creation.

Ethics Panel

Data can be immensely useful. It can also be potentially harmful to vulnerable groups. The same can be said for the algorithms that power data science and emerging programming. An ethics panel, much like an institutional review board, can act to protect people from some of the side effects of digital life.

Limitations of Government Technology

While most public organizations have a technology plan, the limitations of government computing and e-government must be considered. Using advanced technology might be difficult in such a situation. Fortunately, data for good, public interest technology, and civic technology can address some of those limitations (McNutt & Ban, 2023). These efforts bring skilled volunteers into carefully created efforts to upgrade government efforts. Also useful are hackathons and data dives, efforts that are designed to get technologists to develop new efforts to meet government needs on a time-limited basis.

A Planning Model

Building on the structure outlined above, the planning model reflects human-centered design principles. Human-centered design envisions a planning process that relies heavily on how people experience the situation (Chen, et al., 2020; Noveck, 2021, 94) and depends on extensive feedback from the population affected. It envisions a sharing of authority and responsibility between government and other actors. The approach has four phases: Mission/Vision, Assessment, Programming/ Implementation, and Evaluation, and then the next planning cycle. While they are presented here as a series of steps, in reality, they are more interactive phases that can reoccur as the situation warrants.

Figure 2 outlines the overall model. Each stage will be discussed in turn in the discussion below:

Figure 2. The planning model

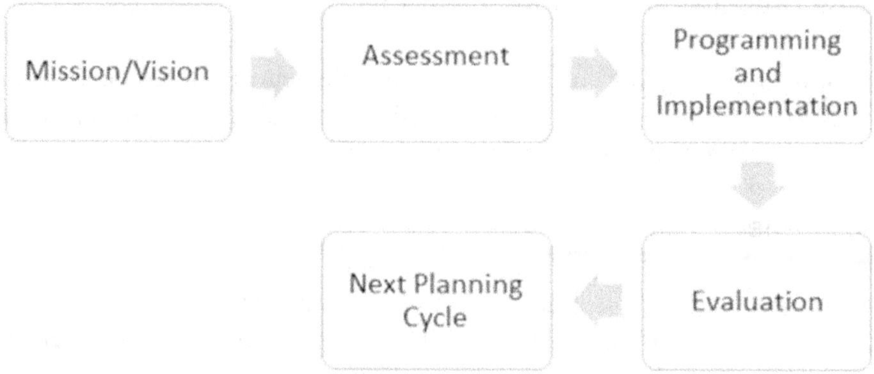

1) Mission/Vision

This phase creates an anchor point or north star for effort. It is built through thick and consistent engagement with community stakeholders. It informs the rest of the planning process.

Tasks at this stage include exploring community consensus, assuring inclusive participation and guiding community members through the visioning process. Technology can assist at this stage by making involvement in the process easier through collaborative technologies and networking methods.

Special care must be taken to address marginalized or disenfranchised communities. Many of these communities have had problematic relationships with public safety organizations.

2) Assessment

This phase takes a deep look at the community, its public safety issues and other community and regional factors. It makes use of the data resources of the community information ecosystem, which includes a wealth of qualitative and quantitative data. Assessment is an ongoing process that functions in a role not unlike the role of business intelligence in commercial organizations.

The assessment process brings together qualitative and quantitative data to paint an accurate portrait of the community and its public safety needs (Noveck, 2021). The toolset at this point includes data, data analysis, data visualization, and data storytelling. While expert analysis is needed, the perspective of those on the ground is critical. This is especially true of those who have knowledge of communities that experience issues with public safety organizations.

The elements in the planning structure are crucial. They facilitate the data process and build systems to address potential problems. The structure, along with developments at the Assessment and Mission/Vision phases become the foundation that underpins programming.

3) Programming and Implementation

This phase takes assessment findings and designs and modifies programs in accordance with the mission/vision statements. Human-centered Design is used in cooperation with other design strategies. This is an ongoing and interactive process.

The structure provides elements that are needed to build the interventions that address the problems identified in the assessment phase. The interventions selected should not only be appropriate to the situation but built on evidence. The programming process is interactive. This means that a wide range of vetted approaches are considered and might be applied tentatively, but the final mix is the product of trial and error.

Some of these interventions are presented in Table 1. This is a limited list for illustration.

Table 1. Potential programming alternatives

• Community Dashboards • Technology, Appropriate Policies • Mental Health Training for Dispatch, Admin, and Officers. • Telemedicine and Telepsychiatry • Mobile Crisis Response Teams • Police Social Workers	• Officer Wellness • Accountability Dashboards • Data Gathering and Review • Citizen Involvement Structure/Boards • Community Engagement

4) Evaluation

This phase looks at the effectiveness of those programs created by the process. Using a variety of methodologies, it seeks to improve existing programs and suggest modifications and continuation for the programs created. The evaluation should be ongoing and interactive with the programming phase.

Evaluation is critical to the planning process. It must be broadly conceived and methodologically pragmatic. This means using a combination of methods like Randomized Controlled Experimental designs and Qualitative studies of process and impact. All methodologies have strengths, but they also have weaknesses. A mixed-methods design is important for creating a substantial and useful evaluation.

CONCLUSIONS AND NEXT STEPS

The past two decades have been challenging ones for public safety organizations. The rise of different types of criminal activity (cybercrime, domestic terrorism, new types of fraud, collective violence) and an increased social service load from a highly stressed population combined with a challenging political and media environment create a perfect storm for public safety executives and their colleagues. Many communities have experienced these issues in very painful situations that will have long-term ramifications.

Redeveloping and modernizing older approaches, such as Police Social Workers and training for police officers, are always important policy options. In addition, a wide variety of new possibilities, such as Mobile Crisis Response Teams (MCRTs), have emerged. The key is finding what works in a given community

Higher education must prepare students for roles in the law enforcement-mental health system. Many mental health professions train primarily for other practice regimes and leave their graduates to learn critical skills on their own. This should be addressed by the creation of specialized educational offerings.

The workforce for such behavioral health response is underdeveloped, and there is a need for new training tracks in Master of Social Work programs for Police Social Workers (Carroll et al., 2021; Logan et al., 2023). Proposals like the one before Valparaiso University to create an MSW program and a Police Social Work/Mobile Crisis certificate, emphasizing micro and macro practice will be important to train social workers for this highly specialized field (Ban, 2023).

Jails and emergency rooms often fall short of providing appropriate mental health care, and police and mental health professionals will need access to drop-in facilities designed to provide mental health and social services, such as “Living Rooms” (Balfour et al., 2022). The best-trained social workers, officers, and mental health professionals in the world will be unable to address housing issues and mental health crises without appropriate and available facilities. Arrests are more likely to happen when officers do not have sufficient options. Jails and prisons have become de facto mental health facilities in the face of the shortage.

Innovation is the way to the future. New techniques allow us to view communities holistically. This means evaluating the need for a new technique and its potential effectiveness. Public safety organizations that work well with their citizens and are trusted by their communities are in a unique position to help meet the mental health challenges of their communities. While adequate 24/7 mental health and social service provision would be ideal, the areas that have this available are rather rare. Reductions in funding for basic services, combined with an uptick in needs could make such a service system further away. Still, communities have an opportunity to lean into these challenges by creating a data and technology-enhanced approach to public safety.

REFERENCES

Ariel, B., Farrar, W. A., & Sutherland, A. (2015). The effect of police body-worn cameras on use of force and citizens' complaints against the police: A randomized controlled trial. *Journal of Quantitative Criminology*, *31*(3), 509–535. doi:10.1007/s10940-014-9236-3

Arizona State University Center for Problem-Oriented Policing. (n.d.). *SARA Model.* Retrieved at https://popcenter.asu.edu/content/sara-model-0

Balfour, M. E., Hahn Stephenson, A., Delany-Brumsey, A., Winsky, J., & Goldman, M. L. (2022). Cops, clinicians, or both? Collaborative approaches to responding to behavioral health emergencies. *Psychiatric Services (Washington, D.C.)*, *73*(6), 658–669. doi:10.1176/appi.ps.202000721 PMID:34666512

Ban, C. C. (2023, July 9). *Proposal for a police social work/mobile crisis certificate and MSW program at Valparaiso University* [Unpublished presentation]. Valparaiso University.

Ban, C. C., & Riordan, J. E. (2023). Re-envisioning public safety through an embedded police social worker (PSW) model: A promising approach for multidisciplinary resource delivery and diversion. *Journal of Contemporary Criminal Justice*, *39*(4), 537–554. doi:10.1177/10439862231189423

Boland, K. M., & McNutt, J. G. (2013). Assessing e-government success strategies using Internet search data. In R. Gil Garcia (Ed.), *E-government success factors and measures: theories, concepts, and methodologies* (pp. 289–307). IGI Global. doi:10.4018/978-1-4666-4058-0.ch016

Brayne, S., & Christin, A. (2021). Technologies of crime prediction: The reception of algorithms in policing and criminal courts. *Social Problems*, *68*(3), 608–624. doi:10.1093/socpro/spaa004

Brudney, J. L., & Prentice, C. R. (2018). A new tool for new times? Using Geographic Information Systems in foundations and other nonprofit organizations. *The Foundation Review*, *10*(4). Advance online publication. doi:10.9707/1944-5660.1442

Burgett, S., & Ban, C. (2022, November 1–3). *Enhancing micro-level police social work by practicing effective macro-level work* [Conference session]. National Association of Public Safety Social Workers Annual Conference, Indianapolis, IN.

Bush, C. L. (2020). Public perceptions of delays in the release of police body-worn camera footage. *Journal of Social Change*, *13*(1), 1–17. doi:10.5590/JOSC.2020.13.1.01

CALEA. (n.d.). Retrieved at https://www.calea.org/

Carroll, A. E., & Hayes, D. (2023). The US mental health system is so broken that even money can't fix it. *JAMA Pediatrics*, *177*(1), 8–10. doi:10.1001/jamapediatrics.2022.4416 PMID:36409471

Carroll, J. J., El-Sabawi, T., Fichter, D., Pope, L. G., Rafla-Yuan, E., Compton, M. T., & Watson, A. (2021, September 8). The workforce for non-police behavioral health crisis response doesn't exist—We need to create it. *Health Affairs Forefront.* https://www.healthaffairs.org/content/forefront/workforce-non-police-behavioral-health-crisis-response-doesn-t-exist-we-need-create

Chen, E., Leos, C., Kowitt, S. D., & Moracco, K. E. (2020). Enhancing community-based participatory research through human-centered design strategies. *Health Promotion Practice*, *21*(1), 37–48. doi:10.1177/1524839919850557 PMID:31131633

DeVylder, J. E., Anglin, D. M., Bowleg, L., Fedina, L., & Link, B. G. (2022). Police Violence and Public Health. *Annual Review of Clinical Psychology*, *18*(1), 527–552. doi:10.1146/annurev-clinpsy-072720-020644 PMID:34890247

Drew, J. M., & Martin, S. (2021). A national study of police mental health in the USA: Stigma, mental health and help-seeking behaviors. *Journal of Police and Criminal Psychology*, *36*(2), 295–306. doi:10.1007/s11896-020-09424-9

Dunham, R. G., Alpert, G. P., & McLean, K. D. (2021). *Critical Issues in Policing* (8th ed.). Waveland Press.

Ellsworth, J. Fish, T., Niesen, & Pitts, N. (2020, April). Police social work in Minnesota: Starting the conversation. In *Social workers and police officers: An essential community partnership.* Mankato State University Social Work Policy Brief.

Feys, Y., Verhage, A., & Boels, D. (2018). A state-of-the-art review on police accountability: What do we know from empirical studies? *International Journal of Police Science & Management*, *20*(3), 225–239. doi:10.1177/1461355718786297

Fiske, Z. R., Songer, D. M., & Schriver, J. L. (2020). A national survey of police mental health training. *Journal of Police and Criminal Psychology*, *36*(2), 236–242. doi:10.1007/s11896-020-09402-1

Ghelani, A. (2022). Knowledge and skills for social workers on mobile crisis intervention teams. *Clinical Social Work Journal*, *50*(4), 414–425. doi:10.1007/s10615-021-00823-x PMID:34803191

Giwa, S. (2018). Community policing in racialized communities: A potential role for police social work. *Journal of Human Behavior in the Social Environment*, *28*(6), 710–730. doi:10.1080/10911359.2018.1456998

Goldkind, L., & McNutt, J. G. (2019). We could be unicorns: Human services leaders moving from managing programs to managing information ecosystems. *Human Service Organizations, Management, Leadership & Governance*, *43*(4), 1–9. doi:10.1080/23303131.2019.1669758

Gramlich, J. (2023). *Mental health and the pandemic: What US surveys have found.* Pew Research Center https://www.pewresearch.org/short-reads/2023/03/02/mental-health-and-the-pandemic-what-u-s-surveys-have-found/

Hannah-Moffat, K. (2019). Algorithmic risk governance: Big data analytics, race and information activism in criminal justice debates. *Theoretical Criminology*, *23*(4), 453–470. doi:10.1177/1362480618763582

Headley, A. M., Guerette, R. T., & Shariati, A. (2017). A field experiment of the impact of body-worn cameras (BWCs) on police officer behavior and perceptions. *Journal of Criminal Justice*, *53*, 102–109. doi:10.1016/j.jcrimjus.2017.10.003

Hougland, S., & Wolf, R. (2017). Accreditation in police agencies: Does external quality assurance reduce citizen complaints? *The Police Journal*, *90*(1), 40–54. doi:10.1177/0032258X16671030

Koen, M. C., Willis, J. J., & Mastrofski, S. D. (2018). The effects of body-worn cameras on police organization and practice: A theory-based analysis. *Policing and Society*, 1–17.

Kuehn, B. M. (2022). Clinician shortage exacerbates pandemic-fueled "mental health crisis". *Journal of the American Medical Association*, *327*(22), 2179–2181. doi:10.1001/jama.2022.8661 PMID:35612873

Lamin, S. A., & Teboh, C. (2016). Police social work and community policing. *Cogent Social Sciences*, *2*(1), 1212636. doi:10.1080/23311886.2016.1212636

Lane, R. (2019). "I'm a police officer not a social worker or mental health nurse": Online discourses of exclusion and resistance regarding mental health-related police work. *Journal of Community & Applied Social Psychology*, *29*(5), 429–442. doi:10.1002/casp.2410

Leipsiger, A., & Hillman, K. (2020). *NASW-Illinois Chapter statement on the call for police reform and the role of social workers.* https://www.naswil.org/post/nasw-illinois-chapter-statement-on-the-call-for-police-reform-and-the-role-of-social-workers

Li, Y., Hyder, A., Southerland, L. T., Hammond, G., Porr, A., & Miller, H. J. (2020). 311 service requests as indicators of neighborhood distress and opioid use disorder. *Scientific Reports, 10*(1), 19579. doi:10.1038/s41598-020-76685-z PMID:33177583

Logan, I., Madden, R., & Solak, M. (2023). Preparing social workers for emerging roles in police social work. *Journal of Social Work Education*, 1–16. Advance online publication. doi:10.1080/10437797.2023.2244999

Machado, M. A., & Lugo, A. M. (2021). A behavioral analysis of two strategies to eliminate racial bias in police use of force. *Behavior Analysis in Practice*, *15*(4), 1221–1231. doi:10.1007/s40617-021-00551-1 PMID:36605163

Marsden, M., Nigam, J., Lemetyinen, H., & Edge, D. (2020). Investigating police officers' perceptions of their role in pathways to mental healthcare. *Health & Social Care in the Community*, *28*(3), 913–921. doi:10.1111/hsc.12922 PMID:31919970

Matthews, J. (2022). *Body-Worn Camera Use and Citizen Behavior During Police–Citizen Encounters* [Doctoral dissertation]. Walden University.

Matthews, J. J., & Lyons, M. L. (2015). Phenomenological experiences of African American men in the aftermath of the Zimmerman trial. *Journal of Counselor Practice*, *6*(2), 76–93.

McKeever, B., Greene, S., MacDonald, G., Tatian, P., & Jones, D. (2018). *Data Philanthropy: Unlocking the Power of Private Data for Public Good*. Urban Institute.

McNutt, J. G. (Ed.). (2018). Technology, Activism and Social Justice in a Digital Age. Oxford University Press.

McNutt, J. G., & Ban, C. C. (2023). Preparing public managers to deal with disruptive innovations through citizen partnerships. In S. Edwards, III & J. Masterson (Eds.), Government Response to Disruptive Innovation: Perspectives and Examinations (pp. 1-19). IGI Global. doi:10.4018/978-1-6684-6429-8.ch001

Michaels, R. A., & Treger, H. (1973). Social work in police departments. *Social Work*, *18*(5), 67–75.

Miller, J., & Chillar, V. F. (2022). Do police body-worn cameras reduce citizen fatalities? Results of a country-wide natural experiment. *Journal of Quantitative Criminology*, *38*(3), 723–754. doi:10.1007/s10940-021-09513-w

Miller, L. (2005). Police officer suicide: Causes, prevention, and practical intervention strategies. *International Journal of Emergency Mental Health*, *7*(2), 101. PMID:16107042

National Association of Social Workers. (2018). Social work in the criminal justice system. In *National Association of Social Workers policy statements* (pp. 302–309). NASW Press. (Original work published 2018)

North County Police Cooperative. (n.d.). Retrieved at https://www.northcountypolice.com/

Noveck, B. S. (2021). *Solving public problems: a practical guide to fix our government and change our world*. Yale University Press.

O'Hare, T. (2019). *Essential skills of social work practice: Assessment, intervention, and evaluation*. Oxford University Press.

O'Hare, T. (2020). *Evidence-based practices for social workers: An interdisciplinary approach*. Oxford University Press.

Office of Community Oriented Policing Services. (2015). *Final report of the president's task force on 21st century policing*. US Department of Justice https://cops.usdoj.gov/pdf/taskforce/taskforce_finalreport.pdf

Patterson, G. T. (2004). Police–social work crisis teams: Practice and research implications. *Stress, Trauma and Crisis*, *7*(2), 93–104. doi:10.1080/15434610490450886

Patterson, G. T. (2008). Police social work: A unique area of practice arising from law enforcement functions. *Police social work: National Association of Social Workers*. Retrieved from www.naswnyc.org/?Page=77

Patterson, G. T. (2021). Treger, Harvey. *Encyclopedia of Social Work*. https://oxfordre.com/socialwork/search?siteToSearch=socialwork&q=treger&searchBtn=Search&isQuickSearch=true

Patterson, G. T. (2023). Police social work and social justice: Lessons for clinical social work practice. *Clinical Social Work Journal*, 1–8. doi:10.1007/s10615-023-00871-5

Patterson, G. T., & Swan, P. G. (2019). Police social work and social service collaboration strategies one hundred years after Vollmer: A systematic review. *Policing*, *42*(5), 863–886. doi:10.1108/PIJPSM-06-2019-0097

Pinals, D. A., Hepburn, B., Parks, J., & Stephenson, A. H. (2020). The behavioral health system and its response to COVID-19: A snapshot perspective. *Psychiatric Services (Washington, D.C.)*, *71*(10), 1070–1074. doi:10.1176/appi.ps.202000264 PMID:32781926

Ray, R. (2020). *How can we enhance police accountability in the United States?* The Vitals: Policy. Brookings Institution.

Reece, J. G., & Macy, J. (2015, October). Citizen advisory boards in contemporary practice: A practical approach in policing. *The Police Chief*, *82*. https://www.policechiefmagazine.org/citizen-advisory-boards-in-contemporary-practice-a-practical-approach-in-policing/

Roberts, A. R. (2007). Police social work: Bridging the past to the present. In A. R. Roberts & D. W. Springer (Eds.), *Social work in juvenile and criminal justice settings* (pp. 126–129). Charles C. Thomas Publisher Ltd.

Rodriguez, R. E. (2020). *The Impact of Agency Accreditation or Certification on Police Misconduct* [Dissertation]. Walden University.

Schlief, M., Saunders, K. R. K., Appleton, R., Barnett, P., Vera San Juan, N., Foye, U., Olive, R. R., Machin, K., Shah, P., Chipp, B., Lyons, N., Tamworth, C., Persaud, K., Badhan, M., Black, C., Sin, J., Riches, S., Graham, T., Greening, J., ... Johnson, S. (2022). Synthesis of the evidence on what works for whom in telemental health: Rapid realist review. *Interactive Journal of Medical Research*, *11*(2), e38239. doi:10.2196/38239 PMID:35767691

SherradenM. (2020, June). *Social work and the future of policing: Key points for changes in policy and practice* (CSD Policy Brief No. 20-14). St. Louis, MO: Washington University, Center for Social Development. doi:10.7936/885h-rh13

Shore, K., & Lavoie, J. A. (2019). Exploring mental health-related calls for police service: A Canadian study of police officers as 'frontline mental health workers. *Policing. Journal of Policy Practice*, *13*(2), 157–171.

Short, T. B. R., MacDonald, C., Luebbers, S., Ogloff, J. R. P., & Thomas, S. D. M. (2014). The nature of police involvement in mental health transfers. *Police Practice and Research*, *15*(4), 336–348. doi:10.1080/15614263.2012.736717

Subramanian, R., & Skrzypiec, L. (2017). *To Protect and Serve: New Trends in State-Level Policing Reform, 2015–2016.* Vera Institute of Justice.

Susha, I., Janssen, M., & Verhulst, S. (2017). Data collaboratives as "bazaars"? A review of coordination problems and mechanisms to match demand for data with supply. *Transforming Government: People. Process and Policy*, *11*(1), 157–172.

Susha, I., Janssen, M., Verhulst, S., & Pardo, T. (2017, June). Data collaboratives: How to create value from data for public problem solving?: Panel. In *Proceedings of the 18th Annual International Conference on Digital Government Research* (pp. 604-606). New York: ACM. 10.1145/3085228.3085309

Syed, S., Ashwick, R., Schlosser, M., Jones, R., Rowe, S., & Billings, J. (2020). Global prevalence and risk factors for mental health problems in police personnel: A systematic review and meta-analysis. *Occupational and Environmental Medicine*, *77*(11), 737–747. doi:10.1136/oemed-2020-106498 PMID:32439827

Thyer, B. A., & Myers, L. L. (2011). The quest for evidence-based practice: A view from the United States. *Journal of Social Work : JSW*, *11*(1), 8–25. doi:10.1177/1468017310381812

Toft, J., Abramovitz, M., & Harty, J. S. (2021). Social work responses to policing in the United States. *Bibliography of Scholarship in Social Welfare History*, *101*(3), 1–21.

Treger, H. (1975). *The police-social work team: A new model for interprofessional cooperation: a university demonstration project in manpower training and development.* University of Illinois, Chicago Circle Paperback.

Treger, H. (1980). Guideposts for community work in police-social work diversion. *Federal Probation*, *44*(3), 3–8.

Umansky, E., & Farooq, U. (2023, Dec. 15). *How police undermined the promise of body cameras.* Retrieved from https://www.propublica.org/article/how-police-undermined-promise-body-cameras

U.S. Mayor's Conference of Cities. (2023, June). *The Mental Health Crisis in America's Cities and Their Responses to It: A 117-City Report.* https://www.usmayors.org/wp/content/uploads/2023/06/USCM-Mental-Health-Survey-2023.pdf

Verhulst, S. G., & Young, A. (2017). The potential of social media intelligence to improve people's lives. *The Governance Lab.* Available at https://www.thegovlab.org/static/files/publications/social-media-data.pdf

Wells, A. S. (1915, May 18). Policewomen. In *Conference of Charities and Corrections, 42nd Annual Meeting Proceedings* (pp. 411-418). Baltimore, MD. University of Michigan Archives. https://quod.lib.umich.edu/n/ncosw/

White, M. D., & Malm, A. (2020). *Cops, Cameras, and Crisis: The Potential and the Perils of Police Body-Worn Cameras*. New York University Press. doi:10.18574/nyu/9781479820177.001.0001

Wike, T. L., Bledsoe, S. E., Manuel, J. I., Despard, M., Johnson, L. V., Bellamy, J. L., & Killian-Farrell, C. (2014). Evidence-based practice in social work: Challenges and opportunities for clinicians and organizations. *Clinical Social Work Journal, 42*(2), 161–170. doi:10.1007/s10615-014-0492-3

Wilson, B. L., Wooten, N. R., & Pitner, R. O. (2023). Examining historical and contemporary policing disparities in the Black community: Implications for social work. *Social Work, 68*(1), 8–17. doi:10.1093/sw/swac049 PMID:36346331

Won, H. H., Myung, W., Song, G. Y., Lee, W. H., Kim, J. W., Carroll, B. J., & Kim, D. K. (2013). Predicting national suicide numbers with social media data. *PLoS One, 8*(4), e61809. doi:10.1371/journal.pone.0061809 PMID:23630615

Wood, J. D., Watson, A. C., & Barber, C. (2021). What can we expect of police in the face of deficient mental health systems? Qualitative insights from Chicago police officers. *Journal of Psychiatric and Mental Health Nursing, 28*(1), 28–42. doi:10.1111/jpm.12691 PMID:32966680

ADDITIONAL READING

Davis, A. J. (2017). *Policing the black man: Arrest, prosecution, and imprisonment*. Pantheon Books.

Dunham, R. G., Alpert, G. P., & McLean, K. D. (2021). *Critical Issues in Policing* (8th ed.). Waveland Press.

Noveck, B. S. (2021). *Solving public problems: a practical guide to fix our government and change our world*. Yale University Press.

Patterson, G. T., & Swan, P. G. (2019). Police social work and social service collaboration strategies one hundred years after Vollmer: A systematic review. *Policing, 42*(5), 863–886. doi:10.1108/PIJPSM-06-2019-0097

The President's Task Force on 21st Century Policing. (2015, May). *Final Report.* https://cops.usdoj.gov/pdf/taskforce/taskforce_finalreport.pdf

Toft, J., Abramovitz, M., & Harty, J. S. (2021). Social work responses to policing in the United States. *Bibliography of Scholarship in Social Welfare History, 101*(3), 1–21.

KEY TERMS AND DEFINITIONS

Accountability Dashboards: These are regularly updated electronic webpages or websites using technology to employ visual representations of progress on police reform and other police data. These are meant to be a public communication tool and can be maintained by law enforcement or by an independent agency. These are externally focused and accessible by the community.

Citizen Advisory Board: This is a board of elected or appointed community members that provide advisory recommendations to the local law enforcement agency. This type of board does not have authority over the law enforcement agency, but may hold considerable influence.

Citizen Review/Oversight Board: This is a board of community members that has authority over some law enforcement policies and practices, especially in cases of misconduct. Typically, seats are appointed by the mayor or other oversight authority (like the Department of Justice).

Commission on Accreditation for Law Enforcement Agencies (CALEA): National accrediting body for law enforcement agencies. National law enforcement accreditation is optional. Only about 2,000 agencies out of nearly 18,000 choose to be nationally accredited.

Human-Centered Planning: A planning technique that involves the people affected in the planning process.

Mobile Crisis Response Teams (MCRTs): These crisis response teams employ social workers or mental health professionals outside of a police department and often coordinate with a police department.

Police Social Workers (PSWs): Refer to social workers who are embedded within police departments and are hired by the police department. PSWs can be second responders and provide case management during or after an incident. The police social work approach is involved in group (mezzo) and community, organization, or policy-level (macro) work.

Chapter 9
Reintegration of Offenders Into Communities:
Restorative Justice Models

Alev Ozeroglu
Ozyegin University, Turkey

ABSTRACT

Punishing offenders and the type of punishment to be given has been one of the fundamental questions of criminal law. The concept of punishment has been associated with revenge in history; however, after the 1940s, it has been formed through a different understanding of the idea of rehabilitating offenders and reintegrating them into society. After the 1970s, with the concept of "reparation," models emerged in which offenders analyze the consequences of the act committed within the scope of restorative justice and display a constructive attitude towards eliminating the damage. Therefore, the understanding of making offenders pay for, atone for, or compensate for the consequences of the act committed, the question of what the punishment given over time or the result of the criminal justice system reveals for offenders has also begun to be asked. At this point, the question asked within the scope of the study is how effective restorative justice models are in reconciling and reintegrating offenders with society.

1. INTRODUCTION

Restorative justice models, which have emerged in Canada since the 1970s, have started to be applied both in countries applying the Anglo-Saxon legal system and in countries in the continental European legal system. Although there are differences between countries in terms of the stage of implementation and the manner of

DOI: 10.4018/978-1-6684-8569-9.ch009

implementation of these models, these methods have similar characteristics in terms of their common points and objectives. Although restorative justice practices basically offer a victim-oriented approach, these models also produce results in favor of offenders (Marshall, 1999; Vogel, 2007).

Offender is not only spared the harsh consequences of the criminal justice system, but also reintegrates into society as a law-abiding citizen. Since offender makes an effort to repair the damage caused by the criminal act on victim and society, this situation also allows offender to repair the relationship with society (Daly, 2002; Dandurand, 2016; Marshall, 1999).

In the judicial system, offenders are judged and a final decision is given about offender at the end of a process in which offender is not included actively in the outcome. Therefore, although participating in the process, offender does not have a decisive word in the outcome and exists as a passive subject. Therefore, there is a situation where both offender and victim are not satisfied with the outcome of the proceedings. Indeed, victims may perceive that their damages are not compensated or that they are not sufficiently listened to and understood; similarly, offenders might think that their situation and the reasons that led them to commit the crime are not sufficiently discussed and that they are treated unfairly (e.g. Marshall, 1999).

The presence of models where offenders like victims, can explain themselves and discuss the reasons leading them to commit crimes has significance, especially for young offenders in terms of age group.

Alternative dispute resolution methods and restorative justice models are preferred procedures in terms of providing an active participation role that judicial system cannot provide to the subjects of the crime. In criminal proceedings, victim, as well as offender, has a role that is not active enough in the process and cannot influence the outcome of the proceedings, mostly as a witness in practice. Since these models are based on interviews in the presence of offender, by using various communication models, offender takes part in the criminal justice system as an active person instead of being a passive subject who is judged in the judicial process. Especially in models such as conference models and circle processes, involvement of people from community in interview process contributes to the rehabilitation of offenders and continue their lives in harmony with society (Marshall, 1999).

2. RELATION BETWEEN RESTORATIVE JUSTICE MODELS AND REINTEGRATION OF OFFENDERS

2.1 Impact of Restorative Justice Models on Offenders

According to the comprehensive definition made by Marshall; "Restorative justice is a process whereby parties with a stake in a specific offense collectively resolve how to deal with the aftermath of that offense and its implications for the future" (Marshall, 1999; Dignan, 2005). The elements included in this definition constitute a common feature for all restorative justice models. Therefore, in all restorative justice-based programs, there is a process in which the parties make decisions together.

In programs within the criminal justice system, once an offender enters the criminal justice system, instead of going to trial, there are meetings with the victim to resolve the dispute. Such meetings reduce the burden on the state in terms of both resources and time allocated to cases (Umbreit, 2001).

The implementation of these models is especially important for the reintegration of young offenders into society. This is mainly for offenders under the age of 18 are less experienced in fully understanding the meaning and consequences of the act they have committed. At this point, giving this opportunity to the young offenders to correct and repair the consequences of the act they committed makes it possible for offenders to continue their perspective on re-offending and to continue their life in society without having a crime on their criminal record. Because, in cases where this opportunity is not provided, young offenders who are sentenced as a result of the trial or even if they are not sentenced to a sentence of imprisonment, may have problems in getting an education, getting a job, and the bond between them and society may be problematic at the beginning of their adult lives (Dandurand, 2016).

Through these models, offenders can gain awareness in understanding of the impact of the crime on the victim. Such awareness also helps young offenders to assume responsibility (Wright, p. 77). The restorative justice approach focuses on the needs of the perpetrator and the improvement of the situation arising from the offense, rather than focusing on the offender's culpable intentions or crime (Wright, 1999; Alkon, 2019).

Another perspective on the issue is that restorative models focus on the offender ignore the victim and do not take into account the needs of the victim. However, this concern is unfounded as restorative justice models have a victim-oriented approach. Since the victim, who takes part in the judicial process as a witness, is actively involved in the process with these interview models and has the right to speak, the needs of the victim are not ignored.

Restorative justice models are also peaceful practices in the sense that they do not cause perpetrators to feel excluded from society. This is because a perpetrator who feels excluded from society is likely to feel anger towards society and commit new crimes. On the matter of this, offenders is the perception of the consequences of the act committed by the offender during the application of these models and the sense of shame that arises in the offenders due to the wrongfulness of their act, as well as taking responsibility. This shame is expressed as a helpful and necessary feeling for offenders to not commit the criminal act again and to continue their lives as an individual in harmony with society (Wright, p. 177). A genuine acceptance of responsibility for one's action also brings with it an uncomfortable feeling of regret (Braithwaith, 2006). Therefore, it has a crime prevention function in terms of fostering a sense of shame.

Another gain of restorative justice models is the reduction in the use of penal institutions. Since the implementation of restorative models allows the perpetrator to take responsibility and compensate for the damage he/she has caused, the fact that he/she does not have to enter penal institutions, even for a short period, leads to a decrease in the number of people in these institutions and thus the resources allocated by the state for this purpose. Therefore, it can be stated that these models benefit both the offender and society in terms of the use of public resources (Wright, p. 80). These models are considered useful in the doctrine in terms of reducing the recidivism rates of offenders who commit minor offenses (Umbreit, 1994; Ward et al., 2014).

Restorative justice models reveal a different perspective in terms of the questions they ask. This different perspective is a perspective that emphasizes the possibility of reparation instead of prosecuting or punishing the perpetrator. In criminal justice, when a crime is committed, questions such as "Who did it?, What laws have been broken?, What does the perpetrator deserve?" are asked, while restorative justice models focus on who has been harmed, what is needed and what obligations the offender may have (Umbreit, 1994; Zehr, 2015). Therefore, restorative justice models, which focus on the harm and how to repair it rather than the crime, are victim-oriented approaches. However, being victim-oriented does not mean that they do not create positive outcomes for the perpetrator or that they do not serve the perpetrator's recovery. In these models, the needs, capabilities, and suggestions of the perpetrator are also listened to while deciding how and with which obligations the damage caused by the crime will be remedied. Therefore, obligations that are both possible for the perpetrator and in his/her favor, where there is a gain for him/her at the end of the process, are decided. During this decision-making process, the perpetrator and the victim, and in some models, other subjects participating in the process can make a decision together, and actions that help the perpetrator to become an individual who is at peace with society again can also be agreed upon (Zehr, 2015).

Restorative justice, from the perpetrator's perspective, is expressed as "making things right" (Zehr, 2015). This putting things right also emphasizes the offender's efforts to take responsibility and compensate for the harm. It is also usual for the offender, especially in the younger age group, not to know the possible consequences of the crime he/she committed due to his/her young age. In the implementation of these models, young offenders' "making things right" provides a chance for them to take responsibility, learn and see the consequences of their actions, and continue their lives as law-abiding citizens (Dandurand, 2016; e.g. Zehr, 2005).

In restorative justice models, when the victim has the chance to ask questions directly to the perpetrator, it helps the perpetrator to see the human dimension of the impact of the crime (Vogel, 2007). For example, when the victim asks the offender why the crime has committed the crime, why the victim has chosen, or when the victim shares the difficulties and troubles that the victim has experienced, the offender can establish a direct connection with the victim and see the impact of the crime concretely. For example, in an incident in the case where the windows of the victim's car were smashed, a meeting between the perpetrator and the victim, in which the victim describes the difficulties experienced regarding the purchase of the car and how this affected the victim, may contribute to the perpetrator seeing the consequences of the act more clearly.

As a result of restorative justice-based programs, offender fulfills certain obligations. These programs, which are based on restoration instead of punishment, impose various acts instead of punishment as a result. These acts may be in the form of material compensation or moral acts (Dignan, 2005). In material acts, the offender may be expected to compensate for damage caused by the offense in material terms. For example, if the offender breaks the victim's glasses during a fight, the offender may be expected to compensate for this damage as a result of the interview, or if the victim had to go to the hospital because of the offender, the offender may be expected to cover the hospital expenses. As a moral act, the offender may apologize to the victim for the harmful consequence. This apology may be verbal, in writing, or, in cases where the victim wishes it to be published or displayed in a certain place, on a platform determined jointly by the victim and the offender. The act of apology can help the victim to end the bad consequences of the incident and move on with their lives. As for offenders, it is seen as an opportunity for them to take responsibility for the crime in terms of morale and to compensate for their crime, especially for young perpetrators who do not have an income (Dignan, 2005).

As a result of these meetings, the perpetrator may be assisted in matters related to the obligations imposed on the perpetrator or in matters related to the main reasons that push the perpetrator to commit the crime. The reasons that push the perpetrator to commit the crime can also be discussed and even the issues related to taking steps to eliminate these reasons or to change the conditions can be discussed and educational obligations can be imposed on the perpetrator in this regard. In these models based on value-based negotiations, the perpetrator has an active role in determining the obligation and participates in the negotiations (Vogel, 2007).

For example, if the offender has an addiction or a disorder (such as anger management, or control disorder), the offender may be obliged to undergo treatment, therapy, or receive training on a certain subject. Similarly, if offender's motivation for committing the offense is, for example, unemployment, the perpetrator may be obliged to join or work in a certain place. With these acts, offenders can reduce the reasons that push them to commit crimes by receiving education on subjects that will improve themselves or by participating in certain programs.

It should be noted that restorative justice models should be applied not only within the criminal justice system but also in terms of preventive criminal law. Therefore, in cases where the crime has not yet occurred, but the dispute arises as a disciplinary problem, for example in schools, it also has a structure that can prevent crime. The application of models such as public meetings and conferences to disciplinary boards in disputes such as property damage, bullying or fighting in schools can prevent such disputes from turning into more serious crimes later on, and at the same time, it provides an educational restoration model for young people (e.g. Hoyle, 2008). Therefore, these models can be applied within the criminal justice system as well as in a complementary structure within the scope of preventive practices.

The impact of restorative justice-based approaches on offenders may not always be positive. For example, the offender may feel that he/she is not punished for the act he/she committed and that he/she can get away with it, or restorative justice-based models may not be beneficial for repeat offenders. At this point, it should be noted that these models may not be suitable for every offender. In particular, these programs may not be respectful to recidivists or habitual offenders. It is also worth considering the possibility that these models may not be useful for those who commit serious and violent crimes. Therefore, these interview models may not apply to every offender and every offense and may not bring positive results. In this respect, the criteria for sending the files to the relevant centers or practitioners should be well evaluated.

2.2 Examples of Restorative Justice Models and the Role of Offenders in These Models

Restorative justice models are not limited to several groups, although they are grouped below based on the main models in terms of their impact on the rehabilitation of offenders. There are other similar models using terminologies such as crime repair crews, various dialogue models, offender competency development programs, community-based support groups, and victim panels (Ward et al., 2014).

It should be noted that the implementation of restorative justice models varies from country to country and from state to state in the USA. While some of the restorative justice models are implemented outside the criminal justice system, some models are implemented within the criminal justice system, together with the existing system. Particularly in terms of the continental European legal system, there are restorative justice models that are implemented together with the prosecutor's office. Therefore, it is worth noting that not all models are necessarily applied within the criminal system, on a perpetrator registered in the system. Some models are implemented before offender enters the law enforcement system, in the form of resolving the conflict between the offender and the victim through various dialogue and conference boards in the region; others are implemented after the end of the trial, when the offender is in the execution phase. These models are more therapeutic and provide an opportunity for the victim to express themselves (Umbreit, 2001; Zehr, 2015).

i. Conference Models and Family/Community Group Conferencing

The family/group conference model, a model originating from New Zealand, was created as a method aimed to be implemented for the juvenile justice system. This model, which is said to have its historical roots in Maori natives, was enacted in New Zealand in 1989 and then influenced other countries. In these models, which are mainly applied for children, it is also possible for public units or child welfare departments to participate in the process (Amstutz, 2009).

In conference models, the perpetrator and victim are directly involved in the process and come together to discuss the harm caused by the crime. The involvement of family members or members of the community in these discussions does not limit the discussions to the parties to the crime but also includes members of the community. What is meant by community members here is the members of the community who live in the neighborhood where the crime was committed whose peace has been disturbed by the crime and who feel themselves in danger. The participation of the offender and victim's families and community members in the process creates the effect that the offender is not excluded from society, and at the same time provides a clearer picture of the effects of the consequences of the crime he/she has committed. It is also possible for social workers, professionals, or lawyers to participate in these conference calls; they can help both offender and victim to express themselves, protect their rights, and take part in the process (e.g. Amstutz, 2009).

For example, in a conference call for damaging a victim's property, the victim and his/her family have the opportunity to express the harm and fear they have suffered as a result of the crime, and to present a payment plan to pay for the damage. The perpetrator, on the other hand, has the opportunity to discuss the reasons that led him or her to do what they did and to take responsibility and make reparation for the harm. Members of the community and other professionals present at the conference can advise the perpetrator on the impact of the offense on society and give their views on this issue (Amstutz, 2009).

These models, which can be especially useful for young offenders in terms of creating the opportunity to make amends for the crime they have committed and giving them the chance to make an effort in this regard by feeling remorse, can contribute to society as well as the offender in terms of members of the community coming together to solve a problem. The model in question is also practiced in Australia under the name of Wagga Wagga and these conferences are attended by law enforcement and officials from the school of the child offender. The Wagga Wagga model, on which the US model is based, is based on the reintegrative shaming theory. According to this theory, the perpetrator feels shame by seeing the impact of the crime on the victim and the damage it has caused, and this shame prevents him from committing the crime again. (Braithwaite, 2006) The shame felt by offenders help them to take responsibility together with the feeling of regret. Therefore, there is a structure based on the view that the offender, who is ashamed in front of the victim, the victim's family, the offender's own family, and community members, will learn from this and will not commit the same act again.

It should be noted that some family/community - conference models may differ in the stages of implementation. For example, in cases where the police department can transfer the incoming file to the relevant unit or center for a conference call without notification, it may also be possible to close the file outside the criminal justice system. Another method, for cases that go to court, is for the judge to refer the file to the relevant center to conduct conference calls. Thus, the implementation of a conferencing model may differ in terms of where and from which unit the file originates (Maxwell/Morris, p. 2; Bazemore/Umbreit, 2001).

Family/group conference models, like other restorative justice models, find application for minor crimes. These models, which are applied in crimes such as theft, simple injury, and property damage, differ from other models in that the perpetrator is mostly a child/youth.

Another type of program within the conferencing models is police-led conferencing. These models, which are integrated with law enforcement, are implemented at the pre-trial stage when the dispute has already reached law enforcement. The police-led conferencing model, whose main focus is on the community and community representation, is based on reintegrative shaming theory, as in family-community conferences (Braithwaite, 2006; Dignan, 2005). In this model, where the active participation of the parties is sought, the perpetrator is also actively involved in the process.

These negotiations include approaches that use different methods or different terminology. For example, restorative caution as practiced in the Thames Valley in the UK is one such approach. In restorative caution, the police officer can be directly involved in the negotiations as soon as the conflict is brought to his/her attention. It should be noted that this method can also be applied in crimes where the victim is not present. For example, in a case involving the possession of cannabis by an adult offender, the offender and the police officer will be present in the negotiations, since there is no specific victim. In cases where there is a specific victim of the crime, the victim or the victim's representative is present in the interviews, as in other models (Dignan, 2005; Hoyle, 2008; Marshall, 1999).

ii. Sentencing Circles

Circle processes referred to as sentencing circles, are interview models in which the perpetrator and the victim come together with all members of the community to reach an agreement. In this model, not only members of the community living in the place where the crime was committed but also law enforcement, relevant public officials, family members, and even members of the judiciary are involved. Thus, everyone involved in the interview is part of a circle, discussing the offense between the offender and the victim, and is involved in finding a solution. Sentencing circles differ from other models in terms of the diversity and multiplicity of participants. Therefore, almost every layer of society is brought together through these interviews. The victim and the community affected by the crime are present in the interviews, as well as the subjects who would be involved if the case in question had come before the judicial authorities (Vogel, 2007).

Sentencing circles are expressed as effective models for the social integration of the perpetrator into society. Since there is a view of listening and healing the offender instead of judging him/her, a structure in which the offender is understood, and reconciled with the society and at the same time everyone affected by the crime is healed. In this respect, punitive rings can be considered to bring the offender closer to society (Vogel, 2007). As well as focusing on the damage caused by the crime committed by the perpetrator, the people in the circle also focus on the perpetrator and listen to the offender. Therefore, an environment in which responsibility is shared and society gains sensitivity towards the offender and crime can also be formed in this way. The new situation of the offender created by the crime is understood by all the subjects in the circle and is also beneficial for sharing social values and finding solutions together (Bazemore/Umbreit, 2001). Therefore, the bond between the offender and society, which was disrupted by the crime, can be repaired through these meetings.

In sentencing circles, the offender speaks in an environment in which the victim, the victim's family, and community members are present and listen to the harm experienced by the victim in this environment. In circle processes, which can create an environment in favor of the perpetrator in terms of not feeling isolated from society, the offender also has the opportunity to discuss the reasons leading to committing the crime. Sentencing circle models are also beneficial in terms of achieving more flexible results (Dandurand, 2016; Amstutz, 2009). The offender and the victim, together with the people participating in the negotiations, can determine an act and an obligation as they wish.

It should be underlined that sentencing circles are not only about reaching a limited agreement on how the offender will compensate the victim. They aim at a broader conversation that focuses on the criminal act committed by the offender and explores its causes, effects and consequences for the community. (Aertsen& Willemsens, 2001)

Sentencing circles have some basic elements. The main elements of the interview include a ceremony process, the determination of the guidelines to be followed in the interview, the speaking process, the facilitation phase, and consensus decision-making (Pranis, 2005). In these phases, the main purpose of the interview and the basic values are reminded with an opening speech, followed by the determination of the basic rules to be followed in the interview, and then the conversation phase in which the actions and effects of the perpetrator are discussed. In this respect, by reminding the basic values and emphasizing that a decision will be made together with the community, public interviews raise awareness of the perpetrator to take responsibility and compensate for the consequences (Amstutz, 2009; Pranis, 2005).

iii. Victim-Offender Mediation

Victim-offender mediation refers to a model in which the perpetrator and the victim meet through a third party, the mediator (Umbreit, 1994). In victim-offender mediation, as in other models, the external participants are quite limited. Therefore, there is no participation of family members, community members, or other people in these meetings and it is not a common practice to have participation in the meetings other than the direct party of the crime.

Victim-offender mediation is not a model in which the perpetrator and the victim must come face to face. In victim-offender mediation, which differs from other models in this respect, the parties can have a remote meeting with each other by conveying their views and wishes to the mediator without ever coming face to face. In this model, which is called shuttle diplomacy, the parties send their views to the other party verbally or in writing to the conciliator without sitting around a table or seeing each other at all (Umbreit, 2001). Although it is not very compatible with the main purpose of the model, in practice, there may be cases where some victims are afraid to face the perpetrator and want to express their views through the mediator. Likewise, the offender may be afraid of the reactions that may come from the victim or avoid coming together with the perpetrator because they do not know what kind of environment they will encounter. In these cases, with the help of the mediator, the parties can meet and convey their demands, wishes, and feelings to each other (Zehr, 2015).

In victim-offender mediation, mediator contacts the parties after receiving the file. There is no clear practice regarding which party the conciliator should contact first. In some models, the mediator first contacts the victim, informs the victim about mediation asks whether victim wants to participate in the meeting, and then contacts the offender. The main reason for this is that it would be more reasonable not to create an expectation in the offender from the beginning and to contact the offender according to the response of the victim. However, the common preference in practice is to contact the offender first, and after the offender accepts the process, the victim is offered an interview. The reason behind this preference is to prevent the possibility of the victim feeling victimized again if the victim accepts the process and the offender does not want it (Umbreit, 2001).

3. THE IMPACT OF POLICE ON RESTORATIVE JUSTICE MODELS AND RECOMMENDATIONS

This aspect of the offender can be seen by the victim as much as the offender actively participates in the process and sees the harm caused by the crime and the victim sees the human side of the offender affected by it. The offender may be a person who has committed a crime or has been pushed to commit a crime because of certain internal motivations. Especially in cases where this person is a first-time offender or a young person and the crime is a minor offense, restorative models can offer an opportunity to reintegrate the perpetrator into society. In the process of evaluating this opportunity, police has different duties both in the process of directing the file to the relevant center before the meeting and in direct meetings in some models. Indeed, police officers are the first contact between the perpetrator and the victim after the dispute. The attitude of the police at this point and the way they handle the dispute is in a position to influence the sending of the file to the relevant places for the implementation of restorative justice models and the achievement of positive results in this process. The fact that the police force is in a more passive structure that observes, follows the process, and intervenes where necessary, without taking on a judgmental role like a judge, both before and during the meetings, may help the offender to be reintegrated into society (e.g. O'Mahony&Doak, 2004).

Although there is a possibility that the presence of police officers may prevent the offender and the victim from expressing themselves openly, the presence of law enforcement may benefit the process in terms of reducing security concerns for both parties. Indeed, offenders, just like victims, may also feel security concerns about how the other party will react and whether there will be a reaction from the other party and whether the other party will take an attitude against them in anger. In this respect, the presence of the police at the meetings can be considered a safe element in terms of relieving this concern.

In some legal systems where restorative justice models are applied, police officers also take part in the process and sometimes meet with the offender and the victim as a mediator and sometimes as a participant in these meetings. It is quite normal for the police force, which is the first person that the victim who has filed a complaint, especially in terms of minor crimes, to take part in the process in which these models are applied. However, various conference, public, and reconciliation models, which enable the offender to re-establish a lawful bond with society, bring along various discussions in terms of the involvement of the police in the process. This issue has also been discussed in foreign legal literature and it has been emphasized whether and at what stage the police should be involved in the implementation of these models.

The role of police in restorative justice models is very important. For example, in terms of conference meetings, in terms of forwarding a file to the relevant conference model without entering it into the system, the police should have a good command of the restorative justice model system and be aware of which files will be referred and under which conditions.

At this point, it should be noted that law enforcement has a great duty in terms of the effective implementation of restorative justice models and the harmonization of offenders to society. First of all, law enforcement agencies and police should have a good command of restorative justice models and should be aware of the main purpose and benefit of these models; they must be made aware of this issue. In addition, since the models in question are constantly changing, it would also be beneficial to organize regular training. It would also be meaningful to organize regular symposiums, conferences, and workshops, especially in the US, to see the different models implemented in different states and to share statistics and positive aspects. This would be beneficial not only for the US but also for other countries in terms of sharing information and collecting healthy data on the effective use of these models, regardless of the legal system.

4. CONCLUSION

Restorative justice models are a new understanding that allows victim and offender to repair the relationship between them arising from crime. Offender and victim, who are directly in the decision-making position, decide how the process will be concluded with the help of a third party. Restorative justice models, which are one of the auxiliary factors in the rehabilitation of offender, when applied in the criminal justice system, it is seen that there are different subjects in the process. In some models, only offender and victim have a closed and confidential meeting with the mediator. In contrast, in other models, victim and offender may be accompanied by family members, friends, and community members who wish to participate in the process. Among these meetings, there are also large-scale models in which professional officials also participate in the process.

Especially in terms of minor offenses and young offenders, addressing the issue by treating the offender as an individual with a high potential to assume responsibility and approaching the offender with the understanding of reintegrating the offender into society will have a positive impact on the victim and society as well as the offender. Indeed, how the relationship between victim and society responds to the relationship disrupted by the crime closely affects how offenders who continue their lives after the closure of the file subject and also affects how offenders will be integrated into society or what kind of relationship they will have with society.

In conclusion, as Howard Zehr states, "Restorative justice is a compass, not a map" (Zehr, 2015). Therefore, the users of this compass and those who seek a path in the criminal justice system in this way should be compatible with the basic principles of this understanding and use this compass in accordance with the basic values for both offender, victim, and society.

REFERENCES

Aertsen, I., & Willemsens, J. (2001). The European Forum for Victim-Offender Mediation and Restorative Justice. *European Journal on Criminal Policy and Research*, *9*(3), 231–300. doi:10.1023/A:1011604620022

Alkon, C., & Schneider, A. K. (2019). *Negotiating Crime*. Carolina Academic Press.

Amstutz, L. S. (2009). *The Little Book of Victim Offender Conferencing*. Good Books- Skyhorse Publishing.

Bazemore, G., & Umbreit, M. (2001). *A Comparison of Four Restorative Conferencing Models*. Juvenile Justice Bulletin. doi:10.1037/e304232003-001

Braithwaite, J. (2006). *Crime, Shame and Reintegration, 16th Printing*. Cambridge University Press.

Daly, K. (2002). Restorative Justice. *Punishment & Society*, *4*(1), 55–59. doi:10.1177/14624740222228464

Dandurand, Y. (2016). Alternative Approaches to Preventing Recidivism: Restorative Justice and the Social Integrarion of Offenders. In *Women and Children as Victims and Offenders: Background, Prevention, Reintegration* (Vol. H, pp. 283–299). doi:10.1007/978-3-319-28424-8_11

Dignan, J. (2005). *Understanding Victims and Restorative Justice*. Open University Press.

Fortune, C. A., Ward, T., & Willis, G. M. (2011). The Rehabilitation of Offenders: Reducing Risk and Promoting Better Lives. *Psychiatry, Psychology, and Law : an Interdisciplinary Journal of the Australian and New Zealand Association of Psychiatry, Psychology and Law*, *19*(5), 1–16.

Hoyle, C. (2008). Restorative Justice, Victims and the Police. In *The Handbook of Policing (Tim Newburn)* (pp. 794–823). Routledge.

Miers, D. (2001). *An International Review of Restorative Justice, Crime Reduction Research Series Paper 10*. Crown Copyright.

Mousourakis, G. (2020). Restorative Justice. *Domestic and International Perspectives*, *33*(1), 55–86.

O'Mahony, D., & Doak, J. (2004). Restorative Justice - Is More Better? The Experience of Police-Led Restorative Cautioning Pilots in Northern Ireland. *Howard Journal of Criminal Justice*, *43*(5), 484–505. doi:10.1111/j.1468-2311.2004.00344.x

Pranis, K. (2005). *The Little Book of Circle Processes*. Good Books- Skyhorse Publishing.

Umbreit, M. S. (1994). *Victim Meets Offender*. Willow Tree Press Inc.

Umbreit, M. S. (2001). *The Handbook of Victim Offender Mediation*. Jossey-Bass Inc.

Vogel, H. J. (2007). The Restorative Justice Wager: The Promise and Hope of a Value- Based Dialogue- Driven Approach to Conflict Resolution for Social Healing. *Cardozo Journal of Conflict Resolution*, *8*, 565–609.

Ward, T., Fox, K. J., & Garber, M. (2014). Restorative Justice, Offender Rehabilitation and Desistance. *Restorative Justice*, *2*(1), 24–42. doi:10.5235/20504721.2.1.24

Wright, R. (1999). *Restoring Respect for Justice*. Waterside Press.

Zehr, H. (2015). *The Little Book of Restorative Justice*. Good Books- Skyhorse Publishing.

ADDITIONAL READING

Barton, C. (2000). Theories of Restorative Justice. *Australian Journal of Professional and Applied Ethics*, *2*(1), 41–53.

Christie, N. (1977). Conflicts as Property. *British Journal of Criminology*, 17.

McCold, P., & Wachtel, T. (2003). In Pursuit of Paradigm: A Theory of Restorative Justice. *XIII World Congress of Criminology*, Brazil.

Petrucci, C. J. (2002). Apology in the Criminal Justice Setting: Evidence for Inclıding Apology as an Additional Component in the Legal System. *Behavioral Sciences & the Law*, *20*(4), 337–362. doi:10.1002/bsl.495 PMID:12210972

Pollard, C. (2002). Restorative Justice and the Role of the Police, Restorative Justice and Its Relation to the Criminal Justice System. *Second Conference of the European Forum for Victim-Offender Mediation and Restorative Justice*, Belgium.

Umbreit, M. S., & Coates, R. (1999). Multicultural Implication of Restorative Justice. *Federal Probation*, *63*(2), 44–52.

Umbreit, M. S., Vos, B., Coates, R., & Brown, K. (2003). *Victim-Offender Dialogue in Violent Cases: The Texas and Ohio Experience*. VOMA Connections.

Chapter 10
Piloting Body-Worn Cameras in Northern Canada

Ariane Khanizadeh
Royal Canadian Mounted Police, Canada & Carleton University, Canada

https://orcid.org/0009-0006-2437-3356
Royal Canadian Mounted Police, Canada & Carleton University, Canada

Simon Baldwin
https://orcid.org/0000-0002-4145-2930
Royal Canadian Mounted Police, Canada & Carleton University, Canada

Audrey MacIsaac

Genevieve Brook
Carleton University, Canada

Liana Lanzo
Carleton University, Canada

Craig Bennell
Carleton University, Canada

ABSTRACT

The Royal Canadian Mounted Police (RCMP) are implementing body-worn cameras (BWCs) across the country. This chapter reports on a pilot project designed to evaluate the implementation of these cameras that was conducted in Iqaluit, Nunavut, a remote northern Canadian community. Findings from several surveys – one focusing on community members and the others focusing on RCMP officers – are presented, and the impact on operational data (e.g., crime trends) is discussed. These findings suggest that BWCs are generally supported by the public and although crime and use-of-force rates during the pilot project did not differ from historical trends, BWCs were generally perceived to increase public safety and help improve police-public relations. RCMP officers are also generally satisfied with their BWCs and their BWC training. The authors believe this pilot project helped develop community trust around the use of BWCs by RCMP officers and they hope the project description provides a blueprint for other agencies to implement their own culturally sensitive and community-focused BWC program.

DOI: 10.4018/978-1-6684-8569-9.ch010

INTRODUCTION

The Royal Canadian Mounted Police (RCMP) is Canada's national policing service. The RCMP currently employs about 19,000 police officers and 11,000 civilians and provides policing services on municipal, provincial/territorial, and federal levels (including international policing, border integrity, and national security). The RCMP polices over 75% of Canada's landmass and over 22% of Canada's population and provides local law enforcement for 8 provinces, 3 northern territories, around 150 municipalities, and more than 600 Indigenous communities. One of the RCMP's current priorities, which is relevant to the current chapter, is to build relationships and trust with the Indigenous peoples of Canada, partially through the development and delivery of culturally aware and engaged services designed to deliver high-quality policing to Indigenous communities.

The RCMP is currently in the process of implementing body-worn cameras (BWCs) across the country. With the support and cooperation of the Government of Nunavut, one of the three territories making up Canada's north, a BWC pilot project was conducted in Iqaluit. Iqaluit is the capital city of Nunavut, and its largest community, with a population of 7,429 in 2021 (*Statistics Canada*, 2023). It is the community with the largest population of Inuit people in Canada, with over 52% of residents identifying as Inuk (Inuit) and 30% indicating Inuktut (Inuit) languages as their mother tongue (*Statistics Canada*, 2023). Inuit are an original people of Canada, with ancestry on the land dating back several millennia (*Inuit Tapiriit Kanatami, 2004*). Canadian Inuit have close ties with the Yupik and Inupiat of Alaska and Russia and with the Inuit of Greenland (*Inuit Tapiriit Kanatami, 2004*). Iqaluit has a geographical area of approximately 32 square miles (52 km^2) and is only accessible by air and sea. It is at a similar latitude to Fairbanks (Alaska), Reykjavík (Iceland), and Arkhangelsk (Russia). It has an average daily temperature of -17°F (-27.2°C) in January and February and 46°F (7.7 °C) in July and August (*Government of Canada*, 2023).

As the environment in Nunavut presents a set of unique challenges for the RCMP (e.g., lack of technological infrastructure, extreme climate conditions, limited personnel for administrative support, remote location, and language and cultural barriers), this BWC pilot project was essential for addressing the applicability of existing RCMP processes and practices, including community acceptance and support for the BWC program. On November 30th, 2020, Nunavut began equipping officers with BWCs using a phased approach (i.e., the number of officers wearing BWCs increased over time). This scaled approach was used so that information and feedback from earlier users could inform changes as the pilot project progressed. The pilot project lasted six months and ended on May 31st, 2021. It aimed to identify best practices and clarify lessons learned to inform RCMP policy and training, and to allow for a framework to be developed to ensure that the national rollout of BWCs would be culturally-sensitive and community-focused.

To ensure the pilot project's success, RCMP officials at the territorial and national levels established a robust internal working group to support awareness, consultation, and evaluation activities. This working group included RCMP leadership from the territory of Nunavut and Iqaluit, the local RCMP BWC Project Manager and BWC Coordinator, as well as representatives from national RCMP units responsible for Indigenous relations, youth, media, diversity, operational computer systems, and research.

In this chapter, we report on the outcomes of the RCMP's pilot project. We first discuss the community consultation process undertaken to facilitate the project and describe the results from community surveys, which speak to citizens' perceptions towards BWCs. We then present the results from surveys of RCMP officers, which examined their satisfaction with the RCMP's BWC training and their BWCs more generally. Finally, we will present operational data and other outcome variables (e.g., crime trends) that were examined during the pilot project. We believe the steps undertaken for this pilot project helped develop community trust around the use of BWCs by RCMP officers in Iqaluit, and we hope that the description of these steps within this chapter provides a blueprint for other agencies to follow as they work through their own implementation of BWCs.

COMMUNITY CONSULTATION AND ENGAGEMENT

The community consultation and engagement process associated with the BWC pilot project consisted of several key components, each of which is briefly described in this section.

Literature on BWCs and Community Engagement

As a first step, a review of the literature was conducted to better understand (1) challenges that might arise in remote and Indigenous communities should BWCs be worn by RCMP officers in Nunavut, (2) benefits that may be associated with the use of BWCs in these communities, and (3) best practices for obtaining the opinions of diverse populations about BWC use (i.e., socioeconomically, racially, geographically). Several relevant challenges and benefits were identified in the literature, which were considered when developing the pilot project and should be considered when BWCs are to be deployed in remote and racialized communities. These are listed in Table 1.

Table 1. Challenges and benefits of BWC implementation identified in the literature

Challenges	Benefits
• Racial bias and profiling (e.g., Murphy, 2018) • The failure of BWCs to capture systemic issues/ contextual factors (e.g., Glasbeek et al., 2020) • The necessity for broader commitments to police-community reparation, over and above camera deployment • Unique environmental hazards • Resource availability to deal with BWC data • Privacy and reliability • The inability of BWCs to change the power dynamics between the police and members of the public • Issues of transparency (e.g., videos capturing children, youth, and bystanders, availability/release of the footage, etc.).	• Increased safety (e.g., Jennings et al., 2014, Dockstader et al., 2022) • Increased public trust and/or legitimacy in police (e.g., Demir et al., 2020) • Increased transparency and accountability (e.g., Jennings et al., 2015) • Exposing the realities and challenges of policing • Reduced public complaints (e.g., Ariel et al., 2015) • Enhanced evidence collection (e.g., Blaskovits & Bennell, 2020)

In general, the available research suggested that perceptions of BWCs could be improved by ongoing public awareness and communication between the police and the public (e.g., town halls, open discussions). For BWC implementation to have positive effects on police-community relations, the literature also recommended the use of "inclusionary policing practices," such as community policing strategies (e.g., proactive and continual collaboration between the public and police around community needs), continuous engagement of stakeholders (e.g., bi-annually), and ensuring that BWC policy is aligned with community needs and interests (e.g., ongoing identification of community needs through examination of outcomes and modifications to BWC policy as required; St. Louis et al., 2019).

Several suggestions were outlined in the literature for obtaining the opinions of members of the public who experience marginalization. Key suggestions include: (1) engaging the community and allowing them to fully participate in the implementation process and (2) tailoring material to each specific community and their unique barriers. For example, O'Donnell and Beaton (2018) emphasize the importance of producing knowledge jointly to create critical interpretations of the world that are actionable, accessible, and understandable to everyone involved. Similarly, Lewis and colleagues (2016) explain that multiple distribution methods (e.g., door-to-door information packages, online surveys, community newsletters, word of mouth) can increase the response rate in Indigenous communities.

Environmental Scan of BWC Awareness Material

An environmental scan was conducted to determine what types of awareness materials other police agencies (e.g., in Canada, the United States, the United

Kingdom, Australia) were sharing about the rollout of BWCs. This identified standard methods of information sharing such as pamphlets, posters, and websites. It also identified messaging themes around transparency, safety, how BWCs are used, as well as open access to agency BWC policy. Public awareness material was produced using information from the environmental scan. Updates were made based on the consultations that took place, which are described in the next section.

Consultations With Stakeholders

Consultations occurred with government officials, Indigenous leaders, and organizations at both the local and national levels throughout the planning for the pilot project. For example, various drafts of awareness materials (including pamphlets, posters, and website) were prepared and shared with several national Indigenous organizations in Canada for their review and feedback. These groups did not report any concerns and were pleased to see the representation of Indigenous RCMP officers within the materials and requested that the cultural component in these materials (including the inukshuk[1] that is displayed on the flag of Nunavut) be retained. The RCMP also consulted with its National Youth Advisory Committee (NYAC), which is comprised of approximately 125 diverse youth (aged 13-21) across Canada, about the materials. Overall, members of the NYAC were relatively unanimous in their opinion that BWCs would increase transparency and safety. In addition to consultations with these stakeholders, an external BWC working group was formed and met regularly prior to the start of the pilot. This working group consisted of various Canadian government officials at the municipal, provincial, and federal levels, various Inuit organizations, an Inuit police force that serves 14 remote northern communities, as well as representatives from the RCMP in Nunavut.

Consultation with stakeholders benefitted the pilot project as it led to changes in the content included on the RCMP's awareness materials. For example, some of the national Indigenous organizations raised questions about BWC video retention and privacy implications for members of the public – information that was then added to the public-facing website and materials (e.g., frequently asked questions). The NYAC raised questions about video ownership and privacy concerns around the video footage, which led to the inclusion of links to the executive summary of the pilot project's Privacy Impact Assessment[2] on the RCMP's website.

Unfortunately, in-person community awareness and consultation initiatives such as town halls could not be conducted during the pilot period due to COVID-19 restrictions.

Community Awareness of the BWC Initiative

To raise awareness about the RCMP's use of BWCs in Iqaluit and the pilot project, various initiatives were undertaken including the development of an awareness campaign and media interviews.

Awareness Campaign

Based on the insights from the literature review, environmental scan, and consultations, an awareness campaign was launched so that information could reach as many people in Iqaluit as possible. This involved publishing and distributing the posters, pamphlets, and website that served as an information hub and facilitated sharing of the BWC policy, press releases, and answers to frequently asked questions with the public, stakeholders, and the media.

Two versions of the poster were developed, one featuring an Inuit female RCMP officer and one featuring an Inuit male RCMP officer. These posters informed the public that RCMP officers would now be wearing BWCs in their community (see Figure 1). For more information, links were included on the poster so individuals could send an email to the RCMP, view a public RCMP website, or visit the RCMP in Nunavut's Facebook page. Once the pilot project commenced, the designated email was monitored by the BWC Coordinator in Iqaluit. The posters were printed in

Figure 1. BWC posters distributed in Iqaluit informing residents of the pilot project

English, French, and Inuktut, encompassing both Inuktitut (syllabics) and Inuinnaqtun (Roman orthography).

Pamphlets in a similar design were also created and included the following additional information:

- Dates when officers would begin wearing BWCs
- How many officers would have BWCs in each phase of the pilot project
- Why the RCMP was considering the rollout of BWCs (e.g., to increase trust between police and the communities they serve)
- How officers will use their BWCs (i.e., when they turn them on and off, whether civilians will be informed a camera is on, what happens if a bystander is caught on tape, and how to request a copy of the video)
- How one can request Nunavut's BWC policy

As with the posters, the pamphlets were printed in English, French, and Inuktut and solicited feedback from the community about the use of BWCs in a variety of ways, including Facebook, email, in-person at the Iqaluit RCMP detachment, and by completing a confidential online or paper-based survey (see Figure 2). The posters and pamphlets were placed in three grocery stores, six convenience stores, five hotels, four restaurants, two shelters (one for men and one for women), three financial institutions, and 12 other spaces that included auto mechanics, the airport, the post office, an Elder's[3] home, a liquor store, a soup kitchen, and the Iqaluit Legion, among others.

The public RCMP website served as a central information hub for the pilot project and contained information about the phased rollout of BWCs and similar information as in the pamphlet concerning how officers would be using the cameras (see Figure 3). Feedback was obtained on the website through the confidential survey, Facebook, email, and in-person at the RCMP Iqaluit detachment. The language of the website could be toggled to change between English, French, or Inuktut.

Local independent Inuit businesses in Iqaluit were employed to translate the material (i.e., posters, pamphlets, website) whenever possible. The information for all the materials was also reviewed to ensure it was understandable in all languages, and comprehensible by various age groups and reading levels.

Media Interviews

In addition to the formal awareness campaign, the RCMP officers from Iqaluit participated in several media interviews. Prior to the rollout of BWCs, in November 2020, a press conference was held in Iqaluit and broadcasted online, with questions being answered in English and Inuktut. Moreover, prior to and throughout the pilot

Figure 2. BWC pamphlets distributed in Iqaluit informing residents of the details of the pilot project

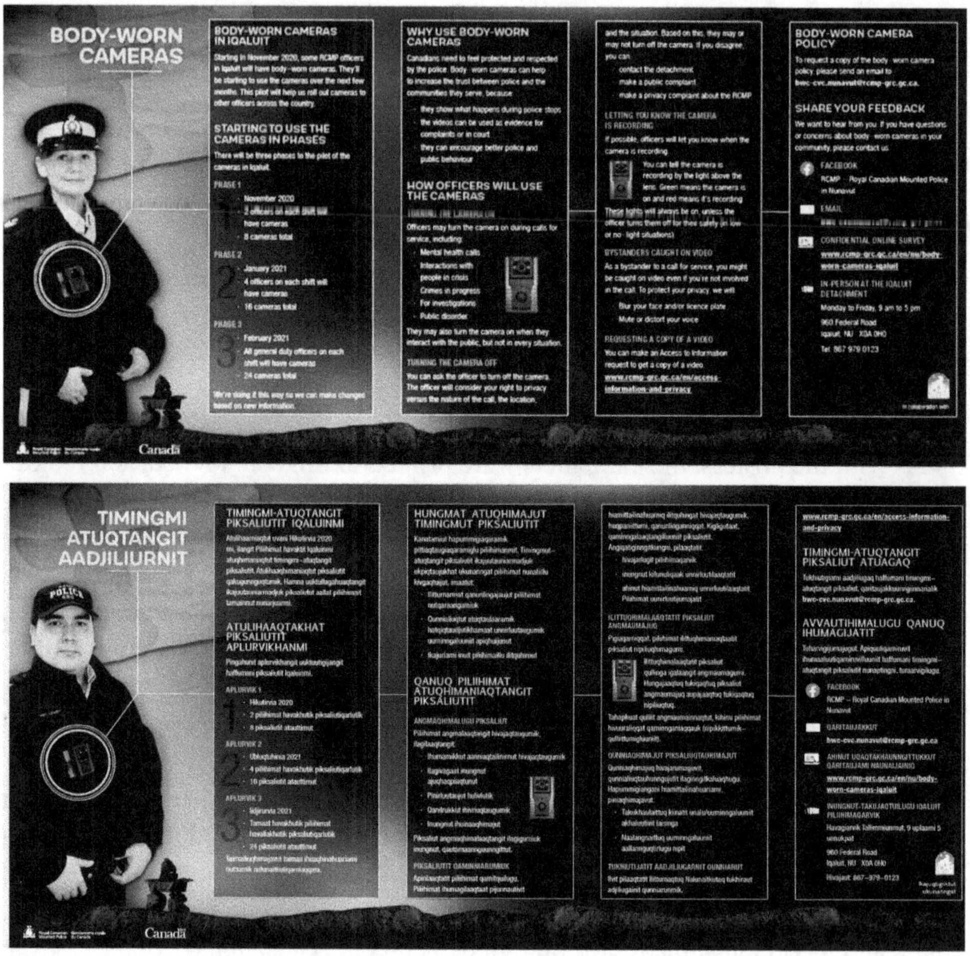

project, the RCMP worked with local media to increase public awareness and solicit public perceptions and feedback on BWCs and the pilot project. Below is a list of some of the interviews that were conducted:

- RCMP to begin using body-worn cameras in Iqaluit next month (Nunatsiaq News, October 22, 2020)
- Iqaluit RCMP provides details for body-worn camera pilot project (Nunatsiaq News, October 30, 2020)
- Iqaluit RCMP to begin wearing body cameras on Monday as pilot project gets underway (Nunavut News, November 27, 2020)

Figure 3. Public-facing BWC pilot project webpage

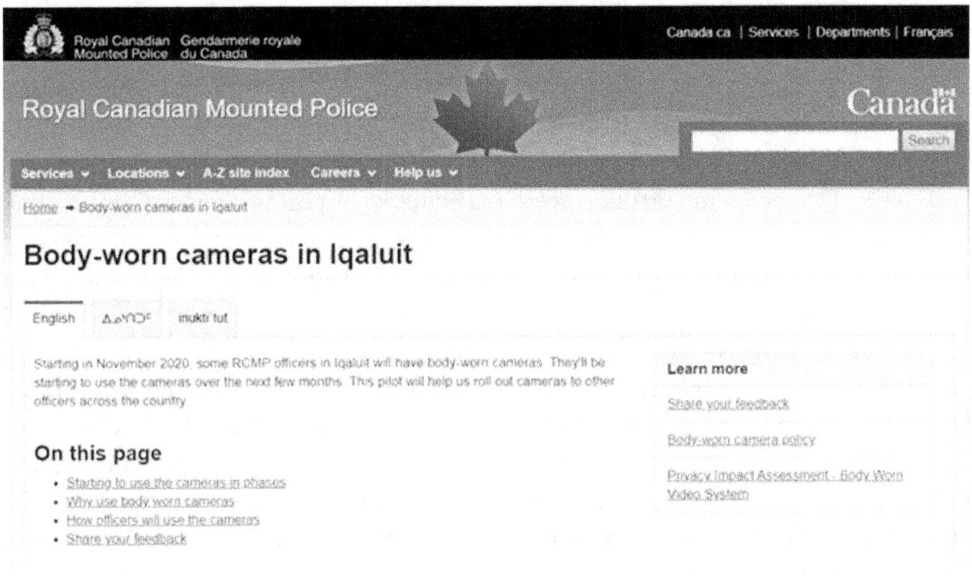

- Iqaluit RCMP want public feedback on body-worn camera pilot project (Nunatsiaq News, December 15, 2020)
- Increasing trust and transparency requires more than just cameras, says RCMP inspector (Nunatsiaq News, January 27, 2021)
- RCMP to evaluate body camera program, seek community input (Nunatsiaq News, May 26, 2021)

Community Survey: Perceptions of BWCS

The community survey was developed specifically to solicit information from local community members about the pilot project and the use of BWCs more broadly. It provided real-time information from residents, establishing an important feedback loop to inform agency policy, training, and procedures. The survey was advertised on pamphlets distributed in Iqaluit in RCMP detachments and neutral locations throughout the community (e.g., grocery stores) and promoted through the media. It was accessible in-person (paper copy) for individuals who attended the detachment or had been taken into custody and were waiting to be processed for release, as well as online in English, French, and Inuktut. The survey was subject to the Government of Canada's Public Opinion Research Process and was approved by the Commissioner of the RCMP, The Privy Council Office (PCO), and the Public Opinion Research Directorate (PORD) at Public Services and Procurement Canada (PSPC).

A literature review was conducted to help with the development of the survey. Based on this review, several themes were identified as particularly pertinent to include in the survey. They included: (1) the impact that BWCs have on community trust, (2) citizens' perceptions of BWCs and privacy, (3) the extent to which BWCs improve police transparency, (4) whether BWCs increased perceptions of safety (e.g., by reducing use of force), and (5) cultural or spiritual concerns with regard to BWCs. Two academic articles were particularly important, one by Sousa et al. (2018) and the other by Crow et al. (2017), as they included measures encompassing these themes. Questions from within these articles were used and adapted for the community survey.

The community survey also included open-text boxes to allow individuals to provide additional or general comments, should they have any, and it collected brief demographic information on the individuals completing the questions. The survey was released near the start of the pilot project and remained open throughout the duration of the project; it continued to be advertised for a period after the pilot project in an attempt to capture citizens' experience of having had officers wear BWCs in their community.

Responses were examined from a total of 70 surveys (61 surveys were completed online and the remaining nine surveys were completed on the paper-based version).

Demographic Characteristics

Half of the respondents reported being male (53.7%, $n = 36$), 30.6% ($n = 21$) reported being female, 2.9% ($n = 2$) reported being two-spirit,[4] 11.4% ($n = 8$) indicated that they *prefer not to say*, and 4.3% ($n = 3$) did not respond. The respondents were fairly evenly distributed with respect to their reported age, with 20.0% ($n = 14$) of respondents aged 18-29, 24.3% ($n = 17$) aged 30-39, 18.6% ($n = 13$) aged 40-49, 12.9% ($n = 9$) aged 50-59, and 5.7% ($n = 4$) aged 60 years or older. When asked their age, an additional 10.0% ($n = 7$) of respondents reported that they *prefer not to say*, and 8.6% ($n = 6$) did not respond.

When asked about race, ethnicity, and Indigeneity, most respondents identified as White (50.0%, $n = 35$), 18.6% ($n = 13$) identified as Inuit,[5] 4.3% ($n = 3$) identified as Métis, and 2.9% ($n = 2$) identified as First Nations. One participant (1.4%) identified as South Asian, one (1.4%) identified as Black, one (1.4%) identified as Filipino, and 5.7% ($n = 4$) selected *other*.[6] Most of the respondents (77.1%, $n = 54$) indicated that they were residents of Nunavut, with 18.6% ($n = 13$) indicating that they were not. Lastly, most respondents ($n = 46$, 65.7%) reported never having interacted with an RCMP officer wearing a BWC, whereas 14.3% of respondents ($n = 10$) reported they had, and 17.1% ($n = 12$) reported not knowing whether they had.

Perceptions of BWCs

Overall, most respondents indicated that they *agreed* or *strongly agreed* that BWCs increase their trust in the police (68.5%), BWCs help the police be more transparent (77.2%), BWCs increase public safety (61.5%), and BWCs improve the relationship between the police and the community (61.4%). Additionally, most respondents *disagreed* or *strongly disagreed* that BWCs are an invasion of their privacy (66.2%) or an invasion of their community's privacy (68.6%). However, responses were mixed regarding whether respondents believed that BWCs decrease police officers' use of force (see Table 2). When negative ratings were received, an open-text box was presented to gather more information from respondents. However, for the sake of brevity, these results have been omitted from the current reporting of the findings.

The last question in the survey asked whether respondents had any cultural, religious, or spiritual concerns with the use of BWCs in their community. Most respondents reported that they had no concerns in this regard (92.9%), while 5.7% indicated that they did.

Lastly, respondents were asked whether they had any final comments, questions, or concerns about BWCs in general. The themes that emerged from these responses centered around policies related to the use of BWCs and how video footage would be stored. In general, there were positive comments about the implementation of BWCs as the community felt it would allow for the public to see the difficult situations that officers encounter. The community members felt that, for BWCs to be effective, they would need to remain turned on, and voiced that there should be regulations in place to share the video footage in a timely manner with the public. However, a

Table 2. Survey results regarding community perceptions of BWCs

	Strongly Agree	Agree	Neutral	Disagree	Strongly Disagree
BWCs increase my trust in the police	31.4%	37.1%	22.9%	5.7%	2.9%
BWCs help the police to be more transparent	38.6%	38.6%	12.9%	7.1%	2.9%
BWCs decrease police officers' use of force	12.9%	22.9%	31.4%	25.7%	7.1%
BWCs increase public safety	28.6%	32.9%	20.0%	11.4%	7.1%
BWCs improve the relationship between the police and the community	37.1%	24.3%	24.3%	10.0%	4.3%
BWCs are an invasion of my privacy	2.9%	13.2%	17.6%	36.8%	29.4%
BWCs are an invasion of my community's privacy	4.3%	8.6%	18.6%	30.0%	38.6%

concern arose regarding the accompanying privacy issues with sharing this footage. There were also conflicting views regarding the safety of the officers when wearing a camera. One comment stated that it would better protect both the subjects and the officers, whereas others worried that wearing a BWC might escalate situations. The comments provided recommendations to use a third-party organization for both the review of footage and the implementation of the BWC survey. Overall, most of the comments suggested that the community was pleased with the steps that were taken for the pilot project (e.g., community consultations).

Temporal Changes in Perceptions Over the Duration of the Pilot Project

Analyses were conducted to examine changes in perceptions as the pilot project progressed. Respondents who submitted the survey in the first three months of the pilot (December to February) were considered to be the "early-pilot" group (n = 24, 34.3%) and those who submitted the survey within the last three months of the pilot and one-month post-pilot (March to June) were considered to be the "end/post-pilot" group (n = 46, 65.7%). Chi-square tests were conducted to examine if any differences existed between these groups.[7] Differences in responses between the early-pilot and end/post-pilot groups were *not* statistically significant.

Race-Based Analysis of Community Survey Results

To examine potential differences between White respondents and Inuit, Indigenous, and/or racialized respondents, the following race-based analysis was conducted. Of the total sample of 70 respondents, 53 (75.7%) reported their race, ethnicity, or Indigeneity. Of those that reported their race/ethnicity/Indigeneity, 60.4% were White (n = 32) and 39.6% were Indigenous and/or racialized (n = 21). The Indigenous and/or racialized group was comprised of any respondent who reported their race/ethnicity/Indigeneity as Inuit, First Nations, Métis, South Asian, Chinese, Black, Filipino, Latin American, Arab, Southeast Asian, West Asian, Korean, and/or Japanese.[8] The race-based analysis was further broken down into Indigenous respondents (n = 17, 32.1%) who identified as Inuit, First Nations, and/or Métis.

As is demonstrated in Table 3, most respondents within each race category indicated that they *agreed* or *strongly agreed* that BWCs increase their trust in the police (White = 66%; Indigenous/racialized = 76%), BWCs help the police be more transparent (White = 85%; Indigenous/racialized = 81%), BWCs increase public safety (White = 66%; Indigenous/racialized = 67%), and BWCs improve the relationship between the police and the community (White = 62%; Indigenous/racialized = 76%). However, responses were mixed regarding whether respondents believed

Table 3. Survey results regarding community perceptions of BWCs for each race category

	Strongly Agree	Agree	Neutral	Disagree	Strongly Disagree
BWCs increase my trust in the police					
White	28%	38%	25%	9%	0%
Indigenous/racialized	38%	38%	19%	5%	0%
BWCs help the police to be more transparent					
White	44%	41%	9%	6%	0%
Indigenous/racialized	38%	43%	14%	5%	0%
BWCs decrease police officers' use of force					
White	9%	19%	38%	28%	6%
Indigenous/racialized	19%	33%	19%	24%	5%
BWCs increase public safety					
White	25%	41%	19%	9%	6%
Indigenous/racialized	43%	24%	19%	10%	5%
BWCs improve the relationship between the police and the community					
White	34%	28%	25%	9%	3%
Indigenous/racialized	57%	19%	14%	10%	0%
BWCs are an invasion of my privacy					
White	0%	13%	13%	38%	38%
Indigenous/racialized	0%	15%	35%	30%	20%
BWCs are an invasion of my community's privacy					
White	0%	9%	9%	31%	50%
Indigenous/racialized	5%	14%	33%	24%	24%

that BWCs decrease police officers' use of force, whether BWCs are an invasion of their privacy, and whether BWCs are an invasion of their community's privacy.

Approximately one-third of participants reported that they believed BWCs decrease police officers' use of force. However, this finding differed based on the participant's race/ethnicity/Indigeneity. Just under one-third (28%) of White respondents believed this compared to approximately half (52%) of Indigenous and racialized respondents. Specifically, 53% of Indigenous respondents (n = 9) and 69% of Inuit respondents (n = 9) *agreed* or *strongly agreed* with this statement. A statistically significant difference between Inuit and non-Inuit respondents was observed ($p = .042$), whereby Inuit respondents believed that BWCs decrease police use of force to a greater degree than non-Inuit respondents.

When asked whether body-worn cameras are an invasion of their *personal* privacy, responses across racial groups varied. Specifically, 75% of White respondents (n = 24) and 50% of Indigenous and racialized respondents (n = 10) *disagreed* or *strongly disagreed*. More specifically, 44% of Indigenous respondents (n = 7) and 33% of Inuit respondents (n = 4) *disagreed* or *strongly disagreed*. A statistically significant difference between Inuit and non-Inuit respondents was observed (p = .033), whereby Inuit respondents indicated greater concern with BWCs being an invasion of their personal privacy than non-Inuit respondents.

Most participants also *disagreed* or *strongly disagreed* that BWCs are an invasion of their own or their *community's* privacy. This finding also differed based on the participant's race/ethnicity/Indigeneity. Fewer Indigenous and racialized participants *disagreed* or *strongly disagreed* that BWCs are invasion of their own or their community's privacy (i.e., Indigenous and racialized participants had more concerns surrounding privacy issues). More specifically, 41% of Indigenous respondents (n = 7) and 38% of Inuit respondents (n = 5) *disagreed* or *strongly disagreed* with this statement. A statistically significant difference between Inuit and non-Inuit respondents was observed (p = .046), whereby Inuit respondents indicated greater concern with BWCs being an invasion of their community's privacy than non-Inuit respondents.

The last statement asked respondents whether they have any cultural, religious, or spiritual concerns with the use of BWCs in their community. Very few participants had cultural, religious, or spiritual concerns with the use of BWCs in their community. However, this response differed based on the participant's race/ethnicity/Indigeneity. No White participants reported having concerns, whereas 10% of Indigenous/racialized participants reported having concerns. Specifically, 12% of Indigenous respondents and 15% of Inuit respondents reported having cultural, religious, or spiritual concerns with the use of BWCs. A statistically significant difference between Inuit and non-Inuit respondents was observed (p = .014), whereby Inuit respondents indicated greater concerns than non-Inuit respondents. A statistically significant difference was also observed between Indigenous and non-Indigenous respondents (p = .041), whereby Indigenous respondents indicated greater concerns than non-Indigenous respondents.

OFFICER SURVEY: PERCEPTIONS OF BWC TRAINING AND BWCS

Two surveys were developed to assess officer perceptions. One of these surveys focused on perceptions of the RCMP BWC training that was provided to officers.

Table 4. RCMP officer ratings of training engagement and clarity

	Strongly Agree	Agree	Neutral	Disagree	Strongly Disagree
I felt actively engaged in learning during this course	10%	60%	10%	15%	5%
The training was well structured and clear	10%	75%	10%	0%	5%

The other survey focused on officer perceptions of BWCs more generally. The results of each survey will be discussed in turn.

BWC Training

The RCMP in Nunavut introduced a new training program for all officers equipped with BWCs during the pilot project. The training focused on how to operate the camera itself, the digital evidence management system, and aspects of the BWC policy. In total, 54 officers completed the training. Following the first wave of training, trainees were asked to complete a training survey. The survey was completed by 20 respondents. The respondents were predominately male (80%), constables (70%), aged 25 to 39 years old (60%), and most had never completed any other kind of BWC training before (60%). Table 4 indicates that most training participants *agreed* or *strongly agreed* that they felt actively engaged in learning during the course (70%) and that the training was well structured and clear (85%).

Concerning their understanding of RCMP BWC policy, the majority of participants *agreed* or *strongly agreed* that they could apply the policy in an operational setting (60%) and that they knew when their BWC should be switched on (95%) and off (75%; see Table 5). Relatedly, the majority of participants *agreed* or *strongly agreed* that they understood their duty to inform members of the public that their BWC was recording (80%), that they knew how their BWC data could be used in judicial proceedings (85%), and that they knew when their BWC data could be used in judicial proceedings (75%). However, it should be noted that 15% of participants also indicated that they *strongly disagreed* when asked if they understood their duty to inform members of the public that their BWC was recording.

General Perceptions of BWCs

All officers who were operational during the BWC pilot project in Iqaluit and used a camera at least once while on-shift were asked to participate in a survey about their experience. The survey asked about their general satisfaction with the performance and configuration of the BWC, how easy it was to use, if they experienced any

Table 5. Ratings of their practical knowledge and understanding of the BWC policy and equipment

	Strongly Agree	Agree	Neutral	Disagree	Strongly Disagree
I can apply the BWC policy in an operational setting	25%	55%	15%	0%	5%
I know when my BWC should be switch on	35%	60%	0%	0%	5%
I know when my BWC should be switched off	25%	50%	15%	5%	5%
I understand my duty to inform members of the public that my BWC is recording	25%	55%	0%	5%	15%
I know how my BWC data can be used in judicial proceedings	10%	75%	5%	5%	5%
I know when my BWC data can be used in judicial proceedings	15%	60%	15%	5%	5%

challenges, their opinion of the mounting location and type of mount they used, the clarity of the BWC policy, and any privacy issues they experienced. Officers were also asked to provide opinions of various camera features that impacted comfort and functionality (e.g., weight, video quality, range of coverage, audio, battery life, display screen). Additionally, officers were asked how the BWC impacted certain aspects of their safety, such as switching the camera from their soft to their hard body armour, and their access to their intervention equipment. Lastly, the survey asked the officers questions about any perceived changes they noticed in themselves or in the public since wearing the camera. Follow-up questions about BWC training were also included. Results for each of these sections are presented below.

The survey was sent to 51 RCMP officers and had a response rate of 25.5% (n = 13).[9] The respondents were predominately male (62%) and at the rank of constable (62%). Where missing values were observed, samples (n) and percentages were adjusted accordingly.

General Satisfaction With the BWC

The first section of the survey asked RCMP officers about their general satisfaction with the BWC. As demonstrated in Table 6, most respondents indicated that they were *very satisfied* or *somewhat satisfied* with the overall performance of the BWC (92.3%), the configurations of the buttons on the BWC (61.5%), the ease of use of the BWC (61.5%), and the molle[10] mount (83.3%). Next, officers were asked whether

Table 6. General satisfaction with the BWC

	Completely Satisfied	Very Satisfied	Somewhat Satisfied	Neutral	Somewhat Unsatisfied	Completely Unsatisfied
How satisfied are you with the overall performance of the BWC?	15.4%	30.8%	46.2%	0.0%	7.7%	0.0%
How satisfied are you with the configuration of the buttons on the BWC?	7.7%	30.8%	23.1%	30.8%	0.0%	7.7%
How satisfied are you with the ease of use of the BWC?	7.7%	30.8%	23.1%	30.8%	0.0%	7.7%
How satisfied are you with the molle mount?[1]	8.3%	33.3%	41.7%	8.3%	8.3%	0.0%

[1]n = 12

the BWC policy was clear, and if unclear, which part(s). The majority of respondents found the policy *very clear* (46.2%) or *somewhat clear* (38.5%).

The final questions in the first section asked officers about possible privacy issues with the camera (see Table 6). Approximately 30.8% of officers said they encountered privacy issues that affected themselves, 23.1% encountered issues affecting other officers' privacy, 23.1% encountered issues with the public's privacy, and 15.4% said they encountered other privacy issues (e.g., the use of BWCs in healthcare settings like hospitals). Respondents (n = 12) were also asked if they thought the RCMP should adopt BWCs for all frontline officers, and nearly all officers responded *yes* (91.7%); only one responded *no* (8.3%).

Comfort and Functionality

The second section of the survey asked respondents (n = 12) questions related to comfort and functionality. Most respondents reported that the BWC was *very comfortable* or *moderately comfortable* (75.1%). Other questions related to the acceptability of various features of the BWC (see Table 7). Briefly, most respondents indicated that the following features were between *somewhat acceptable* and *completely acceptable:* the weight of the BWC (91.7%), the video quality of the BWC (100.0%), the range of coverage captured by the BWC (e.g., periphery; 75.1%), and the audio quality of the BWC (80.0%). However, the ratings were mixed with regards to the bulkiness of the BWC, the video quality of the BWC in low-light conditions, the display screen of the BWC, and the battery life of the BWC.

Table 7. Acceptability of various features of the BWC

	Completely Acceptable	Very Acceptable	Somewhat Acceptable	Neutral	Somewhat Unacceptable	Very Unacceptable	Completely Unacceptable
How acceptable is the weight of the BWC?	50.0%	16.7%	25.0%	8.3%	0.0%	0.0%	0.0%
How acceptable is the bulkiness of the BWC?	8.3%	16.7%	25.0%	33.3%	8.3%	0.0%	8.3%
How acceptable is the video quality of the BWC?	33.3%	41.7%	25.0%	0.0%	0.0%	0.0%	0.0%
How acceptable is the video quality of the BWC in low-light situations?[1]	0.0%	45.5%	9.1%	27.3%	9.1%	0.0%	9.1%
How acceptable is the range of coverage captured by the BWC (e.g., periphery)?	16.7%	41.7%	16.7%	16.7%	8.3%	0.0%	0.0%
How acceptable is the audio quality of the BWC?[2]	30.0%	20.0%	30.0%	20.0%	0.0%	0.0%	0.0%
How acceptable is the display screen of the BWC?	0.0%	8.3%	16.7%	25.0%	25.0%	16.7%	8.3%
How acceptable is the battery life of the camera?	0.0%	16.7%	41.7%	16.7%	8.3%	8.3%	8.3%

[1]$n = 11$
[2]$n = 10$

Finally, respondents were asked if they experienced any issues switching the BWC from their soft body armour to their hard body armour. The two individuals (16.7%) who indicated that it was a problem, mentioned that it was "hard to install" and that "the mount is already on my molle on my soft body armour. This is not a quick transition to move this mount onto hard body armour in an emergency situation."

Officer Safety

The third section of the survey included questions related to officer safety. Respondents ($n = 12$) were asked whether wearing a BWC made them feel safer on the job, which most respondents *strongly agreed* (33.3%), *somewhat agreed* (33.3%) or *neither agreed nor disagreed* (25.0%). As demonstrated in Table 8, most respondents indicated between *completely acceptable* and *somewhat acceptable* regarding the BWC's noise while running (75.1%) and their access to intervention options while wearing the BWC (100.0%). However, responses were more mixed regarding the acceptability of the recording indicator light.

Behavioural Changes

The fourth section of the survey assessed behavioural changes observed by respondents ($n = 12$) as a result of wearing a BWC. Most respondents indicated that they perceived *no changes* in the public's behaviour (83.3%), nor did they perceive any changes in their own behaviour (91.7%) since wearing a BWC. Additionally, there was a reasonably equal divide in responses when asked whether the implementation of BWCs has had an impact on their confidence in their ability to do their job. Specifically, 50.0% of respondent's *disagreed* with the statement, whereas 41.7% *agreed* with the statement. Additional comments provided by respondents related to the benefits of having video evidence, particularly in the case of public complaints.

Table 8. BWCs and officer safety

	Completely Acceptable	Very Acceptable	Somewhat Acceptable	Neutral	Somewhat Unacceptable	Very Unacceptable
How acceptable is the noise that the camera makes while running?	41.7%	16.7%	16.7%	25.0%	0.0%	0.0%
How acceptable is the recording indicator light?	16.7%	16.7%	16.7%	16.7%	25.0%	8.3%
How acceptable is the access to your intervention options while wearing the BWC?	33.3%	33.3%	33.3%	0.0%	0.0%	0.0%

BWC Training

The last section of the survey followed up with officers on the BWC training they received. First, respondents ($n = 12$) were asked about knowledge acquisition from the BWC training (see Table 9). Most respondents indicated that they *agreed* or *strongly agreed* that the BWC course adequately prepared them for the operational use of a BWC (100.0%), that they acquired knowledge and skills during the BWC training course that they have transferred to their workplace (83.4%), that they can upload their BWC data (100.0%), that they can explain how BWC evidence is managed digitally (81.9%), that they have applied the BWC policy in an operational setting (83.3%), that they know when their BWC should be switched on (100.0%) and off (91.7%), and that they can perform basic troubleshooting for their BWC (75.0%). Respondents ($n = 12$) were also asked if they had utilized any of the skills learned during the BWC training course in their operational duties. Most respondents indicated *yes* (75.0%).

Table 9. Knowledge acquisition from the BWC training

	Strongly Agree	Agree	Neutral	Disagree	Strongly Disagree	Not Applicable
The BWC training course adequately prepared me for operational use of a BWC	50.0%	50.0%	0.0%	0.0%	0.0%	0.0%
I acquired knowledge and skills during the BWC training course that I have transferred to my workplace	41.7%	41.7%	16.7%	0.0%	0.0%	0.0%
I can upload my BWC data	50.0%	50.0%	0.0%	0.0%	0.0%	0.0%
I can explain how BWC evidence is managed digitally[1]	36.4%	45.5%	18.2%	0.0%	0.0%	0.0%
I have applied the BWC policy in an operational setting	50.0%	33.3%	8.3%	0.0%	0.0%	8.3%
I know when my BWC should be switched on	50.0%	50.0%	0.0%	0.0%	0.0%	0.0%
I know when my BWC should be switched off.	41.7%	50.0%	0.0%	8.3%	0.0%	0.0%
I can perform basic troubleshooting for my BWC.	33.3%	41.7%	25.0%	0.0%	0.0%	0.0%

[1]$n = 11$

Table 10. Confidence in abilities related to the use of BWCs

	Extremely Confident	Very Confident	Moderately Confident	Slightly Confident	Not at All Confident
Confidence in ability to use a BWC	33.3%	41.7%	25.0%	0.0%	0.0%
Confidence in ability to follow BWC policy	16.7%	50.0%	25.0%	8.3%	0.0%
Confidence in ability to manage one's BWC footage	33.3%	41.7%	25.0%	0.0%	0.0%
Confidence in ability to upload one's BWC footage	33.3%	41.7%	16.7%	8.3%	0.0%
Confidence in ability to manage digital evidence	8.3%	33.3%	33.3%	16.7%	8.3%
Confidence in ability to work with the records management system when a BWC is involved	8.3%	50.0%	25.0%	8.3%	8.3%

As demonstrated in Table 10, respondents ($n = 12$) were then asked a series of questions related to their confidence in various abilities related to the use of BWCs. Here, most respondents indicated that they were *extremely confident* or *very confident* regarding their ability to use a BWC (75.0%), their ability to manage their BWC footage (75.0%), and their ability to upload their BWC footage (75.0%). However, responses were mixed regarding their confidence in their ability to follow BWC policy, manage digital evidence, and work with the records management system when a BWC is involved. Lastly, respondents ($n = 12$) were asked whether there were any changes they would make to the BWC training course after utilizing BWCs operationally. Nearly everyone said *no* (91.7%).

PILOT PROJECT DATA TRACKING

Operational data and other outcome variables (e.g., the number of occurrences,[11] the number of recordings, the quantity of data required to store digital evidence from BWCs, crime trends, use of force) were measured during the pilot project. This section describes these outcomes over the course of the pilot project.

Police Occurrence Data

There was a total of 5,421 occurrences during the pilot project. May 2021 saw the highest monthly number of occurrences (n = 1,069), though the number of occurrences remained relatively stable over the six-month period. In total, 230 (4.2%) occurrences were cleared by charge,[12] with the highest monthly number of clearances in December 2020 (n = 59). Generally, the number of clearances by charge declined over the duration of the pilot project. A total of 776 (14.3%) occurrences had a BWC code, which was a manual flag used to identify the existence of BWC footage associated with a given file when an officer entered information onto the records management system. Occurrences with the highest rates of the BWC codes included crimes against persons (22.4%), followed by crimes against property (15.6%).

Unfortunately, for this pilot project, there was no automatic process to link or flag BWC footage with occurrence files, and there were no systematic quality checks in place to ensure that all files with associated BWC footage had the code. Based on ad hoc quality assurance reviews by the BWC Project Coordinator, it was noted that some occurrences with BWC footage did not include the BWC code. Reasons included lead investigators not being aware that BWC footage from another officer on scene existed and a lack of supervisory oversight due to staffing shortages. Thus, the actual number of occurrences with associated BWC footage may be underestimated.

BWC Data

There was a total of 3,651 BWC recordings over the course of the pilot project. From November 30th, 2020 to March 2021, there was an average of 653 monthly recordings; however, the number of recordings tapered off in April 2021 (489) and May 2021 (533). This decline was unexpected due to the phased approach of the pilot project, where more officers were equipped with a BWC as the project progressed. Reasons that could explain this decline in recordings included:

1. Staffing issues – the number of officers working on any given shift was rarely over four; therefore, the number of cameras used operationally from the early to late phases of the pilot did not functionally increase.
2. Weather – there are typically fewer calls for service during the winter months, and due to inclement weather, calls may have been handled over the phone rather than in person, where possible.
3. COVID-19 – Nunavut was under COVID-19 pandemic-related restrictions in April and May 2021, which may have resulted in both fewer calls for service and more calls being handled over the phone, where possible.

4. Experience – as the pilot progressed, officers gained experience using BWCs and better understood when it was appropriate to record encounters.

Throughout the six months, a total of 525 hours (1,246.34 GB of data) of footage were recorded. On average, each video lasted roughly 8 minutes and 40 seconds. During the entirety of the pilot, 6% of the total number of hours of BWC video footage (30 hours and 11 minutes) needed to be reviewed and redacted for court purposes. Manual redaction of this footage took 126 hours and 50 minutes. In other words, it took approximately four minutes to redact each minute of BWC footage manually.

Crime Trends

To compare crime rates prior to and during the pilot, we examined monthly police occurrence data from January 2016 to June 2021. Comparing occurrence data from the pilot period to historical data demonstrated that implementing BWCs did not reduce crime; in fact, the monthly number of occurrences during the pilot project was either above or on par with previous years. Similar trends were observed when examining specific occurrence types, including crimes against persons, crimes against property, and other *Criminal Code* crimes.

Use of Force

Similarly, we compared officer use-of-force data prior to and during the pilot – January 2016 to June 2021. This data looked at the application of intervention options as well as whether intervention options were drawn and displayed (used as a deterrent only) by year. No noticeable changes were observed during the pilot period. In addition, two officer-involved shootings took place during the 2016 to June 2021 period (one in December 2018 and one in April 2020), but no shootings took place during the pilot period.

Administrative Outcomes

There were two occurrences during the pilot project where BWCs captured an event related to a public complaint; one was received in March of 2021 and the other in June 2021. It does not appear as though the introduction of BWCs significantly influenced the frequency of public complaints. During the pilot project, there were no Access to Information and Privacy[13] requests involving BWCs, and there were only four media requests related to BWCs, one in December 2020 and three in May 2021.

CONCLUSION

Results from this pilot project suggested that BWCs are generally perceived positively by the public – they appear to have a positive effect on trust in the police and improve perceptions of police transparency. While crime rates during the pilot project did not appear to differ from historical trends, BWCs were generally perceived to increase public safety and help improve police-public relations. RCMP officers who participated in the pilot project were also generally satisfied with the overall performance of their BWCs. Despite some challenges, almost all the officers who provided feedback reported that they believed that all officers should be equipped with a BWC while on duty.

RECOMMENDATIONS/CONSIDERATIONS

Based on the findings from the pilot project, several recommendations and considerations were brought forward that pertain to community awareness and consultation, policy, training, equipment, and planning for future BWC implementation. Key recommendations included the need to implement a culturally-sensitive and community-focused consultation and awareness campaign, the need to ensure a community feedback mechanism (e.g., via a community survey that is continually monitored), the need to engage key community stakeholders in the implementation process, and the need to identify a coordinator in each RCMP detachment to oversee the implementation of BWCs. Other key recommendations included the need to ensure that policy makes clear when officers are required to turn their cameras on and off, standardize if, when, and how footage may be disclosed to the public, and ensure that BWCs have adequate battery life to last the duration of shifts, low-light video quality, and other safety features (e.g., ensuring that the record light can be turned off). For a detailed list of recommendations and considerations that emerged from the pilot project, see the Appendix.

REFERENCES

Ariel, B., Farrar, W. A., & Sutherland, A. (2015). The effect of police body-worn cameras on use of force and citizens' complaints against the police: A randomized controlled trial. *Journal of Quantitative Criminology*, *31*(3), 509–535. doi:10.1007/s10940-014-9236-3

Blaskovits, B., & Bennell, C. (2020). Exploring the potential impact of body worn cameras on memory in officer-involved critical incidents: A literature review. *Journal of Police and Criminal Psychology*, *35*(3), 251–262. doi:10.1007/s11896-019-09354-1

Boivin, R., Gendron, A., Faubert, C., & Poulin, B. (2017). The body-worn camera perspective bias. *Journal of Experimental Criminology*, *13*(1), 125–142. doi:10.1007/s11292-016-9270-2

Crow, M. S., Snyder, J. A., Crichlow, V. J., & Smykla, J. O. (2017). Community perceptions of police body-worn cameras: The impact of views on fairness, fear, performance, and privacy. *Criminal Justice and Behavior*, *44*(4), 589–610. doi:10.1177/0093854816688037

Demir, M., Apel, R., Braga, A. A., Brunson, R. K., & Ariel, B. (2020). Body worn cameras, procedural justice, and police legitimacy: A controlled experimental evaluation of traffic stops. *Justice Quarterly*, *37*(1), 53–84. doi:10.1080/07418825.2018.1495751

Dockstader, J., Patterson, Q., Land, A., & Cunningham, B. C. (2022). *Using BWC footage to promote officer safety: Examples from the field* (Report No. 305292). U.S. Department of Justice, Bureau of Justice Assistance. https://bja.ojp.gov/library/publications/using-bwc-footage-promote-officer-safety-examples-field#:~:text=For%20agencies%20to%20fully%20realize,that%20can%20improve%20officer%20safety

Filice, M. (2023). Two-Spirit. In *The Canadian Encyclopedia*. https://www.thecanadianencyclopedia.ca/en/article/two-spirit

Glasbeek, A., Alam, M., & Roots, K. (2020). Seeing and not-seeing: Race and body-worn cameras in Canada. *Surveillance & Society*, *18*(3), 328–342. doi:10.24908/ss.v18i3.13259

Government of Canada. (2022). *Inukshuk*. https://www.canada.ca/en/canadian-heritage/services/art-monuments/public-art/inukshuk.html

Government of Canada. (2023, November 7). Canadian Climate Normals. https://climate.weather.gc.ca/climate_normals/index_e.html

Hele, K. S. (2021). Indigenous Elders in Canada. In *The Canadian Encyclopedia*. https://www.thecanadianencyclopedia.ca/en/article/indigenous-elders-in-canada

Inuit Tapiriit Kanatami. (2004). *5000 Years of Inuit History and Heritage*. https://www.itk.ca/wp-content/uploads/2016/07/5000YearHeritage_0.pdf

Jennings, W. G., Fridell, L. A., & Lynch, M. D. (2014). Cops and cameras: Officer perceptions of the use of body-worn cameras in law enforcement. *Journal of Criminal Justice*, *42*(6), 549–556. doi:10.1016/j.jcrimjus.2014.09.008

Jennings, W. G., Lynch, M. D., & Fridell, L. A. (2015). Evaluating the impact of police officer body-worn cameras (BWCs) on response-to-resistance and serious external complaints: Evidence from the Orlando police department (OPD) experience utilizing a randomized controlled experiment. *Journal of Criminal Justice*, *43*(6), 480–486. doi:10.1016/j.jcrimjus.2015.10.003

Lewis, D., Castleden, H., Francis, S., Strickland, K., & Denny, C. (2016). Increasing response rates on face-to-face surveys with Indigenous communities in Canada: Lessons from Pictou Landing. *Progress in Community Health Partnerships*, *10*(2), 197–205. doi:10.1353/cpr.2016.0021 PMID:27346765

McHugh, M. L. (2013). The chi-square test of independence. *Biochemia Medica*, *23*(2), 143–149. doi:10.11613/BM.2013.018 PMID:23894860

Murphy, J. R. (2018). Is It Recording?—Racial Bias, Police Accountability, and the Body-Worn Camera Activation Policies of the Ten Largest Metropolitan Police Departments in the USA. Columbia Journal of Race and Law, 9(1), 141–190. https://doi.org/10.7916/cjrl.v9i1.2238

O'Donnell, S., & Beaton, B. (2018). A 'whole-community' approach for sustainable digital infrastructure in remote and northern First Nations. *Northern Public Affairs*, *6*(2), 34–37.

Office of the Privacy Commissioner of Canada. (2020, March). *Expectations: OPC's guide to the privacy impact assessment process*. https://www.priv.gc.ca/en/privacy-topics/privacy-impact-assessments/gd_exp_202003/

Sousa, W. H., Miethe, T. D., & Sakiyama, M. (2018). Inconsistencies in Public Opinion of Body-Worn Cameras on Police: Transparency, Trust, and Improved Police–Citizen Relationships. Policing : A Journal of Policy and Practice, 12(1), 100–108. https://doi.org/10.1093/police/pax015

St. Louis, E., Saulnier, A., & Walby, K. (2019). Police use of body-worn cameras: Challenges of visibility, procedural justice, and legitimacy. *Surveillance & Society*, *17*(3/4), 305–321. doi:10.24908/ss.v17i3/4.8649

Statistics Canada. (2023, February 2). Census Profile, 2021 Census of Population.. https://www12.statcan.gc.ca/census-recensement/2021/dp-pd/prof/details/page.cfm?Lang=E&SearchText=iqaluit&DGUIDlist=2021A00056204003&GENDERlist=1&STATISTIClist=1&HEADERlist=0

ENDNOTES

1 Inukshuks are piled stone markers that are used on the land to warn of danger, help with navigation, mark areas of significance, and assist hunters (*Government of Canada*, 2022).

2 A Privacy Impact Assessment is a risk management tool that helps organizations manage risks related to privacy and ensures that institutions meet legal requirements and understand how their actions may impact people's privacy. The primary goal of such an assessment is to ensure compliance with various legal frameworks, including the *Privacy Act*, legislation governing the institution or program, and directives outlined by the Treasury Board of Canada Secretariat and Government of Canada policies. This adherence significantly mitigates the risk of mishandling personal information, thereby lessening the chances of improper collection, use, disclosure, or retention of such data (*Office of the Privacy Commissioner of Canada*, 2020).

3 Indigenous Elders are those "with enough life experience and knowledge of Indigenous traditions to offer guidance and teachings grounded within that experience and knowledge" (Hele, 2021). Elders have many roles, one of which is to ensure that traditions and culture get passed down from generation to generation (Hele, 2021).

4 The term two-spirit refers to an individual who has both a masculine and feminine spirit; the term is used by some Indigenous individuals to describe their gender, sexual orientation, and spiritual identity (Filice, 2023).

5 It should be noted that while efforts were undertaken to ensure a diverse community representation in survey responses, there was an underrepresentation of Inuit respondents. In the future, a different approach should be taken to ensure more representativeness (e.g., non-police, third-party data collection).

6 Respondents were instructed to check all that apply, which resulted in 74 selections in total. Percentages were calculated out of the total number of respondents ($n = 70$).

7 All assumptions required to use chi-square tests were satisfied, except for the assumption that specifies that at least 80% of the cases need to have a frequency count above 5 (McHugh, 2013). In certain cases, only 50% of cases in all instances had frequency counts above 5.

8 This group also includes two respondents who selected "other" where they could specify their race/ethnicity/Indigeneity. One wrote "mix" and the other wrote "mixed".

9 There were 54 officers who participated in training; thus, all but three officers who participated in the BWC training were sent the officer experience survey. The survey was not sent to these three officers because, following the training,

they were in positions (e.g., specialized investigational units) that did not require/allow for the operational use of BWCs.

10 *Molle* is the acronym used for "modular lightweight load-carrying equipment," which refers to the rows and columns of webbing found on soft body armour. This webbing allows for items to be attached to body armour, such as a BWC.

11 An occurrence refers to a police-related event that is entered into a police records management system. This includes both reactive events (e.g., responding to a call for service) or proactive events (e.g., a traffic stop).

12 An occurrence is cleared by charge when a police investigation leads to the identification of a suspect and the person is formally charged.

13 In Canada, requests can be made to obtain information contained in government records, with some exceptions, and these are called Access to Information and Privacy or ATIP requests.

APPENDIX

Community Awareness and Consultation

1. Engage key stakeholders in the community early on to ensure they can fully participate in the implementation process of BWCs, including those in diverse groups/populations (e.g., LGBTQ2S+, racialized, non-governmental organizations, national, regional, and local Indigenous organizations and leaders).
2. Implement an awareness campaign that is culturally sensitive and focuses on the community's unique needs.
    a. Provide pamphlets, posters, a website (examples of these products are included in this chapter), and leverage TV, radio, and social media (e.g., Facebook and Twitter)
    b. Ensure a particular focus on personal and community privacy, and cultural, religious, and spiritual concerns
    c. Temper public expectations around the impact that BWCs will have on crime trends and the use of force
    d. Ensure clear communication for members of the public regarding when cameras will be turned on and off, who has access to the BWC footage, privacy protections, and under what circumstances footage is released to the public
3. Ensure accessibility of awareness materials.
    a. Ensure materials are translated into local language(s)
    b. Ensure that the language of materials is comprehensible by various age groups and reading abilities
    c. Place materials in neutral locations throughout the community (e.g., grocery stores)
    d. Ensure digital and paper-based versions of materials are available
4. Ensure a community feedback mechanism is in place to inform on-going improvements to policy, training, and processes.
    a. Engage diverse, vulnerable, and marginalized groups to participate in the survey; to do this, consider collaborating with an independent, non-police agency (e.g., community organization) to administer the survey
    b. Ensure digital and paper-based versions of the survey are available
    c. Ensure that surveys include an informed consent form and that it is completed before any participant completes a survey
    d. Ensure that surveys are completed on a voluntary basis

   e. Ensure that the survey includes key metrics (e.g., privacy, transparency; see Sousa et al. 2018 and Crow et al., 2017) and areas that allow participants to provide open-ended comments
   f. Ensure that surveys maintain participant confidentiality and that only limited identifying information (e.g., demographic information) is requested
   g. Ensure that the survey inquires about demographic information, including a participant's age, gender, race, and whether they have any affiliation to the police (e.g., family member)
   h. Conduct a race-based analysis of community survey responses to ensure that the needs of diverse groups are being considered
5. Engage with your local Prosecution Service to determine expectations in relation to disclosure and vetting of BWC footage.
6. Consult the local ATIP or Freedom of Information office to determine what should be vetted for various types of disclosure.
7. Engage with local government officials to ensure collaboration.
8. Ensure proactive disclosure of BWC policy to members of the public.
9. Ensure an officer is available for media interviews and someone who can speak or translate in the local language.
10. Implement a generic email account to allow community members to send any questions, concerns, or feedback related to the use of BWCs.
11. Employ a phased approach to implementing the BWCs.
12. Identify an implementation coordinator at each location (e.g., detachment, station) to oversee the implementation of BWCs, be the point of reference for members of the public, and ensure continued collaboration with community stakeholders.
    a. Consideration should be given to ensuring that this coordinator is a supervisor to allow for proper video administration and management
13. Ensure funding partners (e.g., municipalities) are provided information on the potential return on investment of BWCs (e.g., impact on crime rates and the use of force, impact on perceptions of trust and confidence in police).

Policy

1. Standardize, as much as possible, when officers are required to turn their BWC on and off.
2. Ensure that policy includes items pertaining to the privacy of police officers, the public, and the individuals involved in the interactions and that this is communicated to the public.

3. Include if, how, when, and under what circumstances footage can or will be disclosed to the public.
   a. Consider the implications and the importance of providing context when releasing video footage to the public as some research has shown that negative perceptions of the police and police use of force may ensue after a BWC video is released, even if the officer was justified in their actions (Boivin et al., 2017)
   b. Ensure the process is consistent and equitable (i.e., not only when it serves to benefit the police)
4. Clarify in policy how supervisors should be reviewing (e.g., random vs. systematic review of footage) and using BWC footage (e.g., oversight vs. surveillance tool).
5. Consider the risk of disproportionately capturing community members in BWC footage over the long term in the privacy and redaction protocols, particularly as they relate to small and remote communities.
6. Clarify if and when BWC footage can be reviewed by officers involved in use-of-force encounters (i.e., before or after completing a written or verbal statement) and critical incidents, particularly when it might involve an independent or civilian oversight body.

Training

1. Clarify the policy surrounding the use of BWCs and ensure the policy is communicated accurately to officers.
2. Identify the connections between critical incident stress, memory, vision, and BWCs, including benefits and limitations.
3. Ensure adequate time is spent training on the application of policy in an operational setting, including when to turn the BWC on or off.
4. Dedicate adequate time to ensuring a solid understanding of how BWC evidence is managed digitally and working with records management systems when a BWC is involved.
5. Explore ways to ensure the ease of transfer of the BWC from soft body armour (SBA) to hard body armour (HBA) or outerwear, if needed.
6. Develop procedures that demonstrate what to do if officers are dispatched while their BWC is charging or videos are being uploaded.
7. Consider the creation of heuristics (i.e., mental rules) to increase automaticity in turning the BWC "on" under conditions of high stress (e.g., "seatbelt off, camera on").

Equipment

1. Ensure that any BWCs have adequate (a) battery life, (b) display readability, (c) low light/darkness video quality, and (d) compactness of the camera.
2. Ensure that all BWCs have a "covert mode" to ensure officer safety.
3. Ensure that BWCs can be installed adequately on SBA, HBA, and outerwear.
4. Consider integrating equipment and digital evidence management systems with operational records management systems to allow occurrence files to be automatically flagged with the BWC survey code (instead of manually) if a file has BWC footage associated.

Planning for Broader Implementation

1. Use occurrence, recording time, and redaction time data from a pilot study to help inform estimates for appropriate resourcing.
    a. Consider redaction time as a key element for resourcing given the extensive amount of time it can take to redact BWC footage
2. Ensure that relevant administrative (e.g., public complaints) and operational outcomes (e.g., use of force) are systematically tracked for evaluation purposes.
3. Develop a consultative and engagement framework or guide to assist with the implementation of best practices.

Compilation of References

Abdel Aziz, A. (2010). *Community Policing and Activating Security Performance*. Ph.D. Thesis, College of Graduate Studies, Cairo.

Abdel Qader et al. (2007). *Towards Applying the Concept of Community Policing in Egypt. Community Policing Symposium*. Police Research Center.

Adbel-Moneim, M.E. (2018, Spring). Reporting identity: Social and political implications of adding a MENA category to the U.S. Census. *Bard digital Commons*. 1-72.

Addo, P. C., Jiaming, F., Kulbo, N. B., & Liangqiang, L. (2020). COVID-19: Fear appeal favoring purchase behavior towards personal protective equipment. *Service Industries Journal*, *40*(7–8), 471–490. doi:10.1080/02642069.2020.1751823

Adds, E. (2007). *Contemporary Concepts of Community Policing. Community Policing Symposium*. Police Research Center.

Adubato, B., Sachs, N. M., & Fizzinoglia, D. F. (2021). Gatekeepers: Controlling communication in a time of crisis. *Atlantic Journal of Communication*, *29*(5), 275–291. doi:10.1080/15456870.2020.1779724

Aertsen, I., & Willemsens, J. (2001). The European Forum for Victim-Offender Mediation and Restorative Justice. *European Journal on Criminal Policy and Research*, *9*(3), 231–300. doi:10.1023/A:1011604620022

Ahmed, H. M. (2007). *Community policing - a contemporary scientific vision*. Community policing symposium. Police Academy. Police Research Center.

Al-Alam, S. (2000). Security media and its role in influencing public opinion trends. *Journal of the College of Training and Development*.

Al-Ashmawy, M. (2012). Community policing and its applications in Egypt. Police Research Center Review.

Al-Attar, B. (2011). *Community policing and its impact on reducing crime*. Ph.D. Thesis. College of Graduate Studies.

Al-Dardiri, O. (2007). *Community policing - a contemporary scientific vision. Community Policing Symposium*. Police Research Center.

Alderson, J. (1984). Law and disorder. H. Hamilton, OCLC 12216164.

Aleaziz, H. (2023, January 19). ICE releases thousands of migrants affected by data breach. *Los Angeles times*. https://www.latimes.com/world-nation/story/2023-01-19/ice-leak-personal-information-immigrants-asylum

Al-Hakim. (2002). Police Reconciliation Strategy, Leadership Institute for Police Officers. College of Training and Development. Police Academy.

Alkon, C., & Schneider, A. K. (2019). *Negotiating Crime*. Carolina Academic Press.

Al-Shawa, M. S. (1997). *Mediation and Criminal Justice*. Dar Al-Nahda Al-Arabiya.

Al-Sheemary, B. (2015, March 1). Intra-Arab discrimination in Dearborn. *Open Democracy*.

Al-Shehhi, M. (2018). *A criminological critique of body worn cameras in policing: the case of the United Arab Emirates*. University of Salford.

American Psychological Association (n.d.). *White flight may still enforce segregation*. Author.

Amisano, M., (2022). Prevedere -e non predire- attraverso gli algoritmi e le loro insidie. *Archivio Penale, 2*.

Amstutz, L. S. (2009). *The Little Book of Victim Offender Conferencing*. Good Books- Skyhorse Publishing.

Andersen, P., & Guerrero, L. (1998). Principles of Communication and Emotion in Social Interaction. In P. A. Andersen & L. K. Guerrero (Eds.), *Handbook of Communication and Emotion* (pp. 49–96). Academic Press.

Anonymous. (2023, May 5). *CDCR issues recidivism report*. Correctional News. https://correctionalnews.com/2023/05/05/cdcr-issues-recidivism-reports/

Apel, D. (2020, January). *Between two worlds: Arab Americans in Detroit*. Academic Press.

Ariel, B. (2016). Police body cameras in large police departments. *The Journal of Criminal Law & Criminology, 106*(4), 729–768.

Ariel, B., Farrar, W. A., & Sutherland, A. (2015). The effect of police body-worn cameras on use of force and citizens' complaints against the police: A randomized controlled trial. *Journal of Quantitative Criminology, 31*(3), 509–535. doi:10.1007/s10940-014-9236-3

Arizona State University Center for Problem-Oriented Policing. (n.d.). *SARA Model*. Retrieved at https://popcenter.asu.edu/content/sara-model-0

Arnold, M. B. (1960). *'Emotion and Personality'. Psychological Aspects, 1*. Columbia University Press.

Artwohl, A. (2002). Perceptual and memory distortion during officer-involved shootings. *FBI L. Enforcement Bull.*, *71*, 18.

Audet, A. (2020, July 7). The racist, segregationist history behind Dearborn's Orville Hubbard status. Retrieved. *WDET 101.9.*

Badr, A. M. M. (1996). The Policeman, the Citizen, and Alienation. Alfikr AlShurti Periodical.

Badran, H. M. (2007). *The concept of community policing*. Community policing symposium. Police Research Center.

Balfour, M. E., Hahn Stephenson, A., Delany-Brumsey, A., Winsky, J., & Goldman, M. L. (2022). Cops, clinicians, or both? Collaborative approaches to responding to behavioral health emergencies. *Psychiatric Services (Washington, D.C.)*, *73*(6), 658–669. doi:10.1176/appi.ps.202000721 PMID:34666512

Ban, C. C. (2023, July 9). *Proposal for a police social work/mobile crisis certificate and MSW program at Valparaiso University* [Unpublished presentation]. Valparaiso University.

Ban, C. C., & Riordan, J. E. (2023). Re-envisioning public safety through an embedded police social worker (PSW) model: A promising approach for multidisciplinary resource delivery and diversion. *Journal of Contemporary Criminal Justice*, *39*(4), 537–554. doi:10.1177/10439862231189423

Barnert, E. S., Lopez, N., & Chung, P. J. (2020). Barriers to health care for Latino youths during community reentry after incarceration: Los Angeles County, California, 2016–2018. *American Journal of Public Health*, *110*(S1), S63–S70. doi:10.2105/AJPH.2019.305374 PMID:31967868

Bazemore, G., & Umbreit, M. (2001). *A Comparison of Four Restorative Conferencing Models*. Juvenile Justice Bulletin. doi:10.1037/e304232003-001

Beeble, M. L., & Hampton, C. (2021). Community reintegration of repeat female offenders in county jails. *Women & Criminal Justice*, *31*(6), 518–535. doi:10.1080/08974454.2021.1947441

Bender, K. (2018). Education Opportunities in Prison Are Key to Reducing Crime. *Advancing Racial Equity and Justice, Criminal Justice Reform, Education*. https://www.americanprogress.org/article/education-opportunities-prison-key-reducing-crime/

Berdjis, N. (2016). *A descriptive study on police body cameras and civil liability cases* [Master's thesis]. University of Colorado.

Berghuis, M. (2018). Reentry programs for adult male offender recidivism and reintegration: A systematic review and meta-analysis. *International Journal of Offender Therapy and Comparative Criminology*, *62*(13), 4655–4676. doi:10.1177/0306624X18778448 PMID:29890873

Bernstein, M. (2023). Disputed Portland police body camera policy draws questions from federal judge. *The Oregonian.*

Berry, M. C., & Wiener, R. L. (2020). Exoffender housing stigma and discrimination. *Psychology, Public Policy, and Law*, *26*(2), 213–232. doi:10.1037/law0000225

Bertot, J. C., Jaeger, P. T., Munson, S., & Glaisyer, T. (2010). Social Media Technology and Government Transparency. *Computer*, *43*(11), 53–59. doi:10.1109/MC.2010.325

Bertus, F. (1996). *The Use and Effectiveness of Community Policing in a Democracy.* National Institute of Justice.

Beshears, M. L., Beshears, M. L., & Bond, M. (2019). Improving police social media use practices. *International Journal of Social Science Studies*, *7*(5), 34–42. doi:10.11114/ijsss.v7i5.4449

Bill of Rights Institute. (n.d.). *Letter from the Birmingham Jail.* Letter from Birmingham Jail - Bill of Rights Institute.

Binnall, J. M., Scott-Hayward, C. S., Petersen, N., & Gonzalez, R. M. (2022). Taking roll: College students' views of their formerly incarcerated classmates. *Journal of Criminal Justice Education*, *33*(3), 347–367. doi:10.1080/10511253.2021.1962932

Bird, M., Lofstron, M., Martin, B., Raphael, S., & Nguyen, V. (2018), *The impact of Proposition 47 on crime and recidivism.* https://www.ppic.org/wp-content/uploads/r_0618mbr.pdf

Blaskovits, B., & Bennell, C. (2020). Exploring the potential impact of body worn cameras on memory in officer-involved critical incidents: A literature review. *Journal of Police and Criminal Psychology*, *35*(3), 251–262. doi:10.1007/s11896-019-09354-1

Board of State and Community Corrections. (2022). *Realignment.* https://www.bscc.ca.gov/m_realignment/

Boivin, R., & Gendron, A. (2022). An experimental study of the impact of body-worn cameras on police report writing. *Journal of Experimental Criminology*, *18*(4), 747–764. doi:10.1007/s11292-021-09469-8

Boivin, R., Gendron, A., Faubert, C., & Poulin, B. (2017). The body-worn camera perspective bias. *Journal of Experimental Criminology*, *13*(1), 125–142. doi:10.1007/s11292-016-9270-2

Boland, K. M., & McNutt, J. G. (2013). Assessing e-government success strategies using Internet search data. In R. Gil Garcia (Ed.), *E-government success factors and measures: theories, concepts, and methodologies* (pp. 289–307). IGI Global. doi:10.4018/978-1-4666-4058-0.ch016

Bonkiewicz, L., & Ruback, R. B. (2012). The Role of the Police in Evacuations. *Police Quarterly*, *15*(2), 137–156. doi:10.1177/1098611112442808

Bowleg, L. (2012, July). The problem with the phrase women and minorities: Intersectionality—an important theoretical framework for public health. *American Journal of Public Health*, *107*(7), 1267–1273. doi:10.2105/AJPH.2012.300750 PMID:22594719

Bowman, E. I., & Ely, K. (2020). Voices of returning citizens: A qualitative study of a supportive housing program for ex-offenders in a rural community. *The Prison Journal*, *100*(4), 423–446. doi:10.1177/0032885520939273

Braithwaite, J. (2006). *Crime, Shame and Reintegration, 16th Printing*. Cambridge University Press.

Brayne, S., & Christin, A. (2021). Technologies of crime prediction: The reception of algorithms in policing and criminal courts. *Social Problems, 68*(3), 608–624. doi:10.1093/socpro/spaa004

Brinser, K. L., & King, W. R. (2016). Organizational Permeability to Environmental Conditions. *Police Quarterly, 19*(4), 387–409. doi:10.1177/1098611115626409

Brogden, M., & Nijhar, P. (2013). *Community policing.* Routledge. doi:10.4324/9781843925798

Brooks, C. (2022). *Federal Law Enforcement Officers, 2020-Statistical Tables.* Academic Press.

Brown, K. (2018). *A life-history approach to community reintegration: Female ex-offenders & experiences of facilitators and barriers of successful community reintegration.* https://www.academia.edu/98834039/A_Life_History_Approach_to_Community_Reintegration_Female_Ex_Offenders_Experiences_of_Facilitators_and_Barriers_of_Successful_Community_Reintegration

Brown, L. and Wycoff, M.D. (1978). Policing Houston: Reducing fear and improving services. *Crime and Delinquency*, 71–89.

Brown, C. (2011). Vocational psychology and ex-offenders' reintegration: A call for action. *Journal of Career Assessment, 19*(3), 333–342. doi:10.1177/1069072710395539

Brown, G. R. (2020). Police body-worn cameras in the Canadian context: Policing's new visibility and today's expectations for police accountability. In *Police on Camera* (pp. 122–148). Routledge. doi:10.4324/9780429439759-8

Brudney, J. L., & Prentice, C. R. (2018). A new tool for new times? Using Geographic Information Systems in foundations and other nonprofit organizations. *The Foundation Review, 10*(4). Advance online publication. doi:10.9707/1944-5660.1442

Buchanan, A., Marks, R., & Figueroa, M. A. (2016, September). 2015 forum on ethnic groups from the Middle East and North Africa. *U.S. Census Bureau, Population Division.* https://www.census.gov/content/dam/Census/library/working-papers/2015/demo/MENA-Forum-Summary-and-Appendices.pdf

Buller, D., & Burgoon, J. (1998). Emotional Expression in the Deception Process. In P. A. Andersen & L. K. Guerrero (Eds.), *Handbook of Communication and Emotion* (pp. 381–402). Academic Press.

Bullock, K. (2013). Community, intelligence-led policing and crime control. *Policing and Society, 23*(2), 125–144. doi:10.1080/10439463.2012.671822

Burgett, S., & Ban, C. (2022, November 1–3). *Enhancing micro-level police social work by practicing effective macro-level work* [Conference session]. National Association of Public Safety Social Workers Annual Conference, Indianapolis, IN.

Burgoon, J. (1993). Interpersonal Expectations, Expectancy Violations, and Emotional Communication. *Journal of Language and Social Psychology, 12*(1-2), 30–48. doi:10.1177/0261927X93121003

Bush, C. L. (2020). *Public Perceptions of Delays in the Release of Police Body-Worn Camera Footage* [Doctoral dissertation]. Walden University.

Bush, C. L. (2020). Public perceptions of delays in the release of police body-worn camera footage. *Journal of Social Change, 13*(1), 1–17. doi:10.5590/JOSC.2020.13.1.01

Buzarov, V. V. (1998). *Essentials of Conversational English Syntax.* Crone-press.

CALEA. (n.d.). Retrieved at https://www.calea.org/

California Department Corrections Rehabilitation. (2023). *Corrections, and workforce partnership agreement.* https://cwdb.ca.gov/wp-content/uploads/sites/43/2018/02/Corrections-Workforce-Partnership-for-the-Prison-to-Employment-Initiative_.pdf

California Department of Corrections and Rehabilitation. (2023). *Office of Correctional Education.* https://www.cdcr.ca.gov/rehabilitation/oce/

California Department of Corrections and Rehabilitation. (2023). *Office of Research.Offender recidivism.* https://www.cdcr.ca.gov/research/offender-outcomes-characteristics/

California Department of Corrections and Rehabilitation. (2023). *Recidivism report.* https://www.cdcr.ca.gov/research/wp-content/uploads/sites/174/2023/04/Recidivism-Report-for-Offenders-Released-in-Fiscal-Year-2017-18.pdf

California Workforce Development Board. (2023). *Prison to employment.* https://cwdb.ca.gov/wp-content/uploads/sites/43/2021/10/P2E-Interim-Report_ACCESSIBLE.pdf

Cananzi, F. (2022). Dall'emergenza alla legge delega al governo: verso un processo penale veramente telematico? *Sistema penale, 3.* https://www.sistemapenale.it/pdf_contenuti/1648540299_cananzi-2022a-processo-penale-telematico-emergenza-legge-delega.pdf

Canzio, G. (2021). *Le linee del modello "Cartabia".* Una prima lettura, in Sistema penale. https://www.sistemapenale.it/it/opinioni/canzio-riforma-cartabia-prima-lettura?out=print

Cao, L. (2015). Differentiating confidence in the police, trust in the police, and satisfaction with the police. *Policing; Bradford, 38*(2), 239-249.

Carmichael, M. (2010, February 14). Why racial disparities in health care persist. *Newsweek.*

Carmichael, J., David, J., Helou, A., & Pererira, C. (2020). Déterminante of citizen's perceptions of police behavior during traffic and pedestrian stops. *Criminal Justice Review, 46*(1), 99–118. Advance online publication. doi:10.1177/0734016820952523

Carroll, J. J., El-Sabawi, T., Fichter, D., Pope, L. G., Rafla-Yuan, E., Compton, M. T., & Watson, A. (2021, September 8). The workforce for non-police behavioral health crisis response doesn't exist—We need to create it. *Health Affairs Forefront.* https://www.healthaffairs.org/content/forefront/workforce-non-police-behavioral-health-crisis-response-doesn-t-exist-we-need-create

Carroll, A. E., & Hayes, D. (2023). The US mental health system is so broken that even money can't fix it. *JAMA Pediatrics, 177*(1), 8–10. doi:10.1001/jamapediatrics.2022.4416 PMID:36409471

Carson, E. A. (2021). *Prisoners in 2021 – statistical tables*. United States Department of Justice. Office of Justice Programs. Bureau of Justice Statistics.

Centers for Disease Control and Prevention (CDC). (2019). *CERC: Psychology of a crisis*. https://emergency.cdc.gov/cerc/ppt/CERC_ Psychology_of_a_Crisis.pdf

Cesari, C., (2019). *L'impatto delle nuove tecnologie sulla giustizia penale – un orizzonte denso di incognite*. file:///C:/Users/Laptop02%20Unical/Downloads/Dialnet-Editoriale-7169241%20(1).pdf

Champlin, C. (2020, April 10). I am Arab, I am American, I matter. *LAist*. https://laist.com/news/2020-census-arab-americans

Chen, Y., Ignasiak, C., Nieske, M., & Whipp (n.d.). *The Southend District: Vision plan and economic development strategy* [Presentation]. Academic Press.

Chen, E., Leos, C., Kowitt, S. D., & Moracco, K. E. (2020). Enhancing community-based participatory research through human-centered design strategies. *Health Promotion Practice*, *21*(1), 37–48. doi:10.1177/1524839919850557 PMID:31131633

Chriss, J. J. (2016). Beyond community policing: from early American beginnings to the 21st century. Routledge. OCLC 931534901.

Christian, J. (2022). The promise and challenge of local initiatives that support reentry and reintegration. *The Annals of the American Academy of Political and Social Science*, *701*(1), 191–203. doi:10.1177/00027162221115380

Civinini, M. G. (2021). *Il "nuovo ufficio per il processo" tra riforma della giustizia e PNRR. Che sia la volta buona!* Questione Giustizia. www.questionegiustizia.it/rivista/articolo/il-nuovo-ufficio-per-il-processo-tra-riforma-della-giustizia-e-pnrr-che-sia-la-volta-buona

Clarke, R. V., & Eck, J. E. (2005). Crime Analysis for Problem Solvers: 60 Small Steps. Office of Community Oriented Policing Services, US Department of Justice.

Clear, T. R., Rose, D. R., & Ryder, J. A. (2001). Incarceration and the community: The problem of removing and returning offenders. *Crime and Delinquency*, *47*(3), 335–351. doi:10.1177/0011128701047003003

Coleman, J. S. (1990). Foundations on Social Theory. The Belknap Press and Harvard University Press.

Communication from the Commission to the European Parliament. (n.d.). *2030 Digital Compass: the European way for the Digital Decade*. https://eur-lex.europa.eu/legal-content/EN/TXT/HTML/?uri=CELEX:52021DC0118&rid=4

Community Policing Consortium. (1994). Understanding Community Policing: A Framework for Action, Monograph, NCJ 148457, Bureau of Justice Assistance.

Coombs, W. (2005). Crisis and crisis management. In R. L. Heath (Ed.), *Encyclopedia of public relations* (Vol. 2, pp. 218-221). Sage. https://doi-10.4135/9781412952545.n103

Cordner, G. (2014). Community policing. The Oxford Handbook of police and policing, 148–171.

Cordner, G. W. (1997). Community policing: Elements and effects. *Critical issues in policing: Contemporary readings, 5*, 401-418.

Correia, M. E. (2000). The conceptual ambiguity of community in community policing – Filtering the muddy waters. *Policing, 23*(2), 218–233. doi:10.1108/13639510010333840

Coudert, F., Butin, D., & Le Métayer, D. (2015). Body-worn cameras for police accountability: Opportunities and risks. *Computer Law & Security Report, 31*(6), 749–762. doi:10.1016/j.clsr.2015.09.002

Council of State Governments Justice Center and the National Reentry Resource Center. (2017). *Workforce Innovation and Opportunity Act.* https://csgjusticecenter.org/wp-content/uploads/2020/02/6.13.17_WIOA_What-Corrections-and-Reentry-Agencies-Need-to-Know.pdf

Council Recommendation on the 2020 National Reform Programme of Italy and delivering a Council opinion on the 2020 Stability Programme of Italy, COM (2020) 512 final, del 20 maggio 2020, cons. 24.

Cox, S. M., & Fitzgerald, J. D. (1996). *Police in Community relations: Critical issues*. Brown & Benchmark.

Crescencio, A. (2022). Metro Nashville Police employees altered body camera footage without authorization, officials said. *News Channel 5 Nashville.*

Croce, B. (1947). Progresso tecnico e morale, Corriere della Sera, 21 settembre

Crow, M. S., Snyder, J. A., Crichlow, V. J., & Smykla, J. O. (2017). Community perceptions of police body-worn cameras: The impact of views on fairness, fear, performance, and privacy. *Criminal Justice and Behavior, 44*(4), 589–610. doi:10.1177/0093854816688037

Crump, J. (2011). What are the police doing on Twitter? Social media, the police and the public. *Policy and Internet, 3*(4), 1–27. doi:10.2202/1944-2866.1130

Curzio, P. (2022). Relazione sull'amministrazione della giustizia nell'anno 2021. Considerazioni finali, Corte Suprema di Cassazione, Roma, 21 gennaio, https://www.cortedicassazione.it/cassazione-resources/resources/cms/documents/Cassazione_Relazione_2022.pdf

Daly, K. (2002). Restorative Justice. *Punishment & Society, 4*(1), 55–59. doi:10.1177/14624740222228464

Dandurand, Y. (2016). Alternative Approaches to Preventing Recidivism: Restorative Justice and the Social Integrarion of Offenders. In *Women and Children as Victims and Offenders: Background, Prevention, Reintegration* (Vol. H, pp. 283–299). doi:10.1007/978-3-319-28424-8_11

Dearborn Police Department. (n.d.). *The Dearborn Police Department transparency dashboard*. Author.

Delaney, N. (2019). *Strong, Cheap, and Ready Access to Body-worn Camera Footage under New Jersey's Open Public Records Act (OPRA)*. Will Promote Police Accountability and Transparency.

Delvecchio, F., (2021). L'informatizzazione della giustizia penale, in Diritto penale contemporáneo. *Rivista trimestrale, 2*.

Delvecchio, F., (2022). Prospettive e tempi della digitalizzazione del proceso. *Processo penale e giustizia, Fascicolo, 1*.

Demir, M., Apel, R., Braga, A. A., Brunson, R. K., & Ariel, B. (2020). Body worn cameras, procedural justice, and police legitimacy: A controlled experimental evaluation of traffic stops. *Justice Quarterly*, *37*(1), 53–84. doi:10.1080/07418825.2018.1495751

Denef, S., Bayerl, P. S., & Kaptein, N. A. (2013). Social media and the police. *Proceedings of the SIGCHI Conference on Human Factors in Computing Systems*. 10.1145/2470654.2466477

Detroit Historical Society. (n.d.). *Encyclopedia of Detroit*. Academic Press.

Deutsch, M. (1958). Trust and suspicion. *The Journal of Conflict Resolution*, *2*(4), 265–279. doi:10.1177/002200275800200401

DeVylder, J. E., Anglin, D. M., Bowleg, L., Fedina, L., & Link, B. G. (2022). Police Violence and Public Health. *Annual Review of Clinical Psychology*, *18*(1), 527–552. doi:10.1146/annurev-clinpsy-072720-020644 PMID:34890247

Dignan, J. (2005). *Understanding Victims and Restorative Justice*. Open University Press.

Divakaran, B., Bloch, N., Sinha, M., Steiner, A., & Shavit, S. (2023). The reentry health care hub: Creating a California-based referral system to link chronically ill people leaving prison to primary care. *International Journal of Environmental Research and Public Health*, *20*(10), 5806. doi:10.3390/ijerph20105806 PMID:37239534

Dockstader, J., Patterson, Q., Land, A., & Cunningham, B. C. (2022). *Using BWC footage to promote officer safety: Examples from the field* (Report No. 305292). U.S. Department of Justice, Bureau of Justice Assistance. https://bja.ojp.gov/library/publications/using-bwc-footage-promote-officer-safety-examples-field#:~:text=For%20agencies%20to%20fully%20realize,that%20can%20improve%20officer%20safety

Doherty, S., Forrester, P., Brazil, A., & Matheson, F. (2014). Finding their way: Conditions for successful reintegration among women offenders. *Journal of Offender Rehabilitation*, *53*(7), 562–586. doi:10.1080/10509674.2014.944740

Dong, B., & Wu, X. (2022). Reaching and engaging people: Analyzing tweeting practices of large U.S. police departments pre- and post- the killing of George Floyd. *PLoS One*, *17*(7), e0269288. doi:10.1371/journal.pone.0269288 PMID:35834505

Dos Passos, J. (1921). *Three Soldiers*. Modern Library.

Dowidar, S. N. (2007). *Police and Society: Towards a New Concept of Security. Community Policing Symposium*. Police Research Center.

Drew, J. M., & Martin, S. (2021). A national study of police mental health in the USA: Stigma, mental health and help-seeking behaviors. *Journal of Police and Criminal Psychology*, *36*(2), 295–306. doi:10.1007/s11896-020-09424-9

Dunham, R. G., Alpert, G. P., & McLean, K. D. (2021). *Critical Issues in Policing* (8th ed.). Waveland Press.

Dunkle, S. (2021). The air was blue with perjury: Police lies and the case for abolition. *NYUL Rev.*, *96*, 2048.

Earle, H. H. (1970). *Police-Community Relations: Crisis in Our Time*. Charles C Thomas Publisher, Ltd.

Ed.gov. (1991). *Institute of Educational Sciences*. https://files.eric.ed.gov/fulltext/ED330818.pdf

Ekhator-Mobayode, U. E., & Hoogeveen, J. (2002, January 13). *Microdata collection and openness in the Middle East and North African (MENA): Introducing the MENA microdata access indicator*. Academic Press.

Ekman, P. (1979). About Brows: Emotional and Conversational Signals. In M. von Cranach, K. Foppa, W. Lepenies, & D. Ploog (Eds.), *Human Ethology: Claims and Limits of a New Discipline: Contributions to the Colloquium* (pp. 169–248). Cambridge University Press.

Ekman, P. (2004). *Emotions Revealed: Recognizing Faces and Feelings to Improve Communication*. Henry Holt and Company. doi:10.1136/sbmj.0405184

Ekman, P., & Friesen, W. (1975). *Unmasking the Face: A Guide to Recognizing Emotions from Facial Clues*. Prentice-Hall.

El-Kady, R. (2010). *Mediation as an alternative to Criminal proceedings - A comparative study*. PhD thesis. Faculty of Law. Cairo University.

El-Kady, R. (2012). Community partnership in confronting the phenomenon of bullying. A symposium on (security, media, and society shared responsibility). Police Academy.

El-Kady, R. (2013). Police reconciliations and ways to activate their role in achieving security. *Police Research Center Review*, (44).

El-Kady, R. (2023). The Role of the Police in Criminal Mediation. *International Journal of Police Science*. https://doi.org/ doi:10.56331/19122023/ijps

El-Kady, R. (2013). *Police conciliations - An analytical study of the role of the police in resolving criminal disputes*. Dar Al-Nahda Al-Arabiya.

El-Kady, R. (2020). *Criminal Mediation in Comparative Legislation*. Center for Arab Studies for Printing and Publishing.

Ellison, K. (2021). The Death of George Floyd, the Trial of Derek Chauvin, and Deadly- Force Encounters with Police: Have We Finally Reached an Inflection Point? Or Will the Cycle of Inaction Continue? *Ann. Rev. Crim. Proc.*, *50*, i.

Ellsworth, J. Fish, T., Niesen, & Pitts, N. (2020, April). Police social work in Minnesota: Starting the conversation. In *Social workers and police officers: An essential community partnership*. Mankato State University Social Work Policy Brief.

Elphick, C., Philpot, R., Zhang, M., Stuart, A., Walkington, Z., Frumkin, L. A., Pike, G., Gardner, K., Lacey, M., Levine, M., Price, B., Bandara, A., & Nuseibeh, B. (2021). Building trust in digital policing: A scoping review of community policing apps. *Police Practice and Research*, *22*(5), 1469–1491. doi:10.1080/15614263.2020.1861449

El-Shorbagy, A. (2005). *The efforts of the public security sector in preventing criminal crime*. Symposium on the role of civil society in preventing crime. Police Research Center.

Erickson, S. (2021). Communication in a Crisis and the Importance of Authenticity and Transparency. *Journal of Library Administration*, *61*(4), 476–483. doi:10.1080/01930826.2021.1906556

Eriksson, M., & Olsson, E. (2016). Facebook and Twitter in crisis communication: A comparative study of crisis communication professionals and citizens. *Journal of Contingencies and Crisis Management*, *24*(4), 198–208. doi:10.1111/1468-5973.12116

Escutia, X. (2016). *Body-worn cameras, procedural justice, and police legitimacy*. California State University.

Ethridge, G., Dowden, A. R., Brooks, M., Kwan, N., & Harley, D. (2020). Employment and earnings among ex-offenders with disabilities: A multivariate analysis of RSA-911 data. *Journal of Vocational Rehabilitation*, *52*(3), 279–289. doi:10.3233/JVR-201077

European judicial systems – CEPEJ Evaluation report. (2022). https://www.coe.int/en/web/cepej/special-file-report-european-judicial-systems-cepej-evaluation-report-2022-evaluation-cycle-2020-data-?p_p_id=56_INSTANCE_Pec933yX8xS5&p_p_lifecycle=0&p_p_state=normal&p_p_mode=view&p_p_col_id=column-4&p_p_col_pos=1&p_p_col_count=2

European Parliamentary Research Service. (2022). *Digitalising cross-border judicial cooperation*. https://www.europarl.europa.eu/RegData/etudes/BRIE/2022/739256/EPRS_BRI(2022)739256_EN.pdf

Executive Order 2020-47 (2020). Executive Orders (michigan.gov)

Executive Order 2020-78 (2020). Executive Orders (michigan.gov)

Fallik, S. W., Deuchar, R., & Crichlow, V. J. (2020). Body-worn cameras in the post- Ferguson era: An exploration of law enforcement perspectives. *Journal of Police and Criminal Psychology*, *35*(3), 263–273. doi:10.1007/s11896-018-9300-2

Farmer, A. (2016). *Copwatchers: citizen journalism and the changing police-community dynamic* [Doctoral dissertation]. University of Delaware.

Farrar, W., & Ariel, B. (2013). *Self-awareness to being watched and socially desirable behavior: A field experiment on the effect of body-worn cameras and police use of force*. Police Foundation.

Feigenberg, B., Glaser, J., Packis, E. (2021). Implicit bias training for police. *UChicago Urban Labs.*

Feys, Y., Verhage, A., & Boels, D. (2018). A state-of-the-art review on police accountability: What do we know from empirical studies? *International Journal of Police Science & Management*, *20*(3), 225–239. doi:10.1177/1461355718786297

Fielding, N. (1995). *Community policing, Clarendon Studies in Criminology*. Oxford University Press.

Fielding, N. G. (2023). Police communications and social media. *European Journal of Criminology*, *20*(1), 316–334. doi:10.1177/1477370821998969

Filice, M. (2023). Two-Spirit. In *The Canadian Encyclopedia*. https://www.thecanadianencyclopedia.ca/en/article/two-spirit

Fineman, S. (Ed.). (2000). *Emotion in Organizations*. Sage. doi:10.4135/9781446219850

Fineman, S. (Ed.). (2008). *The Emotional Organization: Passions and Power*. Blackwell.

Fiske, Z. R., Songer, D. M., & Schriver, J. L. (2020). A national survey of police mental health training. *Journal of Police and Criminal Psychology*, *36*(2), 236–242. doi:10.1007/s11896-020-09402-1

Florida Career Source. (2022). *Workforce Innovation Opportunities Act Unified Plan.* https://careersourceflorida.com/about-us/policies-and-initiatives/wioa/

Florida Department of Corrections. (2022). *Bureau of Education, Community Transition Unit.* https://fdc.myflorida.com/development/programs.html

Florida Department of Corrections. (2022). *Bureau of Program Development.* https://fdc.myflorida.com/development/applied.html

Florida Department of Corrections. (2022). *Recidivism Report.* https://fdc.myflorida.com/pub/recidivism/FDC%20Recidivism%20Report%202018%20Cohort.pdf

Florida Department of Education. (2018-2019). *Funding opportunities, Carl D. Perkins Career and Technical Education, Department of Corrections.* https://www.fldoe.org/academics/career-adult-edu/funding-opportunities/2023-2024-funding-opportunities/perkins.stml

Fortune, C. A., Ward, T., & Willis, G. M. (2011). The Rehabilitation of Offenders: Reducing Risk and Promoting Better Lives. *Psychiatry, Psychology, and Law : an Interdisciplinary Journal of the Australian and New Zealand Association of Psychiatry, Psychology and Law, 19*(5), 1–16.

Fouad, M. A. (2007). *The Community Policing Experience. Community Policing Symposium.* Police Research Center.

Gaines, L. K., & Kappeler, V. E. (2011). *Policing in America.* Routledge.

Galgani, B. (2021). *Digitalizzazione e processo penale: riflessioni sul dover essere di una nuova "cartografia".* disCRIMEN, fascicolo 2. https://discrimen.it/wp-content/uploads/disCrimen-2-2021.pdf

Galgani, B. (2022). *Il processo penale in "ambiente" digitale: ragioni e (ragionevoli) speranze.* Questione Giustizia. https://www.questionegiustizia.it/articolo/il-processo-penale-in-ambiente-digitale-ragioni-e-ragionevoli-speranze

Garapon, A. (2021). *La despazializzazione della giustizia.* Mimesis.

Gatta, G. L. (2021). *Riforma della giustizia penale: contesto, obiettivi e linee di fondo della "legge Cartabia".* Sistema penale. https://www.sistemapenale.it/it/scheda/gatta-legge-2021-134-delega-riforma-giustizia-penale-cartabia

Gaub, J. E., White, M., Malm, A., Watts, S., & Brown, K. L. (2022). Investigating the prevalence and utility of police body-worn cameras in the George Floyd protests. *Policing: An International Journal.*

Gau, J. M. (2010). *Wilson, James Q., and George L. Kelling: Broken Windows Theory. In Encyclopedia of Criminological Theory.* SAGE Publications, Inc. doi:10.4135/9781412959193.n281

Ghelani, A. (2022). Knowledge and skills for social workers on mobile crisis intervention teams. *Clinical Social Work Journal, 50*(4), 414–425. doi:10.1007/s10615-021-00823-x PMID:34803191

Giffin, E. (2011). *Something Borrowed.* Arrow Books.

Gimenez, M. (2007). *The Colour of Law.* Sphere.

Giwa, S. (2018). Community policing in racialized communities: A potential role for police social work. *Journal of Human Behavior in the Social Environment, 28*(6), 710–730. doi:10.1080/10911359.2018.1456998

Glasbeek, A., Alam, M., & Roots, K. (2020). Seeing and not-seeing: Race and body-worn cameras in Canada. *Surveillance & Society, 18*(3), 328–342. doi:10.24908/ss.v18i3.13259

Goldkind, L., & McNutt, J. G. (2019). We could be unicorns: Human services leaders moving from managing programs to managing information ecosystems. *Human Service Organizations, Management, Leadership & Governance, 43*(4), 1–9. doi:10.1080/23303131.2019.1669758

Goldstein, H. (1990). *Problem-Oriented Policing.* McGraw-Hill Publishing.

Goleman, D. (1995). *Emotional Intelligence*. Bantam Books.

Gonzalez, A. (2021). Successful transition to life after incarceration: A pilot program. *The American Journal of Occupational Therapy*, *75*(Supplement_2), 1–1. doi:10.5014/ajot.2021.75S2-RP222

Goodstein, J. (2019). Firms, ex-offenders, and communities: A stakeholder capability enhancement perspective. *Business Ethics Quarterly*, *29*(4), 491–518. doi:10.1017/beq.2018.48

Government of Canada. (2022). *Inukshuk*. https://www.canada.ca/en/canadian-heritage/services/art-monuments/public-art/inukshuk.html

Government of Canada. (2023, November 7). Canadian Climate Normals. https://climate.weather.gc.ca/climate_normals/index_e.html

Grabiner, G. (2016). Who polices the police? *Social Justice (San Francisco, Calif.)*, 58–79.

Graffam, J., Shinkfield, A., Lavelle, B., & Mcpherson, W. (2004). Variables affecting successful reintegration as perceived by offenders and professionals. *Journal of Offender Rehabilitation*, *40*(1/2), 147–171. doi:10.1300/J076v40n01_08

Gramlich, J. (2023). *Mental health and the pandemic: What US surveys have found.* Pew Research Center https://www.pewresearch.org/short-reads/2023/03/02/mental-health-and-the-pandemic-what-u-s-surveys-have-found/

Grann, M., Danesh, J., & Fazel, S. (2008). The association between psychiatric diagnosis and violent reoffending in adult offenders in the community. *BMC Psychiatry*, *8*(1), 92. Advance online publication. doi:10.1186/1471-244X-8-92 PMID:19032787

Graziano, N., (2021). Investimenti e riforme indirizzate a "tagliare" la durata dei giudizi. L'Ufficio del processo, in Guida al Diritto, 26 giugno, n. 25.

Grice, P. (1969). *Utterer's Meaning and Intentions: Philosophical Review*. Academic Press.

Gualtieri, S. (2009). *Between Arab and White: Race and ethnicity in early Syrian-American diaspora*. University of California Press.

Haney-Lopez, I. (2006). White by law: The legal construction of race (Rev. and updated 10th anniversary ed.). New York, NY: New York University Press.

Hannah-Moffat, K. (2019). Algorithmic risk governance: Big data analytics, race and information activism in criminal justice debates. *Theoretical Criminology*, *23*(4), 453–470. doi:10.1177/1362480618763582

Harb, A. (2016). Arab American cops leaving Dearborn police force. *The Arab American News.*

Harb, A. (2017). *Arabs and African Americans: A complicated relationship*. Academic Press.

Harding, D. J., Morenoff, J. D., & Wyse, J. B. (2019). *On the outside:Prisoner reentry and reintegration*. University of Chicago Press. doi:10.7208/chicago/9780226607788.001.0001

Harjanto, L. & Batalova, J. (2022, January 13). Middle Eastern and North Africa immigrants in the United States. *Migration Policy Institute*.

Harley, D. A., Cabe, B., Woolums, R., & Turner-Whittaker, T. (2014). Vulnerability and marginalization of adult ex-offenders with disabilities in community and employment reintegration. *Journal of Applied Rehabilitation Counseling*, *45*(4), 4–14. doi:10.1891/0047-2220.45.4.4

Hassan, A. (2005). *The Community Policing System and the Role of Voluntary Work in Achieving It*. Symposium organized by Naif Arab University for Security Sciences & Dubai Police Academy on The Concept of Community Policing.

Hassan, Y. (2007). *Community policing - a contemporary scientific vision*. Community policing symposium. Police Research Center.

Headley, A. M., Guerette, R. T., & Shariati, A. (2017). A field experiment of the impact of body-worn cameras (BWCs) on police officer behavior and perceptions. *Journal of Criminal Justice*, *53*, 102–109. doi:10.1016/j.jcrimjus.2017.10.003

Helms, J. E. (1994). The conceptualization of racial identity and other "racial" constructs. In E. J. Trickett & R. J. Watts (Eds.), *Human diversity: Perspectives on people in context* (pp. 285–311). Jossey-Bass.

Hemmer, J. W. (2017). *Exploring Police Beliefs in Community Oriented Policing and Community Trust: A Multiple Case Study* [Doctoral dissertation]. Northcentral University.

Herbert, S. K. (2006). *Citizens, cops, and power: recognizing the limits of community*. University of Chicago Press. doi:10.7208/chicago/9780226327358.001.0001

Heverin, T., & Zach, L. (2010). Twitter for city police department information sharing. *Proceedings of the American Society for Information Science and Technology*, *47*(1), 1–7. doi:10.1002/meet.14504701277

Hicks, D. L., Comartin, E. B., & Kubiak, S. (2022). Transition planning from jail: Treatment engagement, continuity of care, and rearrest. *Community Mental Health Journal*, *58*(2), 288–299. doi:10.1007/s10597-021-00820-x PMID:33835278

Hill, R., Quill, G., & Ellis, K. (2004). The Montgomery County CIT model: Interacting with people with mental illness. *FBI Law Enforcement Bulletin*, *73*(7), 18–25.

Hine, K. A., & Bragias, A. (2020). Effective communication during major crises: A systematic literature review to identify best practices for police. *Police Practice and Research*, *22*(5), 1492–1507. doi:10.1080/15614263.2020.1821681

Hochschild, A. R. (1983). *The Managed Heart: Commercialization of Human Feeling*. University of California Press.

Holland, J. H., & Miller, J. H. (1991). Artificial adaptive agents in economic theory. *The American Economic Review*, *81*(2), 365.

Hougland, S., & Wolf, R. (2017). Accreditation in police agencies: Does external quality assurance reduce citizen complaints? *The Police Journal*, *90*(1), 40–54. doi:10.1177/0032258X16671030

Hoyle, C. (2008). Restorative Justice, Victims and the Police. In *The Handbook of Policing (Tim Newburn)* (pp. 794–823). Routledge.

Hu, X. (2020). Electronic Community-Oriented Policing: Theories, Contemporary Efforts, and Future Directions. Lexington Books.

Hudson, D. (2014). *The first significant legislative reform of our job-training system in a number of years: The White House President Barack Obama.* https://obamawhitehouse.archives.gov/blog/2014/07/22/first-significant-legislative-reform-our-job-training-system-number-years

Hunter, G. (2021, February 3). *Dearborn police confront city's racist past, critics.* detroitnews.com

Hunter, B. A., Lanza, A. S., Lawlor, M., Dyson, W., & Gordon, D. M. (2016). A strengths-based approach to prisoner reentry: The fresh start prisoner reentry program. *International Journal of Offender Therapy and Comparative Criminology*, *60*(11), 1298–1314. doi:10.1177/0306624X15576501 PMID:25805715

Hunt, S. R. (2000). *Drug addiction and alcoholism as qualifying impairments for Social Security disability benefits: The history, controversies, and congressional response.* Brandeis University, The Heller School for Social Policy and Management.

Hu, X., Rodgers, K., & Lovrich, N. P. (2018). We are more than crime fighters": Social media images of police departments. *Police Quarterly*, *21*(4), 544–572. doi:10.1177/1098611118783991

IACP, International Association of Chiefs of Police. (2016). *Social media survey results.* Retrieved March 4, 2023, from https://www.theiacp.org/resources/technology-and-social-media

IACP. (2007). Building trust between the police and the citizens they serve: An internal affairs promising practices guide for local law enforcement. *International Association of Chiefs of Police.* https://www.theiacp.org/sites/default/files/all/b/BuildingTrust.pdf

Inuit Tapiriit Kanatami. (2004). *5000 Years of Inuit History and Heritage.* https://www.itk.ca/wp-content/uploads/2016/07/5000YearHeritage_0.pdf

Ippolito, F. (2018). *Recuperare la fiducia e non rincorrere il consenso.* Questione giustizia. https://www.questionegiustizia.it/rivista/articolo/recuperare-la-fiducia-e-non-rincorrere-il-consenso_597.php

Jaegers, L. A., Skinner, E., Conners, B., Hayes, C., West-Bruce, S., Vaughn, M. G., Smith, D. L., & Barney, K. F. (2020). Evaluation of the jail-based occupational therapy transition and integration services program for community reentry. *AJOT: American Journal of Occupational Therapy*, *74*(3). https://link.gale.com/apps/doc/A623794160/HWRC?u=nu_main&sid=bookmark-HWRC&xid=0bccfcdf

Janmohamed, Z. (2019, January 10). *The divisiveness that permeates Detroit's communities of color*. https://www.theguardian.com/us-news/2019/jan/09/detroit-arab-african-american-discrimination-race

Jannetta, J., Esthappan, S., Fontaine, J., Lynch, M., & La Vigne, N. (2019). *Learning to Build Police-Community Trust*. The Urban Institute.

Jennings, W. G., Fridell, L. A., & Lynch, M. D. (2014). Cops and cameras: Officer perceptions of the use of body-worn cameras in law enforcement. *Journal of Criminal Justice*, *42*(6), 549–556. doi:10.1016/j.jcrimjus.2014.09.008

Jennings, W. G., Lynch, M. D., & Fridell, L. A. (2015). Evaluating the impact of police officer body-worn cameras (BWCs) on response-to-resistance and serious external complaints: Evidence from the Orlando police department (OPD) experience utilizing a randomized controlled experiment. *Journal of Criminal Justice*, *43*(6), 480–486. doi:10.1016/j.jcrimjus.2015.10.003

Jilani, Z. (2023, June 6). New York City community policed itself for five days [news report]. Chicago, IL: NewsNation.

Jouppi, S. (2017, August 8*). CuriosiD: How did Detroit become a center for Arabs in the United States*. Academic Press.

Jungblut, M., Kümpel, A. S., & Steer, R. (2022). Social media use of the police in crisis situations: A mixed-method study on communication practices of the German police. *New Media & Society*, *0*(0). Advance online publication. doi:10.1177/14614448221127899

Khaled, A. A. A. M. (2010). *Community policing and activating security performance*. PhD thesis, College of Graduate Studies.

Khalifeh, H. (2017, July 7). Local Yemenis feel marginalized as Lebanese brethren gain momentum. *The Arab American News*.

Kim, B., Gerber, J., & Beto, D. R. (2010). Listening to law enforcement officers: The promises and problems of police-adult probation partnerships. *Journal of Criminal Justice*, *38*(4), 625–632. doi:10.1016/j.jcrimjus.2010.04.035

Knapp, M., & Comadena, M. (1979). Telling It Like It Isn't: A Review of Theory and Research on Deceptive Communications. *Human Communication Research*, *5*, 270–285. doi:10.1111/j.1468-2958.1979.tb00640.x

Koen, M. C., Willis, J. J., & Mastrofski, S. D. (2018). The effects of body-worn cameras on police organization and practice: A theory-based analysis. *Policing and Society*, 1–17.

Kohring, M., & Matthes, J. (2007). Trust in news media: Development and validation of a multidimensional scale. *Communication Research*, *34*(2), 231–252. doi:10.1177/0093650206298071

Kuehn, B. M. (2022). Clinician shortage exacerbates pandemic-fueled "mental health crisis". *Journal of the American Medical Association*, *327*(22), 2179–2181. doi:10.1001/jama.2022.8661 PMID:35612873

Kumaus, T. (n.d.). *Historical timeline of the Arab community of Dearborn, MI*. Academic Press.

Lamin, S. A., & Teboh, C. (2016). Police social work and community policing. *Cogent Social Sciences*, *2*(1), 1212636. doi:10.1080/23311886.2016.1212636

Lane, R. (2019). "I'm a police officer not a social worker or mental health nurse": Online discourses of exclusion and resistance regarding mental health-related police work. *Journal of Community & Applied Social Psychology*, *29*(5), 429–442. doi:10.1002/casp.2410

Leech, N. (2017, July 5). How Dearborn, Michigan became the heart of the Arab America. *The National News*. https://www.thenationalnews.com/arts/how-dearborn-michigan-became-the-heart-of-arab-america-1.117177

Leipsiger, A., & Hillman, K. (2020). *NASW-Illinois Chapter statement on the call for police reform and the role of social workers*. https://www.naswil.org/post/nasw-illinois-chapter-statement-on-the-call-for-police-reform-and-the-role-of-social-workers

Leverentz, A. (2011). Barriers to reintegration. In L. Gideon & H.-E. Sung (Eds.), *Rethinking corrections: Rehabilitation, reentry, and reintegration* (pp. 359–381). Sage Publications, Inc. doi:10.4135/9781452230474.n14

Lewicki, R. J., & Bunker, B. B. (1995). Trust in Relationships: A Model of Development and Decline. In B. B. Bunker, J. Z. Rubin, & ... (Eds.), *Conflict, Cooperation, and Justice*. Jossey-Bass Publishers.

Lewis, D., Castleden, H., Francis, S., Strickland, K., & Denny, C. (2016). Increasing response rates on face-to-face surveys with Indigenous communities in Canada: Lessons from Pictou Landing. *Progress in Community Health Partnerships*, *10*(2), 197–205. doi:10.1353/cpr.2016.0021 PMID:27346765

Lews, J. (1985). Trust as a Social Reality. *Social Forces*, *53*(4), 967–985. doi:10.2307/2578601

Licht, I. H. (2018). How body cameras may result in a more proactive and community- engaged police force. *Chicago Policy Review*.

Lieberman, J. D., Koetzle, D., & Sakiyama, M. (2013). Police departments' use of Facebook: Patterns and policy issues. *Police Quarterly*, *16*(4), 438–462. doi:10.1177/1098611113495049

Little, B. (2021, June 4). *How American icon Henry Ford fostered anti-semitism*. Academic Press.

Li, Y., Hyder, A., Southerland, L. T., Hammond, G., Porr, A., & Miller, H. J. (2020). 311 service requests as indicators of neighborhood distress and opioid use disorder. *Scientific Reports*, *10*(1), 19579. doi:10.1038/s41598-020-76685-z PMID:33177583

Logan, I., Madden, R., & Solak, M. (2023). Preparing social workers for emerging roles in police social work. *Journal of Social Work Education*, 1–16. Advance online publication. doi:10.1080/10437797.2023.2244999

Lortz, M. (2016). *What is Community Policing?* Everbridge.

Lu, C., Ahmed, R., Lamri, A., & Anand, S. S. (2022, September 15). Use of race, ethnicity, and ancestry data in health research. *PLOS Global Public Health*, *2*(9). Advance online publication. doi:10.1371/journal.pgph.0001060 PMID:36962630

Lutze, F. E., Rosky, J. W., & Hamilton, Z. K. (2014). Homelessness and reentry: A multisite outcome evaluation of Washington State's reentry housing program for high-risk offenders. *Criminal Justice and Behavior*, *41*(4), 471–491. doi:10.1177/0093854813510164

MacDonald, J. M. (2002). The effectiveness of community policing in reducing urban violence. *Crime and Delinquency*, *48*(4), 592–618. doi:10.1177/001112802237131

Machado, M. A., & Lugo, A. M. (2021). A behavioral analysis of two strategies to eliminate racial bias in police use of force. *Behavior Analysis in Practice*, *15*(4), 1221–1231. doi:10.1007/s40617-021-00551-1 PMID:36605163

Maghbouleh, N., Schachter, A., & Flores, R. D. (2022, February 15). Middle Eastern and North African Americans may not be perceived, not perceive themselves, to be White. *Proceedings of the National Academy of Sciences of the United States of America*, *119*(7), e2117940119. Advance online publication. doi:10.1073/pnas.2117940119 PMID:35131945

Mahmoud, M. M. A. (2015). *Mechanisms for implementing community policing* (Vol. 24). Alfikr AlShurti Periodical.

Mahran, A. J. A. (2020). Community transformations towards community partnership, the community police approach - a field study of the repercussions of the June 30 Revolution. *Journal of the Faculty of Arts*, *80*(3).

Marandola, A. (2022). "Riforma Cartabia" e rito penale. La Legge Delega tra impegni europei e scelte valoriali, Cedam, Padova.

Marsden, M., Nigam, J., Lemetyinen, H., & Edge, D. (2020). Investigating police officers' perceptions of their role in pathways to mental healthcare. *Health & Social Care in the Community*, *28*(3), 913–921. doi:10.1111/hsc.12922 PMID:31919970

Maskaly, J., Donner, C., Jennings, W. G., Ariel, B., & Sutherland, A. (2017). The effects of body-worn cameras (BWCs) on police and citizen outcomes: A state-of-the-art review. *Policing*, *40*(4), 672–688. doi:10.1108/PIJPSM-03-2017-0032

Mastrofski, S. D., Reisig, M. D., & McCluskey, J. D. (2002). Police disrespect toward the public: An encounter-based analysis. *Criminology*, *40*(3), 519–552. doi:10.1111/j.1745-9125.2002.tb00965.x

Mastrofski, S. D., Willis, J. J., & Kochel, T. R. (2007). The challenges of implementing community policing in the United States. *Policing. Journal of Policy Practice*, *1*(2), 223–234.

Mateescu, A., Rosenblat, A., & Boyd, D. (2016). Dreams of accountability, guaranteed surveillance: The promises and costs of body-worn cameras. *Surveillance & Society*, *14*(1), 122–127. doi:10.24908/ss.v14i1.6282

Matheny, K., & Laitner, B. (2018, January 18). Utility wants to add 1,000-plus tons of air pollutants to Dearborn's skies. *Detroit Free* Press. https://www.freep.com/story/news/local/michigan/wayne/2018/01/16/utility-wants-add-1-000-plus-tons-air-pollutants-dearborns-skies/1029332001/

Mather, K., & Zahniser, D. (2016). Deal to spend $57.6 million on LAPD body cameras clears key hurdle. *Los Angeles Times*.

Matthews, J. (2022). *Body-Worn Camera Use and Citizen Behavior During Police–Citizen Encounters* [Doctoral dissertation]. Walden University.

Matthews, J. J., & Lyons, M. L. (2015). Phenomenological experiences of African American men in the aftermath of the Zimmerman trial. *Journal of Counselor Practice*, *6*(2), 76–93.

Maury, K. J. (2016). Police body-worn camera policy: Balancing the tension between privacy and public access in state laws. *The Notre Dame Law Review*, *92*, 479.

Mayes, L. (2021). Social media and community-oriented policing: Examining the organizational image construction of municipal police on Twitter and Facebook. *Police Practice and Research*, *22*(1), 903–920. doi:10.1080/15614263.2020.1843459

McCarthy, B., Hagan, J., & Herda, D. (2020). Neighborhood climates of legal cynicism and complaints about abuse of police power. *Criminology*, *58*(3), 510–536. doi:10.1111/1745-9125.12246

McElroy, J. (2019). *Uncovering the police: Converging trends threaten public accountability of local and state law enforcement across the United States.* Middle Tennessee State University: College of Media and Entertainment. https://www.mtsu.edu/seigenthaler/UncoveringThePolice.pdf

McHugh, M. L. (2013). The chi-square test of independence. *Biochemia Medica*, *23*(2), 143–149. doi:10.11613/BM.2013.018 PMID:23894860

McKeever, B., Greene, S., MacDonald, G., Tatian, P., & Jones, D. (2018). *Data Philanthropy: Unlocking the Power of Private Data for Public Good.* Urban Institute.

McNutt, J. G. (Ed.). (2018). Technology, Activism and Social Justice in a Digital Age. Oxford University Press.

McNutt, J. G., & Ban, C. C. (2023). Preparing public managers to deal with disruptive innovations through citizen partnerships. In S. Edwards, III & J. Masterson (Eds.), Government Response to Disruptive Innovation: Perspectives and Examinations (pp. 1-19). IGI Global. doi:10.4018/978-1-6684-6429-8.ch001

Meitl, M. B. (2021). Four thousand voices: Self-reported barriers to reentry. *Federal Probation*, *85*(2), 16–21.

Michaels, R. A., & Treger, H. (1973). Social work in police departments. *Social Work*, *18*(5), 67–75.

Miers, D. (2001). *An International Review of Restorative Justice, Crime Reduction Research Series Paper 10.* Crown Copyright.

Miller, A. H. (1974). Political issues and trust in government, 1964-1970. *The American Political Science Review*, *68*(3), 951–972. doi:10.2307/1959140

Miller, H. V., Miller, J. M., & Barnes, J. C. (2016). Reentry programming for opioid and opiate involved female offenders: Findings from a mixed methods evaluation. *Journal of Criminal Justice*, *46*, 129–136. doi:10.1016/j.jcrimjus.2016.04.001

Miller, J., & Chillar, V. F. (2022). Do police body-worn cameras reduce citizen fatalities? Results of a country-wide natural experiment. *Journal of Quantitative Criminology*, *38*(3), 723–754. doi:10.1007/s10940-021-09513-w

Miller, L. (2005). Police officer suicide: Causes, prevention, and practical intervention strategies. *International Journal of Emergency Mental Health*, *7*(2), 101. PMID:16107042

Miller, L. (2007). Crisis intervention strategies for treating law enforcement and mental health professionals. In F. M. Dattilio & A. Freeman (Eds.), *Cognitive-behavioral strategies in crisis intervention* (3rd ed., pp. 93–121). The Guilford Press.

Ministry of Justice. (n.d.). *Implementation of PNRR measures.* file:///C:/Users/Laptop02%20 Unical/Downloads/12_PNRR_Giustizia.pdf

Monk, E. P. Jr. (2021). The unceasing significance of colorism: Skin tone stratification in the United States. *Daedalus*, *150*(2), 76–90. doi:10.1162/daed_a_01847

Moore, M. H. (1992). Problem-solving and community policing. *Crime and Justice*, *15*, 99–158. doi:10.1086/449194

Moorman, Ch., Deshpande, R., & Zaltman, G. (1993, August). Factors Affecting Trust in Market Research Relationships. *Journal of Marketing*, *57*(1), 81–101. doi:10.1177/002224299305700106

Moreau, G. (2022). *Police-reported crime statistics in Canada, 2021*. Statistics Canada. https://www150.statcan.gc.ca/n1/pub/85-002-x/2022001/article/00013-eng.htm

Mousourakis, G. (2020). Restorative Justice. *Domestic and International Perspectives*, *33*(1), 55–86.

Mullinax, B. J. (2016). Silent Witness-Reconstruction from Body Worn Camera Videos. *Accident Reconstruction Journal, 26*(5).

Murphy, J. R. (2018). Is It Recording?—Racial Bias, Police Accountability, and the Body-Worn Camera Activation Policies of the Ten Largest Metropolitan Police Departments in the USA. Columbia Journal of Race and Law, 9(1), 141–190. https://doi.org/10.7916/cjrl.v9i1.2238

Murray, J. (2006). Criminal exploitation of women and children and the important role of community policing. *Police Practice and Research*, *7*(2), 125–134. doi:10.1080/15614260600676791

NA. N. (2016). Community policing: Comparative perspectives and prospects.Springer.

Naber, N. (2000). Ambiguous insiders: An investigation of Arab American invisibility. *Ethnic and Racial Studies*, *23*(1), 37–61. doi:10.1080/014198700329123

National Association of Social Workers. (2018). Social work in the criminal justice system. In *National Association of Social Workers policy statements* (pp. 302–309). NASW Press. (Original work published 2018)

National Conference of State Legislatures (NCSL). (2021). Body-Worn Camera Laws Database. *April Report.*

National Institute of Justice. (2022). *Recidivism.* https://www2.ed.gov/about/offices/list/ovae/pi/AdultEd/correctional-education.html

National Museum of African American History & Culture (n.d.). *Social identities and systems of oppression.* Author.

North County Police Cooperative. (n.d.). Retrieved at https://www.northcountypolice.com/

Noveck, B. S. (2021). *Solving public problems: a practical guide to fix our government and change our world.* Yale University Press.

O'Connor, C. D., & Zaidi, H. (2021). Communicating with purpose: Image work, social media, and policing. *The Police Journal, 94*(3), 333–352. doi:10.1177/0032258X20932957

O'Donnell, S., & Beaton, B. (2018). A 'whole-community'approach for sustainable digital infrastructure in remote and northern First Nations. *Northern Public Affairs, 6*(2), 34–37.

O'Hair, D., & Cody, M. (1994). Deception. In W. R. Cupach & B. H. Spitzberg (Eds.), *The Dark Side of Interpersonal Communication* (pp. 181–213). Lawrence Erlbaum. doi:10.4324/9781315807010-8

O'Hare, T. (2019). *Essential skills of social work practice: Assessment, intervention, and evaluation.* Oxford University Press.

O'Hare, T. (2020). *Evidence-based practices for social workers: An interdisciplinary approach.* Oxford University Press.

O'Mahony, D., & Doak, J. (2004). Restorative Justice - Is More Better? The Experience of Police-Led Restorative Cautioning Pilots in Northern Ireland. *Howard Journal of Criminal Justice, 43*(5), 484–505. doi:10.1111/j.1468-2311.2004.00344.x

O'Neill, M., van der Giessen, M., Bayerl, P. S., Hail, Y., Aston, E., & Houston, J. (2023). Conditions, Actions, and Purposes (CAP): A dynamic model for community policing in Europe. Policing. *Journal of Policy Practice, 17*, paad014.

Obaidat. (1996). *Scientific Research Methods and Techniques.* Sanaa Publishing House.

Office of Community Oriented Policing Services. (2015). *Final report of the president's task force on 21st century policing.* US Department of Justice https://cops.usdoj.gov/pdf/taskforce/taskforce_finalreport.pdf

Office of Policy Development and Research, State of the Cities Data Systems (n.d.). *SOCDS Census data: Output for Detroit city, MI.* Academic Press.

Office of the Privacy Commissioner of Canada. (2020, March). *Expectations: OPC's guide to the privacy impact assessment process*. https://www.priv.gc.ca/en/privacy-topics/privacy-impact-assessments/gd_exp_202003/

Paat, Y.-F., Hope, T. L., Lopez, L. C., Zamora, H. Jr, & Salas, C. M. (2017). Hispanic exconvicts' perceptions of challenges and reintegration. *Journal of Offender Rehabilitation, 56*(2), 87–109. doi:10.1080/10509674.2016.1268233

Padovani, T., (2021). La "sottile linea rossa" della riforma condizionata dai nodi organizzativi. *Guida al Diritto, 40.*

Pagni, I. (2021). *L'Ufficio per il processo: l'occasione per una (ulteriore) osmosi virtuosa tra teoria e pratica, con uno sguardo alle riforme processuali in cantiere*. Questione Giustizia. www.questionegiustizia.it/articolo/l-ufficio-per-il-processo

Parry, M. M. (2017). *Watching the Watchmen: How Videos of Police-Citizen Encounters Influence Individuals' Perceptions of the Police*. Arizona State University.

Paternoster, R., Brame, R., Bachman, R., & Sherman, L. W. (1997). Do fair procedures matter? The effect of procedural justice on spouse assault. *Law & Society Review, 31*(1), 163–204. doi:10.2307/3054098

Patterson, G. T. (2008). Police social work: A unique area of practice arising from law enforcement functions. *Police social work: National Association of Social Workers.* Retrieved from www.naswnyc.org/?Page=77

Patterson, G. T. (2021). Treger, Harvey. *Encyclopedia of Social Work.* https://oxfordre.com/socialwork/search?siteToSearch=socialwork&q=treger&searchBtn=Search&isQuickSearch=true

Patterson, G. T. (2004). Police–social work crisis teams: Practice and research implications. *Stress, Trauma and Crisis, 7*(2), 93–104. doi:10.1080/15434610490450886

Patterson, G. T. (2023). Police social work and social justice: Lessons for clinical social work practice. *Clinical Social Work Journal*, 1–8. doi:10.1007/s10615-023-00871-5

Patterson, G. T., & Swan, P. G. (2019). Police social work and social service collaboration strategies one hundred years after Vollmer: A systematic review. *Policing, 42*(5), 863–886. doi:10.1108/PIJPSM-06-2019-0097

Paulsen, D. (2016). *Public opinion about police use of body-worn cameras* [Dissertation]. Retrieved from ProQuest Dissertations & Theses Global. (UMI No. 10163614).

Perkins Collaborative Resource Network. (2020). *State profiles.* https://cte.ed.gov/profiles/national-summary

Perkins Collaborative Resource Network. (2022). *State allocations, estimated fiscal year (FY) (2022).* https://cte.ed.gov/grants/state-allocations

Perkins, C. D. (1976). Educational equality. *Journal of Teacher Education, 27*(4), 296–296. doi:10.1177/002248717602700406

Pinals, D. A., Hepburn, B., Parks, J., & Stephenson, A. H. (2020). The behavioral health system and its response to COVID-19: A snapshot perspective. *Psychiatric Services (Washington, D.C.), 71*(10), 1070–1074. doi:10.1176/appi.ps.202000264 PMID:32781926

Pohl, J. G. (1999). Some notions of complex adaptive systems and their relationship to our world. In *Proceedings of InterSymp-1999: The 11th International Conference On Systems Research* (p. 9). Informatics and Cybernetics. https://digitalcommons.calpoly.edu/cadrc/34

Poulin, L. I. L., Colibaba, A., Skinner, M. W., Balfour, G., Byrne, D., & Dieleman, C. (2023). Lost in transition? Community residential facility staff and stakeholder perspectives on previously incarcerated older adults' transitions into long-term care. *BMC Geriatrics, 23*(1), 180. doi:10.1186/s12877-023-03807-3 PMID:36978019

Pranis, K. (2005). *The Little Book of Circle Processes.* Good Books- Skyhorse Publishing.

Pratt, B. M., Hixson, L., & Jones, N. A. (n.d.). Measuring race and ethnicity across the decades: 1970-2010 mapped to 1997 U.S. Office of Management and Budget Classification Standards. The United States Census Bureau.

President's Task Force on 21st Century Policing. (2015). Final report of the president's task force on 21st century policing. *Office of Community Oriented Policing Services.* https://cops.usdoj.gov/pdf/taskforce/taskforce_finalreport.pdf

Prison Policy Initiative. (2020). *50 state profiles.* https://www.prisonpolicy.org/profiles/CA.html

Prison Policy Initiative. (2020). *United States profile.* https://www.prisonpolicy.org/profiles/

Procter, R., Crump, J., Karstedt, S., Voss, A., & Cantijoch, M. (2013). Reading the riots: What were the police doing on Twitter? *Policing and Society, 23*(4), 413–436. doi:10.1080/10439463.2013.780223

Pryor, M., Heydari, F., Goff, P.A., & Friedman, B. (n.d.). *Collecting, analyzing, and responding to stop data: A guidebook for law enforcement agencies, government, and communities.* Academic Press.

Quandt, T. (2012). What's Lest of Trust in a Network Society? An Evolutionary Model and Critical Discussion of Trust and Societal Communication. *European Journal of Communication, 27(1), 7-21.*

Ray, J. M. (1963). Rethinking community policing. OCLC 892799678.

Ray, R. (2020). *How can we enhance police accountability in the United States?* The Vitals: Policy. Brookings Institution.

Razali, A., Mustaffa, J., & Kamsani, S. R. (2021). Reducing recidivism among former offenders: Strategies to increase success in social reintegration. *Turkish Online Journal of Qualitative Inquiry, 12*(3), 5672–5685.

Reece, J. G., & Macy, J. (2015, October). Citizen advisory boards in contemporary practice: A practical approach in policing. *The Police Chief, 82.* https://www.policechiefmagazine.org/citizen-advisory-boards-in-contemporary-practice-a-practical-approach-in-policing/

Reisig, M. D., & Parks, R. B. (2004). Can community policing help the truly disadvantaged? *Crime and Delinquency, 50*(2), 139–167. doi:10.1177/0011128703253157

Remington, F. J. (1965). The role of police in a democratic society. *The Journal of Criminal Law, Criminology, and Police Science, 56*(3), 361–365. doi:10.2307/1141253

Roberts, A. R. (2007). Police social work: Bridging the past to the present. In A. R. Roberts & D. W. Springer (Eds.), *Social work in juvenile and criminal justice settings* (pp. 126–129). Charles C. Thomas Publisher Ltd.

Rodriguez, R. E. (2020). *The Impact of Agency Accreditation or Certification on Police Misconduct* [Dissertation]. Walden University.

Rojek, J., & Smith, M. R. (2007). Law Enforcement Lessons Learned from Hurricane Katrina. *The Review of Policy Research, 24*(6), 589–608. doi:10.1111/j.1541-1338.2007.00301.x

Rosenbaum, D. P. (1994). The challenge of community policing. *Sage (Atlanta, Ga.).*

Rosenbaum, D. P., & Lurigio, A. J. (1994). An inside look at community policing reform: Definitions, organizational changes, and evaluation findings. *Crime and Delinquency, 40*(3), 299–314. doi:10.1177/0011128794040003001

Rostomyan, A. (2013a). Management Techniques of Emotions in Communicative Conflict Reduction. In Communication and Management, Communication: Breakdowns and Breakthroughs, Probing the Boundaries. Inter-disciplinary Press.

Rostomyan, A. (2022a). *The Ultimate Force of Emotions in Communication: A linguo-cognitive Analysis of Verbal and Non-verbal Expressions of Emotions (on the material of English).* Dissertation (Yerevan State University). Düren: Shaker Verlag.

Rostomyan, A. (2009). *Means of Expressing Emotive Emphasis in Conversational English. Foreign Languages in Armenia, 10.*

Rostomyan, A. (2012). *'The Vitality of Emotional Background Knowledge in Court', Italian Association for the Study of Law and Literature. Polemos, 6(2).*

Rostomyan, A. (2020a). *Business Communication Management: The Key to Emotional Intelligence.* Tredition.

Rostomyan, A. (2020b). *Your Guide to Becoming a Successful Leader.* Tredition.

Rostomyan, A. (2022b). *Emotional Intelligence as a Keystone towards Success.* Generis Publishing.

Roy, A. (2014). *On-officer video cameras: Examining the effects of police department policy and assignment on camera use and activation*. Arizona State University.

Ruggieri, F. (2020). *Il processo penale al tempo del Covid-19: modelli alternativi di gestione della crisi*. La legislazione penale. https://www.lalegislazionepenale.eu/wp-content/uploads/2020/05/Ruggieri-sistema-delle-fonti-1.pdf

Salbu, S. R. (2002). The European Union Data Privacy Directive and International Relations. *Vand. J. Transnat'l L.*, *35*, 655.

Salem, B. E., Kwon, J., Ekstrand, M. L., Hall, E., Turner, S. F., Faucette, M., & Slaughter, R. (2021). Transitioning into the community: Perceptions of barriers and facilitators experienced by formerly incarcerated, homeless women during reentry—a qualitative study. *Community Mental Health Journal*, *57*(4), 609–621. doi:10.1007/s10597-020-00748-8 PMID:33387178

Sampson, R. (1994). *Problem Solving, Neighborhood-oriented Policing in Rural Communities: A Program Planning Guide*. Bureau of Justice Assistance, Office of Justice Programs, US Department of Justice.

Santana, A. G., Caplan, J. & Kennedy, L. (n.d.). *Data-informed community engagement: the Newark Public Safety Collaborative*. Academic Press.

Saulnier, A., Bagg, J., & Thompson, B. (2021). Canadian policing and body-worn cameras: Factors to contemplate in developing body-worn camera policy. *Canadian Public Policy*, *47*(2), 131–157. doi:10.3138/cpp.2020-096

Scheider, M. C., Chapman, R., & Schapiro, A. (2009). Towards the unification of policing innovations under community policing. *Policing*, *32*(4), 694–718. doi:10.1108/13639510911000777

Schlief, M., Saunders, K. R. K., Appleton, R., Barnett, P., Vera San Juan, N., Foye, U., Olive, R. R., Machin, K., Shah, P., Chipp, B., Lyons, N., Tamworth, C., Persaud, K., Badhan, M., Black, C., Sin, J., Riches, S., Graham, T., Greening, J., ... Johnson, S. (2022). Synthesis of the evidence on what works for whom in telemental health: Rapid realist review. *Interactive Journal of Medical Research*, *11*(2), e38239. doi:10.2196/38239 PMID:35767691

Schmerler, K., Perkins, M., Phillips, S., Rinehart, T., & Townsend, M. (1998). Problem-solving Tips: A Guide to Reducing Crime and Disorder through Problem-solving Partnerships. Office of Community Oriented Policing Services, US Department of Justice.

Schneider, C. J. (2021). Police use of social media as bureaucratic propaganda: Comments on state violence and law enforcement use of social media in 2020. *Criminology, Criminal Justice, Law & Society*, *22*(2), 1–8.

Scott, M., & Goldstein, H. (2005). Shifting and Sharing Responsibility for Public Safety Problems. Office of Community Oriented Policing Services, US Department of Justice.

Searle, J. R. (1969). *Speech Acts: An Essay in The Philosophy of Language*. Cambridge University Press. doi:10.1017/CBO9781139173438

Sellers, R. M., Smith, M. A., Shelton, J. N., Rowley, S. A., & Chavous, T. M. (1998). Multidimensional model of racial identity: A reconceptualization of African American racial identity. *Personality and Social Psychology Review*, *2*(1), 18–39. doi:10.1207/s15327957pspr0201_2 PMID:15647149

Shaaban, H. (2009). Community Police (Reality and Expectations). *Security Studies Journal.*

SherradenM. (2020, June). *Social work and the future of policing: Key points for changes in policy and practice* (CSD Policy Brief No. 20-14). St. Louis, MO: Washington University, Center for Social Development. doi:10.7936/885h-rh13

Shore, K., & Lavoie, J. A. (2019). Exploring mental health-related calls for police service: A Canadian study of police officers as 'frontline mental health workers. *Policing. Journal of Policy Practice*, *13*(2), 157–171.

Short, T. B. R., MacDonald, C., Luebbers, S., Ogloff, J. R. P., & Thomas, S. D. M. (2014). The nature of police involvement in mental health transfers. *Police Practice and Research*, *15*(4), 336–348. doi:10.1080/15614263.2012.736717

Silk, D. (2012). Community policing to prevent violent extremism. *FBI L. Enforcement Bull.*, *81*, 1.

Simonds, R., Reisig, M. D., Trinkner, R., & Holtfreter, K. (2021). The effect of prior incarceration on trust and social support: Results from two factorial vignette studies. *Journal of Offender Rehabilitation*, *60*(7), 464–484. doi:10.1080/10509674.2021.1966154

Simplification ActF. A. F. S. A. (2023). https://fsapartners.ed.gov/knowledge-center/library/dear-colleague-letters/2023-08-04/fafsa-simplification-act-changes-implementation-2024-25

Sivasubramaniam, D., Burke, K. C., Saulnier, A., Szabo, R., Agius, E. J., & Bottoms, B. L. (2021). International perspectives on procedural justice: Trust and respect matter even when body-worn cameras are present. *Law and Human Behavior*, *45*(5), 440–455. doi:10.1037/lhb0000454 PMID:34871016

Skogan, W. G. (2000). Community policing: Chicago style. Oxford University Press. OCLC 490662808.

Skogan, W. G., & Hartnett, S. M. (1999, December 2). *Community Policing, Chicago Style*. Oxford University Press.

Skogan, W. G., & Hartnett, S. M. (2019). Community policing. *Police innovation: Contrasting perspectives*, 27-44.

Skogan, W. G. (1995). *Community participation and community policing*. Center for Urban Affairs and Policy Research, Northwestern University.

Skogan, W. G. (2005). Citizen satisfaction with police encounters. *Police Quarterly*, *8*(3), 298–321. doi:10.1177/1098611104271086

Skogan, W. G. (2006). Asymmetry in the impact of encounters with police. *Policing and Society*, *16*(02), 99–126. doi:10.1080/10439460600662098

Skolnick, J. H., & Bayley, D. H. (1988). *Community policing: Issues and practices around the world.* US Department of Justice, National Institute of Justice, Office of Communication and Research Utilization.

Skolnick, J. H., & Bayley, D. H. (1988). Theme and Variation in Community Policing. *Crime and Justice*, *10*, 1–37. doi:10.1086/449142

Smith, J. J. (2019). To adopt or not to adopt: Contextualizing police body-worn cameras through structural contingency and institutional theoretical perspectives. *Criminal Justice Review*, *44*(3), 369–385. doi:10.1177/0734016819847267

Smykla, J. O., Crow, M. S., Crichlow, V. J., & Snyder, J. A. (2016). Police body-worn cameras: Perceptions of law enforcement leadership. *American Journal of Criminal Justice*, *41*(3), 424–443. doi:10.1007/s12103-015-9316-4

Sottani, S. (2021). *Le norme del PNRR in tema di giustizia: opportunità e nuovi problema.* Questione Giustizia. www.questionegiustizia.it/articolo/le-norme-del-pnrr-in-tema-di-giustizia-opportunita-e-nuovi-problemi

Sousa, W. H., Miethe, T. D., & Sakiyama, M. (2018). Inconsistencies in Public Opinion of Body-Worn Cameras on Police: Transparency, Trust, and Improved Police–Citizen Relationships. Policing : A Journal of Policy and Practice, 12(1), 100–108. https://doi.org/10.1093/police/pax015

Spelman, W., & Eck, J. E. (1989). Sitting ducks, ravenous wolves, and helping hands: new approaches to urban policing. Public Affairs Comment, School of Public Affairs, University of Texas.

St. Louis, E., Saulnier, A., & Walby, K. (2019). Police use of body-worn cameras: Challenges of visibility, procedural justice, and legitimacy. *Surveillance & Society*, *17*(3/4), 305–321. doi:10.24908/ss.v17i3/4.8649

Statistical Atlas. (n.d.). *Ancestry in Dearborn.* The Demographic Statistical Atlas of the United States - Statistical Atlas.

Statistics Canada. (2023, February 2). Census Profile, 2021 Census of Population.. https://www12.statcan.gc.ca/census-recensement/2021/dp-pd/prof/details/page.cfm?Lang=E&SearchText=iqaluit&DGUIDlist=2021A00056204003&GENDERlist=1&STATISTIClist=1&HEADERlist=0

Steele, J. L., & Blau, N. (2023). An Analysis of Police Department Crisis Communication via social media. *Police Quarterly*, *0*(0), 520–544. Advance online publication. doi:10.1177/10986111221150505

Stenson, K. (1993). Community policing as a governmental technology. *Economy and Society*, *22*(3), 373–389. doi:10.1080/03085149300000025

Sterling, G. (2013, June 5). *Marketing Land.* Retrieved October 3, 2013, from Pew: 61 Percent In US Now Have Smartphones: http://marketingland.com/pew-61percent-in-us-now-have-smartphones-46966

Stewart, L. A., Farrell-MacDonald, S., & Feeley, S. (2017). The impact of a community mental health initiative on outcomes for offenders with a serious mental disorder. *Criminal Behaviour and Mental Health*, *27*(4), 371–384. doi:10.1002/cbm.2005 PMID:27272741

Subramanian, R., & Skrzypiec, L. (2017). *To Protect and Serve: New Trends in State-Level Policing Reform, 2015–2016*. Vera Institute of Justice.

Sun, I. Y., & Wu, Y. (2018). From invisibility to unwanted spotlight: Arab Americans' perception of the police. Race, Immigration, and Social Control. In C. Cunneen, K. Russell-Brown, S. L. Gabbidon, & S. Garner (Eds.), *Race, immigration, and social control. Palgrave studies in race, ethnicity, indigeneity and criminal justice*. Palgrave Macmillan. doi:10.1057/978-1-349-95807-8_6

Susha, I., Janssen, M., & Verhulst, S. (2017). Data collaboratives as "bazaars"? A review of coordination problems and mechanisms to match demand for data with supply. *Transforming Government: People. Process and Policy*, *11*(1), 157–172.

Susha, I., Janssen, M., Verhulst, S., & Pardo, T. (2017, June). Data collaboratives: How to create value from data for public problem solving?: Panel. In *Proceedings of the 18th Annual International Conference on Digital Government Research* (pp. 604-606). New York: ACM. 10.1145/3085228.3085309

Susskind, R. (2019). Online court and the future of Justice. Oxford University Press.

Sveinsdottir, V., & Bond, G. R. (2020). Barriers to employment for people with severe mental illness and criminal justice involvement. *Journal of Mental Health (Abingdon, England)*, *29*(6), 692–700. doi:10.1080/09638237.2017.1417556 PMID:29265941

Syed, Z. (2019, January 10). ME/NA identify boxes now included in Rackham applications. *The Michigan Daily*. https://www.michigandaily.com/news/academics/mena-identity-boxes-now-included-rackham-applications/

Syed, S., Ashwick, R., Schlosser, M., Jones, R., Rowe, S., & Billings, J. (2020). Global prevalence and risk factors for mental health problems in police personnel: A systematic review and meta-analysis. *Occupational and Environmental Medicine*, *77*(11), 737–747. doi:10.1136/oemed-2020-106498 PMID:32439827

Taleb-Agha, K. (2020, December). *History of Arab Americans in Dearborn (1975-)*. Academic Press.

Taylor, E., & Lee, M. (2020). The camera never lies?: Police body-worn cameras and operational discretion. In *Police on Camera* (pp. 80–94). Routledge. doi:10.4324/9780429439759-6

Tehranian, J. (2009). *Whitewashed: America's invisible Middle Eastern minority*. New York University Press.

Texas Department of Criminal Justice. (2022). *Biennial reentry and reintegration services report*. https://www.tdcj.texas.gov/documents/rid/RID_Reentry_Biennial_Report_09_2022.pdf

Texas Department of Criminal Justice. (2022a). *Website to work, how it works.* https://reentry.tdcj.texas.gov/index.php/how-it-works/

Texas Department of Criminal Justice. (2022b). *Website to work, success stories.* https://reentry.tdcj.texas.gov/index.php/success-stories/

Texas Workforce Commission. (2018). *Workforce Innovation and Opportunity Act Report.* https://www.twc.texas.gov/files/partners/wioa-annual-report-2018-twc.pdf

The Dearborn Historical Commission (1979, Winter). *The Dearborn History, 1*(1), 1-35.

Thomas, E. (2016). The privacy case for body cameras: The need for a privacy-centric approach to body camera policymaking. *Colum. JL & Soc. Probs., 50*, 191.

Thornton-Lugo, M. A., & Rupp, D. E. (2021). The Communication of Justice, Injustice, and Necessary Evils: An Empirical Examination. *SAGE Open, 11*(3). Advance online publication. doi:10.1177/21582440211040796

Thyer, B. A., & Myers, L. L. (2011). The quest for evidence-based practice: A view from the United States. *Journal of Social Work : JSW, 11*(1), 8–25. doi:10.1177/1468017310381812

Toft, J., Abramovitz, M., & Harty, J. S. (2021). Social work responses to policing in the United States. *Bibliography of Scholarship in Social Welfare History, 101*(3), 1–21.

Toor, M. (2018). *PBA Sues City Over 'Illegal' Releasing Of Body-Camera Footage.* New York City Police Benevolent Association.

Treger, H. (1975). *The police-social work team: A new model for interprofessional cooperation: a university demonstration project in manpower training and development.* University of Illinois, Chicago Circle Paperback.

Treger, H. (1980). Guideposts for community work in police-social work diversion. *Federal Probation, 44*(3), 3–8.

Trojanowicz, R. C., & Bucqueroux, B. (1990). *Community policing: A contemporary perspective.* Anderson Publishing Company.

Tsui, E., Rao, R. C., Carey, A. R., Feng, M. T., & Provencher, L. M. (2020). Using social media to disseminate ophthalmic information during the #COVID19 pandemic. *Ophthalmology, 127*(9), e75–e78. doi:10.1016/j.ophtha.2020.05.048 PMID:32502595

Tyler, T. R. (1990). *Why people obey the law: Procedural justice, legitimacy, and compliance.* Yale University Press.

Tyler, T. R. (2003). Procedural justice, legitimacy, and the effective rule of law. In M. Tonry (Ed.), *Crime and Justice Chicago.* University of Chicago Press. doi:10.1086/652233

U.S. Commission on Civil Rights (2001, May). *Civil rights issues facing Arab Americans in Michigan.* Author.

U.S. Department of Congress, Bureau of Census (1960). *Notice of required information for the 1960 Census of Population and Housing*. Academic Press.

U.S. Department of Congress, Bureau of Census (2000). *Informational Census Form.* Academic Press.

U.S. Department of Justice (2023, May). *Guidance for federal law enforcement agencies regarding the use of race, ethnicity, gender, national origin, religion, sexual orientation, gender identity, and disability*. Academic Press.

U.S. Mayor's Conference of Cities. (2023, June). *The Mental Health Crisis in America's Cities and Their Responses to It: A 117-City Report.* https://www.usmayors.org/wp/content/uploads/2023/06/USCM-Mental-Health-Survey-2023.pdf

Umansky, E., & Farooq, U. (2023, Dec. 15). *How police undermined the promise of body cameras*. Retrieved from https://www.propublica.org/article/how-police-undermined-promise-body-cameras

Umansky, E. (2021). *Judge Says NYPD Illegally Withheld Footage in Police Shootings*. Pro Publica News.

Umbreit, M. S. (1994). *Victim Meets Offender*. Willow Tree Press Inc.

Umbreit, M. S. (2001). *The Handbook of Victim Offender Mediation*. Jossey-Bass Inc.

United States Census Bureau. (2008, December 8). *American Community Survey 5-year data (2009 – 2021)*. Author.

United States Census Bureau. (2020). *2020 Census frequently asked questions about race and ethnicity*. Author.

United States Census Bureau. (n.d.). *Why we ask questions about ancestry*. Author.

United States Department of Education. (2022). *Office of Career Technical, and Adult Education (OCTAE). Correctional education.* https://www2.ed.gov/about/offices/list/ovae/pi/AdultEd/correctional-education.html

United States Department of Education. (2023). *Press Office. U.S. Department of Education to Launch Application Process to Expand Federal Pell Grant Access for Individuals Who Are Confined or Incarcerated.* https://www.ed.gov/news/press-releases/us-department-education-launch-application-process-expand-federal-pell-grant-access-individuals-who-are-confined-or-incarcerated

United States Department of Labor. (2022). *Workforce Innovation and Opportunity Act.* https://www.dol.gov/agencies/eta/wioa/

University of Michigan National Center for Institutional Diversity. (n.d.). *ME/NA box knowledge community*. https://lsa.umich.edu/ncid/engagement-opportunities/knowledge-communities/mena-box.html

University of Michigan. (n.d.). *Environmental justice case study: the Dearborn, Michigan Arab American community and industrial air pollution.* websites.umich.edu/~snre492/berry.html

University of Minnesota Libraries (n.d.). *Conducting research through an anti-racism lens.* Author.

University of Minnesota Libraries. (n.d.). *Conducting research through an anti-racism lens.* https://libguides.umn.edu/antiracismlens

Uricska, E. (2023). *The Relationship between the Framing of Speeding Messages and Changes.* .S2CID 260399463 doi:10.32577/mr.2023.1.16

USLegal (n.d.). *Discrimination law and legal definition.* Academic Press.

Vail, W. L., Niyogi, A., Henderson, N., & Wennerstrom, A. (2017). Bringing it all back home: Understanding the medical difficulties encountered by newly released prisoners in New Orleans, Louisiana - a qualitative study. *Health & Social Care in the Community, 25*(4), 1448–1458. doi:10.1111/hsc.12445 PMID:28370837

Valencia, N., Sanchez, R., Kirkland, P., & Tamsett, M. (2023). Tyre Nichols' family files federal $550 million civil lawsuit against Memphis and police officers. *CNN.* https://www.cnn.com/2023/04/19/us/tyre-nichols-death-lawsuit-memphis-police/index.html

Veil, S. R., & Husted, R. A. (2012). Best practices as an assessment for crisis communication. *Journal of Communication Management (London), 16*(2), 131–145. doi:10.1108/13632541211217560

Verhulst, S. G., & Young, A. (2017). The potential of social media intelligence to improve people's lives. *The Governance Lab.* Available at https://www.thegovlab.org/static/files/publications/social-media-data.pdf

Vogel, H. J. (2007). The Restorative Justice Wager: The Promise and Hope of a Value- Based Dialogue- Driven Approach to Conflict Resolution for Social Healing. *Cardozo Journal of Conflict Resolution, 8*, 565–609.

Voigt, R., Camp, N. P., Prabhakaran, V., Hamilton, W. L., Hetey, R. C., Griffiths, C. M., Jurgens, D., Jurafsky, D., & Eberhardt, J. L. (2017). Language from police body camera footage shows racial disparities in officer respect. *Proceedings of the National Academy of Sciences of the United States of America, 114*(25), 6521–6526. doi:10.1073/pnas.1702413114 PMID:28584085

Walsh, J. P., & O'Connor, C. (2019). Social media and policing: A review of recent research. *Sociology Compass, 13*(1), 1–14. doi:10.1111/soc4.12648

Wang, H. L. (2022, February 17). The U.S. Census see Middle Eastern and North African people as white. Many don't. *NPR.* https://www.npr.org/2022/02/17/1079181478/us-census-middle-eastern-white-north-african-mena

Wang, H.L. (2018, January 29). No Middle Eastern or North African category on 2020 Census, Bureau says. *NPR.*

Wang, H.L. (2023, April 7). New 'Latino" and 'Middle Eastern or North African' checkboxes proposed for U.S. forms. *NPR.*

Ward, T., Fox, K. J., & Garber, M. (2014). Restorative Justice, Offender Rehabilitation and Desistance. *Restorative Justice, 2*(1), 24–42. doi:10.5235/20504721.2.1.24

Warikoo, N. (2020). Statute of former Dearborn Mayor Orville Hubbard taken down. *Detroit Free Press.*

Warikoo, N. (2021, August). Yemeni Americans in Dearborn struggle to be included in city government. *Detroit Free Press.*

Watson, E. M., & Alfred, R. (1998). Strategies for Community Policing. Prentice-Hall Inc.

Wellborn, J. (1999). Responding to individuals with mental illness. *FBI Law Enforcement Bulletin, 68*(11), 6–8.

Wells, A. S. (1915, May 18). Policewomen. In *Conference of Charities and Corrections, 42nd Annual Meeting Proceedings* (pp. 411-418). Baltimore, MD. University of Michigan Archives. https://quod.lib.umich.edu/n/ncosw/

Western, B. (2018). *Homeward: Life in the year after prison.* Russell Sage Foundation. doi:10.7758/9781610448710

Wheeler, R. E. (2016). About microaggressions. *Boston University School of Law Library Journal, 108*(2), 321–329.

Whipple, C. R., Jason, L. A., & Robinson, W. L. (2016). Housing and abstinence self-efficacy in formerly incarcerated individuals. *Journal of Offender Rehabilitation, 55*(8), 548–563. doi:10.1080/10509674.2016.1229713 PMID:28603403

White House. (2015). *Remarks by the President after Meeting with Task Force on 21st Century Policing.* Office of the Press Secretary Speech Transcript.

White House. (2022). *FACT SHEET: President Biden to Sign Historic Executive Order to Advance Effective, Accountable Policing and Strengthen Public Safety.* https://www.whitehouse.gov/briefing-room/statements-releases/2022/05/25/fact-sheet-president-biden-to-sign-historic-executive-order-to-advance-effective-accountable-policing-and-strengthen-public-safety/

White, M. D., & Malm, A. (2020). *Cops, Cameras, and Crisis: The Potential and the Perils of Police Body-Worn Cameras.* New York University Press. doi:10.18574/nyu/9781479820177.001.0001

White, M. D., Todak, N., & Gaub, J. E. (2017). Assessing citizen perceptions of body-worn cameras after encounters with police. *Policing, 40*(4), 689–703. doi:10.1108/PIJPSM-07-2016-0105

Wike, T. L., Bledsoe, S. E., Manuel, J. I., Despard, M., Johnson, L. V., Bellamy, J. L., & Killian-Farrell, C. (2014). Evidence-based practice in social work: Challenges and opportunities for clinicians and organizations. *Clinical Social Work Journal, 42*(2), 161–170. doi:10.1007/s10615-014-0492-3

Williams, T. N. (2019). *Crisis Communication Systems Among K-12 School Principals* (Order No. 13807361). Available from ProQuest One Academic. (2198700438). https://www.proquest.com/dissertations-theses/crisis-communication-systems-among-k-12-school/docview/2198700438/se-2

Williams, M. (2007). Building Genuine Trust through Interpersonal Emotion Management: A Threat Regulation Model of Trust and Collaboration across Boundaries. *Academy of Management Review*, *2*(2), 595–621. doi:10.5465/amr.2007.24351867

Williamson, O. E. (1993). Calculativeness, Trust, and Economic Organization. *The Journal of Law & Economics*, *36*(1), 453–486. doi:10.1086/467284

Williams, T., & Liou, Y.-H. (2023). Framing K-12 school leaders' roles and competencies in times of crisis. *Journal of School Leadership*, *0*(0). Advance online publication. doi:10.1177/10526846231187576

Wilson, L. (1989). *Family structure and dynamics in the Caribbean*. Doctoral Dissertation, University of Michigan.

Wilson, B. L., Wooten, N. R., & Pitner, R. O. (2023). Examining historical and contemporary policing disparities in the Black community: Implications for social work. *Social Work*, *68*(1), 8–17. doi:10.1093/sw/swac049 PMID:36346331

Wilson, J. M. (2013). *Community policing in America*. Routledge. doi:10.4324/9780203830512

Won, H. H., Myung, W., Song, G. Y., Lee, W. H., Kim, J. W., Carroll, B. J., & Kim, D. K. (2013). Predicting national suicide numbers with social media data. *PLoS One*, *8*(4), e61809. doi:10.1371/journal.pone.0061809 PMID:23630615

Wood, J. D., Watson, A. C., & Barber, C. (2021). What can we expect of police in the face of deficient mental health systems? Qualitative insights from Chicago police officers. *Journal of Psychiatric and Mental Health Nursing*, *28*(1), 28–42. doi:10.1111/jpm.12691 PMID:32966680

Wood, S. E. (2017). Police body cameras and professional responsibility: Public records and private evidence. *Preservation. Digital Technology & Culture*, *46*(1), 41–51. doi:10.1515/pdtc-2016-0030

World Population Review. (2023). *Incarceration Rates by Country 2023*. https://worldpopulationreview.com/country-rankings/incarceration-rates-by-country

Wright, B. J., Zhang, S. X., Farabee, D., & Braatz, R. (2014). Prisoner reentry research from 2000 to 2010: Results of a narrative review. *Criminal Justice Review*, *39*(1), 37–57. doi:10.1177/0734016813501192

Wright, R. (1999). *Restoring Respect for Justice*. Waterside Press.

Yalla Count MENA In. (n.d.). https://yallacountmenain.org/

Yates, D., & Paquette, S. (2011). Emergency knowledge management and social media technologies: A case study of the 2010 Haitian earthquake. *International Journal of Information Management*, *31*(1), 6–13. doi:10.1016/j.ijinfomgt.2010.10.001

Yearwood, E. L. (2023). His name this time was Tyre Nichols. *Archives of Psychiatric Nursing*, *43*, A1–A2. doi:10.1016/j.apnu.2023.02.001 PMID:37032025

Zakhari, N. K. (2021, December). *Count MENA: Clarifying the impact of U.S. hate crimes on the Middle Eastern and Nor African Community*. Master of Science Capstone Project. https://jscholarship.library.jhu.edu/bitstream/handle/1774.2/66668/Zakhari-Capstone%20Project-2021.pdf?sequence=1

Zehr, H. (2015). *The Little Book of Restorative Justice*. Good Books- Skyhorse Publishing.

Zhang, J. (2022, December). Body-worn cameras in China: a survey. In *Third International Conference on Computer Science and Communication Technology (ICCSCT 2022)* (Vol. 12506, pp. 943-950). SPIE.

Zhang, J., Xie, C., Chen, Y., Dai, Y. D., & Yi-Jun, W. (2023). The matching effect of destinations' crisis communication. *Journal of Travel Research*, *62*(3), 491–516. doi:10.1177/00472875211067548

Related References

To continue our tradition of advancing information science and technology research, we have compiled a list of recommended IGI Global readings. These references will provide additional information and guidance to further enrich your knowledge and assist you with your own research and future publications.

Abdel-Hameid, S. O., & Wilson, E. (2018). Gender, Organization, and Change in Sudan. In N. Mahtab, T. Haque, I. Khan, M. Islam, & I. Wahid (Eds.), *Handbook of Research on Women's Issues and Rights in the Developing World* (pp. 107–120). Hershey, PA: IGI Global. doi:10.4018/978-1-5225-3018-3.ch007

Abdullahi, R. B. (2018). Volunteerism in Urban Development the Case of Non-Cash, Non-Digital Crowdfunding Growth in Nigeria. In U. Benna & A. Benna (Eds.), *Crowdfunding and Sustainable Urban Development in Emerging Economies* (pp. 188–210). Hershey, PA: IGI Global. doi:10.4018/978-1-5225-3952-0.ch010

Abioye, T. O., Oyesomi, K., Ajiboye, E., Omidiora, S., & Oyero, O. (2017). Education, Gender, and Child-Rights: Salient Issues in SDGS Years in ADO-ODO/OTA Local Government Area of Ogun State, Nigeria. In O. Nelson, B. Ojebuyi, & A. Salawu (Eds.), *Impacts of the Media on African Socio-Economic Development* (pp. 141–154). Hershey, PA: IGI Global. doi:10.4018/978-1-5225-1859-4.ch009

Adalı, G. K. (2022). Measuring the Attitudes of Governmental Policies and the Public Towards the COVID-19 Pandemic. In Ş. Omeraki Çekirdekci, Ö. İngün Karkış, & S. Gönültaş (Eds.), *Handbook of Research on Interdisciplinary Perspectives on the Threats and Impacts of Pandemics* (pp. 163–187). IGI Global. https://doi.org/10.4018/978-1-7998-8674-7.ch009

Adisa, W. B. (2018). Land Use Policy and Urban Sprawl in Nigeria: Land Use and the Emergence of Urban Sprawl. In A. Eneanya (Ed.), *Handbook of Research on Environmental Policies for Emergency Management and Public Safety* (pp. 256–274). Hershey, PA: IGI Global. doi:10.4018/978-1-5225-3194-4.ch014

Afolabi, O. S., Amao-Kolawole, T. G., Shittu, A. K., & Oguntokun, O. O. (2018). Rule of Law, Governance, and Sustainable Development: The Nigerian Perspective. In K. Teshager Alemu & M. Abebe Alebachew (Eds.), *Handbook of Research on Sustainable Development and Governance Strategies for Economic Growth in Africa* (pp. 273–290). Hershey, PA: IGI Global. doi:10.4018/978-1-5225-3247-7.ch015

Agyemang, O. S. (2018). Institutional Structures and the Prevalence of Foreign Ownership of Firms: Empirical Evidence From Africa. In K. Teshager Alemu & M. Abebe Alebachew (Eds.), *Handbook of Research on Sustainable Development and Governance Strategies for Economic Growth in Africa* (pp. 455–479). Hershey, PA: IGI Global. doi:10.4018/978-1-5225-3247-7.ch024

Aham-Anyanwu, N. M., & Li, H. (2017). E-State: Realistic or Utopian? *International Journal of Public Administration in the Digital Age*, *4*(2), 56–76. doi:10.4018/IJPADA.2017040105

Al Balushi, T., & Ali, S. (2020). Theoretical Approach for Instrument Development in Measuring User-Perceived E-Government Service Quality: A Case of Oman E-Government Services. *International Journal of Electronic Government Research*, *16*(1), 40–58. doi:10.4018/IJEGR.2020010103

Al-Jamal, M., & Abu-Shanab, E. (2018). Open Government: The Line between Privacy and Transparency. *International Journal of Public Administration in the Digital Age*, *5*(2), 64–75. doi:10.4018/IJPADA.2018040106

Alsaç, U. (2017). EKAP: Turkey's Centralized E-Procurement System. In R. Shakya (Ed.), *Digital Governance and E-Government Principles Applied to Public Procurement* (pp. 126–150). Hershey, PA: IGI Global. doi:10.4018/978-1-5225-2203-4.ch006

Amadi, L. A., & Igwe, P. (2018). Open Government and Bureaucratic Secrecy in the Developing Democracies: Africa in Perspective. In A. Kok (Ed.), *Proliferation of Open Government Initiatives and Systems* (pp. 1–28). Hershey, PA: IGI Global. doi:10.4018/978-1-5225-4987-1.ch001

Arble, E., & Arnetz, B. B. (2021). Four Fundamental Principles to Enhance Police Performance and Community Safety. In E. Arble & B. Arnetz (Eds.), *Interventions, Training, and Technologies for Improved Police Well-Being and Performance* (pp. 231–245). IGI Global. https://doi.org/10.4018/978-1-7998-6820-0.ch015

Arora, G. C. (2020). The Problem of Climate-Induced Displacement: Analyzing the International Framework on Protection of Rights of Climate Migrants. In R. Das & N. Mandal (Eds.), *Interdisciplinary Approaches to Public Policy and Sustainability* (pp. 67–82). IGI Global. https://doi.org/10.4018/978-1-7998-0315-7.ch004

Arora, T., & Mehra, N. (2021). Administration of Civil Justice in India: Ancient and Modern Perspectives. In E. Yin & N. Kofie (Eds.), *Advancing Civil Justice Reform and Conflict Resolution in Africa and Asia: Comparative Analyses and Case Studies* (pp. 17–45). IGI Global. https://doi.org/10.4018/978-1-7998-7898-8.ch002

Arteta, A. (2019). *Democracy and Government: Making Decisions*. IGI Global. doi:10.4018/978-1-5225-7558-0.ch001

Asante, M., & Botchway, T. P. (2021). Shielding Members of Parliament Against Court Summons: Interrogating the Question of Parliamentary Immunity. In E. Yin & N. Kofie (Eds.), *Advancing Civil Justice Reform and Conflict Resolution in Africa and Asia: Comparative Analyses and Case Studies* (pp. 210–229). IGI Global. https://doi.org/10.4018/978-1-7998-7898-8.ch012

Ateş, V. (2021). Critical Antecedents of Trust in E-Government Services in Turkey. In C. Babaoğlu, E. Akman, & O. Kulaç (Eds.), *Handbook of Research on Global Challenges for Improving Public Services and Government Operations* (pp. 94–116). IGI Global. https://doi.org/10.4018/978-1-7998-4978-0.ch006

Ayeni, A. O. (2018). Environmental Policies for Emergency Management and Public Safety: Implementing Green Policy and Community Participation. In A. Eneanya (Ed.), *Handbook of Research on Environmental Policies for Emergency Management and Public Safety* (pp. 40–59). Hershey, PA: IGI Global. doi:10.4018/978-1-5225-3194-4.ch003

Ayodele, J. O. (2017). The Influence of Migration and Crime on Development in Lagos, Nigeria. In G. Afolayan & A. Akinwale (Eds.), *Global Perspectives on Development Administration and Cultural Change* (pp. 192–230). Hershey, PA: IGI Global. doi:10.4018/978-1-5225-0629-4.ch009

Baarda, R. (2017). Digital Democracy in Authoritarian Russia: Opportunity for Participation, or Site of Kremlin Control? In R. Luppicini & R. Baarda (Eds.), *Digital Media Integration for Participatory Democracy* (pp. 87–100). Hershey, PA: IGI Global. doi:10.4018/978-1-5225-2463-2.ch005

Balakrishnan, K. (2017). The Rationale for Offsets in Defence Acquisition from a Theoretical Perspective. In K. Burgess & P. Antill (Eds.), *Emerging Strategies in Defense Acquisitions and Military Procurement* (pp. 263–276). Hershey, PA: IGI Global. doi:10.4018/978-1-5225-0599-0.ch015

Banerjee, S. (2017). Globalization and Human Rights: How Globalization Can Be a Tool to Protect the Human Rights. In C. Akrivopoulou (Ed.), *Defending Human Rights and Democracy in the Era of Globalization* (pp. 1–16). Hershey, PA: IGI Global. doi:10.4018/978-1-5225-0723-9.ch001

Bessant, J. (2017). Digital Humour, Gag Laws, and the Liberal Security State. In R. Luppicini & R. Baarda (Eds.), *Digital Media Integration for Participatory Democracy* (pp. 204–221). Hershey, PA: IGI Global. doi:10.4018/978-1-5225-2463-2.ch010

Bhat, M. Y. (2020). Environmental Problems of Delhi and Governmental Concern. In M. Merviö (Ed.), *Global Issues and Innovative Solutions in Healthcare, Culture, and the Environment* (pp. 133–167). IGI Global. https://doi.org/10.4018/978-1-7998-3576-9.ch008

Bhat, R. A. (2021). Identification of Various Dimensions and Indicators of Immigrant Integration Into Global Scenarios. In M. Mafukata (Ed.), *Impact of Immigration and Xenophobia on Development in Africa* (pp. 247–260). IGI Global. https://doi.org/10.4018/978-1-7998-7099-9.ch014

Boachie, C. (2017). Public Financial Management and Systems of Accountability in Sub-National Governance in Developing Economies. In E. Schoburgh & R. Ryan (Eds.), *Handbook of Research on Sub-National Governance and Development* (pp. 193–217). Hershey, PA: IGI Global. doi:10.4018/978-1-5225-1645-3.ch009

Boachie, C., & Adu-Darko, E. (2018). Socio-Economic Impact of Foreign Direct Investment in Developing Countries. In V. Malepati & C. Gowri (Eds.), *Foreign Direct Investments (FDIs) and Opportunities for Developing Economies in the World Market* (pp. 66–81). Hershey, PA: IGI Global. doi:10.4018/978-1-5225-3026-8.ch004

Bogdanoski, M., Stoilkovski, M., & Risteski, A. (2020). Novel First Responder Digital Forensics Tool as a Support to Law Enforcement. In I. Management Association (Ed.), *Improving the Safety and Efficiency of Emergency Services: Emerging Tools and Technologies for First Responders* (pp. 239-270). IGI Global. https://doi.org/10.4018/978-1-7998-2535-7.ch011

Borràs, S. (2017). Rights of Nature to Protect Human Rights in Times of Environmental Crisis. In C. Akrivopoulou (Ed.), *Defending Human Rights and Democracy in the Era of Globalization* (pp. 225–261). Hershey, PA: IGI Global. doi:10.4018/978-1-5225-0723-9.ch010

Bouaziz, F. (2021). E-Government and Digital Transformation: A Conceptual Framework for Risk Factors Identification. In K. Sandhu (Ed.), *Disruptive Technology and Digital Transformation for Business and Government* (pp. 67–90). IGI Global. https://doi.org/10.4018/978-1-7998-8583-2.ch004

Bradford, A. C., McElroy, H. K., & Rosenblatt, R. (2019). Social Climate Change and the Modern Police Department: Millennials, Marijuana, and Mass Media. In I. Management Association (Ed.), *Police Science: Breakthroughs in Research and Practice* (pp. 34-51). IGI Global. https://doi.org/10.4018/978-1-5225-7672-3.ch003

Brusca, I., Olmo, J., & Labrador, M. (2018). Characterizing the Risk Factors for Financial Sustainability in Spanish Local Governments. In M. Rodríguez Bolívar & M. López Subires (Eds.), *Financial Sustainability and Intergenerational Equity in Local Governments* (pp. 206–223). Hershey, PA: IGI Global. doi:10.4018/978-1-5225-3713-7.ch009

Budd, J. R., & Littrell, M. W. (2021). Law Enforcement Challenges to Gathering Intelligence in the Street: The Fourth Amendment. In E. de Silva & A. Abeyagoonesekera (Eds.), *Intelligence and Law Enforcement in the 21st Century* (pp. 18–40). IGI Global. https://doi.org/10.4018/978-1-7998-7904-6.ch002

Bush, C. L. (2021). Policing Strategies and Approaches to Improving Community Relations: Black Citizens' Perceptions of Law Enforcement Efforts to Intentionally Strengthen Relationships. In M. Pittaro (Ed.), *Global Perspectives on Reforming the Criminal Justice System* (pp. 56–75). IGI Global. https://doi.org/10.4018/978-1-7998-6884-2.ch004

Canto Moniz, G. (2020). Is There Anything Left of the Portuguese Law Implementing the GDPR?: The Decision of the Portuguese Supervisory Authority. In M. Tzanou (Ed.), *Personal Data Protection and Legal Developments in the European Union* (pp. 125–139). IGI Global. https://doi.org/10.4018/978-1-5225-9489-5.ch007

Casoria, M., & AlSarraf, E. M. (2020). The Impact of the GDPR on Extra-EU Legal Systems: The Case of the Kingdom of Bahrain. In M. Tzanou (Ed.), *Personal Data Protection and Legal Developments in the European Union* (pp. 224–237). IGI Global. https://doi.org/10.4018/978-1-5225-9489-5.ch011

Chaves, A. (2022). Government Response Capacity to the COVID-19 Pandemic: Estimating the Impact of Lockdown Measures in Colombia. In G. Antošová (Ed.), *Innovative Strategic Planning and International Collaboration for the Mitigation of Global Crises* (pp. 114–137). IGI Global. https://doi.org/10.4018/978-1-7998-8339-5.ch008

Chen, M., & Su, F. (2017). Global Civic Engagement as an Empowering Device for Cross-Ethnic and Cross-Cultural Understanding in Taiwan. In R. Shin (Ed.), *Convergence of Contemporary Art, Visual Culture, and Global Civic Engagement* (pp. 24–45). Hershey, PA: IGI Global. doi:10.4018/978-1-5225-1665-1.ch002

Chigwata, T. C. (2017). Fiscal Decentralization: Constraints to Revenue-Raising by Local Government in Zimbabwe. In E. Schoburgh & R. Ryan (Eds.), *Handbook of Research on Sub-National Governance and Development* (pp. 218–240). Hershey, PA: IGI Global. doi:10.4018/978-1-5225-1645-3.ch010

Chowdhury, M. A. (2017). The Nexus Between Institutional Quality and Foreign Direct Investments (FDI) in South Asia: Dynamic Heterogeneous Panel Approach. In T. Dorożyński & A. Kuna-Marszałek (Eds.), *Outward Foreign Direct Investment (FDI) in Emerging Market Economies* (pp. 293–310). Hershey, PA: IGI Global. doi:10.4018/978-1-5225-2345-1.ch015

Christopher, M. E., & Tsushima, V. G. (2017). Police Interactions with Persons-in-Crisis: Emergency Psychological Services and Jail Diversion. In C. Mitchell & E. Dorian (Eds.), *Police Psychology and Its Growing Impact on Modern Law Enforcement* (pp. 274–294). Hershey, PA: IGI Global. doi:10.4018/978-1-5225-0813-7.ch014

Ciftci, D. (2022). Digital Citizenship and E-Government Integration: The Case of North Cyprus. In E. Öngün, N. Pembecioğlu, & U. Gündüz (Eds.), *Handbook of Research on Digital Citizenship and Management During Crises* (pp. 34–55). IGI Global. https://doi.org/10.4018/978-1-7998-8421-7.ch003

Citro, F., Lucianelli, G., & Santis, S. (2018). Financial Conditions, Financial Sustainability, and Intergenerational Equity in Local Governments: A Literature Review. In M. Rodríguez Bolívar & M. López Subires (Eds.), *Financial Sustainability and Intergenerational Equity in Local Governments* (pp. 101–124). Hershey, PA: IGI Global. doi:10.4018/978-1-5225-3713-7.ch005

Correa de Mello, M. B. (2019). The Information Access Law as a Full Constitutional Citizenship Instrument. In A. Melro & L. Oliveira (Eds.), *Constitutional Knowledge and Its Impact on Citizenship Exercise in a Networked Society* (pp. 55–72). IGI Global. https://doi.org/10.4018/978-1-5225-8350-9.ch003

Covell, C. E. (2018). Theoretical Application of Public Sector Planning and Budgeting. In M. Rodríguez Bolívar & M. López Subires (Eds.), *Financial Sustainability and Intergenerational Equity in Local Governments* (pp. 248–279). Hershey, PA: IGI Global. doi:10.4018/978-1-5225-3713-7.ch011

Cunha, A. M., Ferreira, A. D., & Fernandes, M. J. (2018). The Impact of Accounting Information and Socioeconomic Factors in the Re-Election of Portuguese Mayors. In G. Azevedo, J. da Silva Oliveira, R. Marques, & A. Ferreira (Eds.), *Handbook of Research on Modernization and Accountability in Public Sector Management* (pp. 406–432). Hershey, PA: IGI Global. doi:10.4018/978-1-5225-3731-1.ch019 da Rosa, I., & de Almeida, J. (2017). Digital Transformation in the Public Sector: Electronic Procurement in Portugal. In R. Shakya (Ed.), *Digital Governance and E-Government Principles Applied to Public Procurement* (pp. 99–125). Hershey, PA: IGI Global. doi:10.4018/978-1-5225-2203-4.ch005

Daramola, O. (2018). Revisiting the Legal Framework of Urban Planning in the Global South: An Explanatory Example of Nigeria. In K. Teshager Alemu & M. Abebe Alebachew (Eds.), *Handbook of Research on Sustainable Development and Governance Strategies for Economic Growth in Africa* (pp. 258–271). Hershey, PA: IGI Global. doi:10.4018/978-1-5225-3247-7.ch014

Dau, L. A., Moore, E. M., Soto, M. A., & LeBlanc, C. R. (2017). How Globalization Sparked Entrepreneurship in the Developing World: The Impact of Formal Economic and Political Linkages. In B. Christiansen & F. Kasarcı (Eds.), *Corporate Espionage, Geopolitics, and Diplomacy Issues in International Business* (pp. 72–91). Hershey, PA: IGI Global. doi:10.4018/978-1-5225-1031-4.ch005

De Man, P. (2019). In-Situ Resource Utilization: Legal Aspects. In A. Nakarada Pecujlic & M. Tugnoli (Eds.), *Promoting Productive Cooperation Between Space Lawyers and Engineers* (pp. 211–224). IGI Global. https://doi.org/10.4018/978-1-5225-7256-5.ch013

Drenner, K. (2017). Introduction to Faith in State Legislatures: Land of the Brave and the Home of the Free – The Star-Spangled Banner. In *Impacts of Faith-Based Decision Making on the Individual-Level Legislative Process: Emerging Research and Opportunities* (pp. 1–25). Hershey, PA: IGI Global. doi:10.4018/978-1-5225-2388-8.ch001

Drenner, K. (2017). The Holy Wars of Marriage. In *Impacts of Faith-Based Decision Making on the Individual-Level Legislative Process: Emerging Research and Opportunities* (pp. 92–116). Hershey, PA: IGI Global. doi:10.4018/978-1-5225-2388-8.ch004

Drenner, K. (2017). The Implications of Religious Liberty. In *Impacts of Faith-Based Decision Making on the Individual-Level Legislative Process: Emerging Research and Opportunities* (pp. 143–162). Hershey, PA: IGI Global. doi:10.4018/978-1-5225-2388-8.ch006

Duncan, S. T., & Geczi, H. (2021). Body-Worn Cameras: Panacea or Distraction for Increased Police Use of Force Accountability? In M. Pittaro (Ed.), *Global Perspectives on Reforming the Criminal Justice System* (pp. 1–25). IGI Global. https://doi.org/10.4018/978-1-7998-6884-2.ch001

Duran, D. Ş. (2019). Reflections of the Multi-Level Governance Approach on the Turkish Metropolitan Municipality System: Evaluations on the Metropolitan Law No 6360. In T. Uysal & C. Aldemir (Eds.), *Multi-Level Governance in Developing Economies* (pp. 52–91). IGI Global. https://doi.org/10.4018/978-1-5225-5547-6.ch003

Durnalı, M., & Eriçok, B. (2019). Legal Challenges on Developing Education Policy for Immigrants in Turkey. In I. Management Association (Ed.), *Immigration and Refugee Policy: Breakthroughs in Research and Practice* (pp. 223-237). IGI Global. https://doi.org/10.4018/978-1-5225-8909-9.ch013

Ehalaiye, D., Redmayne, N. B., & Laswad, F. (2020). The Case of Accounting Information for Infrastructural Assets Reporting: Local Government Borrowings and Investment Choices in the Context of Moral Hazard and Local Government Politics. In A. Cunha, A. Ferreira, M. Fernandes, & P. Gomes (Eds.), *Financial Determinants in Local Re-Election Rates: Emerging Research and Opportunities* (pp. 176–201). IGI Global. https://doi.org/10.4018/978-1-5225-7820-8.ch007

Elena, S., & van Schalkwyk, F. (2017). Open Data for Open Justice in Seven Latin American Countries. In C. Jiménez-Gómez & M. Gascó-Hernández (Eds.), *Achieving Open Justice through Citizen Participation and Transparency* (pp. 210–231). Hershey, PA: IGI Global. doi:10.4018/978-1-5225-0717-8.ch011

Eneanya, A. N. (2018). Integrating Ecosystem Management and Environmental Media for Public Policy on Public Health and Safety. In A. Eneanya (Ed.), *Handbook of Research on Environmental Policies for Emergency Management and Public Safety* (pp. 321–338). Hershey, PA: IGI Global. doi:10.4018/978-1-5225-3194-4.ch017

Erickson, G. S. (2019). Sharing Knowledge With the Government: Implications of FOIA Requests. In Y. Albastaki, A. Al-Alawi, & S. Abdulrahman Al-Bassam (Eds.), *Handbook of Research on Implementing Knowledge Management Strategy in the Public Sector* (pp. 143–158). IGI Global. https://doi.org/10.4018/978-1-5225-9639-4.ch007

Essien, E. D. (2018). Strengthening Performance of Civil Society Through Dialogue and Critical Thinking in Nigeria: Its Ethical Implications. In S. Chhabra (Ed.), *Handbook of Research on Civic Engagement and Social Change in Contemporary Society* (pp. 82–102). Hershey, PA: IGI Global. doi:10.4018/978-1-5225-4197-4.ch005

Eweida, A. M. (2021). Urban Laws in Harmony or at Odds With Knowledge-Based Urban Policies: A Case Study on Egypt. In A. Galaby & A. Abdrabo (Eds.), *Handbook of Research on Creative Cities and Advanced Models for Knowledge-Based Urban Development* (pp. 23–40). IGI Global. https://doi.org/10.4018/978-1-7998-4948-3.ch002

Fanaian, T. (2017). The Theocratic Deception Trap: Khomeini's Persuasion Techniques and Communication Patterns in His Books, Guardianship of the Jurist 1979 and Testament 1989. In E. Lewin, E. Bick, & D. Naor (Eds.), *Comparative Perspectives on Civil Religion, Nationalism, and Political Influence* (pp. 62–105). Hershey, PA: IGI Global. doi:10.4018/978-1-5225-0516-7.ch003

Faura-Martínez, U., & Cifuentes-Faura, J. (2020). Does E-Government Promote Transparency and the Fight Against Corruption in the European Union? *International Journal of Electronic Government Research, 16*(4), 42–57. https://doi.org/10.4018/IJEGR.2020100103

Fawsitt, J. (2020). Government Policy and the Disintegration of Village Community Life and Individual Identity in Urbanising Japan. In M. Merviö (Ed.), *Recent Social, Environmental, and Cultural Issues in East Asian Societies* (pp. 76–94). IGI Global. https://doi.org/10.4018/978-1-7998-1807-6.ch005

Fidanoski, F., Sergi, B. S., Simeonovski, K., Naumovski, V., & Sazdovski, I. (2018). Effects of Foreign Capital Entry on the Macedonian Banking Industry: Two-Edged Sword. In B. Sergi, F. Fidanoski, M. Ziolo, & V. Naumovski (Eds.), *Regaining Global Stability After the Financial Crisis* (pp. 308–338). Hershey, PA: IGI Global. doi:10.4018/978-1-5225-4026-7.ch015

Franconi, A. I. (2018). Economic Variations and Their Impact on Labor Legislation Throughout History in Argentina. In S. Amine (Ed.), *Employment Protection Legislation in Emerging Economies* (pp. 77–98). Hershey, PA: IGI Global. doi:10.4018/978-1-5225-4134-9.ch004

Friedrich, P., & Chebotareva, M. (2017). Options for Applying Functional Overlapping Competing Jurisdictions (FOCJs) for Municipal Cooperation in Russia. In M. Lewandowski & B. Kożuch (Eds.), *Public Sector Entrepreneurship and the Integration of Innovative Business Models* (pp. 73–107). Hershey, PA: IGI Global. doi:10.4018/978-1-5225-2215-7.ch004

Garad, A., & Qamari, I. N. (2021). Determining Factors Influencing Establishing E-Service Quality in Developing Countries: A Case Study of Yemen E-Government. *International Journal of Electronic Government Research, 17*(1), 15–30. https://doi.org/10.4018/IJEGR.2021010102

Garita, M. (2018). The Negotiation and Effects of Fiscal Privileges in Guatemala. In M. Garita & C. Bregni (Eds.), *Economic Growth in Latin America and the Impact of the Global Financial Crisis* (pp. 119–137). Hershey, PA: IGI Global. doi:10.4018/978-1-5225-4981-9.ch008

Gascó-Hernández, M. (2017). Digitalizing Police Requirements: Opening up Justice through Collaborative Initiatives. In C. Jiménez-Gómez & M. Gascó-Hernández (Eds.), *Achieving Open Justice through Citizen Participation and Transparency* (pp. 157–172). Hershey, PA: IGI Global. doi:10.4018/978-1-5225-0717-8.ch008

Gáspár-Szilágyi, S. (2017). Human Rights Conditionality in the EU's Newly Concluded Association Agreements with the Eastern Partners. In C. Akrivopoulou (Ed.), *Defending Human Rights and Democracy in the Era of Globalization* (pp. 50–79). Hershey, PA: IGI Global. doi:10.4018/978-1-5225-0723-9.ch003

Gavrielides, T. (2017). Reconciling Restorative Justice with the Law for Violence Against Women in Europe: A Scheme of Structured and Unstructured Models. In D. Halder & K. Jaishankar (Eds.), *Therapeutic Jurisprudence and Overcoming Violence Against Women* (pp. 106–120). Hershey, PA: IGI Global. doi:10.4018/978-1-5225-2472-4.ch007

Gechlik, M., Dai, D., & Beck, J. C. (2017). Open Judiciary in a Closed Society: A Paradox in China? In C. Jiménez-Gómez & M. Gascó-Hernández (Eds.), *Achieving Open Justice through Citizen Participation and Transparency* (pp. 56–92). Hershey, PA: IGI Global. doi:10.4018/978-1-5225-0717-8.ch004

Gerger, A. (2021). Technologies for Connected Government Implementation: Success Factors and Best Practices. In Z. Mahmood (Ed.), *Web 2.0 and Cloud Technologies for Implementing Connected Government* (pp. 36–66). IGI Global. https://doi.org/10.4018/978-1-7998-4570-6.ch003

Germann, S. K. (2019). The International Space Station: Legal Aspects. In A. Nakarada Pecujlic & M. Tugnoli (Eds.), *Promoting Productive Cooperation Between Space Lawyers and Engineers* (pp. 96–113). IGI Global. doi:10.4018/978-1-5225-7256-5.ch007

Gillath, N. (2017). Avoiding Conscription in Israel: Were Women Pawns in the Political Game? In E. Lewin, E. Bick, & D. Naor (Eds.), *Comparative Perspectives on Civil Religion, Nationalism, and Political Influence* (pp. 226–256). Hershey, PA: IGI Global. doi:10.4018/978-1-5225-0516-7.ch009

Górski, J. (2019). Northern Sea Route: International Law Perspectives. In V. Erokhin, T. Gao, & X. Zhang (Eds.), *Handbook of Research on International Collaboration, Economic Development, and Sustainability in the Arctic* (pp. 292–313). IGI Global. https://doi.org/10.4018/978-1-5225-6954-1.ch014

Grant, B., Woods, R., & Tan, S. F. (2017). Subnational Finance in Australia and China: The Case for Municipal Bond Banks. In E. Schoburgh & R. Ryan (Eds.), *Handbook of Research on Sub-National Governance and Development* (pp. 150–166). Hershey, PA: IGI Global. doi:10.4018/978-1-5225-1645-3.ch007

Gurpinar, B. (2018). Supporter, Activist, Rebel, Terrorist: Children in Syria. In C. Akrivopoulou (Ed.), *Global Perspectives on Human Migration, Asylum, and Security* (pp. 97–114). Hershey, PA: IGI Global. doi:10.4018/978-1-5225-2817-3.ch005

Gussen, B. F. (2018). The United States. In *Ranking Economic Performance and Efficiency in the Global Market: Emerging Research and Opportunities* (pp. 109–136). Hershey, PA: IGI Global. doi:10.4018/978-1-5225-2756-5.ch005

Halder, D., & Bhati, D. (2021). Culture, Ethnicity, and Hate Crimes: A Comparative Analysis of Preventive Laws Between India and the USA. In M. Pittaro (Ed.), *Global Perspectives on Reforming the Criminal Justice System* (pp. 236–245). IGI Global. https://doi.org/10.4018/978-1-7998-6884-2.ch013

Haque, T. (2018). Women-Friendly Working Environment in Bangladesh: Critical Analysis. In N. Mahtab, T. Haque, I. Khan, M. Islam, & I. Wahid (Eds.), *Handbook of Research on Women's Issues and Rights in the Developing World* (pp. 52–68). Hershey, PA: IGI Global. doi:10.4018/978-1-5225-3018-3.ch004

Heuva, W. E. (2017). Deferring Citizens' "Right to Know" in an Information Age: The Information Deficit in Namibia. In N. Mhiripiri & T. Chari (Eds.), *Media Law, Ethics, and Policy in the Digital Age* (pp. 245–267). Hershey, PA: IGI Global. doi:10.4018/978-1-5225-2095-5.ch014

Hwangbo, Y. (2022). Government Challenges Over Global Electronic Commerce Using FinTech: Design of Consumer Payment Tax (CPT) System. In M. Anshari, M. Almunawar, & M. Masri (Eds.), *FinTech Development for Financial Inclusiveness* (pp. 197–213). IGI Global. https://doi.org/10.4018/978-1-7998-8447-7.ch011

Ibrahim, F., Suhip, H., Kura, K. M., & Noor, H. M. L. (2022). Exploratory Study on User Satisfaction of E-HRM: Evidence From Brunei Government Employee Management System (GEMS). In P. Ordóñez de Pablos (Eds.), *Handbook of Research on Developing Circular, Digital, and Green Economies in Asia* (pp. 243-271). IGI Global. https://doi.org/10.4018/978-1-7998-8678-5.ch014

Islam, M. R. (2018). Abuse Among Child Domestic Workers in Bangladesh. In I. Tshabangu (Ed.), *Global Ideologies Surrounding Children's Rights and Social Justice* (pp. 1–21). Hershey, PA: IGI Global. doi:10.4018/978-1-5225-2578-3.ch001

Jankovic-Milic, V., & Džunić, M. (2017). Measuring Governance: The Application of Grey Relational Analysis on World Governance Indicators. In J. Stanković, P. Delias, S. Marinković, & S. Rochhia (Eds.), *Tools and Techniques for Economic Decision Analysis* (pp. 104–128). Hershey, PA: IGI Global. doi:10.4018/978-1-5225-0959-2.ch005

Jenkins, B., Semple, T., Quail, J., & Bennell, C. (2021). Optimizing Scenario-Based Training for Law Enforcement. In E. Arble & B. Arnetz (Eds.), *Interventions, Training, and Technologies for Improved Police Well-Being and Performance* (pp. 18–37). IGI Global. https://doi.org/10.4018/978-1-7998-6820-0.ch002

Jiménez-Gómez, C. E. (2017). Open Judiciary Worldwide: Best Practices and Lessons Learnt. In C. Jiménez-Gómez & M. Gascó-Hernández (Eds.), *Achieving Open Justice through Citizen Participation and Transparency* (pp. 1–15). Hershey, PA: IGI Global. doi:10.4018/978-1-5225-0717-8.ch001

Karatzimas, S., & Miquela, C. G. (2018). Two Approaches on Local Governments' Financial Sustainability: Law vs. Practice in Catalan Municipalities. In M. Rodríguez Bolívar & M. López Subires (Eds.), *Financial Sustainability and Intergenerational Equity in Local Governments* (pp. 58–81). Hershey, PA: IGI Global. doi:10.4018/978-1-5225-3713-7.ch003

Khachaturyan, M., & Klicheva, E. (2021). Risks of Introducing E-Governance Into Strategic Management Systems of Russian Companies in the Context of the Pandemic. *International Journal of Electronic Government Research, 17*(4), 84–102. https://doi.org/10.4018/IJEGR.2021100105

Khan, S. A., & Alag, A. (2020). Arbitration in Patent Disputes: To What Extent Is It Possible? In N. Dewani & A. Gurtu (Eds.), *Intellectual Property Rights and the Protection of Traditional Knowledge* (pp. 76–102). IGI Global. https://doi.org/10.4018/978-1-7998-1835-9.ch004

Kirsanov, S., Safonov, E., Tuzcuoglu, F., & Mammadov, Z. (2022). Modern Problems of Staff Training for State and Municipal Services in Russia. In O. Kulaç, C. Babaoğlu, & E. Akman (Eds.), *Public Affairs Education and Training in the 21st Century* (pp. 325–337). IGI Global. https://doi.org/10.4018/978-1-7998-8243-5.ch021

Kita, Y. (2017). An Analysis of a Lay Adjudication System and Open Judiciary: The New Japanese Lay Adjudication System. In C. Jiménez-Gómez & M. Gascó-Hernández (Eds.), *Achieving Open Justice through Citizen Participation and Transparency* (pp. 93–109). Hershey, PA: IGI Global. doi:10.4018/978-1-5225-0717-8.ch005

Kuatova, A., Bekbasarova, T., & Abdrashev, R. (2020). Introducing E-Government in Kazakhstan: The Concept of E-Democracy for the State-Public Interaction. In G. Tazhina & J. Parker (Eds.), *Toward Sustainability Through Digital Technologies and Practices in the Eurasian Region* (pp. 1–16). IGI Global. https://doi.org/10.4018/978-1-7998-2551-7.ch001

Kumari, S., Patil, Y., & Rao, P. (2017). An Approach to Sustainable Watershed Management: Case Studies on Enhancing Sustainability with Challenges of Water in Western Maharashtra. In P. Rao & Y. Patil (Eds.), *Reconsidering the Impact of Climate Change on Global Water Supply, Use, and Management* (pp. 252–271). Hershey, PA: IGI Global. doi:10.4018/978-1-5225-1046-8.ch014

Kumburu, N. P., & Pande, V. S. (2018). Decentralization and Local Governance in Tanzania: Theories and Practice on Sustainable Development. In K. Teshager Alemu & M. Abebe Alebachew (Eds.), *Handbook of Research on Sustainable Development and Governance Strategies for Economic Growth in Africa* (pp. 131–148). Hershey, PA: IGI Global. doi:10.4018/978-1-5225-3247-7.ch007

Kunock, A. I. (2017). Boko Haram Insurgency in Cameroon: Role of Mass Media in Conflict Management. In N. Mhiripiri & T. Chari (Eds.), *Media Law, Ethics, and Policy in the Digital Age* (pp. 226–244). Hershey, PA: IGI Global. doi:10.4018/978-1-5225-2095-5.ch013

Kurebwa, J. (2019). Young People-Sensitive and Participatory Governance Approaches: Lessons for the Zimbabwean Government. In J. Kurebwa & O. Dodo (Eds.), *Participation of Young People in Governance Processes in Africa* (pp. 80–99). IGI Global. https://doi.org/10.4018/978-1-5225-9388-1.ch005

Lawrie, A. (2017). The Subnational Region: A Utopia? The Challenge of Governing Through Soft Power. In E. Schoburgh & R. Ryan (Eds.), *Handbook of Research on Sub-National Governance and Development* (pp. 96–115). Hershey, PA: IGI Global. doi:10.4018/978-1-5225-1645-3.ch005

Lentzis, D. (2020). Revisiting the Basics of EU Data Protection Law: On the Material and Territorial Scope of the GDPR. In M. Tzanou (Ed.), *Personal Data Protection and Legal Developments in the European Union* (pp. 19–33). IGI Global. https://doi.org/10.4018/978-1-5225-9489-5.ch002

Leote, F. J., Teixeira, N. M., & Galvão, R. (2021). Entrepreneurship and Unemployment: Government Grants and Challenges in a Pandemic Context. In N. Teixeira, & I. Lisboa (Eds.), *Handbook of Research on Financial Management During Economic Downturn and Recovery* (pp. 20-40). IGI Global. https://doi.org/10.4018/978-1-7998-6643-5.ch002

Lewin, E., & Bick, E. (2017). Introduction: Civil Religion and Nationalism on a Godly-Civil Continuum. In E. Lewin, E. Bick, & D. Naor (Eds.), *Comparative Perspectives on Civil Religion, Nationalism, and Political Influence* (pp. 1–31). Hershey, PA: IGI Global. doi:10.4018/978-1-5225-0516-7.ch001

Luyombya, D. (2018). Management of Records and Archives in Uganda's Public Sector. In P. Ngulube (Ed.), *Handbook of Research on Heritage Management and Preservation* (pp. 275–297). Hershey, PA: IGI Global. doi:10.4018/978-1-5225-3137-1.ch014

Mabe, M., & Ashley, E. A. (2017). The Local Command Structure and How the Library Fits. In *In The Developing Role of Public Libraries in Emergency Management: Emerging Research and Opportunities* (pp. 44–60). Hershey, PA: IGI Global. doi:10.4018/978-1-5225-2196-9.ch004

Macilotti, G. (2020). Online Child Pornography: Conceptual Issues and Law Enforcement Challenges. In A. Balloni & R. Sette (Eds.), *Handbook of Research on Trends and Issues in Crime Prevention, Rehabilitation, and Victim Support* (pp. 226–247). IGI Global. https://doi.org/10.4018/978-1-7998-1286-9.ch013

Maher, C. (2018). Legal Framework, Funding, and Procurement Polices to Accelerate the Growth of the Social Enterprise Ecosystem. In *Influence of Public Policy on Small Social Enterprises: Emerging Research and Opportunities* (pp. 52–83). Hershey, PA: IGI Global. doi:10.4018/978-1-5225-2770-1.ch003

Mahmood, M. (2019). Transformation of Government and Citizen Trust in Government: A Conceptual Model. In A. Molnar (Ed.), *Strategic Management and Innovative Applications of E-Government* (pp. 107–122). IGI Global. https://doi.org/10.4018/978-1-5225-6204-7.ch005

Mahmood, Z. (2021). Cloud Computing Technologies for Connected Digital Government. In Z. Mahmood (Ed.), *Web 2.0 and Cloud Technologies for Implementing Connected Government* (pp. 19–35). IGI Global. https://doi.org/10.4018/978-1-7998-4570-6.ch002

Malik, I., Putera, V. S., & Putra, I. E. (2018). Traditional Leaders in the Reconciliation of Muslim-Christian Conflicts in Moluccas. In A. Campbell (Ed.), *Global Leadership Initiatives for Conflict Resolution and Peacebuilding* (pp. 235–248). Hershey, PA: IGI Global. doi:10.4018/978-1-5225-4993-2.ch011

Martin, S. M. (2017). Transnational Crime and the American Policing System. In M. Dawson, D. Kisku, P. Gupta, J. Sing, & W. Li (Eds.), Developing Next-Generation Countermeasures for Homeland Security Threat Prevention (pp. 72-92). Hershey, PA: IGI Global. https://doi.org/ doi:10.4018/978-1-5225-0703-1.ch004

Mekonnen, G. A., & Kassie, W. A. (2020). Fiscal Decentralization at Local Government of Ethiopia: Theory vs Practices. In S. Chhabra & M. Kumar (Eds.), *Civic Engagement Frameworks and Strategic Leadership Practices for Organization Development* (pp. 171–197). IGI Global. https://doi.org/10.4018/978-1-7998-2372-8.ch008

Mensah, I. K., Luo, C., & Abu-Shanab, E. (2021). Citizen Use of E-Government Services Websites: A Proposed E-Government Adoption Recommendation Model (EGARM). *International Journal of Electronic Government Research, 17*(2), 19–42. https://doi.org/10.4018/IJEGR.2021040102

Mhiripiri, N. A., & Chikakano, J. (2017). Criminal Defamation, the Criminalisation of Expression, Media and Information Dissemination in the Digital Age: A Legal and Ethical Perspective. In N. Mhiripiri & T. Chari (Eds.), *Media Law, Ethics, and Policy in the Digital Age* (pp. 1–24). Hershey, PA: IGI Global. doi:10.4018/978-1-5225-2095-5.ch001

Mishaal, D. A., & Abu-Shanab, E. A. (2017). Utilizing Facebook by the Arab World Governments: The Communication Success Factor. *International Journal of Public Administration in the Digital Age, 4*(3), 53–78. doi:10.4018/IJPADA.2017070105

Morim, A. C., Inácio, H., & Vieira, E. (2018). Internal Control in a Public Hospital: The Case of Financial Services Expenditure Department. In G. Azevedo, J. da Silva Oliveira, R. Marques, & A. Ferreira (Eds.), *Handbook of Research on Modernization and Accountability in Public Sector Management* (pp. 77–102). Hershey, PA: IGI Global. doi:10.4018/978-1-5225-3731-1.ch005

Mupepi, M. G. (2017). Developing Democratic Paradigms to Effectively Manage Business, Government, and Civil Society: The African Spring. In E. Schoburgh & R. Ryan (Eds.), *Handbook of Research on Sub-National Governance and Development* (pp. 432–462). Hershey, PA: IGI Global. doi:10.4018/978-1-5225-1645-3.ch020

Mwakisisya, H. J., Rugeiyamu, R., & Cyprian, S. (2021). Blending Local Government Authorities and Grassroots for Industrial Economy Through Participatory Development Communication in Tanzania. In F. Nafukho & A. Boniface Makulilo (Eds.), *Handbook of Research on Nurturing Industrial Economy for Africa's Development* (pp. 74–98). IGI Global. https://doi.org/10.4018/978-1-7998-6471-4.ch005

Naidoo, V., & Nzimakwe, T. I. (2019). M-Government and Its Application on Public Service Delivery. In R. Abassi & A. Ben Chehida Douss (Eds.), *Security Frameworks in Contemporary Electronic Government* (pp. 1–14). IGI Global. https://doi.org/10.4018/978-1-5225-5984-9.ch001

Navaratnam, R., & Lee, I. Y. (2017). Globalization as a New Framework for Human Rights Protection. In C. Akrivopoulou (Ed.), *Defending Human Rights and Democracy in the Era of Globalization* (pp. 17–49). Hershey, PA: IGI Global. doi:10.4018/978-1-5225-0723-9.ch002

Nemec, J., Meričková, B. M., Svidroňová, M. M., & Klimovský, D. (2017). Co-Creation as a Social Innovation in Delivery of Public Services at Local Government Level: The Slovak Experience. In E. Schoburgh & R. Ryan (Eds.), *Handbook of Research on Sub-National Governance and Development* (pp. 281–303). Hershey, PA: IGI Global. doi:10.4018/978-1-5225-1645-3.ch013

Neupane, A., Soar, J., Vaidya, K., & Aryal, S. (2017). Application of E-Government Principles in Anti-Corruption Framework. In R. Shakya (Ed.), *Digital Governance and E-Government Principles Applied to Public Procurement* (pp. 56–74). Hershey, PA: IGI Global. doi:10.4018/978-1-5225-2203-4.ch003

Njie, S. N., Wogu, I. A., Ogbuehi, U. K., Misra, S., & Udoh, O. D. (2021). Rising Global Challenges in Energy Demand and the Politics of Climate Change in Government Operations: Policy and Economic Development Implications. In C. Babaoğlu, E. Akman, & O. Kulaç (Eds.), *Handbook of Research on Global Challenges for Improving Public Services and Government Operations* (pp. 242–263). IGI Global. https://doi.org/10.4018/978-1-7998-4978-0.ch013

Ogunde, O. (2017). Democracy and Child Rights Protection: The Problem of the Nigerian Constitution. In C. Akrivopoulou (Ed.), *Defending Human Rights and Democracy in the Era of Globalization* (pp. 123–144). Hershey, PA: IGI Global. doi:10.4018/978-1-5225-0723-9.ch006

Ojedokun, U. A. (2017). Crime Witnesses' Non-Cooperation in Police Investigations: Causes and Consequences in Nigeria. In S. Egharevba (Ed.), *Police Brutality, Racial Profiling, and Discrimination in the Criminal Justice System* (pp. 89–99). Hershey, PA: IGI Global. doi:10.4018/978-1-5225-1088-8.ch005

Okeke, G. S. (2018). The Politics of Environmental Pollution in Nigeria: Emerging Trends, Issues, and Challenges. In A. Eneanya (Ed.), *Handbook of Research on Environmental Policies for Emergency Management and Public Safety* (pp. 300–320). Hershey, PA: IGI Global. doi:10.4018/978-1-5225-3194-4.ch016

Ökten, S., Akman, E., & Akman, Ç. (2018). Modernization and Accountability in Public-Sector Administration: Turkey Example. In G. Azevedo, J. da Silva Oliveira, R. Marques, & A. Ferreira (Eds.), *Handbook of Research on Modernization and Accountability in Public Sector Management* (pp. 18–39). Hershey, PA: IGI Global. doi:10.4018/978-1-5225-3731-1.ch002

Oladapo, O. A., & Ojebuyi, B. R. (2017). Nature and Outcome of Nigeria's #NoToSocialMediaBill Twitter Protest against the Frivolous Petitions Bill 2015. In O. Nelson, B. Ojebuyi, & A. Salawu (Eds.), *Impacts of the Media on African Socio-Economic Development* (pp. 106–124). Hershey, PA: IGI Global. doi:10.4018/978-1-5225-1859-4.ch007

Olmos, S., & Nares, J. J. (2020). Applying Fault Trees to the Analysis at the Minimum Age for Sexual Consent in the Criminal Law of México. In A. Balloni & R. Sette (Eds.), *Handbook of Research on Trends and Issues in Crime Prevention, Rehabilitation, and Victim Support* (pp. 60–78). IGI Global. https://doi.org/10.4018/978-1-7998-1286-9.ch005

Olukolu, Y. R. (2017). Harmful Traditional Practices, Laws, and Reproductive Rights of Women in Nigeria: A Therapeutic Jurisprudence Approach. In D. Halder & K. Jaishankar (Eds.), *Therapeutic Jurisprudence and Overcoming Violence Against Women* (pp. 1–14). Hershey, PA: IGI Global. doi:10.4018/978-1-5225-2472-4.ch001

Onyebadi, U., & Mbunyuza-Memani, L. (2017). Women and South Africa's Anti-Apartheid Struggle: Evaluating the Political Messages in the Music of Miriam Makeba. In U. Onyebadi (Ed.), *Music as a Platform for Political Communication* (pp. 31–51). Hershey, PA: IGI Global. doi:10.4018/978-1-5225-1986-7.ch002

Osmani, A. R. (2017). Tipaimukh Multipurpose Hydroelectric Project: A Policy Perspective – Indo-Bangla Priorities, Indigenous Peoples' Rights, and Environmental Concerns. In P. Rao & Y. Patil (Eds.), *Reconsidering the Impact of Climate Change on Global Water Supply, Use, and Management* (pp. 227–251). Hershey, PA: IGI Global. doi:10.4018/978-1-5225-1046-8.ch013

Owolabi, T. O. (2018). Free Media and Bank Reforms in West Africa: Implications for Sustainable Development. In A. Salawu & T. Owolabi (Eds.), *Exploring Journalism Practice and Perception in Developing Countries* (pp. 18–39). Hershey, PA: IGI Global. doi:10.4018/978-1-5225-3376-4.ch002

Öztürk, N. K. (2021). Government Systems and Control of Bureaucracy. In C. Babaoğlu, E. Akman, & O. Kulaç (Eds.), *Handbook of Research on Global Challenges for Improving Public Services and Government Operations* (pp. 133–150). IGI Global. https://doi.org/10.4018/978-1-7998-4978-0.ch008

Pacheco, F. M., & Alves, D. R. (2019). The New Paths of Fundamental Rights in the 21st Century: Globalization and Knowledge in a Digital Age as a Proposal. In A. Melro & L. Oliveira (Eds.), *Constitutional Knowledge and Its Impact on Citizenship Exercise in a Networked Society* (pp. 1–26). IGI Global. https://doi.org/10.4018/978-1-5225-8350-9.ch001

Panda, P., & Sahu, G. P. (2017). Public Procurement Framework in India: An Overview. In R. Shakya (Ed.), *Digital Governance and E-Government Principles Applied to Public Procurement* (pp. 229–248). Hershey, PA: IGI Global. doi:10.4018/978-1-5225-2203-4.ch010

Pande, V. S., & Kumburu, N. P. (2018). An Overview of Population Growth and Sustainable Development in Sub-Saharan Africa. In K. Teshager Alemu & M. Abebe Alebachew (Eds.), *Handbook of Research on Sustainable Development and Governance Strategies for Economic Growth in Africa* (pp. 480–499). Hershey, PA: IGI Global. doi:10.4018/978-1-5225-3247-7.ch025

Parikh, M., & Krishna, V. S. (2021). Recent Trends and Repercussions in Civil and Criminal Justice Systems: A Comparative Analysis of England, Singapore, and India. In E. Yin, & N. Kofie (Ed.), *Advancing Civil Justice Reform and Conflict Resolution in Africa and Asia: Comparative Analyses and Case Studies* (pp. 230-242). IGI Global. https://doi.org/10.4018/978-1-7998-7898-8.ch013

Pattnaik, P. N., & Shukla, M. K. (2020). Understanding Indian Political Parties Through the Lens of Marketing Management: Towards a Conceptual Political Marketing Model. In S. Kavoğlu & M. Salar (Eds.), *Political Propaganda, Advertising, and Public Relations: Emerging Research and Opportunities* (pp. 170–190). IGI Global. https://doi.org/10.4018/978-1-7998-1734-5.ch008

Paulin, A. A. (2017). Informating Public Governance: Towards a Basis for a Digital Ecosystem. *International Journal of Public Administration in the Digital Age*, *4*(2), 14–32. doi:10.4018/IJPADA.2017040102

Perelló-Sobrepere, M. (2017). Building a New State from Outrage: The Case of Catalonia. In M. Adria & Y. Mao (Eds.), *Handbook of Research on Citizen Engagement and Public Participation in the Era of New Media* (pp. 344–359). Hershey, PA: IGI Global. doi:10.4018/978-1-5225-1081-9.ch019

Pohl, G. M. (2017). The Role of Social Media in Enforcing Environmental Justice around the World. In K. Demirhan & D. Çakır-Demirhan (Eds.), *Political Scandal, Corruption, and Legitimacy in the Age of Social Media* (pp. 123–156). Hershey, PA: IGI Global. doi:10.4018/978-1-5225-2019-1.ch006

Popescu, C. R. (2022). Environmental, Social, and Corporate Governance by Avoiding Management Bias and Tax Minimization: Reaching a General Consensus Regarding a Minimum Global Tax Rate. In C. Popescu (Ed.), *COVID-19 Pandemic Impact on New Economy Development and Societal Change* (pp. 94–132). IGI Global. https://doi.org/10.4018/978-1-6684-3374-4.ch006

Popoola, T. (2017). Ethical and Legal Challenges of Election Reporting in Nigeria: A Study of Four General Elections, 1999-2011. In N. Mhiripiri & T. Chari (Eds.), *Media Law, Ethics, and Policy in the Digital Age* (pp. 78–100). Hershey, PA: IGI Global. doi:10.4018/978-1-5225-2095-5.ch005

Prakash, O. (2020). History, Policy Making, and Sustainability. In R. Das & N. Mandal (Eds.), *Interdisciplinary Approaches to Public Policy and Sustainability* (pp. 1–17). IGI Global. https://doi.org/10.4018/978-1-7998-0315-7.ch001

Provazníková, R., Sobotková, L., & Sobotka, M. (2021). Local Government Development in the Czech Republic: Dilemmas and Challenges. In C. Babaoğlu, E. Akman, & O. Kulaç (Eds.), *Handbook of Research on Global Challenges for Improving Public Services and Government Operations* (pp. 151–171). IGI Global. https://doi.org/10.4018/978-1-7998-4978-0.ch009

Qawasmeh, F. A. (2022). Understanding the Field of Public Policy in the Context of Public Administration Evolution. In O. Kulaç, C. Babaoğlu, & E. Akman (Eds.), *Public Affairs Education and Training in the 21st Century* (pp. 22–44). IGI Global. https://doi.org/10.4018/978-1-7998-8243-5.ch002

Rahman, M. S. (2017). Politics-Administration Relations and the Effect on Local Governance and Development: The Case of Bangladesh. In E. Schoburgh & R. Ryan (Eds.), *Handbook of Research on Sub-National Governance and Development* (pp. 256–279). Hershey, PA: IGI Global. doi:10.4018/978-1-5225-1645-3.ch012

Ramachandran, M., Chelliah, P. R., & Soundarabai, P. B. (2021). Towards Connected Government Services: A Cloud Software Engineering Framework. In Z. Mahmood (Ed.), *Web 2.0 and Cloud Technologies for Implementing Connected Government* (pp. 113–135). IGI Global. https://doi.org/10.4018/978-1-7998-4570-6.ch006

Ravotti, N. (2020). In the [Source] C\ode of the Conquerors: On the Need for Culturally-Minded Tribal Law Research Databases. In S. Edwards III, & D. Santos (Eds.), *Digital Transformation and Its Role in Progressing the Relationship Between States and Their Citizens* (pp. 124-137). IGI Global. https://doi.org/10.4018/978-1-7998-3152-5.ch006

Razzante, R. (2020). The Fight Against Corruption. In A. Balloni & R. Sette (Eds.), *Handbook of Research on Trends and Issues in Crime Prevention, Rehabilitation, and Victim Support* (pp. 167–186). IGI Global. doi:10.4018/978-1-7998-1286-9.ch010

Reddy, P. S. (2017). Political-Administrative Interface at the Local Sphere of Government with Particular Reference to South Africa. In E. Schoburgh & R. Ryan (Eds.), *Handbook of Research on Sub-National Governance and Development* (pp. 242–255). Hershey, PA: IGI Global. doi:10.4018/978-1-5225-1645-3.ch011

Rombo, D. O., & Lutomia, A. N. (2018). Tracing the Rights of Domestic and International Kenyan House Helps: Profiles, Policy, and Consequences. In N. Mahtab, T. Haque, I. Khan, M. Islam, & I. Wahid (Eds.), *Handbook of Research on Women's Issues and Rights in the Developing World* (pp. 1–18). Hershey, PA: IGI Global. doi:10.4018/978-1-5225-3018-3.ch001

Rouzbehani, K. (2017). Health Policy Implementation: Moving Beyond Its Barriers in United States. In N. Wickramasinghe (Ed.), *Handbook of Research on Healthcare Administration and Management* (pp. 541–552). Hershey, PA: IGI Global. doi:10.4018/978-1-5225-0920-2.ch032

Ryan, R., & Woods, R. (2017). Decentralization and Subnational Governance: Theory and Praxis. In E. Schoburgh & R. Ryan (Eds.), *Handbook of Research on Sub-National Governance and Development* (pp. 1–33). Hershey, PA: IGI Global. doi:10.4018/978-1-5225-1645-3.ch001

Sabao, C., & Chingwaramusee, V. R. (2017). Citizen Journalism on Facebook and the Challenges of Media Regulation in Zimbabwe: Baba Jukwa. In N. Mhiripiri & T. Chari (Eds.), *Media Law, Ethics, and Policy in the Digital Age* (pp. 193–206). Hershey, PA: IGI Global. doi:10.4018/978-1-5225-2095-5.ch011

Saidane, A., & Al-Sharieh, S. (2019). A Compliance-Driven Framework for Privacy and Security in Highly Regulated Socio-Technical Environments: An E-Government Case Study. In R. Abassi & A. Ben Chehida Douss (Eds.), *Security Frameworks in Contemporary Electronic Government* (pp. 15–50). IGI Global. https://doi.org/10.4018/978-1-5225-5984-9.ch002

Sandill, S. (2020). Law, Equality, and Entrepreneurship Through a Gendered Lens: Bridging the Gap Between Academia, Legislature, and Politics. In T. Moeke-Pickering, S. Cote-Meek, & A. Pegoraro (Eds.), *Critical Reflections and Politics on Advancing Women in the Academy* (pp. 124–149). IGI Global. https://doi.org/10.4018/978-1-7998-3618-6.ch008

Santos, H. R., & Tonelli, D. F. (2019). Smart Government and the Maturity Levels of Sociopolitical Digital Interactions: Analysing Temporal Changes in Brazilian E-Government Portals. In A. Molnar (Ed.), *Strategic Management and Innovative Applications of E-Government* (pp. 176–199). IGI Global. https://doi.org/10.4018/978-1-5225-6204-7.ch008

Saponaro, A. (2021). "Visible" and "Invisible" Victims in the Criminal Justice System: Victim-Oriented Paradigms and Models. In R. Blasdell, L. Krieger-Sample, & M. Kilburn (Eds.), *Invisible Victims and the Pursuit of Justice: Analyzing Frequently Victimized Yet Rarely Discussed Populations* (pp. 1–23). IGI Global. doi:10.4018/978-1-7998-7348-8.ch001

Shaikh, A. K., Ahmad, N., Khan, I., & Ali, S. (2021). E-Participation Within E-Government: A Bibliometric-Based Systematic Literature Review. *International Journal of Electronic Government Research, 17*(4), 15–39. https://doi.org/10.4018/IJEGR.2021100102

Shakya, R. K., & Schapper, P. R. (2017). Digital Governance and E-Government Principles: E-Procurement as Transformative. In R. Shakya (Ed.), *Digital Governance and E-Government Principles Applied to Public Procurement* (pp. 1–28). Hershey, PA: IGI Global. doi:10.4018/978-1-5225-2203-4.ch001

Shambare, R. (2019). Facilitating Consumers' Adoption of E-Government in South Africa: Supply Side-Driven Virtuous Cycles. In A. Gbadamosi (Ed.), *Exploring the Dynamics of Consumerism in Developing Nations* (pp. 243–265). IGI Global. https://doi.org/10.4018/978-1-5225-7906-9.ch011

Siphambe, H., Kolobe, M., & Oageng, I. P. (2018). Employment Protection Legislation and Unemployment in Botswana. In S. Amine (Ed.), *Employment Protection Legislation in Emerging Economies* (pp. 157–191). Hershey, PA: IGI Global. doi:10.4018/978-1-5225-4134-9.ch008

Song, M. Y., & Abelson, J. (2017). Public Engagement and Policy Entrepreneurship on Social Media in the Time of Anti-Vaccination Movements. In M. Adria & Y. Mao (Eds.), *Handbook of Research on Citizen Engagement and Public Participation in the Era of New Media* (pp. 38–56). Hershey, PA: IGI Global. doi:10.4018/978-1-5225-1081-9.ch003

Sood, P., Malhotra, M., & Nijjer, S. (2021). Government Policies During Lockdown: Indian vs. International Perspective. In V. Kumar & G. Malhotra (Eds.), *Stakeholder Strategies for Reducing the Impact of Global Health Crises* (pp. 18–39). IGI Global. https://doi.org/10.4018/978-1-7998-7495-9.ch002

Stacey, E. (2018). Networked Protests: A Review of Social Movement Literature and the Hong Kong Umbrella Movement (2017). In S. Chhabra (Ed.), *Handbook of Research on Civic Engagement and Social Change in Contemporary Society* (pp. 347–363). Hershey, PA: IGI Global. doi:10.4018/978-1-5225-4197-4.ch020

Stamatakis, N. (2017). Authority and Legitimacy: A Quantitative Study of Youth's Perceptions on the Brazilian Police. In S. Egharevba (Ed.), *Police Brutality, Racial Profiling, and Discrimination in the Criminal Justice System* (pp. 151–213). Hershey, PA: IGI Global. doi:10.4018/978-1-5225-1088-8.ch009

Steinert, S. W. (2021). An Interview With Chief Sargent of the Worcester, MA Police Department. In E. Arble & B. Arnetz (Eds.), *Interventions, Training, and Technologies for Improved Police Well-Being and Performance* (pp. 185–197). IGI Global. https://doi.org/10.4018/978-1-7998-6820-0.ch011

Sugars, J. M. (2017). Refoulement and Refugees. In C. Akrivopoulou (Ed.), *Defending Human Rights and Democracy in the Era of Globalization* (pp. 181–197). Hershey, PA: IGI Global. doi:10.4018/978-1-5225-0723-9.ch008

Takaya-Umehara, Y. (2019). Suborbital Spaceflight: Legal Aspects. In A. Nakarada Pecujlic & M. Tugnoli (Eds.), *Promoting Productive Cooperation Between Space Lawyers and Engineers* (pp. 64–78). IGI Global. https://doi.org/10.4018/978-1-5225-7256-5.ch005

Tan, S. F. (2017). Local Representation in Australia: Preliminary Findings of a National Survey. In E. Schoburgh & R. Ryan (Eds.), *Handbook of Research on Sub-National Governance and Development* (pp. 368–384). Hershey, PA: IGI Global. doi:10.4018/978-1-5225-1645-3.ch017

Tavares, M. D., & Rodrigues, L. L. (2018). Strategic Responses of Public Sector Entities to GRI Sustainability Reports. In G. Azevedo, J. da Silva Oliveira, R. Marques, & A. Ferreira (Eds.), *Handbook of Research on Modernization and Accountability in Public Sector Management* (pp. 159–188). Hershey, PA: IGI Global. doi:10.4018/978-1-5225-3731-1.ch008

Thakre, A. G. (2017). Sexual Harassment of Women in Workplace in India: An Assessment of Implementation of Preventive Laws and Practicing of Therapeutic Jurisprudence in New Delhi. In D. Halder & K. Jaishankar (Eds.), *Therapeutic Jurisprudence and Overcoming Violence Against Women* (pp. 135–146). Hershey, PA: IGI Global. doi:10.4018/978-1-5225-2472-4.ch009

Tiwary, A. (2017). Key Elements of CEAF. In *Driving Efficiency in Local Government Using a Collaborative Enterprise Architecture Framework: Emerging Research and Opportunities* (pp. 25–61). Hershey, PA: IGI Global. doi:10.4018/978-1-5225-2407-6.ch002

Toscano, J. P. (2017). Social Media and Public Participation: Opportunities, Barriers, and a New Framework. In M. Adria & Y. Mao (Eds.), *Handbook of Research on Citizen Engagement and Public Participation in the Era of New Media* (pp. 73–89). Hershey, PA: IGI Global. doi:10.4018/978-1-5225-1081-9.ch005

Trompetter, P. S. (2019). A History of Police Psychology. In I. Management Association (Eds.), *Police Science: Breakthroughs in Research and Practice* (pp. 377-402). IGI Global. https://doi.org/10.4018/978-1-5225-7672-3.ch019

Tryma, K., & Salnikova, N. (2021). The Influence of Religion on Political Parties of the European Union. In E. Alaverdov & M. Bari (Eds.), *Global Development of Religious Tourism* (pp. 98-112). IGI Global. https://doi.org/10.4018/978-1-7998-5792-1.ch007

Tsabedze, V. W. (2020). Strategies for Managing E-Records for Good Governance: Reflection on E-Government in the Kingdom of Eswatini. In M. Rodríguez Bolívar & M. Cortés Cediel (Eds.), *Digital Government and Achieving E-Public Participation: Emerging Research and Opportunities* (pp. 63–86). IGI Global. https://doi.org/10.4018/978-1-7998-1526-6.ch004

Tshishonga, N. (2017). Operation Sukuma-Sakhe: A New Social Contract for Decentralized Service Delivery and Responsive Governance in KwaZulu-Natal. In E. Schoburgh & R. Ryan (Eds.), *Handbook of Research on Sub-National Governance and Development* (pp. 304–323). Hershey, PA: IGI Global. doi:10.4018/978-1-5225-1645-3.ch014

Tsygankov, S., & Gasanova, E. (2017). Electronification of the Public Procurement System: A Comparative Analysis of the Experience of the Russian Federation and Ukraine. In R. Shakya (Ed.), *Digital Governance and E-Government Principles Applied to Public Procurement* (pp. 267–277). Hershey, PA: IGI Global. doi:10.4018/978-1-5225-2203-4.ch013

Tüzünkan, D. (2018). The International Migration Movements and Immigrant Policies From the Ottoman Empire 1299 to Republican Turkey 2016. In Ş. Erçetin (Ed.), *Social Considerations of Migration Movements and Immigration Policies* (pp. 13–45). Hershey, PA: IGI Global. doi:10.4018/978-1-5225-3322-1.ch002

Ullah, Z. (2022). Violent Extremism and the Politics of Education in Pakistan: An Analysis of the Links Between Anti-Terror Laws, the Curriculum, and the Islamised Public Sphere. In O. Kulaç, C. Babaoğlu, & E. Akman (Eds.), *Public Affairs Education and Training in the 21st Century* (pp. 256–275). IGI Global. https://doi.org/10.4018/978-1-7998-8243-5.ch017

Valenzuela, R., & Ochoa, A. (2018). Open Mexico Network in the Implementation of National Open Data Policy. In A. Kok (Ed.), *Proliferation of Open Government Initiatives and Systems* (pp. 50–67). Hershey, PA: IGI Global. doi:10.4018/978-1-5225-4987-1.ch003

Valera-Ordaz, L., & Humanes, M. L. (2022). What Drives Selective Exposure to Political Information in Spain? Comparing Political Interest and Ideology. In D. Palau-Sampio, G. López García, & L. Iannelli (Eds.), *Contemporary Politics, Communication, and the Impact on Democracy* (pp. 93–112). IGI Global. https://doi.org/10.4018/978-1-7998-8057-8.ch006

van der Vliet-Bakker, J. M. (2019). Environmentally Forced Migration and Human Rights. In I. Management Association (Eds.), *Immigration and Refugee Policy: Breakthroughs in Research and Practice* (pp. 336-362). IGI Global. https://doi.org/10.4018/978-1-5225-8909-9.ch019

Waller, P. (2017). Co-Production and Co-Creation in Public Services: Resolving Confusion and Contradictions. *International Journal of Electronic Government Research, 13*(2), 1–17. doi:10.4018/IJEGR.2017040101

Wodecka-Hyjek, A. (2017). Co-Operation between the Public Administration and Non-Profit Organisations as a Condition of the Development of Public Entrepreneurship: On the Example of the Selected World Solutions. In V. Potocan, M. Üngan, & Z. Nedelko (Eds.), *Handbook of Research on Managerial Solutions in Non-Profit Organizations* (pp. 253–275). Hershey, PA: IGI Global. doi:10.4018/978-1-5225-0731-4.ch012

Yang, K. C., & Kang, Y. (2017). Social Media, Political Mobilization, and Citizen Engagement: A Case Study of the March 18, 2014, Sunflower Student Movement in Taiwan. In M. Adria & Y. Mao (Eds.), *Handbook of Research on Citizen Engagement and Public Participation in the Era of New Media* (pp. 360–388). Hershey, PA: IGI Global. doi:10.4018/978-1-5225-1081-9.ch020

Yang, K. C., & Kang, Y. (2020). Will Microblogs Shape China's Civil Society Under President's Xi's Surveillance State?: The Case of Anti-Extradition Law Protests in Hong Kong. In V. Kumar & G. Malhotra (Eds.), *Examining the Roles of IT and Social Media in Democratic Development and Social Change* (pp. 156–184). IGI Global. https://doi.org/10.4018/978-1-7998-1791-8.ch007

Yasmeen, H., Wang, Y., Zameer, H., & Ismail, H. (2020). Modeling the Role of Government, Firm, and Civil Society for Environmental Sustainability. In I. Management Association (Ed.), *Developing Eco-Cities Through Policy, Planning, and Innovation: Can It Really Work?* (pp. 62-83). IGI Global. https://doi.org/10.4018/978-1-7998-0441-3.ch003

Yavuz, N., Karkın, N., & Sevinç Çubuk, E. B. (2020). Explaining Government Crowdsourcing Decisions: A Theoretical Model. In M. Rodríguez Bolívar & M. Cortés Cediel (Eds.), *Digital Government and Achieving E-Public Participation: Emerging Research and Opportunities* (pp. 159–183). IGI Global. https://doi.org/10.4018/978-1-7998-1526-6.ch008

Zhaleleva, S., Zhaleleva, R., & Pasternak, A. (2020). Evolution of Business-Government Interaction Models: Their Use and Management. In G. Tazhina & J. Parker (Eds.), *Toward Sustainability Through Digital Technologies and Practices in the Eurasian Region* (pp. 17–35). IGI Global. https://doi.org/10.4018/978-1-7998-2551-7.ch002

Zhao, B. (2018). A Privacy Perspective of Open Government: Sex, Wealth, and Transparency in China. In A. Kok (Ed.), *Proliferation of Open Government Initiatives and Systems* (pp. 29–48). Hershey, PA: IGI Global. doi:10.4018/978-1-5225-4987-1.ch002

About the Contributors

Christopher Lee Bush is an adjunct professor at Allen County Community College providing instruction in Criminal Justice course work (Introduction to Criminal Justice, Law Enforcement Operations and Procedures, Criminal Investigations and Criminal Law). Dr. Bush also has been invited to be an adjunct at Kansas Wesleyan University to teach a course on Multiculturalism. Dr. Bush professional fulltime work experience in state government (Kansas). Dr. Bush has a published article (fall 2020) in the Journal of Social Change and a book chapter in Global Perspective on Reforming the Criminal Justice System published in IGI global that have been indexed in Scopus. Dr. Bush is an active member of Kappa Alpha Psi Fraternity Inc., with the Topeka (KS) local chapter. Dr. Bush is a member of the National Honor Society Leadership/ Criminal Justice and Walden University- Sigma Alpha Pi/Alpha Phi Sigma and a Member of the 2011 Greater Topeka Leadership. Dr. Bush resides in Topeka, KS with his wife and two sons.

Jennifer Matthews is a renowned public speaker, educator, and thought leader dedicated to inspiring individuals and organizations to reach their full potential. With a unique blend of expertise in law enforcement, psychology, communication, and leadership development, Dr. Matthews captivates audiences with her dynamic presentations and empowers them with practical strategies for personal and professional growth. She has 16 + years of hands-on and educational experience in the field of criminal justice and I'm third third-generation law enforcement professional as well. Dr. Jennifer Matthews is a driving force behind digital transformations to solve cases quickly with body-worn cameras. Body Worn Cameras create a safer world, help victims fight for justice, and protect the lives of the innocent.

* * *

Evelyn L. Anderson, Ph.D., MBA, is an adjunct of Law and Public Service, Public Administration, Organizational Leadership, and Criminal Justice Management professor at National University. She also serves as a development director for Path of Life, Chief Executive Officer for a consulting group, and vice president for the Southern California Black Chamber of Commerce. Dr. Anderson is also a retired Sergeant of a local Sheriff's department. Her research interests include areas in the administration of justice, nonprofit management, and grant development.

Maria Anastasia Arcuri is a PhD student in "Theory of Contracts, Services and Markets" at the Department of Management and Law of the University of Rome "Tor Vergata". She graduated in Law with top marks in 2022. After graduating she immediately joined the "Office for Trial and Criminal Justice" research group of the Department of Legal Sciences of the University of Salerno. She is a member of the Editorial Committee of the journal "Teoria e Prassi del Diritto", she practices law and is registered in the Register of Trainee Lawyers at the Council of Lawyers of Cosenza.

Simon Baldwin is the manager of the research unit of one of the largest law enforcement agencies in North America and has worked in the areas of police use of force and evidence-based policing for the last 15 years. He is an Adjunct Research Professor at Carleton University in Ottawa, Ontario, Canada and holds a Ph.D. in Psychology from Carleton University's Police Research Lab. His research focuses on the areas of police training, stress physiology and performance, crisis intervention and de-escalation, body-worn cameras, and the prevention of arrest-related deaths.

Caroline Ban is the Program Director and an Assistant Professor for the Social Work Program at Valparaiso University, in Indiana. Caroline received her bachelor's degree in psychology at Carleton College, her MSW at Washington University in St. Louis, and she is a DSW student at St. Thomas/St. Kate's. Caroline's passions and experience include police and community relations, police social work, lobbying, advocacy, municipal and state government, collaborations and consolidations, community development and economic development. Caroline was instrumental in developing the first police social work position in Valparaiso City Police Department in 2021. Caroline was selected as one of eight Indiana Humanities Action Fellows (2019-2022), focused on policing and social work. Caroline was recently appointed to be a new co-director for the Welcome Project, a Northwest Indiana story collection on belonging, homelessness, and flight paths created by Allison Schuette and Liz Wuerffel: . To learn more about Caroline, please visit her Valparaiso University page: .

Angelo Brown received his master's at Arizona State University and his Ph.D. Criminal Justice and Criminology at Washington State University. His research and teaching in criminal justice and criminology are primarily on policy and policing from a comparative and intersectional perspective.

Ramy El-Kady is an Associate Professor of Criminal Law at the Police Academy and holds the position of the Head of the Criminal Law Dept. he a rewarded with the State Encouragement Award in Legal and Economic Sciences, Citizenship and Human Rights Branch, on the topic of (The right of persons cooperating with justice for protection in international conventions and national legislation). He graduated from the Police College in 1999. He obtained a postgraduate diploma in criminal sciences and public law, which is equivalent to a master's degree in criminal law in 2003. He obtained a PhD in criminal law from the Faculty of Law, Cairo University, on the topic of (Mediation as an alternative to a criminal case, a comparative study). He currently teaches criminal law subjects to college students. He supervised numerous research submitted for doctoral degrees and higher diplomas and authored a host of research in the criminal law field. He has previously judged numerous research papers in a number of refereed regional scientific journals. He published a host of research in refereed and indexed periodicals and took part in a number of international and local conferences and symposia.

Ana M. Gamez, Ph.D., MBA, is a Professor of Psychology at California Baptist University with 20 years of teaching experience. Dr. Gamez is the Chief Executive Officer for Badge of Life, 501 (C)(3), an agency that provides comprehensive services to first responders—promoting their physical and psychological well-being through awareness, support, evidenced-based training, and education. Dr. Gamez provides nonprofit leadership to community organizations to facilitate their fulfillment of their mission and vision. Dr. Gamez is a licensed clinical psychologist specializing in police and public safety. She is a retired Industrial/Organizational Consultant with the Los Angeles County Sheriff's Department, where she provided organizational consultations to department executives, program development, training, employee wellness, curriculum development for the California Peace Officers Standards and Training (CA POST), emergency response, and clinical services. Dr. Gamez has served as a national grant reviewer, published author, and researcher. Her research interests include forensic and police psychology, trauma, ethics, police misconduct and corruption, substance abuse, immigration, diversity, inclusion, and leadership. She earned a Ph.D. in clinical psychology (LLU), an MBA in general business (WTAMU), an M.S. in forensic psychology (CSULA), a B.A. in psychology (CSULA), and a graduate certificate in diversity and inclusion from Cornell University.

Audrey MacIsaac is a PhD student in the Department of Psychology at Carleton University. Her research primarily examines de-escalation, with a particular focus on officer safety, and police interactions with persons in crisis.

John G. McNutt is Professor Emeritus in the Joseph R. Biden, Jr. School of Public Policy and Administration at the University of Delaware. Dr. McNutt is a specialist in the application of high technology to political and social engagement. His work focuses on the role of technology in lobbying, e-government and e-democracy, political campaigning and deliberation, organizing and other forms of political participation. He has conducted research on professional associations, child advocacy groups, consumer and environmental protection groups, social action organizations and legislative bodies. His most recent work looks at political change technology and e-government and data science Dr. McNutt has co-edited or co-authored eight books and many journal articles, book chapters and other publications. He regularly presents at National and International conferences and sits on several editorial boards.

Chloe Robinson is an Assistant Professor in the Criminal Justice department at Indiana University South Bend. She holds a PhD in Criminal Justice from North Dakota State University, an MA in Criminal Justice from the University of Illinois at Chicago, an MS in Academic Advising from Kansas State University and a BA in Criminology and Law Studies from Marquette University.

Tomicka N. Williams is an Assistant Department Chair in the College of Social and Behavioral Science at Purdue University Global. Her research and passion focus on educational leadership, crisis leadership, crisis communication, and strategies to enhance growth and development in academic and public safety settings.

Index

T

U

www.ingramcontent.com/pod-product-compliance
Lightning Source LLC
LaVergne TN
LVHW061546290926
849162LV00004B/927